Eyewitness testimony

Eyewitness testimony

Psychological perspectives

Edited by

GARY L. WELLS AND ELIZABETH F. LOFTUS

The right of the
University of Cambridge
to print and sell
all manner of books
was granted by
Henry VIII in 1534.
The University has printed
and published continuously
since 1584.

CAMBRIDGE UNIVERSITY PRESS

Cambridge

London   New York   New Rochelle

Melbourne   Sydney

Published by the Press Syndicate of the University of Cambridge
The Pitt Building, Trumpington Street, Cambridge CB2 1RP
32 East 57th Street, New York, NY 10022, USA
10 Stamford Road, Oakleigh, Melbourne 3166, Australia

First published 1984
Reprinted 1985, 1987

Printed in the United States of America

Library of Congress Cataloging in Publication Data

Main entry under title:

Eyewitness testimony.

Includes bibliographical references and index.

1. Witnesses—Psychology.   2. Visual perception.
3. Judicial error.   4. Psychology, Forensic.
I. Wells, Gary L.   II. Loftus, Elizabeth F., 1944–
[DNLM: 1. Criminal psychology.   2. Expert testimony.
3. Memory.   HV 6080 E97]
BF241.E93   1984   347′.066′019   83-7615
ISBN 0 521 25564 3   342.766019

Contents

Contributors

Ray Bull
Department of Psychology
North East London Polytechnic
Stratford, England

Brian R. Clifford
Department of Psychology
North East London Polytechnic
Stratford, England

Patricia G. Devine
Department of Psychology
Ohio State University
Columbus, Ohio

David F. Dinges
Institute of Pennsylvania
  Hospital and
University of Pennsylvania
Philadelphia, Pennsylvania

Howard E. Egeth
Department of Psychology
Johns Hopkins University
Baltimore, Maryland

Hadyn D. Ellis
Department of Psychology
King's College
Aberdeen, Scotland

Joseph D. Grano
Law School

Wayne State University
Detroit, Michigan

David F. Hall
Department of Psychology
Thiel College
Greenville, Pennsylvania

Frank Horvath
School of Criminal Justice
Michigan State University
East Lansing, Michigan

Kenneth R. Laughery
Department of Psychology
Rice University
Houston, Texas

David R. Lenorovitz
Computer Technology Assoc., Inc.
Denver, Colorado

Elizabeth F. Loftus
Department of Psychology
University of Washington
Seattle, Washington

Roy S. Malpass
Department of Psychology
State University of New York,
  Plattsburgh
Plattsburgh, New York

Michael McCloskey
Department of Psychology
Johns Hopkins University
Baltimore, Maryland

Donna M. Murray
Department of Psychology
University of Alberta
Edmonton, Canada

Emily Carota Orne
Institute of Pennsylvania
    Hospital and
University of Pennsylvania
Philadelphia, Pennsylvania

Martin T. Orne
Institute of Pennsylvania
    Hospital and
University of Pennsylvania
Philadelphia, Pennsylvania

David A. Soskis
Institute of Pennsylvania
    Hospital and
University of Pennsylvania
Philadelphia, Pennsylvania

James P. Tousignant
Department of Psychology
University of Washington
Seattle, Washington

Gary L. Wells
Department of Psychology
University of Alberta
Edmonton, Canada

A. Daniel Yarmey
Department of Psychology
University of Guelph
Guelph, Canada

Preface

EYE·WIT·NESS, *n*. 1. A person who actually sees some act, occurrence, or thing and can give a firsthand account of it. [*The Random House Dictionary of the English Language*]

Testimony by an eyewitness can be an event of profound importance. In one case it can be the event that saves a community from the terror of future rapes or muggings by being the key evidence against their perpetrator. In another case it can be the principal basis on which an innocent person is convicted of another's heinous crime. In other words, it has positive effects when it leads to the successful conviction of guilty people, but it has negative effects when it leads to the conviction of the innocent. Those in our society who are strongly concerned with crime control think more about the positive effects. Those whose primary interest is "due process" think more about the negative effects, as did William Blackstone, who in 1769 said, "It is better that ten guilty escape than one innocent suffer."

We must be concerned about the successes of eyewitnesses, as well as their failures, for it is highly unlikely that eyewitness testimony will ever be eliminated as a form of evidence. We might, then, profitably concentrate our efforts on building a research base to guide us in understanding the errors of eyewitnesses and in developing procedures that produce the least amount of error or distortion in eyewitness reports. This book provides a step in this direction.

Our hope in compiling these chapters was to provide psychologists, attorneys, judges, jurors, and police with the most thorough treatment to date of the psychology of eyewitness testimony. Each chapter has been written by an expert who is not only intimately familiar with the available data but also has served as a principal contributor of the data. We cannot claim that any or all chapters are free of influence from personal values of the contributors; nor can such a claim be made about any other work in the social and behavioral sciences. In some places the experts disagree. A prime example of this is on the topic of expert testimony. Whether this disagreement is due to the relative lack of data on the effects of expert testimony, differences in philosophy about how perfect the research must be before it should be applied to real problems, or differences in the degree to which the contributors endorse Blackstone's thesis, we cannot say. Nevertheless, the disagreement is a healthy one, we are convinced, because it improves the chances that needed research will be conducted.

We have been impressed with the extent to which the arguments and conclusions of our colleagues have been driven by empirical data. Some readers will feel that certain chapters overgeneralize from available data, and other readers will feel that authors have been unduly hesitant to make conclusions. Whatever the readers' reactions, we believe that this book presents a fair picture of the complexities inherent in the psychology of eyewitness testimony.

1   Eyewitness research: then and now

Gary L. Wells and Elizabeth F. Loftus

Robert Dillen, a free-lance photographer, was arrested July 17, 1979, and subsequently charged with indecent exposure and open lewdness. Robert's crime: relieving himself in the bushes at a park after finding the door to the lavatory locked. Little did Robert know this small mistake would lead to loss of his job, heavy financial burdens, and finally, a divorce.

Robert was photographed and fingerprinted at police headquarters and eventually released on his own recognizance. He and his wife decided to pay the fine and forget the whole incident, but the next day he was arrested for armed robbery after his photo had been selected from a batch of 10 by a young victim. Robert spent 2 days in jail, hired a lawyer, and agreed to take a lie detector test and appear in a lineup to clear himself. The lie detector test showed no evidence he was lying, but he was picked out of the lineup several times by eyewitnesses to various offenses.

Released on bail, Robert was again arrested several days later and charged with armed robbery, kidnapping, and rape. During the next 3 months, four different robbery charges were filed and dismissed against him and he was scheduled to appear in court for the remaining robbery – kidnap – rape count. With a strong alibi and the ability of a young attorney to disprove the only witness for the prosecution, Robert was acquitted, but not before he had begun to question his own sanity. One year later, with his marriage broken and career ruined, Robert Dillen moved to a different state to begin anew. (Another man was eventually arrested and confessed to charges laid against Robert Dillen.) At his lawyer's advice Robert kept a diary of all his waking hours. Eventually he hopes to rebuild his career and recover the almost $30,000 that his defense cost his family (see Fincher, 1981).

What went wrong in the instance of Robert Dillen's ordeal? Was there something about police procedures that produced this unfortunate series of events? Is there something about the lack of ability on the part of humans to be good eyewitnesses that led to the faulty accusations? Both of these possi-

1

bilities could have played a role. As described in various chapters of this book, procedures used for testing the memories of eyewitnesses are critical to the outcome. In Dillen's case we could question many procedural aspects, one of which is the adequacy of the original lineup from which several eyewitnesses identified Dillen. The lineup was produced hastily and seemed to lack the important criteria necessary for fairness. We also might question why the eyewitness identifications of Dillen carried so much weight. Are people overly willing to believe eyewitness identification evidence? How could an eyewitness be certain and definitive and yet be incorrect? How could an eyewitness identify a man whose appearance was relatively dissimilar to the actual perpetrator? Can faces undergo changes in the memory of a witness? Should not the lie detector test have exonerated Dillen to a point of reasonable doubt? Would hypnotizing the eyewitnesses have uncovered the witnesses' errors? Are there legal perspectives on how to protect the innocent from mistaken eyewitness testimony? Chapters in this book relate to each of these points.

We might also ask what went "right" in Robert Dillen's case. What went right was that Robert Dillen was found not guilty each time. It was fortunate for Dillen that he had a strong alibi and other circumstantial exonerating evidence to aid his defense. Without this, and the eventual confession by another man, Dillen's life would probably now be very different.

Concerns about eyewitnessing are not restricted to criminal cases. The outcomes of civil trials, safety investigations, or virtually any inquiry in which witnesses can help clarify facts can be affected by the nature of eyewitness testimony. The testimony of John Dean during the Senate Watergate hearings in 1973 is a case in point. Dean made repeated claims during his testimony that he had met with Herbert Kalmbach in the coffee shop of the Mayflower Hotel in Washington, D.C. Dean further claimed that he and Kalmbach had gone upstairs to Kalmbach's room. Other evidence, however, suggested to people that Dean was lying. In particular it was noted that Kalmbach had not been registered at the Mayflower on the date in question. Dean continued to assert that his testimony was correct and suggested that Kalmbach had possibly registered under a false name. Eventually the story was cleared up when it was learned that another hotel, the Statler Hilton Hotel, has a coffee shop called the Mayflower Doughnut Coffee Shop and that Kalmbach was registered at the Statler at the time in question (see Neisser, 1981).

Civil cases often rely on eyewitnesses for information. Important outcomes in civil trials can hinge, for example, on a witness's recollection of whether a traffic light was red or green at a particular time, how many people were present at an incident, or what time someone was seen at an event. After the Air Florida crash of January 13, 1982, in Washington, D.C., for example, a crucial question put to survivors was, "How much time passed between the last de-icing and take off?" The plane had been de-iced more than once by airport personnel while the 78 passengers were aboard. The time between de-icings was critical for clarifying matters in preliminary investigations (McKean, 1982). How good are people at estimating time durations of this sort?

The psychology of eyewitness testimony is obviously not restricted to criminal cases nor is it restricted to identifications of people. The psychology of eyewitness testimony concerns the study of factors that influence people's reports of their previous experiences. Although legal applications seem to be the rallying point around which most eyewitness testimony research is conducted, much of the research can also be applied to nonlegal, social situations, such as processes involved in rumor transmission (Allport & Postman, 1947).

Our purpose in putting together this book is to organize present knowledge in the psychology of eyewitness testimony into one volume. We do so at this particular time because much empirical research has been conducted on the topic in the last few years that has direct relevance for criminal justice usage. A second purpose of this book is to help clarify the ascendance of this research and set the stage for what might fruitfully be accomplished by eyewitness researchers during the next decade. Although we have come a long way, we admit willingly that the existing state of knowledge in eyewitness testimony research is far from perfect.

Early research

We estimate that over 85% of the entire published literature has surfaced since 1978. Yet, eyewitness research as an empirical interest of psychologists is not a new concern. Events that were of relevance to eyewitness testimony were being staged by psychologists as early as 1908. American psychology's earliest advocate of the use of experimental psychology in judging eyewitness testimony was Hugo Munsterberg, author of *On the Witness Stand*. Munsterberg (1908) strongly argued that his experiments and other researchers' work in perception and memory were invaluable to the courts. He openly criticized legal experts for ignoring the empirical evidence of psychologists with regard to the process of evaluating eyewitness testimony.

Munsterberg's arguments, while at times carrying the flavor of proselytism, were concretely stated:

The jurymen and the judge do not discriminate, whether the witness tells that he saw in late twilight a woman in a red gown or one in a blue gown. They are not expected to know that such a faint light would still allow the blue colour sensation to come in, while the red colour sensation would have disappeared. They are not obliged to know what directions of sound are mixed up by all of us and what are discriminated; they do not know, perhaps, that we can never be in doubt whether we heard on the country road a cry from the right or from the left, but we may be utterly unable to say whether we heard it from in front or from behind. They have no reason to know that the victim of a crime may have been utterly unable to perceive that he was stabbed with a pointed dagger; he may have felt it like a dull blow. We hear the witnesses talking about the taste of poisoned liquids, and there is probably no one in the jury-box who knows enough of physiological psychology to be aware that the same substance may taste quite differently on different parts of the tongue. We may hear quarreling parties in a civil suit testify as to the size and length and form of a field as it appeared to them, and yet there is no one to remind the court that the same distance must appear quite differently under a hundred different conditions. The judge listens, perhaps, to a description of things which the witness has secretly seen through the keyhole of the door; he does not understand why all the judgments as to the size of objects and their place are probably erroneous under such circumstances. The witness may be sure of having felt something wet, and yet he may have felt only some smooth, cold metal. In short, every chapter and sub-chapter of sense psychology may help to clear up the chaos and the confusion which prevail in the observation of witnesses. (1908, pp. 32–33)

The ideas of Munsterberg were not, however, universally embraced. The superb wit of Dean J. H. Wigmore, rivaling that of Munsterberg, was mustered to argue that Munsterberg's claim of psychological knowledge had been exaggerated (Wigmore, 1909). Wigmore was, nevertheless, openminded in many respects. He felt that psychological research *could* make contributions and even suggested some ways to achieve such a goal (e.g., via the use of the "talking film," Wigmore, 1937). In some respects Wigmore was correct; Munsterberg had probably overstepped the bounds of generalization. In other respects, however, Wigmore seemed naive. He boldly claimed, for example, that when psychology has something to offer, the legal world will be ready to receive it.

Munsterberg was not the first person to press the need for empirical studies of testimony. The French psychologist Alfred Binet in his book *La suggestibilité* (1900) argued for "the advantage that would accrue from the creation of a practical science of testimony." The German psychologist Louis William Stern was publishing and editing studies of eyewitness testimony as early as 1902. In 1903, Stern was admitted to German courts of law to testify as an expert on eyewitness testimony, one of the first psychologists to appear in a courtroom on the subject. The same year Stern began publishing *Beitrage zur Psychologie der Aussage* (1903–1906), which contained reviews and reports by numerous individuals such as Jaffa, Cramer, Lobsien, Lipmann, Borst, Bogdanoff, Rodenwalt, Oppenheim, Kosog, Weindriner, Gunther, and Gottschalk. Much of this early work was of the "classification" type. For example, Stern classified questions that might be asked of an eyewitness into six types: determinative, completely disjunctive, incompletely disjunctive, expectative, implicative, and consecutive. Other contributions to Stern's periodical were empirical. Marie Borst, for example, reported empirical work on the range and errors of positive statements, sworn statements, unsworn statements, certain statements, and uncertain statements. Not surprisingly the early empirical work was not of the quality and precision that exists in psychology today. Indeed, some of this imprecision led to mild conflicts, such as that between Louis Stern and Marie Borst. Stern argued from his data that men gave more accurate reports than women, whereas Marie Borst reported the opposite. Modern research suggests that these different results may be due to the type of stimulus materials used in the differing studies (e.g., see Powers, Andriks, & Loftus, 1979).

Controversy also existed in this early work with regard to the adequacy with which experimental procedures reflected the actual workings of legal procedure. For example, Stern and Borst documented that interrogatory reports (a series of prearranged questions) produce greater range but less accuracy than narrative reports (free or open accounts by the witness without comment by the questioner). H. Gross (author of the influential book (*Kriminalpsychologie*, 1897), however, argued that such a result "does not accord with the facts of legal procedure, and argued that it merely shows that psychologists do not know how to ask questions" (quotation attributed to Gross by Whipple, 1909, p. 165). Subsequent research (e.g., Cady, 1924; Marston, 1924; Whitely & McGeoch, 1927), however, supported the basic conclusions of Stern and Borst on this point.

Guy Montrose Whipple (1909, 1910, 1911, 1912) played a strong role in the history of the psychology of eyewitness testimony. His principal contribution was that of bringing the Aussage tradition (developed in Germany and France) into English terminology. Although Whipple did some empirical work on the psychology of eyewitness testimony (e.g., on the estimation of temporal durations and size), his chief contribution was to translate, summarize, and interpret the works of Stern, Borst, Lobsien, Binet, Gross, and others of the Aussage tradition for English-speaking audiences. Whipple did this in a series of *Psychological Bulletin* articles beginning in 1909.

The research in the early years of this century seemed to be setting the stage for an explosion of useful research on the psychology of eyewitness testimony. Such an explosion did not occur, however, until the latter half of the 1970s. Indeed, the research output on the psychology of eyewitness testimony dwindled. This is not to say that there was no relevant research in the

1930s, 1940s, 1950s, and 1960s, but contributions were sparse. In the 1930s research was carried out by Burtt (1931) and by Stern (1939). In the 1940s, Snee and Lush (1941) followed up on the narrative–interrogative issue, and Allport and Postman (1947) worked on the psychology of information transmission. In the 1950s, Hastorf and Cantrill (1954) demonstrated the effects of personal prejudice on perception. Why the amount of research on eyewitness testimony was so low during these decades is debatable. It seems clear, however, that psychological research during that time was oriented primarily toward theoretical issues with little focus on practical questions. This is not to say that practical and theoretical issues need be opposing concerns (see Loftus, 1981b). We believe that practical and theoretical approaches *can* be complementary, as several chapters in the current volume illustrate. Still, researchers whose main concern is with theory per se usually select their stimuli, designs, and procedures so as to test the theory itself with little or no regard for how these stimuli are encountered in real-world settings. Although much excellent research was conducted during these decades in the areas of perception and memory, real-world aspects were not of much interest to experimental researchers.

Thus, our view is that the decline in eyewitness testimony research (1930–1970) was due to a preference for theory and hypothesis testing without regard for immediate practicality. Sporer (1981), on the other hand, suggests that this decline was probably due to zealous overgeneralizations drawn from experimental studies that did not meet adequately the demands of complex courtroom reality. "Jurist-practitioners and forensic psychiatrists...were reluctant to accept the blanket rejection of witness testimony.... This, and the rise of World War II, of course, led to the decline of the experimental psychology of eyewitness testimony" (Sporer, 1981, p. 15). Sporer might be correct at one level, since some of these early researchers made extreme claims, but, many of the early eyewitness researchers (e.g., Stern, 1939) were moderates by most standards. Most eyewitness researchers today are acutely aware of the limits of generalization and usually qualify their conclusions accordingly. Although we do not claim to speak for the entire coterie of modern researchers, we think most do not believe that eyewitness testimony is useless in any general sense. Instead, modern eyewitness research focuses on two general issues: (a) Under what conditions is eyewitness testimony reliable and when might it not be reliable? and (b) How can we structure situations that will improve the accuracy of eyewitness testimony? From these two general questions other, related issues surface, such as, How much do triers of fact already know about eyewitness memory problems? and Does expert testimony help triers of fact (e.g., jurors) in their decisions about eyewitness testimony?

Thus, eyewitness researchers do not argue that eyewitness test erally unreliable; instead we research variables that help estima eyewitness accuracy (Wells, 1978).

What then accounts for the rise in interest in eyewitness rese 1970s? A major impetus was the forcefulness of the view that understanding human memory and social behavior requires a new ...pnasis on observations made in natural contexts. Such observation does not mean abandonment of the experimental method or the laboratory. It does mean representing the task, stimuli, and responses in a form that captures the essence of real-world settings. This view was expressed strongly by Ulric Neisser in his book *Cognition and Reality* (1976) and can be found in his new book *Memory Observed: Remembering in Natural Contexts* (1982). The latter work is a series of reprinted articles dealing with how we remember and forget in everyday settings. We agree with Neisser that the findings from "real-life studies" can be used to illustrate and extend theoretical issues, as well as be of practical importance.

This volume

Chapters in this volume are divided into three general sections. The first section (Chapters 2–8) deals with the general issue of the reliability of testimony. This section encompasses a broad range of subissues covering visual memory for people (Chapters 2–4), memory for voices (Chapter 5), how new information affects original memories (Chapter 6), the effects of age on eyewitness memory (Chapter 7), and the relationships between eyewitness confidence and eyewitness accuracy (Chapter 8). The second section deals with special techniques for discerning witness information, namely hypnosis (Chapter 9) and devices for detecting deception (Chapter 10). The third section deals with the eyewitness in the legal system. This section includes evidence on how much knowledge triers of fact have about eyewitness matters (Chapter 11), the use of experts in the court (Chapters 12–14), and legal perspectives on eyewitness testimony (Chapter 15).

The identification and recall of faces is of paramount import in eyewitnessing. As described by Hadyn Ellis in Chapter 2, there is an extensive body of research directed at the issues of memory for faces. Clearly, nothing in Ellis's chapter would lead us to think that memory for faces is inherently reliable or unreliable. Instead, memory for faces strongly depends on the conditions of acquisition, storage, and retrieval. Any conclusions about how well an eyewitness can remember faces must consider these conditions as they apply to the particular eyewitness in question.

In criminal investigations eyewitnesses are frequently asked to search a mug file to identify a face from memory. In Chapter 3, David Lenorovitz and Kenneth Laughery describe a witness–computer interactive system for searching mug files. The computer-assisted photographic search and retrieval (CAPSAR) system developed by Lenorovitz and Laughery shows significant improvement over the traditional linear search process in terms of both increasing accurate identifications and decreasing false identifications. Although there are many practical aspects of CAPSAR to be examined, this prototype model of a computerized mug-file search system seems to hold great promise.

Mug files are usually used only when police investigators do not have a specific suspect. If there is a specific suspect in a case, investigators will typically use either a subset of photographs (somewhere between 5 and 11 photographs being most common) or conduct a live lineup (containing up to 11 or 12 individuals). The structure of photo arrays and lineups varies widely, as do the instructions given to eyewitnesses. As Roy Malpass and Patricia Devine describe in Chapter 4, the structure and procedures used in photo-array and lineup identification tasks can have strong effects on identification accuracy and response biases of eyewitnesses.

Memory for voices, an issue of import in many cases, such as extortion, bomb threats, or kidnapping, is the topic of Chapter 5. As Ray Bull and Brian Clifford point out, memory for voices has many parallels to memory for visual information. For example, time, disguise, typicality, distractor similarity, and so on have effects on the recognition and recall of voices similar to those on the recognition and recall of faces.

The interrogation of eyewitnesses for purposes of establishing facts is indispensable. Yet, questions asked of eyewitnesses are forms of "postevent information" that can affect later memory reports. Postevent information is information acquired by witnesses of an event that can later be "confused" with their memory of it. As David Hall, Elizabeth Loftus, and James Tousignant describe in Chapter 6, the postevent information can be incorrect and thus create false memory reports. The crucial question addressed in this chapter is how the postevent information competes with the original information (i.e., does it *replace* the original memory or does it simply *add* a new memory that competes at the time of retrieval with the original memory?). The answer to this question will, of course, have implications for the techniques that might be used to elicit accurate information from a witness.

Age as a factor in the validity of eyewitness reports was of considerable interest to early researchers (e.g., Binet, 1900; Borst, 1906; Stern, 1902). This early work, however, was exclusively restricted to the differences between young children and adults. In Chapter 7, Daniel Yarmey discusses the eyewitness abilities of the elderly as well as the young. As Yarmey points out, views of the elderly as being poor eyewitnesses is a conclusion that needs qualification. Differences in age may not be as important as differences in other factors, such as testing conditions.

Chapter 8 deals with the issue of eyewitness confidence. As Gary Wells and Donna Murray note, the measurement of eyewitness confidence can be quite reliable under certain circumstances, but the validity of eyewitness confidence for predicting accuracy seems poor at best. The studies show that the value of eyewitness confidence for inferring eyewitness accuracy is especially poor when factors that occur in the real world (e.g., perpetrator-absent lineups, witness–attorney interactions, and arousal) enter into the analysis.

Hypnosis is widely used in psychology, medicine, and dentistry and has for years been portrayed in literature and films as having extraordinary effects on humans, including that of "total recall." As Martin Orne, David Soskis, David Dinges, and Emily Orne note in Chapter 9, there is remarkably little scientific evidence to support this view. Orne, Soskis, Dinges, and Orne outline the scientific evidence on the effects of hypnosis on eyewitness accuracy and confidence. In addition, Chapter 9 discusses the probative value of "hypnotically refreshed" testimony as well as its likely effects on jurors.

For the most part, eyewitness research deals with situations in which the person giving testimony has nothing to gain or lose from the testimony. That is, eyewitness research generally focuses on "pure" errors in memory. In Chapter 10, however, Frank Horvath reminds us that many aspects of false testimony are the result of motivated distortions. Although the polygraph and other devices for detecting deception have been regarded with strong skepticism by the courts, recent studies give high marks to certain measures of deception. It seems that the lie detection techniques might have precisely the opposite problem of eyewitness testimony in one respect: Lie detection techniques seem to be regarded with more skepticism than scientific evidence would lead us to believe that they should, whereas eyewitness testimony might be regarded with less skepticism than scientific data would indicate it should.

A great deal of research on eyewitness testimony is predicated on the assumption that the findings can be of benefit to the trier of fact. This is not a necessary assumption for most eyewitness research, because one's findings could be used for other purposes (e.g., to help police investigators improve their methods of obtaining testimony). Nevertheless, the question of whether eyewitness research evidence can be of use to triers of fact has become a central question of late. In Chapter 11, Gary Wells reviews evidence on how much people know about the factors that relate to the accuracy of eyewitness testimony. The literature shows that there might be numerous factors misunderstood by the lay trier of fact, but, as Wells points out, eyewitness researchers have only recently started addressing this issue. We must examine carefully the research procedures used to find out what lay people know about eyewitness problems and how people perform in judging eyewitness testimony.

Chapters 12, 13, and 14 address the issue of psychologists' giving expert testimony on eyewitness matters in court. In Chapter 12, Elizabeth Loftus reasons that the courts often have a need for expert knowledge. Although the psychologist may not have all the answers, there are times when empirical findings can reduce ambiguity on some issue. Loftus readily acknowledges that more research is needed to assess the effects of expert testimony on deliberation processes. She argues that expert testimony can be given in such a way that it does not invade the province of the jury, yet helps the jury evaluate the eyewitness testimony.

Howard Egeth and Michael McCloskey (Chapter 13) take a somewhat different perspective. In general, Egeth and McCloskey argue that there is a dearth of empirical evidence suggesting that jurors are overbelieving of eyewitness testimony or that jurors misunderstand the effects of certain factors on eyewitness testimony. Psychologists, they state, should not be giving expert testimony in the courts unless or until such testimony can be shown empirically to have beneficial effects on the judgments rendered by the jurors. Among other things, Egeth and McCloskey maintain that expert testimony could result in jurors' becoming too skeptical of eyewitness evidence, and it is their opinion that this should be strongly avoided.

In Chapter 14 the issue of expert testimony is readdressed by Gary Wells. Although acknowledging imperfections in the strength of current evidence, Wells argues that people may be overbelieving of eyewitness testimony under certain conditions. In addition, Wells says, expert testimony is not wedded to the concept of making jurors skeptical of eyewitness testimony in general. Rather, expert testimony, which could include testimony that enhances the jurors' perceptions of eyewitness accuracy under certain conditions, should be designed to improve the decisions of jurors.

Joseph Grano offers a legal perspective on eyewitness testimony in Chapter 15. The law itself has recognized that identification evidence may be suspect because of inherent deficiencies in human perception and memory and because of suggestive pretrial and trial identification procedures. Because of these inherent dangers the courts have imposed some restrictions on identification procedures. In this chapter, Grano discusses not only these restrictions but also other avenues that may be pursued to help ensure that identification evidence is subject to appropriate challenge before the trier of fact.

It has been our aim in this book to describe what is known and, equally important, what is not known about the psychology of eyewitness testimony. We hope that those who must deal with practical matters of eyewitness testimony, be they attorneys, triers of fact, police, or psychologists, will find this book useful. The literature on the psychology of eyewitness testimony is neither perfect nor complete, and we have attempted here to help eyewitness researchers formulate better conceptual ideas as well as to encourage more and better empirical research on the issues.

2   Practical aspects of face memory

Hadyn D. Ellis

Background

Interest in the scientific study of face memory has a long history, but only in the last two decades has it become a major topic for psychological research. The literature on face memory has grown accordingly, partly because faces constitute a convenient, ecologically valid set of stimuli, and partly because they are themselves of intrinsic scientific interest (Ellis, 1981a). This increased research output means that any reviews of the area must to some extent be selective; the present one will concentrate exclusively on work that has a bearing upon forensic psychology. In other words, I will confine myself to discussing experiments on both face recognition and face recall that might interest those involved in various aspects of the judicial process. Other, more general reviews of the face memory literature can be found in Clifford and Bull, 1978; Davies, 1978; Ellis, 1975, 1981c; Goldstein and Chance, 1981; and Yarmey, 1979a. More specific reviews of face memory may be found as follows: the development of face memory, Carey (1981), Fagan (1979); the neurophysiology of face recognition, Benton (1980), Ellis (in press), Hécaen (1981), Meadows (1974), Sergent and Bindra (1981); social factors in face memory, Shepherd (1981); and specific reviews of face recall techniques may be found in Davies (1981) and Laughery, Rhodes, and Batten (1981).

Review plan

Memory for anything, including faces, is traditionally reduced to the minimum three distinct processes shown in Figure 2.1: encoding or acquisition, storage, and retrieval. The last stage, as depicted in Figure 2.1, can be

I should like to acknowledge the assistance of my colleagues John Shepherd, Graham Davies, Jean Shepherd, Rhona Flin, and Alan Milne, all of whom are involved in projects on practical aspects of face memory sponsored by the British Home Office. Colin Gray read parts of the paper and tried to improve the English.

Figure 2.1. Stages in the process of memory for faces

subdivided usefully into two parts, recognition and recall. The following review of forensic aspects of face memory will examine each stage, beginning with the initial encounter and ending with a retrieval of information that may help to secure a criminal conviction or, alternatively, provide an important piece of alibi evidence. In the main the review will stick to studies wherein the faces of strangers have been presented and tested for subsequent retrieval, but occasionally it will be necessary to consider episodic memory for familiar faces. All of the studies mentioned can be classified as laboratory experiments, and for the most part they involve the presentation of photographic stimuli that typically show full-face head and shoulders portraits. A discussion of any limitations to generalizing from such studies will be postponed until later.

The allocation of material to one of the three principal stages cannot always be made unequivocally – indeed one should always bear in mind the possibility that stages are interactive, that encoding will influence storage characteristics, which, in turn, will affect retrieval.

Encoding

Before giving an account of what face encoding seems to entail, I state what it is not. Face encoding does not appear to be mediated by verbal processes (Bruce, 1982; Ellis, 1975; Goldstein & Chance, 1971). It would seem that language is too imprecise to be of much use in acquiring the subtle information regarding each face we encounter. When asked to describe faces, people usually resort to simple general labels (e.g., "crafty-looking") or select a few salient features (e.g., "large nose and red hair"). As we shall later see in the section on retrieval, verbal descriptions of faces are not without practical interest. Still, there is no reason to suppose that such descriptions play any significant part in the initial encoding of facial features.

When we look at a face, we see it as a whole percept rather than as a set of discrete visual features. The experience, however, may derive from a preconscious pattern analysis that involves sequential processing of the different features (Ellis, 1981c). Whatever the underlying analysis, the conscious experience is of seeing a whole face. This does not mean that each facial area is accorded equal attention. A considerable body of evidence indicates that some features are given more attention than others, which may enhance their particular encoding.

Cue saliency

The most direct evidence for such differences in the amount of attention given to various parts of the face ought to be found in eye-movement studies. Unfortunately, however, these have not yielded particularly reliable results. Luria and Strauss (1978), for example, found that the nose, followed by the eyes and the mouth, attracted the most attention. Cook (1978) also discovered that central features commanded most visual attention, though he found that the eyes were given a disproportionate amount. This discrepancy may be accounted for in a number of ways. The pose of each face used in eye-fixation studies is likely to affect fixation patterns, as is the actual size of the image employed. Equally, it seems from the work of Walker-Smith, Gale, and Findlay (1977) that the pattern of fixation differs by individuals and by the nature of the task. Furthermore, these authors admit that fixation on central parts of the face may simply serve to provide a reference point for analyzing peripheral details.

If one were, nevertheless, to accept from eye-movement studies that central portions of the face are most salient, one would predict that any changes made to them would be particularly inimical to recognition. Davies, Ellis, and Shepherd (1977) tested this possibility. Using Photofit faces as target stimuli, they required subjects to identify each target from an array of faces in which for each face four features were identical to those in the target face and a fifth feature, in each case different, varied. The changed features had been previously rated as being similar or dissimilar to the ones in the target face. The measure of discriminability used was the number of times each distractor face was erroneously identified as being the target. Under all conditions hair changes led to least confusion, followed by mouth, eyes, chin, and nose changes.

Other studies have looked at the relative salience of facial features by obliterating specific features and noting how well the faces are then recognized. Strictly speaking, these need not be considered as studies of stimulus encoding but may instead be thought of as differential storage for various features. Leaving aside that caveat, however, we find that upper face features (i.e., hair and eyes) are more likely than lower face features to lead to correct recognition (Fisher & Cox, 1975; Goldstein & Mackenberg, 1966; Langdell, 1978).

A similar picture has emerged from studies in which people are invited to describe faces either from memory (Ellis, Shepherd, & Davies, 1980) or with

Table 2.1. *Relative proportions of facial descriptors for descriptions made in the presence of the face and from memory*

	Descriptions	
Features	Face present	Face absent
Hair	.24	.27
Eyes	.13	.14
Nose	.12	.14
Face shape	.09	.13
Eyebrows	.09	.08
Chin	.07	.07
Lips	.06	.06
Mouth	.04	.03
Complexion	.04	.02
Cheeks	.01	.01
Forehead	.02	.01
Others	.02	.04

Sources: Figures for "face present" are from Shepherd, Ellis, and Davies, 1977; figures for "face absent" are from Ellis, Shepherd, and Davies, 1980.

a picture of the face present during the description (Ellis, Deregowski, & Shepherd, 1975; Shepherd, Ellis, & Davies, 1977). Table 2.1 indicates the proportion of descriptions involving different facial areas.

Interestingly, Baddeley and Woodhead (unpublished report, 1982) examined the facial descriptions given by 13 writers of short stories. These also revealed a tendency for upper rather than lower face features to be described. The nose, mouth, lips, teeth, beard, and mustache together only accounted for about 9% of the total number of features reported.

In summary, apart from studies of eye fixations, there is reasonable support for the suggestion that upper face features are encoded better and in preference to lower face features. From a practical point of view this means that a police officer trying to elicit a description of a suspect might concentrate on the witness's ability to give details of hair and eyes and be more skeptical of any proferred description of nose, mouth, and chin – unless they were particularly remarkable. By the same token, the would-be criminal ought to disguise his upper rather than his lower face. Baker (1967) confirmed this by showing that the addition of spectacles caused more identification problems than did the addition of a mustache. As one might expect, a particularly strong effect has been reported for changes in hairstyle (Laughery & Fowler, 1980; Patterson, 1978; and Patterson & Baddeley, 1977). Figure 2.2 presents an example of just how powerful

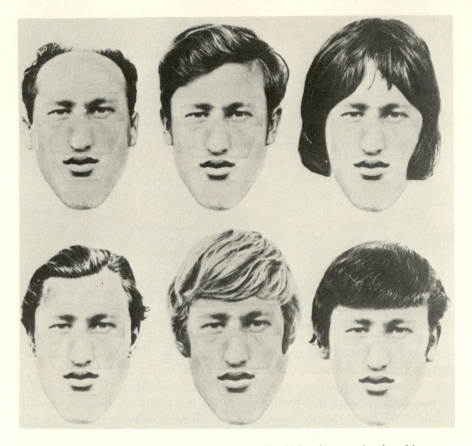

Figure 2.2. An illustration of the ease with which a face may be altered in appearance by a change of hairstyle

changes in hairstyle can be in altering someone's appearance. The basic Photofit face in the illustration becomes quite a different one with each change of wig.

The conclusions drawn about the most salient features only apply to Caucasian people looking at Caucasian faces. Some evidence, based upon analysis of the descriptions of faces given by Africans, shows that Negro subjects attend to rather different facial features — regardless of whether the faces are white or black (Ellis et al., 1975). Shepherd and Deregowski (1981) extended these observations by applying multidimensional scaling techniques to similarity judgments among black or white faces by African and European subjects. Both subject groups tended to use similar attributes for making their judgments. Black faces were compared for skin details, face shape, thickness of lips, and breadth of nose, and white faces were com-

pared principally for details of hair, eye shape, fatness of face, and
ture. Thus when the pool of faces employed is racially homogen
the task required is to group them according to similarity there is n
ference between the judgments of the two races. As Ellis and colleagues
showed, however, when the task is to encode each face verbally, quite large
differences between races occur, regardless of the race of face being described. The implications of this finding will be explored in the following
section.

Race of face

It is a commonplace observation that faces drawn from an unfamiliar race
are more difficult to remember than own-race faces. One possible reason
for this was mentioned at the end of the last section: Under some circumstances individuals from one race may attend to particular, discriminating
facial features that are usually not so suitable for encoding faces of a different race. Other theoretical explanations for the own-race advantage in face
memory have been thoroughly reviewed by Shepherd (1981). For the
present, because cross-racial identification evidence is now fairly commonplace testimony in the courts of many societies, we will confine our attention to the practical implications of the phenomenon.

If we accept the data on face descriptions obtained by Ellis et al. (1975)
from African and European subjects, then it would seem that members of
one race may fail to encode appropriate facial features of members of
another race. Thus most people would be less able to reconstruct (Ellis,
Davies, & McMurran, 1979) or to identify faces of another race than they
would faces of their own race (Elliott, Wills, & Goldstein, 1973; Malpass &
Kravitz, 1969).

Formal training in identifying members of another race may be of some
benefit (Elliott et al., 1973), but such benefit may be transitory. Training,
therefore, may not ensure that professional groups, such as policemen, are
equally skilled in own- and other-race face memory (Malpass, Lavigueur, &
Weldon, 1973).

Training

The efficient acquisition of information from faces is also of practical relevance for those who seek to improve their ability to remember faces of
people from within their race. Most non-psychologists from Leonardo da
Vinci onward have advocated a piecemeal strategy in which the face is analyzed feature by feature (Furst, 1962; Lorayne & Lucas, 1976; Penry, 1971).

Penry's system for analyzing faces was examined in a series of three experiments by Woodhead, Baddeley, and Simmonds (1979). They evaluated a course on improving face recognition based upon Penry's principles, which essentially train the individual to categorize the various features of a face along specific dimensions, starting with a classification of face shape and proceeding to other facial features.

Subjects undergoing a 3-day course on Penry's techniques of face encoding were tested before and afterward on a simple face memory task. A control group was tested with the same tasks but without an intervening training session. The result indicated no improvement in the proportion of correctly identified faces for the experimental groups (60% hits before, 60% hits afterward). The control group revealed similar unchanged scores.

In a second experiment Woodhead and colleagues confirmed the original finding; and in a third experiment they discovered that those who underwent Penry training were actually worse at recognizing faces than those who had not taken the course!

Malpass (1981b) has offered two hypotheses to account for the failure of the experiments of Woodhead and colleagues as well as of his own studies (Malpass et al., 1973) to demonstrate positive training effects. One is that people's ability to recognize faces is overlearned and therefore difficult to improve. The other is that the methods used to train people are inappropriate. He points out that studies in which subjects are enjoined to make global judgments of faces when encountering them, a "personological approach," have shown that face memory can be significantly improved.

The first demonstration of this phenomenon was made by Bower and Karlin (1974) who discovered that asking subjects to make judgments either of the likely honesty or likability of each face produced better subsequent recognition rates than judgments of physical attributes of each face (i.e., male or female). Others quickly confirmed this finding (e.g., Patterson & Baddeley, 1977; Warrington & Ackroyd, 1975). Winograd (1978), however, has pointed out that the main reason that the personological encoding strategy produces better results than the physical trait strategy may simply be that the former ensures overall face analysis, whereas the latter often involves a limited self-termination feature search. Indeed, he has repeatedly shown that requiring subjects to engage in a more extensive scan of each face in search of physical information leads to an improvement in memory comparable to that earlier discovered for personological judgments. Winograd (1981) reported that requiring subjects to look for the most distinctive feature of each face was as effective as asking them to make judgments of friendliness, honesty, or intelligence. Both methods produced significantly better performance than simply asking subjects whether each face has a big nose, straight hair, or a square jaw. Winograd accounts for these and other data by suggesting that global strategies require the individual to scan more features than do piecemeal analyses of single features – particularly because the former are more likely to lead to the encoding of any distinctive features that might be relevant.

Winograd's theoretical analysis is interesting, but it does not explain why training techniques such as Penry's are so singularly unsuccessful. Penry advocates a detailed and systematic scanning of the face, which should reveal the presence of any distinctive features and therefore should yield an improvement in memory. Two reasons for this apparent anomaly immediately present themselves. One is that the subjects studied by Woodhead et al. (1979), although adequately instructed, may have failed to apply the training techniques when under test. Alternatively, Winograd's (1981) data may reveal less about training than it at first seemed. Because no control groups were included in any of the four experiments he reports, it is possible that Winograd has not shown an *improvement* in face memory by ensuring elaborative encoding but, rather less interestingly for the present discussion, has demonstrated that constraining face scanning to a single feature is deleterious to subsequent recognition.

Moreover, Malpass (1981b) reports a study in which he specifically tested the relative efficiency of 12 hour-long training procedures based on: (a) overall feature analysis following Penry's system; (b) global personality ratings, allowing subjects to use as many categories as they wished; (c) examination of groups of faces, similarity judgments being made among them; and (d) repeated experience of conventional face-recognition tests. The results can be briefly summarized: None of the training techniques was better than any other and there was an overall drop in recognition performance from pretraining to posttraining tests.

Malpass's observations are rather discouraging to anyone intent on training face memory skills; but, before meekly accepting them, it is worth reporting that the overall level of mean performance in the pretraining and posttraining tests was modest (A' of .78 and .72, respectively). These levels leave room for improvement, but none of the methods tried yielded any. Perhaps the training necessary to improve a highly learned skill would require far more time than that allowed by Malpass and others who have attempted to do so.

Viewing conditions

Among the many factors that may affect the encoding of facial features are the amount of time for which the face is seen; the amount of attention allocated to it; and, under certain circumstances, the mode in which the face is originally encountered (live, film, or photograph).

The first two factors are probably related. If we assume that a finite period of intensive study is required for the establishment of a new facial "trace" or "engram," then the questions follow as to how long it takes and under what circumstances a robust trace is likely to occur. Needless to say, we have definite answers to neither question. What can be said, however, is that viewing duration is important. Ellis, Davies, and Shepherd (1977) reported that altering viewing durations from .25 second to 4 seconds improved subsequent recognition memory in a log-linear fashion. Others have shown that increasing viewing durations beyond 4 seconds leads to further improvements in memory, but we cannot say whether the function remains log-linear or at what point it becomes asymptotic (Alexander, 1972; Forbes, 1975).

It is tempting simply to assume, all other things being equal, that the longer a witness views a face the better the chances of identification. Although this may, in general, prove to be a reasonable "estimator variable" (Ellis, 1981b; Wells, 1978), the fact remains that the observations reported involve the presentation of photographed heads with no concurrent distractions.

In real life, more than a person's head is viewed within an environment rich in visual and aural detail. Brandt (1945) examined the eye movements of subjects looking at a full-length picture of a man and discovered that only a third of fixations were made to the man's face. In a real criminal encounter it is possible that even less time would be spent looking at, say, an assailant's face. Instead, the victim, as a result of extreme stress, may focus attention upon a weapon or some other detail (Clifford & Bull, 1978; Loftus, 1979). It is not possible practically to separate attention and stress, because they interact; a high degree of arousal is likely to lead to a narrowing of attention and, possibly, a more labile deployment of concentration (see Deffenbacher, 1983, for a discussion of these and related problems). Laboratory studies have shown, however, that it is possible for people to encode facial information while at the same time attending to verbal information (Kellogg, 1980). Thus it may well be that the amount of aural information occurring during a criminal encounter is not an important factor in determining how much facial information is processed.

The medium in which a face is presented has a strong effect on a witness. In real life we usually encounter live faces and see them in a variety of expressions and poses. Sometimes, however, it is necessary to encode a film or picture of a person who is to be sought. This form of presentation is experienced particularly by police officers, but occasionally members of the public are requested to look out for the person presented in a picture.

Shepherd, Ellis, and Davies (1982) presented target people to subjects either live, as a color video recording, as multiple color prints, or as multiple black-and-white prints. The subjects' task was to listen to a 2-minute life story given by the target (a recording of his or her voice was used if the target was not present) and to rate the truthfulness of the tale. Two weeks later, subjects were recalled to the laboratory and asked to identify the target from among nine people and give a confidence judgment on their decisions. These parades were also live, video, color prints, or black-and-white prints. The initial mode of presentation proved to be a highly significant factor in the accuracy of the identification. Generally, live presentations yielded the highest accuracy of identification and greater confidence, regardless of the mode of identity parade. The worst performances were obtained from subjects who initially saw the target in picture form.

The results found by Shepherd et al. are of practical interest, but they may be difficult to apply. Although live presentation may result in higher accuracy of identification, such presentation is often impossible and people have to search for someone with only photographs to guide them. Baddeley (1979) has commented on the fact that Carlos, the international terrorist, though known to police throughout the world from his photograph, nevertheless seems able to move about with impunity, living proof both of the difficulty of encoding a face from photographs and of the efficacy of disguise.

Uniqueness

Not all faces are encoded efficiently, but some faces appear to be more readily remembered (Goldstein & Chance, 1971). A. Peters (1917) found that faces judged to be either pleasant or unpleasant were well remembered. A similar finding was also reported by Shepherd and Ellis (1973), although in their study faces had been independently rated for attractiveness rather than pleasantness.

Light, Kayra-Stuart, and Hollander (1979) gave an interesting theoretical analysis of such observations. They demonstrated that faces judged to be atypical were particularly well remembered regardless of viewing and storage conditions. Essentially their thesis is that faces judged to be typical are easily confused with one another – an argument to which I shall briefly return in the next section. Goldstein and Chance (1981) in their analysis of typicality or uniqueness studies emphasize the similarity between them and studies of the von Restorff effect (i.e., verbal items that in any way are easily distinguished from others in the list, say, by being written in a different colored ink, are well recalled). According to Goldstein and Chance (1981), an "atypical face is perceived to be atypical because it is compared to the observer's memory store (schema) of faces. Possibly scalar judgments are made automatically with every encoding, and atypical faces compared to typical faces may be encoded differently" (pp. 88–89). They go on to suggest that atypical faces may evoke more arousal (cf. Shepherd & Ellis, 1973) or produce different kinds of eye movements from those occurring for faces that are less unusual. These ideas, of course, are speculative. From a practical point of view, though, it is clear that some faces are more easily encoded than others (and subsequently recognized), but the exact parameters and demographic distribution of "unique" faces are unknown. Furthermore it is debatable whether the knowledge that some faces are more easily encoded than other faces would be of any practical value in, say, a court of law dealing with identification evidence. It is interesting to note, however, that the committee headed by Devlin (1976), in their review of English identification laws, recommended that a judge should advise the jury that a defendant's nondescript appearance may reduce the validity of identification.

In summary, the evidence favors the view that, up to some as yet undetermined point, the more time and attention spent looking at a face the more likely it will be later recognized. Upper face features appear to command more attention than lower face features, and therefore disguises involving changes of hairstyle are probably more effective than those involving a mustache or beard. We may encode faces of people from another race rather differently and less efficiently than those from our own race. Training may improve other-race face memory, at least temporarily, but it is difficult to produce any improvement on own-race face memory. We are rather better at encoding information from live faces than from video recordings or photographs, and we encode unique faces more easily than typical ones.

Storage

Once a face has been successfully encoded what then happens to the trace? Does the passage of time inexorably cause forgetting? Is there any evidence that subsequently encountered faces in any way interfere with the trace? Can the trace survive, unaltered, the influence of conflicting or distorting information? Each of these questions is of practical relevance. Suspects are identified from photographs weeks or months after an incident, during which time the witness will have encountered countless new faces. His or her memory of the person may well be colored by stereotypes of criminal faces, or may be affected by suggestions from other witnesses or from investigating officers.

Delay

The first storage characteristic to be addressed concerns the likely effects of the length of the interval between seeing a face and retrieving it. We have just seen the significance of the duration of viewing to the encoding of facial features, but what about the temporal factor following the initial encounter?

One widely cited study by Bahrick, Bahrick, and Wittlinger (1975) will be used to set the scene. It showed that memory for high school classmates' faces is remarkably durable, being reasonably accurate after an average interval of 48 years and virtually unaffected by an interval of up to 35 years. These observations, of course, are not strictly relevant to the present discussion, because we are primarily concerned with memory for strangers' faces. Still, they do illustrate the fact that memory for faces can, under some conditions, involve extraordinary trace strength.

Laughery, Fessler, Lenorovitz, and Yoblick (1974) discovered that memory for a single face did not deteriorate between immediate testing and testing after a week's delay. Similarly, Goldstein and Chance (1971) found no deterioration over a 2-day interval. A longer interval was investigated by Deffenbacher, Carr, and Leu (1981), who not only found no loss in recognition accuracy over 2 weeks, but under some circumstances actually found a small improvement. One of the few exceptions to this rule was the finding by Krouse (1981) that the police officers who were the subjects of her study were less able to recognize 16 faces, each embedded among 3 distractor faces, 2 or 3 days later than they were immediately after they had seen them. Overall identification accuracy was less than 60%, which is rather lower than usual. Krouse argues that task difficulty may be a significant factor, but this is questionable as we shall see in the next study, where identification levels were even lower but delay effects were nonetheless found to be elusive. What should be added, however, is that if the recognition test is made difficult by presenting each alternative for only .25 second, then a deterioration in memory for even a single face occurs over a 3-week interval (Davies, Ellis, & Shepherd, 1978a).

In the earlier-mentioned study on attractiveness by Shepherd and Ellis (1973), some decline was observed in memory for 27 girls' faces after an interval of 5 weeks. This drop in recognition accuracy was confined to faces judged to be of average attractiveness; the high- and low-attractive faces were remembered as well after 5 weeks as they had been upon immediate testing or after a 6-day interval.

It is possible that this result occurred because the faces of intermediate attractiveness are more commonly encountered and are, therefore, more "typical." According to the analysis of Light et al. (1979), mentioned earlier, typical faces have fewer distinguishing features and, presumably, are assimilated more readily into what they term the "facial prototype." Perhaps Krouse's stimuli contained a high proportion of "typical" faces.

Solso and McCarthy (1981) have also examined "prototype" faces using Identikit features. Their results are constrained by the artificiality of the stimuli they used but indicate that some constructive processes may operate during storage so that when people see hair on one face, eyes on another, a nose on another, and so on, they can identify a face uniquely made up of these features and believe that it has already been presented. Ellis (1981c), however, reported no such confusion among subjects shown similar faces and then shown a "prototype" face made according to the Galton technique by photographically superimposing the faces to make a face unique but typical of the group. Ellis (1981c) concluded that during storage of faces no cerebral equivalent of the Galton photographic method took place over time, but despite the negative results found, it may be worthwhile extending the study. People do sometimes complain that when trying to recall a face last seen a long time ago they imagine a face of the same basic structure but different in detail from the one intended. It would be interesting to study this phenomenon over a variety of time periods.

To return now to simple delay studies, a more ambitious set of experiments was reported by Shepherd et al. (1982), who examined delay intervals from 1 week up to 11 months. In one experiment a young man burst in on a psychometric testing session demanding to know the owner of a particular car. The subjects, all members of the general public, were later required to identify the target from a video array of 9 men at intervals of a week, a month, 3 months, or 11 months. No significant decline in accuracy was found over the intervals of 1 week to 3 months, nor was there an increase in false alarm rates. The 11-month delay, however, did cause a significant fall in the number of subjects making a correct identification. Interestingly, there was no change in the false alarm rates across the four delay intervals. In two further experiments no decline in accuracy was found for selecting one or two targets between a week and 4 months. The data from these three experiments are quite consistent in trend; but note that they differ from those reported by Egan, Pittner, and Goldstein (1977), who found that although hit rate was unaffected by a delay of 8 weeks, the tendency to make false identifications did rise over the same period. There are too many differences between the study of Egan and colleagues and those reported by Shepherd et al. (1982) to make a sensible comparison, but perhaps the crucial factor is that Egan and colleagues always employed two target figures but only paraded one of them, which may have contributed to their discovery of a high false identification rate following a long interval.

Generally speaking, delay intervals even as long as weeks or months do not automatically reduce recognition accuracy, which suggests not only that the memory traces involved are durable but that they are fairly robust, being relatively unaffected by other faces that are bound to be seen during the intervening interval.

Interference

Although the evidence from delay studies may suggest that interference among face memory traces is unlikely for intervals of up to 3 or 4 months, does that mean that no distortion or disruption takes place? The short answer would seem to be that under some circumstances changes may occur; but whether these are strictly changes during storage or, instead, reflect distortions at the retrieval stage is often rather difficult to tell.

The earliest experimental evidence that stored facial images may undergo systematic distortion was published by Bartlett (1932). He showed subjects five drawings of men serving in various branches of the British armed services. After various intervals, beginning half an hour later, Bartlett asked his subjects to describe each face. He discovered that the successive descriptions tended to change over time, corresponding more and more to stereotyped impressions of or attitudes toward the British Tommy, the army colonel, the able seaman, and so on. "Even in immediate memory the features of the face often tended to be made more conventional, while in subsequent recall they tended to approach yet more closely the conventional pattern" (p. 54). Here is an example of the process at work: The subject originally described the naval captain's face as being serious-looking and having a heavy chin. Three weeks later the same subject described him as "very serious and determined looking." When eventually Bartlett showed the picture again, the subject was amazed and thought that a new face had been substituted, because in her memory the image had changed to one of grave seriousness and the facial features had altered to accommodate the stereotype of a naval captain.

Bartlett also noted that detail was interchanged among the faces and that totally new detail was sometimes incorporated. He commented that such errors of detail increased considerably the longer the facial images remained in store. Bartlett realized that his methodology may have contributed to some of his results. The so-called Method of Description allows for a verbal contamination that may not normally occur when storing facial images. A very different methodology was introduced by Shepherd, Ellis, McMurran, and Davies (1978) in a study also aimed at investigating the influence of stereotypes on facial recall.

Shepherd and colleagues showed subjects individually a photograph of a male face for 30 seconds. During this observation period half of the subjects were casually informed that the man was a multiple murderer: the other half were informed that he was a lifeboat captain recently decorated for bravery. Each subject then made a Photofit likeness of the face from memory and afterward rated the original face (again from memory) on a series of bipolar scales. The Photofit compositions were also rated on the same bipolar scales by an independent group of judges.

The results indicated that the two groups of subjects made slightly different kinds of facial compositions, the "murderer" group's being generally less favorably rated, particularly with regard to qualities of intelligence and attractiveness. An analysis of the face ratings given from memory by the original subjects showed a much more dramatic difference between the two groups. Here the "murderer" group not only remembered him as being a less attractive and intelligent-looking man, but also one who looked quick-tempered, unpleasant, unsociable, cruel, and lacking in humor.

Although it is not possible to establish whether in the study by Shepherd and colleagues the influence of verbal labeling occurred at the encoding stage, during storage, or even at retrieval, the study does once again demonstrate the malleability of face memory, which may be particularly problematic when witnesses to a crime give a description of the culprit or when they make a composite likeness. Further illustrations of this point were recently provided by Loftus and Greene (1980) in a paper aptly titled "Warning: Even Memory for Faces May Be Contagious."

Pilot work by Loftus and Greene indicated that subjects who saw a face and then heard a description of it given by someone else tended to incorporate the other person's information and make correspondingly erroneous Identi-Kit likenesses. In a series of experiments, Loftus and Greene further explored these tentative findings. They presented targets live, in photographs, or on film. Whatever the mode of presentation, some subjects proved to be unable to ignore the inaccurate information purporting to come from another witness. The study showed that particular details may be altered (e.g., straight hair remembered as curly) or imported (e.g., mustache remembered when none existed). In all cases, whether memory was tested by recall or recognition, the information about a target face held in store could be manipulated, at least for a significant number of subjects.

Loftus and Greene point out that their results are to some extent inconsistent with those found by Davies, Shepherd, and Ellis (1979a), who examined whether simple retroactive interference occurs in face memory. Davies and colleagues showed a videotape of 3 men playing cards. Subjects who subsequently searched a series of 100 faces that did not include the 3 men were found to be significantly less likely than control groups to identify the targets in a recognition test in which all 3 were presented along with 33 foils. Davies et al. (1979a) also discovered that the group who had searched the 100 interpolated faces made fewer false identifications and therefore attributed this and the corresponding drop in hit rate to a shift in response criterion. In other words, they suggested that the experience of the interpolated faces had not distorted or diminished memory for the 3 target faces but, instead, had caused those subjects to be more cautious than control subjects in making a positive response during the recognition test. Further confirmation of this explanation was provided by an examination of the behavior of control subjects during the test. They, too, became significantly more cautious in the second half of the test, which suggests that a criterion shift may automatically occur in response to the experience of so many negative instances.

Loftus and Greene rightly point out that their data cannot be attributed to any simple shifts in response criterion because, like Bartlett, they observed qualitative changes in memory that persisted even when the original faces were shown again. In the study by Deffenbacher et al. (1981), no forgetting of faces occurred as a result of a 2-week interval between presentation and test. In other conditions, however, errors were generated after inspection of interpolated faces. This study is conceptually similar to that of Davies et al. (1979a), but there are also many differences. Without becoming unnecessarily entangled in details of design and analysis, I will summarize the results of present interest. Interpolation of faces reduced face recognition; false alarm levels to novel faces, however, were unaffected by the interpolations. These results are somewhat at variance with those of Davies et al. (1979a). Instead, they perhaps correspond to the idea that faces held in storage can be directly affected or contaminated by various forms of retroactive interference.

This conclusion, albeit a reasonable one in view of the majority of data available, does not quite square with the fact that memory for faces is relatively immune to the passage of time – for, unless a person lives on a desert island, any increase in time will involve a corresponding increase in the number of faces he or she encounters and thus will allow a greater amount of retroactive interference. My colleague John Shepherd points out that what may be critical is the context in which a person encounters other faces and their distribution. If the context differs from the original encounter and other faces are seen sporadically, perhaps little interference ensues.

In the criminal context, it would seem that an image of a miscreant's face could effectively be altered in the memory of a witness by descriptions given by other witnesses or, less surely, by the perusal by the witness of large numbers of mug-shot photographs. There is some evidence to suggest that the longer a face is held in storage the more likely it will conform to some stereotype, say, of a mugger's face or a typical rapist's face, but before firmly accepting such a conclusion we need more empirical work on the topic. It is probable that simply viewing faces in an everyday manner does not lead to any appreciable retroactive interference. Another conclusion from the research reviewed in this section is that memory for some faces may be relatively immune to distortion either from the passage of time or from retroactive interference. The more typical face is most susceptible to distortion, and statistically it is more probable that we will encounter such a face.

Retrieval

Figure 2.1 shows retrieval as involving either recall or recognition, both of which are of prime interest when examining practical, particularly forensic, aspects of face memory. These two aspects of retrieval will be discussed separately before being evaluated together.

Recall

When witnesses to a crime are asked to recall the culprit's facial features, they are confronted with an extremely difficult task. How can a witness convey a complex, possibly incomplete, image to someone else with sufficient clarity that they can be said to share the same knowledge (Ellis & Christie, 1980)? Obviously this is no problem with straightforward verbal information; ideas that are encoded as words can usually be transmitted with virtually errorless ease. Nonverbal information, however, is more difficult to convey. The smell of a rose or the taste of claret cannot easily be described. Similarly the details of someone's face are difficult enough to convey when the face is present (Ellis, Deregowski, & Shepherd, 1975; Shepherd, Davies, & Ellis, 1978); when the witness is drawing upon memory the task is even more daunting. Ellis, Shepherd, and Davies (1980), for example, required subjects to describe two faces from memory, one immediately after seeing it and one after an interval of an hour, a day, or a week. The results quite clearly showed that verbal descriptions of faces became briefer as the interval lengthened and provided a less useful means for other subjects to identify which face was being recalled.

There are, of course, other ways of enabling a witness to externalize a facial image. Methods such as Photofit and Identikit have been reviewed by Davies (1981), so I shall not detail any of the work on the efficiency of such systems. They have generally proved to be rather disappointing techniques insofar as they enable witnesses to convey at best only an approximate image of the original face, even when increased in flexibility by being linked to a powerful computer graphics system (Christie et al., 1981). Moreover, Photofit compositions are no more accurate than freehand drawings made by subjects with no artistic training (Ellis, Davies, & Shepherd, 1978). Indeed, Christie and Ellis (1981) have recently demonstrated that verbal descriptions, for all their undoubted inadequacies, are more likely to be successfully decoded and the intended face selected from a range of alternatives than are Photofit compositions made under the supervision of a highly experienced operator. Whether words or pictures are better retained for delayed identification, however, has yet to be determined.

Other aspects of face recall merit passing mention. The two principal composition methods, Photofit and Identikit, are inadequate but not simply because of any recall difficulty. Subjects using these methods have often been found to be equally good at immediately constructing a face from memory as when the face is present. According to Phillips (1978), almost 90% of subjects shown a picture of a face could, 20 minutes later, experience an image of it. Read (1979) has shown that mental rehearsal of a face image facilitates later recognition, and one practical corollary to this has been explored by Malpass and Devine (1981b).

Malpass and Devine staged an act of vandalism and 5 months later tested some witnesses on their ability to identify the vandal's photograph from among five photographs. Half of the subjects were simply asked to select the culprit from the photo lineup. The other half were given a "guided recollection" interview in which they were encouraged to recall, among other things, the setting of the crime, to visualize their neighbors, the room, the actions of the vandal, and his appearance. Subjects who had thus been encouraged mentally to rehearse all of these things were more likely to select the vandal from the photo lineup than were those who had not been encouraged to recall the various details of the event (60% vs. 40%).

Recognition

As I have already mentioned, memory for photographs of faces when measured by conventional laboratory recognition techniques appears to be very good indeed (Goldstein, 1977; Phillips, 1978), provided the same pictures of the target faces presented initially are shown again at recognition. Such laboratory studies generally reveal an accuracy level of about 80%, the percentage varying according to the number of targets presented and the target–distractor ratio at test (Forbes, 1975; Goldstein, 1977). When a crime is being investigated there are three kinds of recognition "test": (a) the witness searches mug-shot photographs in the hope of seeing the culprit; (b) a suspect is placed among a number of other people (usually corresponding in gross physical characteristics to the suspect) for what is termed corporeal identification, the lineup; and less commonly (c) the suspect alone is surreptitiously shown to the witness in what is called the showup. (Although the last condition, under ideal circumstances, should be sufficient [Wallace, 1980], it is clear that too many biases can influence a witness's willingness to make an identification and thus the showup is not always fair – see the review by Malpass and Devine, Chapter 4 in this volume.) In the real world, of course, the face seen at test is unlikely to be identical to the one seen during initial encounter because of changes in hairstyle, expression, orientation, and so on.

Familiarity

Whatever the actual method for effecting recognition, the essential process underlying each one is that the subject or witness looks at a face and decides whether or not it is familiar. This is not quite as easy as it sounds, for faces that have never been encountered previously will occasionally give rise to feelings of familiarity, and likewise, faces that actually have been encountered may not produce a sufficiently strong feeling of familiarity. The decision process has been likened to those studied in conventional statistical decision theory experiments (Ellis, Davies, & Shepherd, 1977; Hilgendorf & Irving, 1978a). The inevitable consequences of such a process are two kinds of errors: those where a target face fails to elicit strong enough feelings of familiarity (misses); and those occurring when novel faces give rise to strong feelings of familiarity (false alarms). The two types of error are reciprocally related because each depends on the willingness of the subject-witness to make a positive identification. With a lax criterion of familiarity, subjects are unlikely to miss many targets, but false alarm levels may be high; and with a stricter criterion misses will be high and false alarms low.

It may be predicted that faces similar to target faces will be more likely to be misclassified as having been encountered than would dissimilar faces. Goldstein, Stephenson, and Chance (1977) in fact did observe that false alarms are not randomly distributed. They found that some distractors were more likely to evoke erroneous positive identifications. Courtois and Mueller (1981) added that atypical distractors are least likely to be falsely identified. Other relevant findings emerged from a study by Davies, Shepherd, and Ellis (1979b), who performed a series of experiments in which target faces were mixed with faces previously established by cluster analysis as being either similar or dissimilar. In one experiment, Davies et al. (1979b) discovered that almost three-quarters of the false identifications made were to faces drawn from the same cluster as the target faces. Another experiment was performed aimed at reducing errors by instructing subjects only to make an identification if they were certain. This reduced but by no means eliminated errors – particularly in conditions where the recognition test was arranged so that no targets were present. The latter condition is comparable to a lineup containing an innocent person similar in appearance to the culprit. Here the results of Davies et al. (1979b) suggest that there is a definite risk of misidentification.

Unconscious transference

Deciding that a face is familiar is only the first part of the identification procedure. Next must come a process of categorization: The face must be recognized as having been encountered at a particular time and place (Mandler, 1980). As we shall see, a slip at this stage may have dire consequences. That is to say, if a witness discovers that a face presented as a mug shot or in an identity parade is familiar, he or she may indeed have encountered it previously – but not within the context of the crime. An illustration of this kind of faulty recognition is given by Houts (1956). A booking clerk at a railway station was held up at gunpoint. He later identified a man from an identity parade, but the man, a sailor from a nearby camp, had a cast-iron alibi. According to the clerk, the sailor's face looked familiar so he had picked him out. This sense of familiarity resulted from the fact that the sailor had on three separate occasions bought railway tickets from the clerk, who had misclassified the face at the time of the parade, assuming that it was familiar because it belonged to the robber. The phenomenon of wrongly categorizing familiar faces is known as unconscious transference (Williams, 1955).

Loftus (1976) investigated a related phenomenon whereby there is confusion about who among a group actually perpetrated a particular action. Subjects in her experiment were told the details of a crime, and as each of six characters was mentioned his photograph was shown. The fourth character was identified as the one who hit someone with a paperweight. Half the subjects then saw a photo parade of five men, including the miscreant. The other half saw a parade that included one of the other characters in the story plus four new faces. Over 80% of the first group correctly identified the culprit. Of the second group, 60% identified the "bystander" as being the culprit. Loftus explains these data in terms of the "integrative malleable nature of human memory," which we have already encountered in the section on storage.

Further illustration of this process was given by Brown, Deffenbacher, and Sturgill (1977), who presented subjects with live targets and later asked them first to try to select the target persons from a photo parade and then a week later to identify them from a live parade. The live parade contained targets whose faces had appeared in the photo parade, targets whose photographs had not appeared, nontargets whose photographs had appeared in the photo parade, and other nontargets whose faces had not appeared in the photo parade. The most significant finding was that "novel" faces seen as photographs were as likely as target faces not shown as photographs to be selected from the live parade.

The practical implications of the studies are quite important. If an investigating police officer shows pictures of a suspect to a witness and then presents the man at an identity parade, there is a grave risk that he will be picked out even if he is innocent. A convincing illustration of this was provided by the British case of George Ince, who was tried for murder, and, though quite innocent, almost convicted on the evidence of two eyewitnesses who had both been shown pictures of Ince prior to seeing him in an identity parade (Cole & Pringle, 1974).

A theme related to unconscious transference is that of context. As Mandler (1980) points out, upon finding a face to be familiar, we may actively try to retrieve the appropriate context for the face in order to effect full recognition (e.g., do I know him from work? from my neighborhood? the garage? etc.) How much easier recognition would be, one may conjecture, if the appropriate context were provided!

Context effects

Laboratory evidence for the speculation on appropriate context is not very impressive, however. Bower and Karlin (1974) found no context effect at all when pairs of faces shown at study were tested together, alone, or paired with a different face during a later recognition test. Contradictory results were subsequently provided by Watkins, Ho, and Tulving (1976) and Winograd and Rivers-Bulkeley (1977), but the effects reported are small and even the small effects found may not be related to memory sensitivity but to shifts in response criterion (Ellis, 1981c).

It is possible that the reason for weak or absent context effects is that the experiments merely required subjects to make yes-or-no judgments of familiarity. Mandler (1980) maintains that "the initial sense of knowing (the person) is context free." Knowledge of context is independent but combined with familiarity information to achieve full recognition.

Brown, Deffenbacher, and Sturgill (1977) presented faces in two different rooms and at the recognition test asked subjects not only to say whether or not a face was familiar but also to state in which of the two rooms each face had initially occurred. It was found that subjects were not very accurate at saying in which room the faces had been shown. Daw and Parkin (1981) followed up the work of Brown and colleagues by asking some subjects to rate each face for likability during initial presentation. These subjects had relatively good recall for the contextual background face compared with subjects who made judgments about the most salient physical feature of each face. As for the recognition data, there was no difference in performance between the two groups, a finding consistent with that first published by Winograd (1978).

There appears to be an absence of critical experimental evidence on the question of context and identification accuracy. What is required is an investigation of face recognition when the context changes totally, compared with performance when no alterations in context occur. The first condition would approximate the usual situation in which a witness sees a culprit commit a crime and then attempts to select someone from an identity parade. The second condition would be the procedure of showing a suspect to a witness in the same context as that in which the original viewing took place, a procedure not normally followed in real life. If experimental results were to favor the view that substantial improvements in identification performance were to be achieved by retaining the original crime context at parade, then police practice could be altered accordingly. Results from experiments with face–pair contexts, though showing only small effects, nonetheless suggest the possibility that when the total context is manipulated, larger improvements for same-context identifications may occur. A similar conclusion can be reached from the work on guided memory discussed earlier (Malpass & Devine, 1981b).

Pose

One decision concerning the arrangement of mug-shot files is what pose or poses to show of each face. It is likely that a witness to a crime will view the culprit's face from a variety of angles and displaying more than one expression. Two related questions of practical interest are now briefly to be considered: (a) Are people able to identify faces seen in one pose or expression when confronted with the same face from a different angle or showing a different expression? and (b) Is there an optimal pose for displaying faces in a mug-shot file?

Three studies have shown that faces changed in pose (full face to three-quarter profile or vice versa) are as well recognized as when no transformation occurs (Davies, Ellis, & Shepherd, 1978b; Laughery et al., 1971; Patterson & Baddeley, 1977). A change from full face to full profile, however, is not so well handled (Patterson & Baddeley, 1977). Three more recent experiments, on the other hand, have shown that there is a significant deterioration in recognition accuracy following even the small changes in pose between three-quarter profile and full face (Ellis & Deregowski, 1981; Krouse, 1981). Bruce (1982) also noted, contrary to Galper and Hochberg (1971), that a change in expression (smiling to unsmiling) resulted in poorer recognition performance and, furthermore, discovered that a combination of pose and expression changes are particularly detrimental to accuracy.

Krouse has explained the failure of the three earlier studies to find a pose-change effect as being due to the failure of the investigators to use measures of false alarm rates to correct the hit rates for any changes in response criterion. Another possible reason for discrepancies among studies arises from the ever-present problem of relating task difficulty across studies (Ellis, in press). Ellis and Deregowski (1981), for example, found that although subjects showed a small pose-change effect for faces drawn from their own race, by far the greater effect was obtained when subjects tried to match other-race faces that were changed in pose between study and test. This result may reflect the difficulty of the latter task and may indicate that pose-change effects are to some extent contingent upon overall task difficulty.

Is there an ideal pose for use in police records? Krouse (1981) suggests that a three-quarter profile contains most of the information available in a face and that this pose has an advantage over the full-face or full-profile view. Her own data support that assertion.

Normally, of course, a witness to a crime will have an opportunity to view the culprit from more than one aspect. Baddeley and Woodhead (1983) explored this by initially presenting two or three views of a face and testing for recognition by full, three-quarter, or profile views. Again the three-quarter profile proved to be the most efficient – indeed, just as good as a combination of full and profile poses. Baddeley and Woodhead interpret this result to mean that the three-quarter profile possesses advantages over the statistical one already mentioned. They suggest that the three-quarter view allows the viewer to access full-face and profile information as well as their relationship. The three-quarter profile may be said to be the "canonical view" of a face and perhaps therefore ought to be used in police mug-shot systems as a convenient and efficient aid to face recognition.

Face retrieval involves a number of different processes, many of which are of keen interest to criminal investigators. Recalling faces so that others can identify them is a difficult process. Recognition seems much easier, but it, too, has various difficulties that may be ameliorated by the experimental psychologist. More work is urgently needed on the problem of possible context effects in recognition, principally because the performance of witnesses at identity parades is thought to be poor in comparison with laboratory studies of face recognition (Goldstein, 1977; Shepherd, Ellis, & Davies, in press).

Recall and recognition

Recalling a face is usually more difficult than recognizing it. The process of recognition generally involves less cognitive effort and, moreover, is probably exercised more often. True, we do occasionally try to imagine someone's face and we may at times achieve a clear image of a face seen even only once before. The business of making that image public, however, presents great problems – not the least of which is that any recall procedure requires a decomposition of the gestalt image into its constituent parts. From my own introspections on this process, I am persuaded that it is difficult, if not impossible, to simultaneously maintain an image of a face and extract information from it (cf. Brooks, 1968).

Perhaps from a practical viewpoint the ideal solution is to capitalize on the strengths of both forms of retrieval: to encourage a witness mentally to rehearse the face of the wanted person and then to use any crude verbal description or visual composite merely to access an appropriate area of a mug-shot file that the witness can inspect. Such a system has been explored by an interdisciplinary group working at Houston University (Laughery, Rhodes, & Batten, 1981) and is currently being investigated by my colleagues John Shepherd, Graham Davies, and Alan Milne at Aberdeen University in conjunction with the British Home Office.

Individual differences

Not surprisingly there are differences among individuals in their ability to remember faces (Davies, 1978; Ellis, 1975; Shepherd, 1981; Yarmey, 1979a), but whether these differences are due to encoding, storage, or retrieval factors is usually unknown. The four sources just cited give ample accounts of the large literature on individual differences. Futher specialized reviews may be found for age effects (Carey, 1981; Yarmey, Chapter 7, this volume) and sex effects (McKelvie, 1978). Individual differences in witness performance are covered in Shepherd et al. (1982), who also discuss the practical implications of such differences.

Shepherd (1981) points out that one of the problems besetting anyone interested in studying individual differences in face memory is that it is not a very stable ability. Goldstein and Chance (1978) found positive correlations in performance across repeated face recognition tests. Deffenbacher, Brown, and Sturgill (1978) and Shepherd et al. (in press), however, found no significant relationship between accuracy in identifying a target at an identity parade and recognition of faces in photographs. Similarly, Davies et al. (1978a) failed to find a significant correlation between recognizing a face and recalling it using Photofit.

Not only are there difficulties in extending results of laboratory tests to real-life face recognition tasks, but the laboratory data themselves fall short of the sort of consistency required for any practical implementation. Shepherd (1981), for example, cites 17 experiments that revealed a sex difference in face recognition, usually a female superiority; he also cites 18 experiments where no sex difference was observed. Two studies of another independent variable, field dependency, indicate that field dependents are better at face recognition than field independents; another study shows no relationship at all, and two other studies show the opposite effect. A similar lack of agreement among studies may be found for the independent variables of anxiety and intelligence. Thus, even if it were practicable to screen witnesses to a crime on a battery of psychological tests, the results would not yield information of much value to the triers of fact, who are faced with conflicting eyewitness evidence.

Summary and conclusions

This review of the practical aspects of face memory has grouped some of the relevant research into a chain of areas concerned with the perception of faces, their storage, and finally their retrieval, either by recall or recognition. At each stage it has been possible to demonstrate that various factors operate either to facilitate or to impair face memory. Important factors include: cue saliency, particularly upper face features; race; duration of viewing; the uniqueness of the face; what information is given after the face has been seen; and whether it is seen again in the same context. It has been shown that each of these factors may powerfully affect the accuracy of face memory. Others, such as subjects' prior training, delay, and interference, have yielded inconsistent results and may be considered to be rather weak factors.

As I mentioned earlier, some of the reviewed data are too general to be applied directly to the operations of perception and memory of witnesses to crimes. Many of the studies reported were conducted simply to examine theoretical issues with, therefore, little concern for the realism of the procedures. For some years, however, we have known that laboratory studies using identical pictures of people as stimuli at presentation and test produce performance levels far higher than those achieved by witnesses to a live incident. What we have yet to decide is whether there are not only *quantitative* differences between these two methodological approaches but also *qualitative* differences. If the latter are found, then it will be necessary for forensic psychologists, especially those giving expert testimony in courts of law, to base their opinions solely on evidence derived from experiments involving natural stimulus material and to eschew all conclusions arising from studies using photographic face stimuli. This would severely limit the range of material that expert witnesses are presently called upon to provide, and therefore an early resolution to the issue as to whether photographs are acceptable stimuli for the study of criminal identification is of pressing importance.

3   A witness–computer interactive system for searching mug files

David R. Lenorovitz and Kenneth R. Laughery

Most law enforcement people assume that the greater the number of faces a witness searches in a mug file before encountering the target face, the less likely the face will be recognized. Certainly this assumption is consistent with a large body of psychological literature on retroactive interference in memory for verbal materials. Two studies on facial recognition have been reported that bear directly on the issue. Laughery, Alexander, and Lane (1971) exposed subjects to a target face and then had them search through a set of 150 full-face photographs (slides) looking for the target. Significant reductions in identification rates occurred when the target's position varied from 40 to 104 to 140. Davies, Shepherd, and Ellis (1979a) exposed subjects to three target faces and then had them search through a set of 100 interpolated faces followed by a set of 33 faces that contained the targets. Target identification was lower than that of a control group that did not search the set of 100 interpolated faces. A third study also bears on the issue, although somewhat less directly. Laughery et al. (1974) varied the similarity between the target face and the decoy faces that preceded it in the search series. The greater the similarity the poorer the recognition performance.

The results of these studies obviously have implications for the design of mug-file systems as well as for the procedures used in searches. A first strategy would be to try to reduce the size of the picture file to be searched on the basis of information provided by the witness. To a limited degree, this approach is currently possible in that most mug files are organized on the basis of sex and race. Hence, if a witness describes the target as a white male, all females and nonwhite males could be eliminated from the relevant files. Given the size of many mug files, however, even after pruning the set on a sex–race basis, the witness may be faced with thousands of photographs to search.

The work reported here represents an effort to develop a computer-based system for pruning a mug file on the basis of a witness's memory for a face.

38

Several previous efforts have attempted to deal with this problem. Harmon (1973), Bledsoe (1966), and Batten and Rhodes (1978) have developed systems in which a mug file is coded into a computer, an image (such as a sketch or Identikit composite) is generated from a witness's description, and a mug-file search is based upon properties of the sketch or composite. Typically the search consists of computing distance functions from measures of the image and the mug-file faces. On the basis of these distance functions faces from the file are selected as candidates for the target face. To date, the results of these efforts have not been particularly impressive, although work by Harmon and Hunt (1977) with profiles does appear promising.

In this chapter we will argue that systems for retrieving photographs from mug files would benefit from two fundamental changes in the approach just mentioned. First, the system we will describe employs a *matching algorithm* (Laughery, Rhodes, & Batten, 1981); that is, on the basis of information provided by the witness, unlikely alternatives are eliminated, or pruned, from the file. This technique contrasts with the previously used *sequencing algorithms*, which select a sequenced or prioritized set of likely alternatives from the file on the basis of the witness's input. The pruning strategy is potentially more efficient from a practical viewpoint. Because faces can be eliminated on the basis of a single feature mismatch, one feature can be considered at a time. The selection strategy, on the other hand, requires that a face be simultaneously consistent with all available information before being considered a likely alternative. This distinction will be analyzed further in the general discussion section.

A second change concerns the involvement of the witness. In most previous efforts, the witness provided information initially, and this information served as the basis for selection. One problem is that this procedure does not make provision for differences in witnesses' memories for faces. Different witnesses may remember different kinds of information about a face; indeed, a given witness may attend to and remember different aspects of different faces. Search procedures based upon algorithms using invariant weightings for specific aspects of faces may, therefore, be inappropriate when applied to a given witness's input for a specific target. Except for one study by Harmon (1973), previous efforts have used fixed procedures. The Harmon study represents an exception in that the witness indicated which features were most important (useful), and the algorithm gave greater weight to these features. A second problem with the procedure is that it limits the witness's inputs to the beginning of the process. The system developed here is more dynamic in that it permits a continuing witness-algorithm interaction. Such a procedure takes advantage of the witness's constant efforts to remember the target face.

The present system, in which the witness plays an active role in the search process, was designed as follows. A mug file existed in which values for each of 18 facial feature dimensions (e.g., lip thickness or amount of eye separation) were stored in a computer. A *likely* list and an *unlikely* list of faces were created, the likely list consisting of all faces in the file that were candidates for the target and the unlikely one including all those that for some reason had been eliminated as candidates. Initially all faces were on the likely list. As a basis for a preliminary pruning of the likely list, the witness provided the file manager (who was the experimenter and computer terminal operator) with a verbal description of facial features. *Pruning* in this study was defined as moving a face from the likely list to the unlikely list. Following the initial witness input, a face was randomly selected from the likely list and presented to the witness. The witness examined the face and indicated if it was or was not the target. If it was not, the witness was given the opportunity to provide additional information regarding differences between the face and the target. An example of such information might be that the eyebrows were too thick and the mouth was too wide. On the basis of this input the likely list was further pruned. Then another face was randomly selected and presented to the witness, and the process was repeated. This procedure continued until one of the two criteria was met: the target face was encountered or the likely list was pruned to 50 or fewer faces. In the latter case, the remaining faces were presented serially to the witness as in a standard recognition procedure. If a target identification was not made among the remaining faces, the faces on the unlikely list were presented serially on a last in, first out basis.

It should be noted that this work was experimental in the sense that the mug file consisted of artificial faces – Identikit composites. The Identikit consists of a large number of transparent celluloid foils, each containing an image of a facial feature (mouth, nose, eyebrows, eyes, chin and jawline, and hair). Many examples of each feature are available. A face is constructed by superimposing an appropriate example of each of the various features. We used Identikit faces for two reasons. First, considerable information was available or could be easily derived about these faces. The kit contains a limited set of feature examples, a subset of which was selected for this study. Hence, it was possible to determine precisely the extent to which faces in the mug file share common feature examples. This point will be discussed in greater detail later. The second reason is that previous work by Yoblick (1973) determined a set of 18 feature dimensions for the Identikit that represent the manner in which people dimensionalize these types of facial features. This data base provided an extremely useful starting point for the type of search procedure being developed.

The remainder of this chapter is organized as follows. Two experiments will be described that provided data basic to the system's development. In the first experiment we attempted to determine the relative frequency of occurrence in real faces for 25 examples of each Identikit feature so that we could construct a realistic mug file. In the second experiment we scaled the 25 examples of each Identikit feature on the appropriate subset of Yoblick's 18 dimensions in order to be able to apply the pruning rules. A third experiment that will be described was a straightforward recognition study using the Identikit faces. Subjects were shown a target face and then indicated for each face in a series whether it was or was not the target. This experiment was similar to earlier recognition studies with real faces (Laughery, et al., 1971) and was a useful indication of the validity of using Identikit faces. The results of this experiment also served as a comparative basis for evaluating the interactive search system being developed. The interactive search system and the results obtained from applying it to the mug file of artificial faces will then be described. The final section will discuss the results and the potential for such search procedures.

Experiment 1: Feature frequency study

In order to develop an Identikit composite mug file that validly represents real-world faces, an effort was made to estimate the relative frequency of occurrence in actual faces of the various feature examples used in constructing the composite faces. In this experiment representative feature examples of lips, noses, chin/ears, eyebrows, eyes, and hair were assigned consensually validated rank-order scores on the basis of their estimated frequencies of occurrence in the population of adult white male faces. Estimates of the absolute frequencies of occurrence were also obtained.

Method

Subjects. The subjects were 24 students enrolled at the State University of New York at Buffalo. Participation partially fulfilled a course requirement.

Task. The task consisted of sorting a set of 25 Identikit feature examples into a row ordered according to their relative frequencies of occurrence in the faces of adult white males encountered in everyday life. Then the subject was instructed to subdivide the ordered row into seven or fewer groupings and to assign to each group an average frequency-of-occurrence estimate.

Each of the first 12 subjects performed the above task six times, once for each feature. The remaining 12 subjects performed the task once – on a second (mutually exclusive) set of 25 hair examples.

Materials. The stimulus materials were seven sets of 25 feature examples. There was a set of 25 for each of five features – lips, noses, chin/ears, eyebrows, and eyes – and two sets of 25 for hair. All except the second set for hair were the same feature examples used by Yoblick (1973) in his study. The second hair set was introduced for two reasons. First, Yoblick reported that his subjects could accurately discriminate a much larger number of hair examples than any of the other features. Second, pilot work for this study indicated a high level of similarity among composite faces constructed with only the Yoblick examples. Analyses of protocol reports from the pilot work revealed that the excessive similarity was due primarily to the hair feature.

Procedure. Subjects were run individually. Following a set of straightforward, conversationally presented instructions, the subject sat at a large table and was given a randomly ordered set of feature examples. These were to be arranged from least to most frequently seen. Then the subject was asked to subdivide an ordered set into seven or fewer groupings such that the examples in each group occurred approximately equally in the population of real faces. The subject estimated the percentages of occurrence for each group where the ranges available were: 0–5%, 6–10%, 11–15%, 16–20%, 21–25%, 25–30%, and greater than 30%. The subject then moved to another table and repeated the task for another feature set while the experimenter recorded the results of the completed sorting. No time limit was placed on the subject; the average time used was about 8 minutes per set. This procedure continued until all six sets had been completed. The second group of 12 subjects did the sorting task only once, on the second hair set.

Results

A mean percentage value (percentage of population in which it occurs) was computed for each feature example. These values were obtained by assigning each example the midpoint percentage value of the category group into which the subject had placed it (e.g., a value of 8 for examples in the 6–10% group). The mean of this midpoint value from each of the 12 subjects was computed. These mean percentages were then used to compute a cumulative frequency distribution function for each feature. This computation consisted simply of ordering the examples by mean percentage value, summing the values, and dividing each entry by the total.

In order to determine subject agreement in ordering the feature sets, Kendall's concordance coefficient (W) was obtained for each of the seven sets of rankings. The W's ranged from .308 for lips to .423 for chin/ears. Using the chi-square described by Siegel (1956), these concordance levels were all significant ($p < .001$).

Discussion

The purpose of this experiment was to define a basis for constructing a large set of Identikit faces that would more realistically represent the general population of real faces than if the features were randomly combined. The consensual validity of the probability functions lends support to the approach. Of course, selecting component feature examples on this basis in constructing faces does not address other factors that would be potentially relevant, such as feature interactions and dependency relationships. Nevertheless, the idea of weighting feature example selection in this manner does represent a reasonable first approximation to the construction of a realistic composite face set.

Experiment 2: Feature dimension scaling study

The proposed witness–computer interactive system requires that the component features of each face be scaled along a variety of feature dimensions that are both valid and reliable dimensions of facial discriminability. The purpose of this experiment was to scale the examples in each of the feature sets along the appropriate feature dimensions defined by Yoblick.

Method

Subjects. The subjects were 40 students enrolled at the State University of New York at Buffalo. They were paid $2.50 for participating in the 1-hour session.

Task. The task consisted of sorting sets of Identikit feature examples into an ordered row on the basis of a specified feature dimension. Each subject performed a total of five such sortings, each sorting on a different feature set.

Materials. The stimulus materials were the same 175 feature examples described in the feature frequency study. Since the Identikit foils containing the features also contain number codes, 3 × 5-inch photographic prints were prepared in which only the actual feature drawings were visible.

Procedure. Subjects were run in groups of three. Upon arrival at the testing room the subjects were given appropriate instructions. Each subject was then supplied with a selected feature set (e.g., 25 lip examples), a card naming the dimension upon which the feature examples were to be scaled (e.g., lip thickness) and containing instructions as to the desired arrangement of the ordered set (e.g., thinnest lips on the left, medium in center, and thickest lips on the right), and a form to record the identification numbers from the backs of the photographs after they had been ordered.

Scaling information was collected for each of the 18 feature dimensions. There were 3 dimensions each for lips, chin/ears, eyebrows, and eyes; 2 dimensions for nose; and 4 for hair. The names of the 18 dimensions were: lip thickness, mouth width, prominence of teeth, nose shape, nostril separation, facial shape, jowl width, ear prominence, eyebrow size, eyebrow shading, eyebrow shape, area of eye opening, eye shading, eye separation–bridge width, hair shading, hair density, hair length, and hair texture.

No time constraints were placed on the sorting task. The average time per 25-member feature set was 6–8 minutes; hair took longer because the set contained 50 examples. Each subject performed 5 sorts, 1 sort on hair and 1 sort on each of 4 of the other 5 features. The assignment of features and sorting dimensions was counterbalanced to distribute evenly any possible order effects. A minimum of 10 sortings was obtained for each of the 18 feature dimensions.

Results

Position values (1–25) were averaged across subjects for each of the feature examples. Kendall's concordance coefficients (W) were computed for each of the 18 dimension matrices. The obtained W values ranged from .460 for the prominence-of-teeth dimension to .962 for hair shading. All W's were highly significant ($p < .001$).

The ordered feature examples on any particular dimension do not provide information about the magnitude or meaningfulness of the differences between successively ranked examples on the scale. Similarly, although concordance analyses indicate an overall agreement among subject rankings, these analyses do not reflect agreement or disagreement about specified pairs in the ordered set. In order to get at these issues, sign texts were computed for the pairs in each of the feature sets. For each feature example, these analyses resulted in the identification of the next higher and lower ranked feature example consensually judged to differ *significantly* on the given dimension of that feature. The end product of the analysis was a table of feature examples. For each feature example the identities were indicated of adjacently ranked examples that bounded confidence intervals of significantly greater or lesser dimension values.

Discussion

The purpose of this experiment was to provide a data base for the pruning operation in the witness–computer search system. Specifically, the data served as a basis for determining the extent to which feature examples differ along the various feature dimensions. The results possess one very desirable quality for use in a computer-assisted facial recognition system; namely, they can be readily transformed into numerically coded data for efficient storage, processing, and retrieval. The nature of the adopted coding scheme will be described in a later section.

Experiment 3: Linear Search–Position Effect Study

In the third experiment, subjects were exposed to a target face (a composite) and then were shown a sequence of 330 composite faces with instructions to indicate whether each face was or was not the target. The experiment represents the standard procedure for searching a mug file against which the results of the interactive system can be compared, and it is very similar to recognition studies using real faces (Laughery et al., 1971). This latter aspect enables comparisons that to some extent validate the use of the artificial Identikit faces in this initial phase of system development.

Method

Subjects. The subjects were 90 students enrolled at the State University of New York at Buffalo. They were paid $2.50 for participating in the 1-hour session.

Task. The subjects viewed 6 composite faces (slides) projected for 8 seconds each. One of the faces, the 6th, was accompanied by a tone, which identified it as the target. Then 330 composite faces were projected 1 at a time, with the pace controlled by the subject. The subject assigned a rating to each face, which either clearly identified it as the target or reflected the degree of confidence with which it was rejected as being the target.

Materials. The stimulus materials were 35-mm black-and-white slides of 335 composite faces. These faces were constructed from the 175 Identikit feature examples described in Experiments 1 and 2. The feature examples selected for each face were determined by a pseudorandom selection procedure that took into account directly the relative feature frequency estimates obtained in Experiment 1. This selection was accomplished in a straightforward manner using computer-generated random numbers and the obtained frequencies.

This set of faces represents a very small sample of the more than 400 million unique faces possible from the feature example sets. Comparisons of the 335 faces indicated that none of the possible pairs had as many as five feature examples in common. One pair shared four identical features, 66 pairs shared three features, 1,220 shared two features, and 22,372 shared a single matching feature. The remaining pairs had no common feature examples.

Five composite faces were selected from the 335 to be used as targets. The selection was random with the following restrictions: A target could not share more than three feature examples with any face in the total set; a target could not share both hair and chin/ears with any other face; and no face was selected if judged by subjects in a pilot study to have any idiosyncratic or particularly noticeable qualities. These restrictions were minimal, and the first 5 faces selected were acceptable.

Design. A randomized factorial design was employed with two between-subjects variables: target and target position in the search sequence. The target variable consisted of the 5 different faces selected as just described. Position consisted of six equally spaced locations in the 330-item search sequence (54, 108, 162, 216, 270, and 324). Three subjects were run in each of the resulting 30 conditions.

Procedure. The subjects worked individually in a room that was darkened so as to provide good viewing of the slides, but had sufficient light for the experimenter to record subject responses. The subject faced a panel at one end of a table. The viewing distance was about 40 inches. The slides were projected from the rear onto an 8×10-inch frosted glass in the center of the panel.

The target exposure consisted of 6 pictures of composite faces: the target and 5 randomly constructed faces. The target face was always the last (6th) in the sequence and was accompanied by a loud tone, indicating that it was the target. The subjects had not been told how many faces they would see but were instructed to identify the target by the use of the tone. Each face in the exposure series was on the screen for 8 seconds. Subjects had no prior knowledge of the number of faces in the exposure series or which one would be identified as the target.

Following the target exposure series, specific instructions were given regarding the responses to be made during the search series. A 4-point rating scale was used with the following definitions:

1. No, he's definitely not the man I'm looking for. I'd never mistake those two for each other.
2. No, I don't think so. He may bear some resemblance to the target person, but he's not the one.
3. I don't believe it's him, but I'm not certain. I can't completely eliminate him from consideration.
4. Yes, he's the one. I can identify that man. I recognize him as being the target person.

Each of the four response alternatives was printed on a separate card, and the cards were visible to the subject throughout the search series.

The search series contained 330 faces. In order to eliminate response bias shifts when the target appeared late in the series, subjects had been told that the series would contain 360 faces. They were also told the target might appear in any position or might not appear at all. The subject controlled the presentation rate of the slides by pressing a remote projector advance button. Responses were given verbally and recorded by the experimenter.

If at any point in the series the subject identified a face as the target (a 4 response), the experimenter interrupted and confirmed the response while carefully avoiding feedback regarding correctness. The subject was then told that the experimental design required getting ratings of the other faces in the sequence, and that he or she should proceed. The following rules were given for terminating the search:

1. If the identification was correct, another 30 faces were rated (or, if the target position was 324, the series was exhausted).
2. If the identification was wrong and the target had not yet appeared, the sequence continued to 30 faces beyond the target's appearance.
3. If the identification was wrong and the target had occurred earlier, another 30 faces were rated.
4. If no 4 response was given, the series was exhausted. Up to the point where a 4 rating was given, the subject could go back and review any face or set of faces previously seen and, if desired, make changes in the rating.

Finally, at the conclusion of the search series, each subject was asked to report in writing any method used in carrying out the search. In particular the subject was asked to list any facial features or characteristics attended to in making rating decisions.

Results

Several performance measures were analyzed. Hit rate was the percentage of subjects who correctly identified the target. False-alarm rate was the percentage of subjects who falsely identified a decoy (nontarget) face as the target. It should be noted that these measures are based only upon the first response given by a subject. The false alarms were divided into two sets: those given to faces that appeared prior to the 30th face after the target, and those given to faces more than 30 beyond the target. This breakdown will be used for comparisons with the results of the interactive system described in the next section.

The results are presented in Figure 3.1. Hit rate ranged from 60% (9 of 15 subjects) at position 54 to 6.7% (1 of 15 subjects) at position 324 and evidenced a monotonic relationship. The overall hit rate was 32.3% (29 of 90 subjects). Although the relationship between false-alarm rate and target position was not so clear-cut, generally more false alarms occurred when the target appeared late in the sequence. The overall false-alarm rate was 33%.

A third dependent measure was the hit–miss (H–M) score. This score was based upon rating scale values (1–4) assigned to the target faces. A higher value represented better recognition performance. An analysis of variance on these scores showed a significant main effect of position, $F(5, 60) = 5.09$, $p < .01$. There was a significant linear trend for the six positions but no statistical evidence of any higher order trends. Analysis of false-alarm–correct-rejection (FA–CR) scores, ratings assigned to decoy faces, indicated no significant main effects for either the target or position variables.

The protocol data provided by subjects at the end of their search sequences were examined. These reports were in response to a general question about any facial features or characteristics on which the subject may have keyed while searching for the target. Results are shown in Table 3.1. The left column lists the actual feature descriptor responses. The 18 descriptors named by Yoblick (1973) were reported by him to be valid and reliable feature dimensions. They are also the ones used in the feature dimension scaling study. Of the total responses, 48% matched with Yoblick's 18 dimensions. Further, if it is assumed that most of the undifferentiated feature responses (e.g., hair) could be broken down and related to one or more of the specified dimensions or attributes of that feature (e.g., hair shading, hair density, hair length, or hair texture), then as many as 82% of the protocol responses could be accounted for by Yoblick's set of 18.

The column on the right in Table 3.1 lists comprehensive descriptor categories of the type reported by Zavala (1972) and Lenorovitz (1972) in studies using pictures of real faces. These categories were formed by cluster-

Figure 3.1. Hit and false-alarm frequencies for six different search series positions

Table 3.1. *Classified frequency counts of facial feature descriptions given as protocol responses by subjects in linear search–position effect study*

Actual responses	Frequency	Comprehensive descriptors[b]	Frequency
Hair (undifferentiated)	38		
Hair shading[a]	13		
Hair density[a]	17	Hair	94
Hair length[a]	3		
Hair texture[a]	5		
Hair style	18		
Eyes (undifferentiated)	28		
Eye shading[a]	18		
Eye opening[a]	9		
Eye slant	4	Eyes	64
Eye separation[a]	2		
Eye expression	2		
Eye lids	1		
Face shape[a]	38	Face shape	38
Mouth (undifferentiated)	22		
Lip thickness[a]	11		
Mouth width[a]	4	Mouth	38
Mouth expression	1		
Prominence of teeth[a]	0		
Ear prominence[a]	34	Ears	34
Nose (undifferentiated)	17		
Nose shape[a]	11		
Nose lines	3	Nose	34
Nose size	3		
Nostril separation[a]	0		
Chin (undifferentiated)	15	Chin	28
Jowl width[a]	13		
Eyebrows (undifferentiated)	15		
Eyebrow size[a]	8	Eyebrows	25
Eyebrow shading[a]	2		
Eyebrow shape[a]	0		
Hair line	12	Hair line	12
Face shading	1	Face shading	1

[a]18 feature dimensions named by Yoblick (1973).
[b]Descriptor categories used by Lenorovitz (1972) and Zavala (1972).

ing protocol reports into "logically consistent and comprehensive" groups. It may be noted that there is good correspondence between the most frequently reported descriptors for Identikit faces and responses reported by Zavala (1972) for a similar task with pictures of real faces.

Discussion

Experiment 3 had several objectives. One objective was to answer the question as to whether the artificial stimulus materials used in these studies are justifiable for studying facial recognition memory. An indirect answer to this question can be obtained by comparing performance levels with those in a similar study by Laughery et al. (1971), where photographs of real faces were used. Laughery and his colleagues reported hit rates of 65%, 53%, and 41% for target positions 40, 104, and 140, respectively. In the present study the rates were 60%, 53%, and 33% for positions 54, 108, and 162. In addition to demonstrating an equivalent effect of the position variable, these results show similar performance in the absolute values of hit rates.

False alarm rates in the two studies can also be compared. At first glance the overall rate of 9% reported in the earlier study does not seem to compare well with the 25.6% here. In the present experiment, however, false-alarm rates increased markedly when the target position was beyond 200. If just the first three target position conditions (54, 108, and 162) are considered (conditions roughly equivalent to the study by Laughery et al., 1971), the false-alarm rate is a very comparable 11%.

The present study also had the objective of approximating the real-life situation of a witness searching through a mug file. To this end, the study differed from earlier experiments such as those reported by Laughery, et al. (1971, 1974). Some of these differences were: Subjects were run individually; the search sequence was subject-paced; subjects could go back and review previously seen faces; several faces were seen at the time of the target exposure; when the target face appeared in the exposure period, it was accompanied by a loud, piercing, and somewhat obnoxious tone, introducing some amount of shock, annoyance, and anxiety; and the search sequence was lengthened to the point where the task became quite difficult. These aspects of the task may increase the applicability of the results to real-life situations.

A third objective was to establish baseline performance measures for linear search procedures against which alternative search methods could be compared. Certainly the low hit rates and high false-alarm rates that characterize performance in the longer search series argue for the development of more effective procedures. The following section presents an alternative, computer-based, interactive method.

Experiment 4: CAPSAR

In this study facial recognition performance levels were determined for subjects who used an interactive computer system to search for a target face contained in a set of Identikit composites. Comparisons were made between performance using the computer-assisted photographic search and retrieval (CAPSAR) system and performance in the previous experiment using a linear search.

Method

Subjects. Fifteen students at the State University of New York at Buffalo served as subjects. They were paid $2.50 for participating in the session of 60–90 minutes.

Task. The task consisted of searching through a set of Identikit composite photographs in an attempt to locate a previously seen target face. The order in which the set was searched (and thus the position of the target within the sequence) was dynamically and independently determined for each subject at the time of search by the subject's interaction with an on-line computer program. The general procedure was as follows. The subject initially input to the program a description of the most clearly remembered features or characteristics of the target face. The computer then eliminated seemingly irrelevant faces from its "set of most likely faces," a set that initially included the entire face library. The program then randomly selected one of the remaining "likely" faces for presentation, which the subject then either accepted or rejected as being the target. If the face was rejected, additional information was provided to the computer regarding the ways in which the target face was seen as differing significantly from the presented face. On the basis of this input, additional faces were eliminated from the likely set, another face was selected for presentation from those remaining, and the process was repeated. This iterative pruning process continued until the target was identified or a stop criterion was reached. If the latter occurred, the subject then did a linear search through the remaining faces in the likely set. In a manner similar to that described in the previous study, each face was rated on a 4-point scale.

Materials. The stimulus materials used in this study were the same set of target and decoy slides used in the linear search–position effect study. Additional materials included 18 dimension-name cards and a subset of the photographic prints of isolated feature prototypes described in the feature dimension scaling study. These latter items were used to indicate the kinds of facial feature information stored in the computer's memory and to demonstrate the possible range of values along the various dimension scales. The feature prototypes used for each dimension were chosen on the basis of their rankings and sign tests so as best to illustrate the full range of values for the given dimension. Both the highest and lowest ranking prototypes were selected from each dimension along with some (from 1 to 7) of the intermediately ranked prototypes. As many of these midrange values were selected as possible, subject to the restriction that *each* member of the representative scale had to be significantly higher in rank than its next lowest ranking member, and significantly lower in rank than its next highest ranking member.

Apparatus. The equipment included the items described in the linear search–position effect study. Significant changes involved the addition of a computer communications terminal and an experimenter assistant. The assistant was seated at the slide projector and assumed the duties of its loading and operation. The experimenter sat at an IBM Model 2741 communications terminal located adjacent to the subject. The terminal was linked via a data-phone connection to an APL 360 system at the State University of New York at Binghamton. The host computer was an IBM 370-55 machine, offering multiple APL workspaces of 32,000 bytes each.

Procedure and program description. Subjects were run individually and were seated in a chair facing the screen. The procedure was basically the same as that described in the linear search–position effect study up to the point of starting the recognition task (i.e., same exposure series, identifying tone, etc.). One deviation in procedure involved the experimenter's leaving the room while the assistant presented the Identikit familiarization and target exposure series. The experimenter's absence during this initial target exposure, the use of a randomized target selection order not disclosed to the experimenter, and the experimenter's sitting with his back toward the screen during the search constituted a sort of double-bind situation. This was done so as to allow interaction between subject and experimenter while minimizing the likelihood of the experimenter's accidentally disclosing the target when it appeared on the screen.

After the exposure series the experimenter initiated the interactive process by asking the subject what features or characteristics he or she remembered most clearly about the target. Throughout the search, the experimenter acted as messenger and interpreter for the subject and the computer. The experimenter translated feature descriptions into appropriately formatted computer inputs, entered the information on the keyboard, relayed any of CAPSAR's queries for additional information, reentered the subject's replies, and informed the assistant as to which face CAPSAR had selected for projection. The exact procedure and conversational dialogue was unique for each search.

The general strategy followed by the program was first to divide the 330 faces into two subsets – a likely set and an unlikely set. This division was based upon information that the subject remembered about the target's individual facial features. Only feature information reported as being distinctly remembered was considered. For each such "certain" feature, the experimenter determined whether one of the stored feature dimensions corresponded to the information reported about the feature. If the experimenter suggested one of these dimensions and the subject considered it appropriate (i.e., it properly described a remembered aspect of the feature), an ordered row of pictures of prototypes of that isolated feature was then presented. These pictures were a subset of the photographic prints used in the feature dimension scaling study. The prototypes had been selected so as to represent the range of dimension values contained in the face set. The subject's task was to indicate where the target's feature would fall within the presented dimension range. Further, the subject was asked whether any of the sample prototypes could be rejected as representing values much too high or too low on the dimension scale. This information was relayed to CAPSAR and all faces were eliminated from the likely set with dimension values as high (low) or higher (lower) than the rejected sample prototypes.

All unlikely faces thus rejected were eliminated from further consideration unless and until the likely set was exhausted with no identification having been made. A very conservative attitude was stressed in making these dimension scaling reports so as to avoid any premature pruning of the target from the likely set.

This first phase of the search procedure required absolute judgments from subjects about remembered features of the target and then a refinement of these inputs in terms of relative judgments of dimension values of isolated feature prototypes. The second phase of the procedure again involved relative judgments of feature dimension values, but this time they were made in the context of whole faces rather than isolated features. The process started with CAPSAR's randomly selecting a face from the likely set for projection on the screen. The subject indicated whether or not the face was the target by assigning it a rating on the 4-point scale.

If a positive identification was not made, the face was removed from the screen and from the likely set, and the subject was asked to make some relative judgments about the ways in which the target differed from the face just seen (e.g., the target's hair was darker, his eyebrows were bushier). The face was removed from the screen because it seemed that having the projected face staring back at the subject during the sometimes lengthy dialogue unnecessarily degraded or interfered with the subject's memory of the target. The face was not removed, however, until the subject indicated that the needed information had been obtained. The subject was encouraged to take only enough viewing time to make a rating and note obvious feature differences. The projected face was returned to the screen if the subject wished.

The new information was then used to reduce the size of the search set further. This interactive pruning process continued until an identification was made or the size of the likely face set reached a cut-off level of 50 faces or fewer. At that point, the subject did a linear search through the remaining likely faces in much the same manner as that described for the previous study. If no identification occurred from searching the likely face set, the linear search was continued through the unlikely face set. Instead of searching through these previously eliminated but as yet unseen faces in a random order, however, the faces were viewed in a last in, first out order, that is, in the reverse of that in which they had been pruned from the likely set. Finally, if all the faces had been viewed without an identification, the subject was given the option of going back and reviewing any face or set of faces he or she had previously seen, such as all those that had been given a rating of 3.

If at any point in the search the subject gave a rating of 4 to a face, the experiment was stopped and the response was noted. The response was later scored as either a hit, if it was the target's face, or a false alarm, if it was a decoy. A linear search procedure was then carried out on the remaining faces in the likely set (and, if necessary, those in the set of eliminated faces) until one of the search stop criteria described for the previous study was reached. In this way, each subject was given a chance to see and rate the target, even though he or she might have committed a false alarm prior to its appearing on the screen.

CAPSAR data structures and face search algorithms. The data structures used by CAPSAR to store feature information about each of the 350 Identikit faces were derived from information obtained in the feature dimension scaling study. This face "library," or "dictionary" (referred to as FLIB), was represented by a matrix having 330 rows, 1 per stored face, and 18 columns, 1 per stored feature dimension. For example, FLIB (1, 1) would be the cell containing feature information about the lip thickness of the first face.

Individual matrix cell entries consisted of six-digit, coded numbers, reflecting rank-order information about a specified face on a specified dimension. For example, the cell entry for FLIB (1, 1) was 171910 and reflected the following:

1. The first two digits (*17*1910) represented the rank-order value of the lips of the first face (Identikit prototype no. 29) on the lip thickness dimension.
2. The middle two digits (17*19*10) indicated the rank-order number of the first "thicker" ranking lips prototype judged to be of significantly greater value on the lip thickness scale.
3. The last two digits (1719*10*) indicated the rank-order number of the first "thinner" ranking lips prototype to be judged of significantly lower value on the lip thickness scale.

Thus each face was defined by CAPSAR in terms of the relative rank orderings of its component features on the specified dimensions of those features.

The algorithm used by CAPSAR to prune faces from the likely set during the first (isolated feature dimension) phase of the search process may be illustrated as follows. Suppose that the subject reported having clearly remembered something about the lips – in particular, something about the thickness or fullness of the lips. Further, assume that after having been shown the six isolated prototypes of lips in the representative lip thickness scale, the subject was able to restrict the range of possible lip thickness to the middle two pictures – that is, the second and lower ranking prototypes were too thin, and the fifth and higher ranking prototypes were much too thick.

The experimenter would have then fed into CAPSAR the rank-order numbers associated with the second and fifth prototypes. The net result of this action would be for CAPSAR to scan through all the entries in the first column of the FLIB matrix and move those faces with inappropriate lip thickness from the likely set to the unlikely set.

A similar procedure was used to prune the likely face set further during the second phase of the search procedure (screen-face rating and feature-difference reporting). Again, by way of illustration, suppose that Face 1 had been projected on the screen and that the subject had rejected it as being the target, giving it a 2 rating. Further, assume that the subject reported that one of the ways in which the target differed from the screen face was that the target's lips were much thinner than those seen. The experimenter would then enter a coded "greater than" response on the keyboard, and CAPSAR would thus be instructed to separate out the middle two digits of the FLIB (1, 1) cell entry (i.e. 17*19*10). These digits, of course, indicated the rank order of the first lips prototype judged to be significantly higher in rank than the lips of the screen face. CAPSAR would then prune out all likely faces with lips as thick or thicker than those of the indicated reference prototype. Correspondingly, had the subject reported remembering the target's lips thicker than those of the screen face, a "less than" response would have been transmitted to CAPSAR. The program would then have used the last two digits of the FLIB (1, 1) entry (i.e., 1719*10*) to eliminate all faces having lips significantly thinner than those on the screen. Finally, if the subject reported that the target's lips were neither very much thicker nor very much thinner than those of the screen face, but that the target's lips did not look anything like the ones on the screen, an "unequal" response would be transmitted. CAPSAR would then prune out all faces having the same lips prototype as the screen face, that is, all faces with FLIB (1, 1) entries equal 171910.

Results

Several of the dependent measures collected in this study were directly comparable to those reported in the previous linear search–position effect study. The first was hit rate. The number of hits and misses for face-search tasks using CAPSAR were 8 and 7 respectively, whereas for traditional linear search techniques there were 29 hits and 61 misses. These values are collapsed across the various conditions of both the target and (in the case of the linear search data) position variables. Collapsing across the position variable was justified because in a normal mug-file search the target face is equally likely to appear in any of the positions.

The overall hit rate for the linear search conditions was 32.2%, whereas for the CAPSAR trials it was 53%. A one-tailed test of these observed cell frequencies using Fischer's Exact Probability test with Tocher's modification (Siegel, 1956) indicated that the difference was significant at the .05 level.

An even more striking performance improvement with CAPSAR was indicated by the false-alarm frequency counts. The overall false-alarm rate for the linear search was 25.6%, whereas not a single false alarm was committed by subjects who used CAPSAR. Fischer's Exact Probability test indicated that the observed cell distribution frequencies differed significantly at the .18 level.

Comparisons were also made in terms of the H–M and FA–CR scores. Figure 3.2 plots the H–M scores for each of the targets across all seven search conditions. The negative effects of target position in the search sequence is quite evident. It can also be seen that the H–M scores with CAPSAR were comparable to those with linear search when the target appeared in position 108. A one-tailed t ratio comparison supported the a priori hypothesis that the mean CAPSAR H–M scores would be significantly higher than the overall mean of the linear search H–M scores ($p < .05$).

As noted earlier, FA–CR scores in Experiment 3 did not vary significantly as a function of series position. A t-test comparison of CAPSAR FA–CR

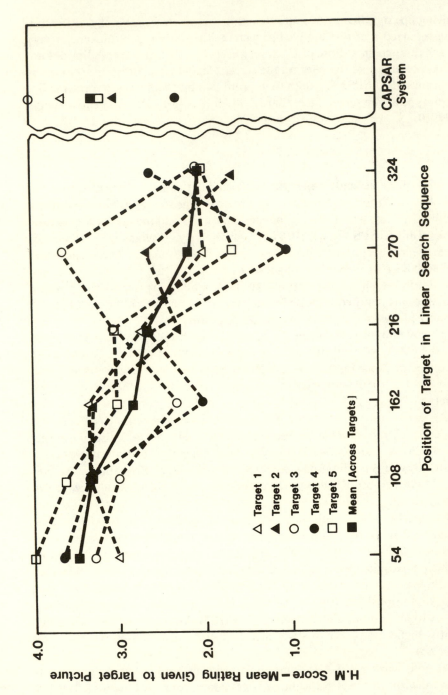

Figure 3.2. Hit–miss scores for linear search and for CAPSAR search

scores with the overall mean of FA–CR scores from the six linear search position levels also failed to reach significance.

In addition to these summary analyses, the performance of individual CAPSAR subjects was examined at a more detailed level. Table 3.2 presents data that permit a number of such observations. First, the effective target position entries indicate that the subjects were able to get the target's picture on the screen fairly early. In fact, 8 of the 15 subjects were able to encounter the target within the first 54 faces, and an additional 3 within the first 162 faces. The median sequence location in which the target appeared was position 52.

If one assumes a face library of 330 faces with a randomly positioned target variable, then the mean number of faces one might expect to search linearly before encountering the target would be 165. Using this "expected" position value as a reference, a Wilcoxon distribution-free signed-rank test (Hollander & Wolfe, 1973) was used to evaluate the target appearance positions obtained with CAPSAR. The results of this test indicated that CAPSAR targets appeared significantly earlier than this midpoint in the search sequence ($p < .004$).

Still, the benefits derived from this early exposure may be questioned. Of the 8 subjects who saw the target no later than position 54, only 4 of them positively identified the target when it did appear. This 50% hit rate at position 54 or earlier falls short of the 60% level attained by the 15 linear search subjects who saw the targets at position 54. Similarly, the mean H–M score for the 8 CAPSAR subjects was only 3.0, whereas for the 15 linear search subjects it was 3.5. On the other hand, the 4 CAPSAR subjects who did not see the target until relatively late in the sequence (by CAPSAR standards) demonstrated a remarkable 100% hit rate. This perfect performance level, of course, surpassed that of any comparable linear search subjects. It may be observed, however, that the reason these particular subjects saw the target so much later was that each of them prematurely pruned the target from the likely face set on either the first or second iteration with CAPSAR. Thus, these "communications breakdowns" greatly delayed the target appearance in the series, even though the subjects apparently did observe and remember enough about the target to be able to recognize him when he finally did appear. Close examination of the specific features or feature dimensions being "erroneously" rated at the time the target was pruned from the set revealed no consistent patterns or meaningful insights as to why the situation occurred.

Finally, it should be noted that relatively few iterations or information exchanges were needed to allow CAPSAR to produce an ordering with which the subject could linearly search the face library in a meaningful and

Table 3.2. *Number of faces left in "likely" set by subjects using the CAPSAR system*

| | Effective target position | | | | | | | | | | | | | | |
| | Target 1 | | | Target 2 | | | Target 3 | | | Target 4 | | | Target 5 | | |
	42	110	203	29	24	218	217	237	30	40	42	44	99	52	126
Iteration 1	289	*8*[a]	*92*[a]	*31*	*29*	200[a]	236	*76*[a]	*34*	294	*31*[a]	*77*	114	*10*[a]	*92*[a]
Iteration 2	243		*77*			165	95[a]	*46*		265		*67*	105		*77*
Iteration 3	220		*63*			162	75			243		*49*	73[a]		*63*
Iteration 4	153		*38*			158	72			184			53		*38*
Iteration 5	116					149	71			159			44		
Iteration 6	82					144	63			150					
Iteration 7	69					136	61			127					
Iteration 8	58					135	59			99					
Iteration 9	46					110	20			53					
Iteration 10						98				*41*					
Iteration 11						94									
Iteration 12						83									
Iteration 13						61									
Iteration 14						60									
Iteration 15						59									
Iteration 16						58									
Iteration 17						57									
Iteration 18						48									
H-M score	4	3	4	1	4	4	4	4	4	3	2	2	3	4	3

Note: Italicized entries indicate the number of faces left in the likely set when the interactive stop criterion was reached (i.e., 50 faces remaining). This was the point at which the linear search process was started.

[a] Point at which the target was prematurely pruned from the likely set.

efficient manner. The number of exchanges needed to reduce the likely set to 50 or fewer faces ranged from 1 to 18, with a median of 3.

Discussion

The CAPSAR system resulted in significantly higher hit rates and mean H–M scores than the linear search technique. Also, with CAPSAR, there was a highly significant drop in false alarms, accompanied by slightly (but not statistically significant) lowered FA–CR scores.

These results speak well for the CAPSAR prototype system, and it is appropriate to note some of the system's more salient features or character- istics. First, the approach differed from a pure linear search in that it initially required the subject to concentrate on the remembered image and to be very specific in describing the features or aspects of the target that were distinctly remembered. Of course, this rehearsal could also have been performed prior to the start of a straight linear type of search. The key fea- ture of the CAPSAR approach, however, is that it had the means of using this information to reorder dynamically the face-search sequence in a way that usually resulted in earlier target appearances.

Another characteristic of CAPSAR is that it does not directly attempt to identify the face or set of faces that best match descriptions of remembered features. Instead, it eliminates faces in an order defined by those faces that appear to have the least fit with the subject's memory. This approach was based on the assumptions that what the subject had available in memory at the time of search was a less-than-perfect image of the target, and what the computer had available in its data base was a matrix of consensually (but not universally) agreed-upon rank-order information about a specific and somewhat restricted set of facial features. In view of these two imperfect or "noisy" system variables it was decided to use an approach eliminating the least likely alternatives, as opposed to one based upon the selection of the most likely alternatives. Further comment on this point is in the next section.

The mechanical aspects of the CAPSAR system as employed in this study could be improved considerably. Certainly, the direct retrieval and display of faces by the computer is an appropriate step and is easily within current technology. Also, eliminating the experimenter (or technician in an actual real-life system) and permitting direct communications between the witness and the computer would be desirable.

General discussion

The present research effort was aimed at developing and testing a prototype computer interactive system to facilitate facial recognition. Given the success of CAPSAR, the question remains as to how successful CAPSAR or similar systems would be in more realistic facial identification situations – specifically, situations using pictures of real faces, and face libraries many times larger than the one used here.

With respect to photographs of real faces and large face libraries, none of the results obtained here suggests that a CAPSAR system would be unworkable. A multidimensional feature-ranking data base could be built for real faces, perhaps using a different approach. For example, prototypes of features representing different points along a particular scale of feature dimensions could serve as referents for an experienced (trained) technician to classify large numbers of faces. Of course, establishing the data base for an already existing large face set, such as an extensive mug file, could be enormously time-consuming. Once the file was created, however, adding new faces to it should be quite manageable. Another approach to this problem would be computerized systems in which the computer scans and classifies facial features. Laughery et al. (1981), however, have recently reviewed the state of the art in this area and concluded that considerable progress is needed to achieve such a working system.

The actual effectiveness of a system like CAPSAR in dealing with a much-expanded set of real faces will probably require an empirical study. Certainly it seems clear that performance levels obtained with traditional linear search techniques will continue to degrade with increased search set sizes. An important factor in the usefulness of CAPSAR may be the ability to decrease the likelihood of the premature pruning of the target face from the likely set. A more conservative pruning rule could accomplish this goal; the price, of course, would be fewer faces being moved to the unlikely list. There are other ways in which the CAPSAR system may potentially be improved. One possibility involves the selection of feature dimensions used for coding faces. Which feature dimensions are most accurately remembered? Several researchers (e.g., Walker-Smith, 1978) have recently been concerned with this question, and some results are beginning to emerge. Which features are most useful in narrowing down the search set? The answer to this question may be reflected by the distributions of feature set values, with more distributed dimensions having greater utility.

The CAPSAR system uses an elimination-of-least-likely-alternatives (pruning) approach. Other systems, such as those of Harmon (1973), Bledsoe (1966) and Batten and Rhodes (1978), have employed a selection-of-most-likely-alternatives strategy. As noted earlier, Laughery et al. (1981) have characterized these approaches as matching and sequencing algorithms, respectively. The difference between these strategies can be viewed in the context of the likely–unlikely sets. In the pruning approach, one is moving faces from the likely set to the unlikely set, whereas in the selecting strategy, faces are moved from the unlikely to the likely set. On the basis of this study, the pruning strategy has greater potential utility. The following two supporting arguments are offered.

First, the likely set can be pruned sequentially on the basis of individual feature dimensions. That is, the first dimension identified can alone serve as a basis for eliminating faces from the likely set, such as mouths whose widths are characterized as significantly wider or narrower than the target's mouth. Then another dimension, perhaps hair texture, can be a basis for further pruning. This process can continue through any number of dimensions, the number being a function of such factors as the confidence of the witness in remembering the information. Furthermore, the pruning criteria for different dimensions can vary. This variation might be appropriate, for example, if one assumes that the dimensions that are most valid are those the witness remembers best and uses first; hence, the criteria could become sequentially more conservative. On the other hand, if the selection strategy employs multiple feature dimensions, the dimensions must be applied simultaneously. They can, of course, be given differential weightings (and they typically are). Most of the researchers who have employed a selection approach have used distance functions that applied variable weightings. This distinction between the approaches can be best understood by noting that a face can be *eliminated* if one feature dimension is different from the target, but a face would not be *selected* unless it is consistent with all dimensions that are considered. This distinction is essentially a practical one. Theoretically the two approaches converge, but in the actual implementation of the strategies the practical difference is important. It permits a witness to interact, on-line, with a computer while dealing with one dimension at a time, a processing requirement that seems much more compatible with human processing abilities than a simultaneous multidimensional analysis.

A second argument is simply empirical. The earlier work of Harmon (1973), Bledsoe (1966), and Batten and Rhodes (1978) employed sequencing algorithms. The success of these efforts can be regarded as limited to poor. In contrast, the results of the CAPSAR approach demonstrated performance clearly superior to a linear search procedure.

Obviously there are numerous questions to answer and much to be done before a system like CAPSAR can be implemented in searching a large mug file containing real faces. On the basis of the success of the prototype system developed here, the approach has considerable potential.

4   Research on suggestion in lineups and photospreads

Roy S. Malpass and Patricia G. Devine

Identification by eyewitnesses of suspected offenders in lineups and photo-spreads is important direct evidence in many criminal trials and is probably an important element in plea bargaining negotiations. Such identification is widely held to be vulnerable to error by judges, legal scholars (Devlin, 1976; Levine & Tapp, 1973; Sobel & Pridgen, 1981; Wall, 1965), and experimental psychologists (Goldstein, 1977). A literature documenting cases of mistaken identification exists (Borchard, 1932; Brandon & Davies, 1973), and the problem has been reviewed in recent books on eyewitness identification (Ellison & Buckhout, 1981; Loftus, 1979; Yarmey, 1979a). In many criminal incidents, eyewitness identification is an important part of the available evidence, and sometimes, such as in rape and other assaults, it may be the only direct evidence available. The challenge to experimental psychologists is to respond effectively to the two major applied issues: avoiding identification of innocent suspects, and facilitating identification of guilty suspects.

Research on identification in lineups and photospreads has been largely oriented to these applied issues, and the degree to which empirical research has been influenced by psychological theory has until recently not been great. We will begin by presenting a conceptualization of the problem of eyewitness identifications in lineups and photospreads that takes account of both the applied issues and psychological thinking about social and cognitive processes.

A conceptualization of the problem

Choosing is the appropriate object of study

There is an important distinction between the witness's act of making or not making a lineup choice and the accuracy of that choice. Choosing is a behavior, whereas accuracy and error are outcomes of choosing. Although

64

Table 4.1. *Outcomes of choice alternatives available to witnesses*

	Witness makes an identification			Witness makes no identification
	Identifies offender	Identifies innocent suspect	Identifies foil	
Offender is present in the lineup	Correct	Impossible[a]	Error	Error
Offender is absent from the lineup	Impossible	Error	Error	Correct

[a]Assuming that the suspect is the offender and that there is only one suspect in any given lineup; the latter is not always the case, especially for photo identifications during the investigation phase of a prosecution.
Source: Adapted from Lindsay and Wells (1980).

choosing and accuracy are loosely related, whether or not a choice is accurate depends partly on whether the offender is actually present in the lineup. Table 4.1, adapted from Lindsay and Wells (1980), illustrates more fully the dependency of accuracy and error on choosing and on the presence of the offender. Accuracy (error) is a complex interaction of the witness's choosing, just who is chosen and whether the offender is actually available to be chosen, rather than being related to the witness's response in any simple way. It is misleading to treat accuracy and error as simple complements of each other or as homogeneous categories. Accuracy when the offender is present is different from when the offender is absent, and the different errors possible in either an offender-present or an offender-absent lineup have very different implications. Also misleading is the ignoring of these distinctions by summing errors together or by focusing exclusively on accuracy, which implicitly accomplishes the aggregation of errors.

The choosing–accuracy distinction has not been made sharply until very recently even though it has been implicit in many psychological discussions of eyewitness identification (Levine & Tapp, 1973; Woocher, 1977) and is implicitly at the core of traditional legal treatment of the problems of eyewitness identification in the concept of "suggestion" (Devlin, 1976; Sobel & Pridgen, 1981; Wall, 1965). It is especially easy to gloss over the distinction between choosing and accuracy because attention is readily drawn to the major applied problems of minimizing errors and enhancing accurate identifications. After all, this is a field of applied research. On the other hand, choosing is the appropriate object of study from a behavioral and theoretical point of view.

Signal detection theory as an orienting conceptualization

A sharp distinction between informational and response decision processes (choosing) is made in signal detection theory (SDT) (Coombs, Dawes, & Tversky, 1970; Egan & Clarke, 1966; Green & Swets, 1966).[1] SDT distinguishes between (a) the degree to which an observer can differentiate previously seen objects from new ones and (b) the amount of evidence of the objects' familiarity the observer requires before *reporting* having observed the object before. The processes underlying differentiation concern the information the observer has about the objects to be recognized, whereas the processes underlying decisions about reporting concern how this and other information will be used to decide what response to make when asked if the object is recognized among those presented. The probability that an observer will claim that the object presented is one previously seen is a function of both the amount of information the witness possesses about the object and the social utility of the available response alternatives. When witnesses are uncertain about whether an individual in a lineup is the one seen before at a particular time and place, they may be either conservative or liberal in their decision whether or not to choose a member of the lineup as the offender. SDT separates this social decision from the factors influencing the amount of information the witness possesses and provides an explicit account of the processes through which social influence may affect the witness's choice behavior.

The role of the witness's information. The information possessed by the witness is an example of what Wells (1978) calls "estimator variables": the quality of the witness's information about the physical appearance of the offender can only be estimated from reports of conditions for observation, the distribution of the witness's attention, and so on. Deffenbacher (1980) lists a number of factors contributing to the "optimality" of the conditions of witnessing for the witness's processing of the information about the offender's appearance: warning of a recognition test to come, moderate situational stress, ample opportunity to observe the offender, brief retention interval, high similarity in the offender's condition (appearance) from first observation to the subsequent test, unbiased testing instructions, and others. Factors such as these influence the degree to which witnesses can discriminate the offender from other persons, and potentially their accuracy as witnesses.

A major contribution of SDT to measuring the accuracy of recognition performance under conditions of uncertainty is in pointing out that the frequency of correct identifications (the hit rate) cannot be used alone as an indicator of accuracy, because high hit rates can also be obtained with only minimal information in combination with a high overall rate of identification responses. The hit rate would be high but so would the rate of making identifications when the object to be recognized is not present (a false alarm). Thus, the hit rate alone is ambiguous information about accuracy, and the false-alarm rate must be considered simultaneously. SDT develops a measure of accuracy, d', that is calculated on the basis of both hits and false alarms. A second index, Beta, is created that is an indication of response bias – the degree to which the observer's decision criterion is strict (conservative) or lax (liberal). SDT was initially seen as an attractive approach to the problem of eyewitness identification precisely because of the measurement refinements it provides by separating response bias from recognition ability. Response bias, however, was seen as a contaminant, preventing a clear examination of the eyewitness's accuracy (Buckhout, 1974), and the problem of the decision criterion was neglected. Hilgendorf and Irving (1978a) point out that underemphasis of the decision criterion aspects of SDT was widespread in its early application to social-psychological problems. We believe that the response bias aspects of eyewitness identification to a very large degree are the phenomena to be studied and that social decision making is the theoretical context in which the problem should be recast.

The social utility of choosing. When the conditions of observation are less than optimal, when it is possible that the offender may be confused with someone else or not recognized, witnesses viewing the lineup clearly face some ambiguity. They must decide whether or not to choose a member of the lineup, and they must take some risks whatever they decide. The relative attractiveness of a choice alternative is a function of the risks and values associated with the various response alternatives available in the judgment of the witness. Consider, for example, the response options available in Table 4.1, and the consequences of the associated outcomes. If the witness chooses the offender, the outcome is a correct identification. The importance of the consequences associated with this outcome depends on the beliefs of the witness. If the salient belief for a witness is that a correct identification will lead to the conviction of a criminal (a positively valued consequence), this belief will contribute a positive quantity to the attractiveness of choosing. On the other hand, the belief that a correct identification will require further participation in somewhat intimidating contacts with the police and perhaps even a confrontation with the offender or the offender's family may reduce the attractiveness of choosing. Likewise if the salient belief for a witness is that an incorrect identification may result in the identified person's being wrongfully convicted of a crime (presumably a negatively valued consequence), choosing may become less attractive. Of course, these consequences are not equally likely: They depend on the probability that the police suspect is actually the offender and the probability that the consequence will occur. Witnesses may well vary considerably in their beliefs about these probabilities.

Similar reasoning can be applied to the response alternative of not choosing someone from the lineup. If the witness believes that the outcome of failing to identify the guilty suspect in a lineup results in freedom for a criminal, then this consequence may make the alternative of not choosing less attractive. On the other hand, if the witness believes that the suspect may in fact not be the offender and that the outcome of a correct rejection has the consequence of freedom for an innocent person, the attractiveness of not choosing may be enhanced. The degree to which not choosing is attractive will depend to an important degree on the witness's belief about the probability that the police suspect is actually the offender.

In general, the subjective expected utility (SEU) of a response alternative equals

$$\sum_{i,j=1}^{n} \{[p\,(\text{outcome}_i)\,p\,(\text{consequence}_{ij}/\text{outcome}_i)]\,[\text{value of consequence}_{ij}]\}$$

A hypothetical example is represented in Table 4.2. The witness's SEU for the two response alternatives (choosing, or not choosing) can be calculated as follows.[2]

First, arbitrary numerical quantities are assigned to different degrees of value: $0 = $ indifference, $1 = $ low, $2 = $ moderate, and $3 = $ high. Positive or negative value determines the algebraic sign.

$$\text{SEU}_{\text{choosing}} = [(.8 \times .6)(+2)] + [(.8 \times .7)(-3)] + [(.2 \times .3)(-2)]$$
$$+ [(.2 \times .7)(-3)] = -1.26$$

$$\text{SEU}_{\text{not choosing}} = [(.8 \times .5)(-2)] + [(.8 \times .7)(-1)] + [(.2 \times .7)(+2)]$$
$$+ [(.2 \times .7)(0)] = -1.08$$

According to the social utility formulation, there are five ways in which witnesses' choice behavior can be influenced:

1. by manipulating the salience to the witnesses of the outcomes of making or not making an identification

Table 4.2. *Hypothetical payoff matrix*

	Suspect is the offender ($p = .80$)	Suspect is not the offender ($p = .20$)
Witness chooses suspect[a]	Outcome: hit Consequences: 1. Criminal brought to justice (moderate positive value, $p \sim .6$) 2. Will have to confront suspect or family in neighborhood (high negative value, $p \sim .7$)	Outcome: false alarm Consequences: 1. Innocent person convicted (moderate negative value, $p \sim .3$) 2. Will have to confront suspect or family in neighborhood (high negative value, $p \sim .7$)
Witness does not choose	Outcome: miss Consequences: 1. Guilty criminal set free (moderate negative value, $p \sim .5$) 2. Police annoyed (low negative value, $p \sim .7$)	Outcome: correct rejection Consequences: 1. Innocent person exonerated (moderate positive value, $p \sim .7$) 2. Police annoyed (indifferent value, $p \sim .7$)

[a]We will assume for the sake of simplicity of exposition that choices are always of the suspect.

2. by manipulating the salience to the witnesses of the consequences of the outcomes of making or not making an identification
3. by manipulating the value the witnesses place on the consequences of the outcomes of their behavior
4. by manipulating the witnesses' estimates of the probability that the suspect is the offender
5. by manipulating the witnesses' estimates of the probability of various consequences occurring given the outcomes of the witnesses' choice decisions.

It is not clear how these components of social decision making are influenced by a given event. For example, were investigators to imply confidence in having apprehended the offender, a witness confronting the lineup might reasonably believe that (a) it is likely that the offender is actually in the lineup, and that (b) the police will be disappointed if the witness either fails to make an identification or makes a wrong identification. The first of these directly affects the witness's subjective assessment of the probability that the suspect is the offender. The second increases the probability of police disapproval given a nonidentification and also indicates that the disapproval will be of a magnitude that reflects the high confidence of the police that they have apprehended the offender. The witness may therefore believe that the police will not merely disapprove of nonidentification but will be annoyed, which would give this consequence a more negative value than before.

Conceptualizing the behavior of eyewitnesses as a decision process and using theoretical accounts of decision-making processes to structure further thinking about eyewitness identifications generate many interesting implications for further research. For example,

> To what extent are witnesses' decisions to make or not make a lineup choice actually independent of the amount of information they possess about the offender's identity? What is the role of this information in determining willingness to choose?
>
> What beliefs do witnesses to real criminal offenses bring with them to the lineup, and what is the structure of the payoff matrix for these real witnesses?
>
> Not all witnesses to offenses are asked to attempt an identification, nor are all attempts to identify reported as evidence. What are the correlates of this selectivity? Is selection done on the basis of the quality of information the witnesses possess, the nature of the witnesses' beliefs, or both? Would this selection produce eyewitness identification evidence based only on particular patterns of beliefs about probabilities and values in the witnesses' decision making?

Whatever the answers to these questions, we suggest that the behavior of eyewitnesses in lineups and photospreads is choice behavior and that it should be viewed as the result of the interplay of the information witnesses have and the witnesses' beliefs about the outcomes of their behavior and the consequences and probabilities of these outcomes.

The difficulty of the lineup as a test of recognition

The specification of the "stimulus" in research on recognition in lineup and photospreads has been neglected. Whereas for the criminal justice system this is a substantive problem – a matter of lineup fairness – for research on lineups and photospreads the quantification of the difficulty of the lineup as a test of recognition is a serious methodological problem. Comparison of studies investigating, for example, the effects of various kinds of staged "crimes," manipulations of the witness's beliefs, or degrees of realism is an important prerequisite for the development of a cumulative body of knowledge. As Wells (1978) points out, however, such comparisons are not meaningful without an index of how difficult it is to discriminate the offender from the other members of a particular lineup. There have been many proposals for measures of the difficulty of a lineup as a one-item test of recognition, ranging from the use of conventional statistical techniques such as chi-square and tests on identification proportions (Doob & Kirshenbaum, 1973; Malpass & Devine, 1983) to indices developed specifically for the eyewitness lineup problem (Malpass, 1981a; Malpass & Devine, 1983; Wells,

Leippe, & Ostrom, 1979). These will be reviewed as part of the discussion of the substantive problem of suggestion in the structure of lineups. At this point it is sufficient to point out that cross-study comparisons as well as absolute levels of choosing, accuracy, or error are not interpretable in the absence of knowledge about the difficulty of the discrimination required of the witnesses.

The importance of manipulating offender presence

Research studies on identification in lineups and photospreads benefit considerably from manipulating the presence of the offender in the lineup for the following reasons.

Generalizability to the criminal justice system. Avoiding the error of identifying an innocent suspect in a lineup is one of the dominant themes in conceptual discussions of eyewitness identification research. The most obvious instance where this error is possible is in lineups where the offender is absent (i.e., the suspect is not the offender). Convicting the innocent is clearly the more important error to avoid, and avoiding it provides the rationale for the bulk of eyewitness identification research. It is all the more surprising then that a great many studies fail to investigate lineups from which the offender is absent, because this is the most common real-world situation that gives rise to wrongful incrimination. Therefore, to examine the effects of any procedure concerning this focal problem, witnesses' behavior in response to offender-absent lineups must be observed.

Separating choosing from accuracy. The rate of correct identifications of an offender in a lineup or photospread is a function of both the witness's ability to discriminate the offender from the foils, and the witness's willingness to make an identification. Therefore, the rate of *correct* identifications in an offender-present lineup cannot be directly interpreted to reflect their accuracy without information about the rate of *false* identifications when the offender is absent. If there is a high rate of identification when the offender is absent then it is likely that a proportion of the identifications of the offender will have resulted from guessing. Knowledge of the rate of choosing when the offender is absent is necessary in order to know the degree to which correct identifications reflect the witness's ability to differentiate the offender from other individuals. The rate of choosing foils in an offender-present lineup does not alone provide this information. Identifying a foil in the presence of the offender may be a different kind of error of judgment from identifying a foil in a lineup where the offender is absent, because it requires the witness both to reject the correct alternative and to choose another one. In order to separate the choosing rate from accuracy, correct identifications when the offender is present must be considered against false identifications when the offender is absent.

Informativeness and diagnosticity. More sophisticated means of examining the separation of choosing and accuracy have been described by Wells and Lindsay (1980; Lindsay & Wells, 1980). Through application of Bayesian statistical thinking they identify two measures of identification performance in lineups. The first is the *informativeness* of identifications and of non-identifications. Informativeness is a measure of the amount of revision of the probability of guilt (or innocence) resulting from knowledge of the rates of identification (or nonidentification) in a lineup. The second measure is the *diagnosticity* of an identification (or nonidentification). Diagnosticity of lineup identifications (the likelihood ratio in Bayesian statistics) is the ratio of the probability of a correct identification of an offender in a lineup to the probability of a false identification of the suspect in an offender-absent lineup. "As the proportion of identifications of the innocent suspect decreases relative to the proportion of identifications of the guilty suspect, the likelihood that an identified suspect is actually guilty increases; or, in other words, the diagnosticity of the lineup increases" (Lindsay & Wells, 1980, p. 309).

These applications of Bayesian thinking provide measures with which to evaluate the changes in the quality of information obtained from eyewitness identifications as a result of experimental manipulations. Lindsay and Wells (1980) in a staged crime study (calculator theft) created offender-present and blank lineups in which the similarity of the foils to the offender (or his substitute) was either high or low. They were able to show that the diagnosticity of both identifications and nonidentifications is higher in high-similarity lineups than in low-similarity lineups.

Malpass and Devine (1981a) found that both identifications and nonidentifications were more diagnostic under unbiased instructions than under biased instructions, indicating that unbiasing instructions in eyewitness lineups provides investigators with more useful information. Other modifications of lineup structure or lineup procedure or both can likewise be evaluated by these informational measures, but information about identifications in offender-absent lineups is required. Although these measurements provide a rich source of information, they cannot easily be applied to actual criminal lineups, because the offender is rarely omitted intentionally. These measurement techniques are important for research, however, because they facilitate evaluation of the effects of procedural and structural attributes of lineups.

Studies that omit blank lineups are therefore limited in direct applicability and in the information they can provide. Malpass and Devine (1981b), for example, studied the effect on recognition of an offender's face of a guided memory interview in which subjects who had witnessed a vandalism in a classroom setting 5 months earlier were reminded of details of the events, their feelings at the time, and the physical context in which the event occurred. Although choosing rates between the two conditions (guided memory interview and no interview) did not differ, correct identifications in an offender-present photospread with unbiased instructions were increased from 40% to 60%. We do not know, however, what effect the interview might have had on choosing in an offender-absent lineup. The criminal justice system is appropriately conservative about introducing new procedures that might introduce a bias to choose, and information about the effects of such procedures in blank lineups is important in determining the applied utility of the findings.

Leippe, Wells, and Ostrom (1978) found that if witnesses had information prior to a theft that supported the inference that the crime was serious, more witnesses accurately identified the thief than if they gained that knowledge after the theft. Still, we do not know the effect of this manipulation on choosing rates in offender-absent lineups. Similarly, Brigham et al. (1982) omitted offender-absent lineups in a study that otherwise presents important basic data on identification rate under conditions of high mundane realism. Even though the accuracy of eyewitness identifications obtained under realistic conditions is of interest, the omission of offender-absent lineups prevents us from observing the prevalence of wrongful identifications and from observing the relationship between such important factors as a witness's confidence and accuracy under these conditions.

Summary

This conceptualization of the problem of eyewitness identification points out some desiderata for research on eyewitness identification.

> Choosing rates should be reported. Studies that do not examine the proportions of choosing in their witnesses or do not present their data in such a way that choosing rates can be examined omit the most theoretically relevant behavioral data.
> The nature of the witnesses' beliefs should be investigated and used in interpreting choosing rates.
> Variables affecting the amount of information witnesses have should be measured (if they vary) and their relationship to choosing and errors examined.
> Information on the difficulty of the discrimination task presented to witnesses by the lineup or photospread should be presented. Studies that

do not provide such information cannot be compared with others in which the difficulty of the discrimination is known, and thus they contribute less than they might to cumulative knowledge in the field.

Data from offender-absent lineups should be obtained. Studies that do not manipulate the presence of the offender fail to provide information on the two conditions in real eyewitness identifications under which errors can occur, fail to provide a baseline against which to interpret correct identification rates, and make it impossible to apply recently developed indices for evaluating the effects of experimental manipulations on witnesses' choice behavior.

Suggestion in eyewitness identifications

The Supreme Court of the United States in its decision in the Wade-Gilbert-Stovall trilogy (Wall, 1965, p. 26) has suggested that "the influence of improper suggestion upon identifying witnesses probably accounts for more miscarriages of justice than any other single factor – perhaps it is responsible for more such errors than all other factors combined." An identification is suggestive if there is an implication to the witness that the police believe that the actual offender is present in the lineup or if the identity of the police suspect is indicated to the witness. Suggestion can be communicated through the procedure of the lineup (through the social interactions of the various persons present) and through the structure of the lineup itself. There is probably an irreducible degree of suggestion inherent in any identification. If witnesses believe that a lineup would not be held if the police thought that they did not have a good suspect, then witnesses will also understand that the police believe it likely that the offender is present in the lineup. In the next section we will review empirical studies and related issues on procedural and structural suggestion in lineups and photospreads. Coverage of the literature is not exhaustive. Rather, we have focused on studies that possess many of the desirable features already noted.

Suggestion in lineup procedure

Many aspects of the lineup situation may suggest that a witness's task is to choose a member of the lineup as the offender (Levine & Tapp, 1973). The aggregate effects of these suggestions have been simulated in laboratory studies by manipulations of the instructions given to witnesses. Malpass and Devine (1981a) manipulated lineup instructions by giving one group of witnesses an instruction indicating that the offender was present in the lineup, at the same time failing to provide a place on a response form for indicating that the witness believed the offender to be absent from the lineup (biased instruction). The other group of witnesses was told that the offender may not be in the lineup and was given the option of indicating on the response form that the offender was not present (unbiased instruction). The biased instruction was expected to lead to higher rates of choosing than the unbiased instruction, which in turn would lead to high error rates when the offender was absent from the lineup and lower error rates when the offender was present. Witnesses were students who had observed a realistically staged destructive event of moderate seriousness. Students from a number of different classes were gathered for a demonstration of psychophysiological measurement techniques in a large lecture hall. During the demonstration a young male confederate of the investigators approached the instructor, carried on a short conversation, and then stood aside, next to a rack of electronics apparatus. The confederate appeared interested in the apparatus and changed dial settings. The instructor responded by asking him to stop. The confederate repeated his action twice more, and the instructor responded in increasingly angry terms. The confederate then shouted an obscenity at the instructor, pushed the electronics equipment rack face-over to the floor, and escaped out a rear door. The audience gasped, and the instructor manifested confusion. After some minutes, the instructor informed the students that the event had been staged. The witnesses were debriefed, and their participation in viewing lineups to be held on each of the following 3 evenings was solicited. Postexperimental questionnaire results indicated that during the minutes following the event, few witnesses were suspicious.

Witnesses viewed a five-person lineup through a one-way mirror. Half of the subjects in each instruction condition saw a lineup containing the offender, and the other half saw a blank lineup. Results in general showed the anticipated effects of instructional bias on both choosing and errors and underscored the importance of focusing on choosing in the study of eyewitness identification. When the offender was present in the lineup, 100% of witnesses chose someone when given a biased instruction (25% in error), whereas 83% chose someone when the instruction was unbiased (all choices were correct; the remaining 17% were erroneous rejections). When the offender was absent from the lineup, however, 78% of the witnesses chose a member of the lineup under the biased instruction, and 33% under the unbiased instruction. Of course, all of these were errors.

Separating choosing from accuracy as a factor of interest allowed Malpass and Devine (1981a) to examine the relation of choosing with both accuracy and the witness's confidence that the offender was in the lineup. Mean confidence ratings were patterned similarly to the choosing proportions, and there was a very strong correlation of confidence ratings with choosing both within experimental conditions and overall $[r\,(100) = .86]$, whereas the overall correlation of confidence with accuracy was $-.06$. They conclude that witnesses' confidence judgments made after their identification reflect their having chosen someone and are a valid indicator only of whether an identification has been made. To know whether the identification is an accurate one, one must know whether the offender was in fact present in the lineup. This, obviously, is what lineups are conducted to find out, and outside of research laboratories it cannot be known in advance.

The entire research literature on procedural suggestion is not very large, and there is an even smaller number of studies that have investigated procedural suggestion and also included offender-absent lineups. Hall and Ostrom (1975) asked subjects to identify the person who had recruited them for an experiment in their psychology class. They found a high rate of choosing when the target was present under both biased (80%) and unbiased (100%) instructions. When the target was absent from the lineup, choosing was moderately low (36%) under biased instructions, but very low (8%) under unbiased instructions, showing that subjects could reject the offender-absent lineup more effectively under unbiased instructions. When the target was present in the lineup, biased instructions led to 40% errors as compared with no errors when the instructions were unbiased. When the offender was absent, errors were the same as choices (36%, 8%).

Egan and Smith (1979) asked subjects to role play being witnesses. Subjects were shown the target person through a one-way mirror and were then (after either 2 or 35 days) asked to indicate whether or not each member of a five-person lineup, in turn, was the target. Subjects were given either "lax" or "strict" instructions, which the authors see as instructions to avoid misses (lax) or avoid false alarms (strict). Data on choosing are not presented but can be inferred from the errors data. With the target present, there was little difference in the error rates for the two instructions (12% and 8% for lax and strict, respectively), which implies choosing rates equal to or greater than 88% and 92%, respectively. With the target absent, there were more choices under lax instructions (79%) than under strict instructions (37%). All of these choices were, of course, errors. Again, the effects of suggestion on both choosing and errors depend on whether the offender is present or absent.

Buckhout (1980) showed subjects a film of a mugging and after 20 minutes asked them to view a photospread under either a "lax" or "strict" criterion instructional set. When the offender was present in the spread, 76% chose under lax instructions and 52% under strict instructions. With the offender absent, the figures were almost identical: 74% choices under lax instructions and 53% under strict. The accuracy rates were in contrast to the other studies: When the offender was present, there were 86% errors under lax instructions, and 90% errors under strict instructions; with the offender absent there were 74% and 53% errors under lax and strict conditions, respectively. Again, however, there was greater differentiation in error rates between instructions when the offender was absent than when present.

Some important if tentative generalizations can be advanced from these laboratory studies of procedural suggestion. There is a strong and consistent effect of instructional biases on both choosing and errors when the offender is not present. When the offender is present, the effects of instructional bias are lessened: Choosing rates are often very high, whereas errors generally are moderately low. Absolute levels of identification are not interpretable, however, because we generally do not know how easy it is for witnesses to pick out the suspect from the lineup.

An important limitation on extrapolation from these studies to the behavior of real eyewitnesses is the substantial lack of realism in these studies. We stated the problem of realism in eyewitness identification research earlier in the following terms:

While the object of the field is to contribute to the understanding of processes occurring in the natural social environment, subjects in eyewitness identification studies have rarely witnessed what appears to be a realistic criminal offense. And when these "witnesses" are asked to view a lineup they know that they are participants in an experiment. They know that neither they nor the "offender" will experience the consequences of either a correct or an incorrect judgement. (Malpass & Devine, 1980, pp. 347–348)

Claims to a high degree of generalizability from laboratory to natural settings have low face validity.

Realism in research on procedural suggestion

Munsterberg (1908) reported on an experiment conducted in the Berlin laboratory of Professor Liszt: Two students who were engaged in a violent argument were joined by the professor, and a pistol was fired. This incident was then used as the basis for a study of eyewitnesses' recollection of the events. Munsterberg continued:

This dramatic psychological experiment of six years ago opened up a long series of similar tests in a variety of places, with a steady effort to improve the conditions. The most essential condition remained, of course, always the complete naivete of the witnesses, as the slightest suspicion on their part would destroy the value of the experiment. It seems desirable even that the writing of the protocol should still be done in a state of belief. (p. 51)

That eyewitness identification studies should place subjects in a social situation that preserves the belief that a genuine event is occurring, rather than a simulation of a genuine event, is not presently thought of as a matter of course. Very few studies attempt to preserve the subjects' perception of the genuineness of the events they are experiencing past the initial incident. Still, concern for realism is reemerging in the eyewitness identification area, and it has been foreshadowed by vigorous discussions of realism in other areas of research on psychology and law (Bray & Kerr, 1979; Konechni & Ebbesen, 1979). Realism is both a matter of the plausibility of the events in which the "witness" participates and the witness's subjective experience. If witnesses believe that the events they experience are genuine rather than staged for research purposes, then realism has been achieved. Many kinds of simulations clearly do not lend themselves to the impression of realism, for example, those using slides, films, or video presentations. Realistic events alone, however, are not enough to ensure meaningful research on procedural suggestion in eyewitness identification. Without a basis in theoretical analysis, or without a concern for generalization to an important applied problem, attaining realism could result in little more than dramatic manipulation. The conceptualization of the processes influencing the choice behavior of eyewitnesses' viewing lineups presented earlier in this chapter provides both a theoretical and applied basis for a concern with realism. If witnesses' decisions about whether or not to make a lineup choice are affected by the salient outcomes and consequences of their behavior and the associated values and probabilities, then we have identified through theory an important dimension of generalization from research to application. If the content and structure of the payoff matrix differs substantially between laboratory studies and the conditions in natural settings in which eyewitnesses confront identification lineups, then important questions can be raised about the ways in which laboratory simulations contribute to understanding the behavior of eyewitnesses in natural settings. Similarly, it is possible that the psychological processes involved in orienting to and observing an event, coding it (or aspects of it) into memory, and rehearsing, retrieving, and reporting a recollection at a later time are affected differently by the social meaning of the natural social environment than they are by the social meaning of the laboratory. If realistic conditions coupled with the belief that an event is genuine affect these processes in a way different from simulations, an argument can be made for the desirability of realistic conditions on the grounds of generalizability to natural environment applications. Realism in eyewitness identification research, then, is a means to implementing empirical research that meets theoretical criteria on which generalization to conditions in natural settings can be based. Realism can be attained during many stages of an eyewitness study. The two that are of immediate interest are the event that the subject witnesses and the situation in which an identification is requested.

"Crimes" in eyewitness identification research: variations on the staged-incident paradigm. Dramatic and mundane events have been employed as demonstrations of fallibility of eyewitness evidence at least since the early years of this century. Munsterberg (1908) reported on two dramatic demonstrations, one in a classroom and the other at a meeting of a scientific association, both involving violent quarrels culminating in the firing of a pistol. He went on to say, "It is not necessary to tell more of these dramatic experiments, which have recently become the fashion and almost a sport, and which will still have to be continued with a great variety of conditions if the psychological laws involved are really to be cleared up" (pp. 53–54).

Another investigator, this time in the United States (H. B. Brown, 1934), arranged for a workman to enter his classroom to check a radiator, and subsequently the witnesses to this event were used to study several questions about eyewitness accuracy. More recently there has been renewed interest in the use of the staged-incident paradigm in eyewitness research. The following, in rough order of "seriousness" or intensity, were staged before groups of witnesses.

1. The target person solicits students as experimental subjects in a classroom (Hall & Ostrom, 1975).
2. The target stands before a group and gives a brief life history (Shepherd, Davies, & Ellis, 1980, Exp. 1).
3. Two target persons enter a testing room to ask directions (Shepherd et al., 1980, Exp. 4).
4. The target person enters a classroom and asks if a wallet has been found (Gorenstein & Ellsworth, 1980).
5. The target person is a "technician" who has just ostensibly destroyed a TV set by accident outside of the view (but within hearing) of witnesses gathered in a classroom (Shepherd et al., 1980, Exp. 3).
6. The target person steals a bag containing an object ostensibly left by a previous experimental subject, dropping the bag on the way out to call attention to himself (Leippe et al., 1978).
7. The target person angrily enters a testing session as an irate driver whose car has been scratched and blocked and who is seeking the owner of the other car (Shepherd et al., 1980, Exp. 2).
8. Two target persons intrude into a classroom to retrieve a left-behind book. One argues with the professor (Loftus & Greene, 1980).
9. The target person enters a classroom to retrieve an object, snatches a woman's purse, and runs out (Buckhout et al., 1974).
10. The target person is a volunteer (or intruder) in a demonstration of psychophysiological and biofeedback measurements. He argues with the professor and damages electronics equipment (Malpass & Devine, 1980; Malpass & Devine, 1981a; Malpass, Devine, & Bergen, 1980).

11. The target person argues with and assaults a professor in the classroom (Buckhout, Figueroa, & Hoff, 1975).

The following, in rough order of seriousness, were staged repeatedly before individual witnesses.

1. The target person waits together with the witness (Hilgendorf & Irving, 1978b).
2. The target person enters a convenience store where the witness is a checkout clerk, and draws attention to himself by, for example, paying for a small purchase with pennies, which are individually counted out, and then asking for directions (Brigham et al., 1982).
3. An object (e.g., a calculator) is stolen by the target during the initial stage of an experiment ostensibly on another topic than eyewitness identification (Lindsay & Wells, 1980; Lindsay, Wells, & Rumpel, 1981; Wells, Ferguson, & Lindsay, 1981; Wells, Lindsay, & Ferguson, 1979).
4. The target person is interrupted by the witness while in the act of stealing a TV set connected to a video game, which is a part of the ostensible experiment (Murray & Wells, 1982).

Other events, of different kinds, have been presented to subjects on film or videotape, sometimes with instructions that might lead subjects to believe that the recorded events were genuine. The events just listed, on the other hand, were carried out with the intention of creating an environment in which subjects were witnesses to a genuine event.

Problems in the staged-incident paradigm. Although we believe the considerations favoring the staging of realistic incidents to be compelling, some issues should be considered in planning a research program.

1. Witnesses to incidents staged before groups discuss the incident with each other, leave the place of the incident together, and if the incident is a dramatic one, may spend additional time together discussing the event. The incident staged by Malpass et al. (1980), for example, was the talk of the campus for days after the event, and its true nature was eventually uncovered. If the perception of an incident's genuineness is to be preserved beyond the ensuing few moments (e.g., until identifications can be arranged), the contact among witnesses may lead to suspicions or beliefs about the incident that will affect the witnesses' subsequent behavior in an identification task. The witnesses' beliefs about the incident – assignment of blame, attributions of intent, beliefs about consequences of their own further participation, and so on – may reasonably be expected to affect behavior in an identification. These and other matters should be investigated at least by means of a postexperiment questionnaire and perhaps through a field or participant observation methodology.

2. Group presentations generally are one-shot occurrences and therefore

are susceptible to criticism on grounds of uniqueness. When a given script is enacted a number of times for individual subjects or for small groups, the unique properties of any particular enactment are spread over experimental conditions, and variations across enactments help to ensure that the resulting data show effects of the experimental script in general rather than the unique properties of a particular enactment. All single-event studies are vulnerable to this criticism and should document the event enacted to preserve it for future analysis if possible. This is not always possible. Malpass et al. (1980) attempted no documentation of their staged vandalism because detection of such an attempt would certainly have undermined the credibility of the subsequent request by the police for eyewitnesses to come forward to view lineups.

3. Staged incidents that involve reenactments of the incident for individuals or small groups do not have the degree of difficulty with generalizability that single enactments have. They possess instead the danger that knowledge of the manipulation will diffuse through the subject population. If experimental naivete is important, then the possibility of diffusion should be investigated. A number of methodologies might be useful, including a postexperimental questionnaire given to a randomly selected subset of subjects across time in synchrony with the running of other conditions of the study for the sole purpose of examining diffusion. Participant observation or other similar techniques might be valuable.

Realism at the point of the eyewitness's decision. Although many studies have used realistic events, rarely is realism preserved in the social environment in which witnesses make their identification decision. Eyewitnesses in the natural environment are confronted with social constraints and influences that may be very different from those existing in laboratory simulations, where subjects are aware that the witnessed events are not genuine. Subjects in eyewitness identification experiments, for example, probably do not anticipate facing the disfavor of either those running the lineup or the person who is identified; they do not risk making an error in the important natural environment senses of having wrongly incriminated someone or having allowed a criminal to go unidentified. They do not risk having to continue what may be perceived to be time-consuming or inconvenient participation in an investigation or trial, and they do not have to confront the question of whether or not to participate in an episode of formal and perhaps intimidating contact with the powerful institutions of authority in our society. The experience of real witnesses in important aspects of their contacts with the criminal justice system may be outside the range of variation attained in nongenuine laboratory simulations on important incentive variables which affect their decisions. For this reason alone, laboratory simulations of identification in lineups or photospreads that do not provide a genuine-appearing social environment in which the eyewitness confronts the identification decision may well provide an inadequate basis for extrapolation to natural environments of eyewitness identifications. Unless we are prepared to ignore theoretical considerations concerning social decision processes, research on witnesses' identification choice behavior must become concerned with the decision-making environment of the research as a basis for extrapolation to natural settings.

Malpass et al. (1980) conducted a study in which witnesses to an act of vandalism on a college campus were asked to attend lineups conducted by police officers. This study was done as an extension of Malpass and Devine (1981a). Although the results in Malpass and Devine (1981a) showed differential instructional bias effects on choosing and errors, depending on the offender's presence or absence, Malpass et al. (1980) were concerned that the artificial conditions of the research placed the subjects in a decision-making environment in which the outcomes of their decision were inherently trivial. This raised the question of the effects of the importance of the consequences of the identification decision, and led Malpass et al. (1980) to design a realistic study in which the seriousness of the outcomes could be manipulated.

During a lecture on biofeedback techniques a volunteer subject for the demonstration became engaged in an argument with one of the lecturers, which culminated in the volunteer's pushing over a rack of electronics equipment associated with the demonstration and escaping through a nearby door. The demonstration was terminated, and the lecture broke up with faculty, students, and administrators milling about on the lecture platform and discussing the events of the evening and what to do about them. The following day, police officers entered the college's student center with a group of six young men and a female police clerk, and persons who had attended the previous evening's demonstration were requested to view a lineup. Over the next day and a half, students who had viewed the demonstration attended lineups individually. Just prior to a witness's moving to the location from which the lineup could be viewed, the lecturer whose equipment had been damaged asked the police officer in charge what would be the likely consequence to the suspect if he was identified. The officer made one of two responses, which were rehearsed manipulations of consequence severity. One response (a severe consequence) indicated that the suspect would be responsible for financial restitution for the damage and perhaps receive a felony conviction and spend time in jail, whereas the other (a trivial consequence) indicated that the incident would probably not go beyond the college and the punishment would be no more than a good talking to from the Dean.

The authors based their expectations for the results of this manipulation on the emphasis on avoiding errors of identification, which has been a dominant theme in the literature on eyewitness identification (Levine & Tapp, 1973; Loftus, 1980b). It is presumed that avoiding errors in eyewitness identification is important, that avoiding the error of incriminating the innocent is the more important error to avoid, and that in general this value is widely agreed upon in American society. The authors expected, therefore, that as the consequences of an identification became more severe, witnesses would become less willing to make an identification. The results, however, were to the contrary: 83% of the witnesses who heard the severe-consequence manipulation made a lineup choice, whereas only 26% of those who heard the trivial-consequence manipulation did so. The effect of these differential choosing rates on identification accuracy was equally dramatic. When the consequences were severe and the rate of choosing was high, 73% of the witnesses were in error when the offender was absent and 25% when he was present. When the consequences were trivial and the rate of choosing was low, 22% of witnesses were in error when the offender was absent, and 70% when he was present.

One can argue after the fact that these results might have been expected had the investigators attended to other, alternative bases for developing expectations, for example, retribution. It seemed clear to Malpass et al. (1980) that the explanation for these results lies in examining the beliefs of the witnesses in the social situation of the vandalism and the lineup. Focusing on identification errors emphasizes the identification consequences associated with those errors to the exclusion of those consequences associated with accuracy, especially with catching and punishing the offender. A belief that the police probably had the right person and a salient value on punishment, coupled with a lack of reflection on the consequences and probability of incriminating an innocent person, might well increase the value of making an identification. Malpass and Devine (1980) suggest that a subjective-expected-utility approach to the problem of the witnesses' identification decision provides a general methodology for understanding a given situation of witnessing an offense. Eyewitnesses in realistic settings may place such positive values on certain outcomes (e.g., identification of the offender) that they overshadow values placed on other outcomes (e.g., identification of an innocent person). A simulation might not elicit such values. The transposition from laboratory studies to more genuine simulations of natural environment events is not entirely straightforward, a realization that supports an emphasis on realism as an important part of a comprehensive research strategy in this area.

Brigham et al. (1982) carried out a study of eyewitness identification that has a high degree of realism and the character of everyday social interaction in the natural social environment. Target persons, either white or black, entered convenience stores and called the attention of the lone store clerk to themselves by paying with pennies (laboriously counted out) or by other plausible means and by then asking for directions to a distant location in the city. "Law interns" visited the store approximately 2 hours later and presented the store clerk with photographic lineups from which the clerks were asked if any one of these individuals had been in their store during the last 24 hours. Under these realistic conditions, and after a delay of only 2 hours, Brigham et al. found (considering white clerks only) that 76.5% chose a white customer, and 82.5% chose a black customer. Of the white clerks, 55% misidentified a black customer, and 35% misidentified a white customer. This difference appears large in an absolute sense, but it is of only marginal statistical significance and lends weak support to the generalizability to natural settings of the fairly robust laboratory finding of a cross-race recognition difficulty (Malpass, 1981b; Shepherd, 1981). As noted previously, however, these results are limited because offender-absent lineups were not included, so interpretation of the identification rates cannot be aided by information about false alarms. There is evidence that experimental manipulations to modify witnesses' beliefs are effective both in simulations (Buckhout, 1980; Egan & Smith, 1979; Hall & Ostrom, 1975; Malpass & Devine, 1981a) and in a realistic study (Malpass et al., 1980). There is no direct evidence, however, that manipulations of realism affect witnesses' beliefs in the way we have suggested: Malpass and colleagues did not directly compare a simulation with a realistic study.

Murray and Wells (1982) compared two highly realistic conditions. Students entered a room for the purpose of participating in a study on computer games just in time to observe the theft of the game equipment. Campus security officers were informed and arrived to display photos of workmen who might have been involved in the theft. Half of the witnesses were told, shortly before the arrival of the investigating officer, that the entire series of events had been staged for research purposes; the remaining witnesses were not so informed. Otherwise, all subjects were treated the same. Uninformed witnesses were more likely to choose a foil, less likely to choose the offender, and had lower correlations between confidence ratings and accuracy scores. These differences were not dramatic, but neither were they trivial. Murray and Wells discuss the degree to which it is necessary to construct highly realistic studies in which the witnesses are induced to believe the events are genuine. They conclude that "there should be some value placed on the general plan of corroborating results from the informed witness procedure by using an uninformed witness procedure." The Murray and Wells (1982) study is the kind of transitional study advocated by Malpass and Devine (1980) and brings us closer to having an empirical base for estimating the generalizability of research on identifications in lineups and photospreads.

If we consider realism as a dimension, ranging from extremely uninvolving simulations (e.g., cryptic printed descriptions) to totally involving and genuine-appearing events in which witnesses are participants, we can ask what conditions are required to bring the witnesses' subjective state close to that attained in a genuine experience of the given type of event. Presumably, genuine events elicit a rich network of associations and related affective processes. How rich in associative elicitation must a simulation be to attain an adequate level of simulation of a genuine experience? The means by which associative elicitation is accomplished by various kinds of simulation attempts is an important question. How effective as simulations are (a) written descriptions, (b) descriptions accompanied by slide shows, (c) slide/tape shows, (d) film or video presentations, (e) dramatic enactments in which the witness is aware that it is a dramatization, or (f) dramatic enactments in which the witness is a participant but is told at some point during the drama that it is a simulation? The last condition, seemingly as rich in associative elicitation as a genuine experience, is the kind of realism manipulation used by Murray and Wells (1982). From the point of view of associative elicitation, the witnesses may find it sufficiently close to a genuine experience that being informed that the events were staged will have only subtle effects on their choice behaviors.

Realism is an important problem in eyewitness identification research for those issues in which there is theoretical reason to believe that the witnesses' beliefs about the genuineness of the events they are participating in may make a difference in the behavior being studied. Still, even in those areas it may not be necessary for the research literature to be totally dominated by realistic studies. There may be ways to construct simulations sufficiently effective to provide a good empirical basis for generalizations and for application in the criminal justice system.

To investigate all of the important issues in the area of identification in lineups and photospreads requires many kinds of studies. A comprehensive research strategy for studying eyewitness identification should contain both descriptive studies to provide information on attributes of genuine events in criminal justice (such as the beliefs of real witnesses about consequences and their values and probabilities) and exploratory studies to evaluate the feasibility of new procedures (e.g., Malpass & Devine, 1981b). Even with respect to studies of lineups and photospreads "we do not believe that laboratory studies on eyewitness identification in which 'witnesses' know they are experimental subjects are of no value or that 'realistic' studies should dominate the literature. But we do need to know whether the results of nonrealistic studies and the theoretical analyses we work from survive the transposition from the laboratory to more realistic contexts" (Malpass & Devine, 1980, p. 356). Although realism is not the *only* issue, and not the *only* strategy of importance, until we know more about the degree to which simulations actually produce results that can be validly applied to genuine events in the natural environment, realism will be an important aspect of psychological research in this area, and its absence will be an important source of reservation about the applicability of the research literature. The section that follows contains a good example of an area of research in which highly realistic research settings are not necessary for obtaining useful and applicable information.

Summary

What have we learned from the small literature on procedural suggestion in eyewitness identification? We have confirmed the expectations derived from the psychological laboratory and literature that witnesses' identification behavior is malleable through social influence and expectations. We have learned, however, that the behavior on which to focus investigation is the witness's decision to choose or not to choose a member of the lineup as the offender. Separating choosing from eyewitness accuracy is an important sharpening of the issues in the study of eyewitness identification. We have also learned that although at high levels of abstraction our theoretical thinking is consistent with data generated in both laboratory and realistic studies, mapping the concrete events of realistic studies and presumably the natural social environment into the more abstract theoretical concepts that guide our research requires the development of explicit theoretically based procedures, and research is needed to bridge the gap from the laboratory to the natural social environment.

Suggestion in lineup structure

Comparison among studies using varying kinds of stimulus events, manipulations of the witness's beliefs, and degrees of realism is an important part of research on eyewitness identification. It certainly is true that such comparisons are of interest, but as Wells (1978) points out they are not presently meaningful because of a basic methodological problem: Lineups are very much like one-item tests in which the item difficulty is unknown. For any given lineup we have until recently had no way of knowing if the choice of the offender was an easy or a difficult task for the witness, given the distractor alternatives (foils) available in the lineup.

Although the problem of the unknown difficulty of a particular lineup is a serious methodological problem in eyewitness identification research, it is an important substantive problem in the criminal justice system. Lineups in which it is "easy" to identify the person who is the police suspect are generally termed "unfair" or "suggestive." Malpass and Devine (1983) describe two principles of lineup fairness abstracted from legal discussions:

1. Lineups should be of a sufficient *size* that the probability of a chance identification of an innocent suspect is low – that the potential for error is distributed across a number of persons. This principle concerns the absolute level of risk to which an innocent suspect is exposed. The larger the lineup, the lesser this risk.
2. The suspect must not be distinctive in comparison with the other members of the lineup. This principle is concerned with the level of risk to which an innocent suspect is exposed *relative* to the other members of the lineup: that no *bias* exists towards or away from the suspect.

These two kinds of fairness – size and bias – are both based on the composite similarity of the members of the lineup to each other and to the suspect. Unfairness in the size sense arises when one or more of the individuals standing in a lineup is actually not a plausible choice alternative for the witness. At the extreme, this person may be of a different race from the suspect (see, for example, Ellison & Buckhout, 1981, p. 116) or may be dissimilar from the suspect in one or more features so that he or she is not a completely plausible choice alternative. To the degree that one or more of the known-to-be-innocent members of the lineup (the foils) are less than plausible choice alternatives, the lineup is in reality smaller than the number of individuals standing in it. If the foils are similar to the police suspect in all important features (e.g., those features mentioned in a witness's description of the offender, or other important characteristics of the suspect), then a witness who possesses good information about the offender's unique appearance should be able to make an identification, whereas witnesses without such information or persons whose knowledge of the offender goes little beyond the verbal descriptions offered to the police should not be able to make an identification with a probability greater than chance.

Unfairness in the bias sense arises when the suspect is more likely to be chosen as the suspect in comparison with the foils, even though none of the foils may be an implausible choice alternative. Clearly these two senses of the term *unfairness* are related. It is necessarily the case that if there is a bias toward the suspect, these additional choices will be drawn away from one or more of the foils, likely resulting in their becoming less than fully plausible lineup alternatives. Still, it is not necessarily the case that if one foil has a low probability of being chosen (is an implausible choice alternative) that the suspect will have higher choice probability as a result.

Malpass and Devine (1983) examined the relationship between the composite similarity of the foils to the suspect and a number of measures of the two kinds of lineup fairness. Similarity was manipulated in the following way. A description was settled upon for the suspect, and individuals who fit that description were photographed, along with others who differed from the suspect in one direction or the other on one or more of six dimensions of variation: hair color, hair style, hair length, general body build, height, and eye color. The composite similarity of the foils to the suspect in the resulting photographic lineups could vary from 0 (when all foils share the same description of the suspect) through 5 (when all 5 foils differed from the suspect on one of the six feature dimensions) to 30 (when all 5 foils differed from the suspect on all 6 feature dimensions). Four lineups were constructed, which had composite similarities of approximately 8.5, 10, 17, and 24. Subjects read a description of a criminal offense (a breaking and entering) that included two repetitions of a description of the "suspect" (brown, medium-length wavy hair; medium height; medium build; and brown eyes).

The results generally showed a decrease in "fairness" as measured by 7 different indicators resulting from increasing suspect–foil dissimilarity. These include some standard statistical tests (chi-square test for deviation of choice frequencies from expectation, z test on proportions to assess bias toward the suspect) and some measures developed specifically for application to the lineup fairness problem. Wells, Leippe, and Ostrom (1979) suggested a measure of the degree of bias toward or away from the suspect. Their index is the reciprocal transformation of the proportion of mock witnesses identifying the suspect: the total number of mock witnesses divided by the number identifying the suspect. A lineup is biased toward the suspect if the index is smaller than the number of individuals in the lineup and is biased away from the suspect if the index is larger. If the number of identifications of the suspect equals chance expectation, the index equals the number of individuals in the lineup. Malpass (1981a) suggested a measure of the "effective size" of a lineup that adjusts the nominal size of the lineup (the number of individuals standing in the lineup) by subtracting from it the degree to which lineup members are chosen less than expected by chance. To obtain this index, the choice frequencies of those lineup members who are chosen less than expected are subtracted from chance expectation, these differences summed and then divided by the frequency expected by chance, and the resulting figure subtracted from the lineup's nominal size.

Malpass and Devine (1983) suggested alternative indicators of fairness that, they argue, are superior because they are more easily understood by laymen without training in statistics and measurement, and because the value judgments they involve are both directly apparent and can be decided in the criminal justice system without complicated technical consultation. They suggest that an interval be constructed around the proportion of identifications expected by chance (expressed as a proportion of chance expectation based on the lineup's nominal size), and that any member of the lineup be considered a less than plausible lineup choice alternative if an observed proportion of identifications falls below the interval. An acceptable foil could then be defined by choosing a proportion such as .90 (or .75 or .50) of chance expectation. Any foil whose choice proportion falls below this cutoff point would be rejected as a plausible foil. This same reasoning applied to lineup bias merely focuses on the suspect. A lineup is biased toward the suspect if the suspect is identified with a proportion of identifications above a certain criterion; it is biased away from the suspect if the proportion of identifications is below a specified criterion.

The latter proportional criterion measure (Malpass & Devine, 1983) has not yet been applied in empirical research, but other measures have. Brigham et al. (1982) found a marginally significant ($p < .10$) rank-order correlation (based on eight lineups) of -65 between the lineup's effective size (Malpass, 1981a) and the frequency of correct identifications.

The fairness measurements we have described are all based on the use of "mock witnesses": witnesses who do not have visual information about the identity of the offender but instead have the kind of general information that is provided in a verbal description. These individuals are then asked to choose the offender (suspect) from a lineup. The rationale behind the use of mock witnesses is based on the need for a means of evaluating the fairness of a lineup independently of the judgment of real witnesses. In the criminal justice system, after all, the lineup is used to test their memory; their memory is not used to test the lineup. One purpose of a fair lineup is to protect innocent suspects from misidentification by witnesses who do not possess very good information about the identity of the offender but who feel they must attempt an identification. If a lineup is fair then witnesses who have only general information about the appearance of the offender should not be able to identify him with a probability greater than that expected by chance, whereas witnesses who do have information about the offender's unique appearance should be able to do so. This rationale and the "mock witness" technique has been used by Doob and Kirschenbaum

(1973), Biederman (1980), and Wells, Leippe, and Ostrom (1979) to evaluate the fairness of lineups in actual criminal cases.

The measures of the informativeness and diagnosticity of an identification developed by Wells and Lindsay (1980; Lindsay & Wells, 1980), discussed earlier, do not require the use of mock witnesses and can be applied in studies using both offender-present and offender-absent lineups. These measures give fuller meaning to the idea of lineups with high composite similarity possessing greater fairness. Although fairness in the informational sense is not a concept found in legal discussion, it is certainly an important contribution of psychological research to the analysis of problems of eyewitness identification. Although the direct applicability of these measures to the criminal justice system is limited, they have the advantage of having a high degree of theoretical relevance to witnesses' decision processes.

Recommendations for future research

Existing psychological theory should be used in increasingly explicit ways to structure the analysis of the natural environment problems in eyewitness identification. This will (a) increase our knowledge of the degree to which existing theory can actually provide useful accounts of natural environment problems, (b) provide directions for research and practical improvements that become apparent through theoretical analysis, and (c) provide means of identifying the important dimensions of contrast between laboratory simulations and the natural environment of criminal justice practices so that research can produce both valid and apparently valid information. More specifically, the implications of a decision-theory approach to the choice behavior of witnesses in lineups or photospreads should be pursued. Interesting avenues of investigation are the decision structure for real eyewitnesses and its relation to their decisions. The results of such investigations would provide ecologically valid criteria against which to design laboratory simulations. Knowledge of the degree to which conditions of eyewitness identification in the natural environment influence choosing and error rates would be an important contribution both to the criminal justice system and the evaluation of the adequacy of psychological theory in this area.

Attention should be given to the desiderata for empirical studies noted earlier and especially to the basic methodological issue of the difficulty (fairness) of a given lineup as a test of witnesses' recognition. Attention to this psychometric aspect of eyewitness identification research will be very helpful to the interpretation of research findings and will add to the body of literature available. The various indicators of lineup fairness discussed should be used as criteria for the construction of lineups in research studies and not merely as a measurement to be taken post hoc and reported.

Finally, we should remember that simulations are intended to simulate something, and the farther we fall short of having obtained the important criteria of simulation the more tenuous will be our claim to an applicable contribution. We should attempt to minimize the number of assumptions necessary to move from our data to a clear generalization that will have an important application in the criminal justice system.

Notes

1 Rigorous application of SDT to the eyewitness identification problem may not be strictly appropriate because the choices open to witnesses generally are not the same as those available to subjects in detection tasks of the kind the theory addresses. Subjects in experiments on recognition memory are asked to choose one (or more) from a number of alternatives, where a correct alternative is always present (a forced-choice task) or are asked to say yes or no to each of a number of serially presented alternatives, one of which, at least, is a correct alternative. Subjects in these studies frequently know the proportion of alternatives that are correct.
2 Subjective expected utility is not the only decision-making strategy that witnesses might apply. In fact, the kind of decision strategy used by witnesses is an interesting research question. We use SEU here because it is close to the analysis used to illustrate the SDT formulation of decision processes in perception and recognition.

5   Earwitness voice recognition accuracy

Ray Bull and Brian R. Clifford

In obscene phone calls, bomb hoaxes, ransom demands, hooded rape, robberies, muggings, or in crimes committed in darkness, the perpetrator's voice may be the only definite piece of evidence available to aid police investigation and court conviction. That most research into witness testimony and identification has been conducted in the visual realm reflects the fact that most identification situations involve a witness using visual clues. The preponderance of such research serves to obscure the fact that in many instances both visual and verbal information is available and in many others only verbal cues exist. The awareness of the existence of the last two types of criminal situation dictates that research into human abilities to recognize voices should not be neglected but rather be rapidly pursued. In this chapter we attempt to "balance the books" by reviewing the state of voice memory research as illustrated by our own work of the last four or five years.

The starting points for voice identification research and those for eyewitness research are the same: the belief, based mainly on personal experiences, that voice identification can be very good and the fact that voice identification is accepted at face value in courts of law. That is, identification testimony based on the sound of a person's voice is treated as direct evidence of identity and therefore is admissible in the courts.

A key point to note, however, is that personal experience of voice recognition is always of familiar voices – the voices that are *not* usually those to be identified in criminal situations. In other words the two situations are not comparable: Identification of familiar and unfamiliar voices constitute two entirely different classes of phenomena.

When we move from "commonsense understanding" to the potentially relevant experimental literature, the way forward is not clear: Experimentalists disagree among themselves. Thus some hold that "the ability of human listeners to identify speakers from their voices has long been known" (Atal, 1972, p. 1687), that "we all know from experience that people can be easily recognized by their voices" (Bunge, 1977, p. 207), and that "identification of speakers by their voices is a common experience" (Compton, 1963, p. 1748). The opposite view has also been expressed, most categorically by Saslove and Yarmey (1980), who argue that long-term speaker identification must be treated with the utmost caution.

How can these contrasting views be reconciled? Most simply, this can be done by pointing out that many studies have, in fact, used familiar voices for generating their speech samples or have examined, often with poor methodology, the efficiency of voiceprints and other electromechanical methods of voice matching. Neither of these two approaches is particularly relevant to the case wherein a witness hears an unfamiliar voice during the commission of a crime and is later asked to attend a voice lineup in order to assert whether a suspect's voice is the same voice as that heard previously.

This is not the place to give a detailed account of voiceprint research, either as an indicative tool for predicting voice identification accuracy of witnesses "in the field," or as a means of gaining understanding concerning how listeners encode, store, and retrieve once-heard unfamiliar voices. (The interested reader is referred to Bull, 1978, 1981, and Clifford & Bull, 1978, for our views on the matter.) Suffice it to say here that in our opinion (a) it is not the best method of advancing forensically relevant knowledge about the man in the street who becomes a witness, and (b) it cannot become a substitute for such research.

The research we will discuss in this chapter does deal with the man in the street in that most of our studies employed subject populations or samples other than undergraduates and tested their ability to identify a once-heard voice by means of listening rather than by viewing graphic representations of that voice or by hearing the voice repeatedly (as can occur in aural-spectral research). In other words, our overall approach was to approximate as closely as possible the voice identification procedures used in real-life criminal cases. To facilitate experimental control, however, approximation to real life was all we set out to achieve.

We entered voice identification research from work we had been doing in visual identification, and thus we did not come to it with a completely open mind. Rather we assumed that, as with visual identification, the reliability and validity of voice identification as evidence was likely to be found to be largely a function of the encoding, storage, and retrieval stages of memory as they interact with the social and situational aspects of the total criminal situation and criminal justice procedure (Clifford & Bull, 1978). It so happened that as our thoughts were moving to the relatively virgin soil of voice memory, the process was given an impetus by the publication of an important document by a legal committee that was to investigate identification evidence (in all its forms) in criminal cases in Great Britain. This committee, referred to as the Devlin Committee, which reported to the U.K. Home Secretary in 1976, stated that as far as its members were concerned no scientific research had been conducted on voice identification but that "research should proceed as rapidly as possible into the practicality of voice parades ... or any other appropriate method" (Devlin, 1976). Now, although it was inaccurate to say that no research had been conducted on voice identification (Bull & Clifford, 1976), it may have been true to say that little directly relevant research had been conducted. In fact, despite the very long history of voice identification in legal cases, formal study and experimentation are fairly recent developments.

The early literature on voice identification has been reviewed by Clifford (1980b) and the interested reader should consult that paper, but the major point to note is that despite the fact that most researchers were concerned to stress that accurate memory depends on many factors and to go on to document these, the state of the art is still in a rudimentary stage. Few if any of the putatively important areas have been adequately investigated or settled. This chapter classifies and reviews existing research, both ours and that of others, under a number of headings that could be of value to the criminal justice system. We hope that it clarifies certain questions and provides data from which future research can proceed. Our research does not pretend to be definitive; it is avowedly exploratory. It needs to be, given the current status of voice research.

Individual differences in earwitnessing

Age of witness

A very difficult question that faces the police and courts daily is whether the testimony of young children and elderly citizens should be accorded the same status as that of middle-aged witnesses. Although some of our own studies have focused on this particular problem, most previous research has concentrated solely on the voice identification powers of children. An exception to this is Yarmey (1979a), who devotes a chapter in his book to the testimony of the young and the aged. Yarmey concludes that "our understanding of the psychology of aging has moved in the last few years from a pessimistic view that aging necessarily involves decrement to one which recognizes changes in abilities and processes over a life span of development" (p. 217). In general this may be a more worthwhile perspective on the effects of aging, but Yarmey made no direct reference to research on the effects of a listener's age on voice identification accuracy. This may well have been due to the dearth of literature on the topic. The literature concerning visual identification is slightly more extensive, but although it suggests that older children may be more accurate in face recognition tasks than younger children, especially when the younger children's propensity for guessing has been taken into account (Clifford & Bull, 1978), we should note that "witnesses at the upper age range have not received as much attention" (Loftus, 1979, p. 163). Smith and Winograd (1977) found people over the age of 60 years to perform more poorly than younger people in a face recognition task, but Loftus (1979) notes that "one might be tempted to conclude from these results that after a certain age (perhaps fifty or sixty) eyewitness reliability will decline with age. This generalization would not be correct" (p. 160). She reminds us that although the efficiency of some processes may decline with age, an increase of efficiency in others could more than compensate. For example, although elderly witnesses may be poorer at providing descriptions, they may be less influenced than children by suggestive or biased questions.

Our own particular interest in the effects of age of witness has been concerned with earwitnessing. There is some evidence that voice recognition ability develops at a very early age (perhaps earlier than face recognition). For example, Friedlander (1970) showed that infants under 6 months could differentiate their mother's voice from that of strangers, and Mehler et al. (1978) found 1-month-old infants to emit an operant sucking response at a higher rate upon hearing their mother's voice. For children of school age, Bartholomeus (1973) reported a study in which it would seem that nursery school children identified the voices of their classmates almost as well as their teachers did. Though not concerned with the recognizing of strangers' voices, this finding could be taken to indicate that only minimal improvement in voice recognition capacity occurs after 4 years of age. A study by Mann, Diamond, and Carey (1979), however, casts a little doubt upon this deduction. Subjects ranging in age from 6 years to 16 years and adults were asked to recognize unfamiliar voices in a forced-choice recognition paradigm. It was found that performance increased with age such that only by age 10 did the children come to achieve adult accuracy rates (there was a somewhat puzzling decrease in performance between ages 10 and 14).

Several of our own voice studies have examined the effects of age of listener, and although each experiment has not had the effects of age as its major focus, many of them were able to incorporate age as a variable. In almost all of our studies the age range has been from 16 years upward. In none of our studies to be reported in this section were the subjects undergraduates (who may, because of test sophistication, provide inflated scores).

In some of our earliest studies (Clifford, Bull, & Rathborn, 1981), which were designed to examine the effects of the number of distractor, nontarget voices in the test array, we built in the factor of age of listener. The subjects were either young adults (aged 16 to 20 years) or middle-aged (21 to 40 years) or old (over 40). (Readers of this chapter who are themselves aged over 20 or over 40 years may be relieved to hear that these categories were decided upon by our youthful research assistant, Harriet Rathborn, who was a mere 21 at the time!) A significant effect of age of listener was found in that the "middle-aged" witnesses were significantly more accurate than were the "old" witnesses. A similar finding was noted in our study of performance under "open" and "closed" conditions. In our study of the effects of disguise on voice identification we found a strong effect ($p < .001$) of age of listener in that with five or seven voices in the test array the performance of the old subjects was considerably poorer than that of the middle-aged and young adults (who did not differ among themselves). The percentage of correct scores were 25% and 42%, respectively (for the five-voice condition), and 17% and 30%, respectively (for the seven-voice condition). For the test arrays containing nine voices (i.e., target plus eight distractors) and for which performance was overall no greater than that expected by chance, age had no effect (18% and 17%, respectively, chance being 11%). Thus the overall finding from our studies employing adult listeners is fairly clear: Listeners aged over 40 years are not so accurate, as a group, as are younger adults. (This is a finding similar to that of Kausler and Puckett [1981], who measured the recall of auditorally presented sentences). Still, as with the majority of psychology's findings on the effects of age (and many other variables), one cannot say that a particular witness who is elderly is necessarily going to be a poorer voice recognizer than a younger adult witness.

We have also examined the performance of schoolchildren. In one of our studies of the effects of speech sample length we were able to use five classroom groups of children from a school. We had no control in this study over the allocation of these subjects to experimental conditions (and so drawing clear conclusions is problematical), but, nevertheless, we found that in the two-sentence speech sample condition, the 13- to 14-year-olds performed more poorly than did the 15- to 16-year-olds (49% and 68%, respectively). Also, in the one-sentence condition the 12- to 13-year-olds did worse than the 15- to 16-year-olds (28% and 66%, respectively). Thus it could be concluded that stranger-voice identification accuracy increases from ages 12 to 16 years. Still, we cannot rule out the possibility that the observed differences may have been due to other factors (e.g., motivational or attentional variables). In one of our studies, which employed the levels-of-processing paradigm, we again found middle-aged witnesses to perform better than children.

From our studies of the effects of listeners' ages upon voice identification accuracy it can be concluded that older adults (aged over 40 years) may not be so accurate as adults aged under 40 and that there is possibly a developmental effect in that only when in their late teens will children have reached their peak of performance. If future earwitness research supports the contention that the individual differences in the age of witness is important, then generalizing to witnesses aged over 40 years from studies employing undergraduates may well be unwarranted. Similarly, generalizing from our "mobile laboratory" studies to real-life criminal instances involving voice identification should be undertaken with caution. Nevertheless, at the present time we would advocate that where a witness is under 16 years of age or over 40 years, extra care should be exercised in cases where voice identification is deemed to be of importance.

Sex of witness

The effect of sex of listener in voice recognition tasks has received considerably less attention than has the effect of sex of eyewitness. By and large, eyewitness research suggests that *if* there is an overall sex effect it may be that females are more accurate than males. This needs to be qualified by the observations that the significant female superiority that is sometimes found (a) is usually one more of consistency than of quantity (Yarmey, 1979a); (b) may be a function of the absence of stress during the task (Clifford & Scott, 1978); and (c) may be influenced by the nature of the information to be recalled (Loftus, 1979), including the sex of the witnessed person (Clifford & Bull, 1978). These limitations also are likely to apply to voice identification.

Since sex of speaker is usually very accurately noted by earwitnesses (Coleman, 1971; Coleman & Lass, 1981; Hartman & Danhauer, 1976; Ingemann, 1968; Lass et al., 1976; Lass, Mertz, & Kimmel, 1978; Nerbonne, 1968; Schwartz, 1968), even under "incidental" conditions (Cole, Coltheart, & Allard, 1974; Craik & Kirsner, 1974; Hintzman, Block, & Inskeep, 1972; Light et al., 1973), the "same-sex" interaction found in some eyewitness research may be expected to exist in earwitnessing. McGehee (1937), however, found this not to be the case. She noted that men were better at identifying female voices than were women (96% vs. 47%) and that male voices were equally well recognized by both sexes (73% vs. 72%). In our own studies, which are reported throughout this chapter, those that have employed both male and female subjects have found female listeners to perform more accurately than males. Whether this female superiority would be found in more stressful conditions than we employed is worthy of investigation. As previously noted, our own studies were designed to provide estimates of the optimum performance that earwitnesses could achieve under certain conditions. Therefore, in some studies only female earwitnesses were used and, in the majority of these, female voices were more accurately identified than male voices. Though this offers some support for the "same-sex" effect found in eyewitnessing, it should be noted that the absolute size of the performance sex differences was rather small and thus they are likely to be of little judicial relevance.

Race of witness

The issue of cross-racial visual identification has been much discussed (e.g., Clifford & Bull, 1978; Lindsay & Wells, 1983; Yarmey, 1979a), and there exist several explanations of cross-racial eyewitnessing difficulty. It may well be that an eyewitness usually finds it more difficult to identify accurately a person from a different race, but, if such an identification were, in fact, correct, the existence of a cross-racial difficulty confers upon such an identification a high degree of informativeness (Lindsay & Wells, 1980). Goldstein et al. (1981) investigated the extent to which cross-racial identification problems may exist in earwitnessing. They stated that "the meagre amount of relevant voice recognition data that is available suggests that recognizing unfamiliar voices is more difficult than recognizing unfamiliar faces" (p. 217). The results of our own studies suggest that in *some* situations identification of unfamiliar voices may be highly accurate, and because (as we have argued elsewhere, Clifford & Bull, 1978) laboratory studies of visual identifying give an inflated estimate of eyewitness accuracy (Clifford, 1978), the statement of Goldstein and colleagues may be in need of some revision. Nevertheless, they do usefully point out: "Direct comparisons of the results of voice recognition studies with those of face recognition studies should be attempted with caution because of the vast differences in procedures employed in the two areas of investigation" (p. 217). Goldstein and colleagues conducted three exploratory studies that examined the possibility that the other-race effect will generalize to voice recognition memory. In their pilot study either American-born or foreign-born speakers provided speech samples in English by reading aloud the same 15-word sentence. In immediate recognition memory tasks (employing target-to-distractor ratios of between 1 in 6 and 1 in 13) the identification accuracy rate for American-born speakers did not differ from that for foreign-born speakers ($M = 55\%$). Goldstein and colleagues suggest that this lack of difference may have been due to the heterogeneity of the voices in their foreign-born group in that the identification of such voices "could have been spuriously enhanced by differences in kinds of accents" (p. 218). For this reason, in their main studies Goldstein and colleagues employed Taiwanese speakers of English.

In their first study Goldstein et al. (1981) used as speakers 12 white Americans, 12 black Americans, and 12 Taiwanese. The listeners were either black or white Americans. The target voice uttered a 14-word sentence and then, immediately afterward, the test trial occurred in which four different speakers (one of which was always the target) uttered a 6-word sentence (which contained different words from the initially heard sentence). Neither the race of the listener (black or white) nor "voice ethnicity" had an effect on performance ($M = 80\%$). Thus Goldstein and colleagues concluded: "These results and the results of the pilot studies imply that, for short retention periods, accented voices, voices that sound 'foreign' are no more difficult to recognize than are unaccented voices" (p. 218).

In their second study, Goldstein et al. (1981) examined whether reducing the length of the speech samples "might affect accented voices more than unaccented voices" (p. 219). In the present chapter we will see from the results of our own studies that reducing the speech samples to below one-sentence in length does have a deleterious effect on recognition accuracy, but we have also noted that if initially only one word from the target voice is heard, performance is still considerably above chance level. In their second study Goldstein and colleagues employed the 36 voices from their first study. On initial hearing the target speaker uttered just the word *impossible* and again in the immediate test trials the voices uttered a 6-word sentence. All the listeners were white. Recognition accuracy for black and white voices was almost identical (55% and 56%, respectively), whereas the Taiwanese English-speakers were correctly recognized significantly less often (37%).

In their third study, Goldstein et al. (1981) used as speakers 10 English-speaking South Americans whose native tongue was Spanish. The 68 listeners (of whom no details are given) heard per trial 2 target persons speaking a sentence in English and on other trials 2 other persons speaking a sentence in Spanish. In the test trials, which occurred after a 10-minute delay and in which the same sentences were used, the listeners heard 10 voices speaking accented English or 10 voices speaking fluent Spanish (the language spoken in each test trial being the same as that initially spoken by the target voices). The listeners were required to indicate which of these voices they had heard previously. The results revealed that listeners identified 58% of the Spanish-speaking voices and 57% of the accented English voices, the false alarm rates associated with these hit rates being identical (18%). Gold-stein and colleagues concluded that "these data demonstrate that accented voices speaking a familiar language are as well remembered as are voices speaking incomprehensible words in a foreign language" (p. 219). If these findings are supported by replication (and La Riviere's 1972 work suggests that they might) then there seems to be here an important factor that needs to be taken into account by any theory of how humans recognize strangers' voices.

Concerning the effects of race, one must conclude from the exploratory work of Goldstein and colleagues that there exists at present no strong evidence of cross-racial problems in speaker identification. Still, further research is needed before psychologists are in a position to advise other professionals (e.g., lawyers, police) about this matter.

The effects of stereotypes

We have argued elsewhere (Bull, 1979; Bull & Green, 1980; Clifford & Bull, 1978) that stereotypic conceptions can have an effect upon eyewitnesses and this may also be the case with earwitnesses. People from different walks of life and from different parts of the same country do speak in a variety of ways and it has been shown that stereotypic judgments are made on the basis of speech (Mulac, Hanley, & Prigge, 1974). Kramer (1963) examined the judgments of personal characteristics based on speech and provided a review of studies that had investigated the existence of vocal stereotypes. It does seem that listeners often reliably agree (sometimes with accuracy) on such things as the physical appearance, profession, and personality they expect certain speakers to have. Given that such vocal stereotypes exist they may have the same biasing influence as visual ones. Bortz (1970) investigated how a witness's own voice may influence his description of others' voices and found that (a) raters with high-pitched voices judged others as having low-pitched voices, and vice versa; and (b) raters with strongly dynamic voices overestimated existing differences of expression in the voices of others, and vice versa. The effects found by Bortz have interesting parallels in visual judgments of skin color (Marks, 1943) and of height (Dunnaway, 1976). Such effects seem not to apply to judgments of a speaker's age (Ptacek & Sanders, 1966; Shipp & Hollien, 1969), which seem usually to be accurate (Nerbonne, 1968).

The voice identification powers of the blind

It may happen only rarely that blind persons are witnesses to crimes, but Bull, Rathborn, and Clifford (in press) decided to investigate their voice recognition powers not only to assess how accurate they were but also to see whether such a study would throw some light on the processes of voice recognition by sighted people. For example if blind listeners were more accurate at voice recognition than sighted listeners, sighted personnel in key positions in which voice identification may be required could possibly improve their skills with suitable training.

The literature on the voice recognition abilities of blind listeners is sparse indeed. William James (1890) noted the common belief that blindness may lead to enhanced perceptual powers in nonvisual modalities, and Cobb, Lawrence, and Nelson (1979) cite Gibson's (1969) belief that "nature compensates in some way for the loss of vision by providing extraordinary sensory gifts of another kind" (p. 363). This rather popular compensation hypothesis has by no means always been supported by research (Cobb et al., 1979; Hayes, 1941; Stankov & Spillsbury, 1978). Stankov and Spillsbury did note that "the auditory channel has been the most popular channel studied and it has been found that there are significant differences between blind and sighted on a number of variables" (p. 491), and they do provide a brief list of studies in which blind subjects performed better than sighted subjects. Still, none of the studies employed a task similar to earwitnessing, and the authors added: "Most variables in which differences occurred belong to the General Auditory Function.... It must be mentioned, however, that in most of the studies quoted degree of vision was not properly controlled. Typically, no distinction was made between totally blind and those with light perception" (p. 491).

The blind subjects in our study were 94 individuals (aged from 16 to 42 years) of varying degrees of blindness from four Centres for the Blind in England; the sighted subjects used for comparison were 98 members of the general public drawn from the same age range. The age factor was deemed important because of our findings from other studies in our research program that, generally, people over 40 years of age were poorer at voice recognition than were people aged 16 to 40. Prior to the study each of the blind subjects was classified into one of the following four categories: totally blind, perception of light, residual sight, goodish sight. The subjects' age at onset of blindness, number of years of blindness, and sex were recorded. The subjects from one of the Centres for the Blind could be divided into those who were receiving training as piano tuners and those who were not. IQ scores for subjects from another Centre were available. No subjects reported having any auditory deficits.

There was a delay interval of only 5 seconds between the subject's first hearing of the target voice and commencement of the voice parade. Although the research program was concerned with voice identification in

criminal settings, these testing conditions were designed to produce an estimate of the optimal voice recognition performance that human listeners
may achieve. Each subject undertook six trials, each of which employed a
different target and different distractors. At the end of each trial the subjects were required to note down the number of the voice in the test array
that they believed to be the target voice. They did this using a braille
machine, a shorthand version of a braille machine, or pencil and paper.
(Those using braille machines were told not to type anything while a trial
was in progress.)

Statistical analysis revealed a significant difference between the performance of the blind subjects and that of the sighted subjects (67% and 52%,
respectively). No significant main effect was found for the number of voices
in the test array (5 vs. 7 vs. 9 voices) and there was no significant interaction
between these two factors.

The data concerning the blind listeners' degree of blindness and their level
of voice recognition performance revealed no effect of the former upon the
latter. For the "totally blind" the mean performance was 66%, for those
with "perception of light" 62%, for those with "residual sight" 73%, and for
those with "goodish sight" 67%. No difference was found between those
receiving training to become piano tuners (who could be regarded as having
particularly acute auditory capabilities) and those who were not. For all the
blind subjects, data on the age of the onset of their blindness (ranging from
0 to 14 years) and their years of blindness (from more than 30 to fewer than
5) were available. Neither of these factors related to voice recognition
accuracy.

Thus we found a significant difference between the voice recognition
accuracy of blind and sighted subjects (both groups' performance being
considerably above that obtainable by guessing or chance). The fact that
degree of blindness did not relate within the blind group to voice recognition accuracy may argue against an explanation of this difference in terms
of a simple compensation hypothesis. Nevertheless, the blind subjects did
perform significantly better than the sighted ones and if future research
established the reliability of this finding and discovered how the superior
performance of the blind subjects was achieved, then perhaps improvement
in the level of voice recognition accuracy of sighted personnel could be
achieved by appropriate training.

Training in voice identification

The possibility of educating the general populace, and personnel in high-
risk professions specifically (e.g., bank employees), in matters of voice

encoding and recognition should be a special focus for psycholegal researchers. The literature on the training or encoding of voices is, however, notable for its dearth. In a very complex study, Nerbonne (1968) failed to find any effect of trained versus untrained groups in voice identification. Nevertheless, the potential for training along at least one dimension has been suggested by Haggard and Summerfield (1982), who showed clearly that a basic difference between good and poor voice identifiers is identifying criteria differences, that is, the proclivity to say yes or no when presented with a target voice at recognition stages of identification, and they point out that this response set is amenable to training.

Another approach that could have practicality in most situations is that suggested by Pear (1931). He observed that whatever the physical sounds produced by a voice, the effect of the total voice gestalt may be to regenerate consciously or unconsciously a memory of a voice that was significant to us in the past, for example, a famous person's voice. A verbal label could then both sustain the memory of the to-be-recognized voice and perhaps aid in communicating information about the voice to other interested personnel. This labeling obviously carries inherent danger, as in the visual identification field (see Clifford & Bull, 1978; Doob & Kirshenbaum, 1973). Still, it is a method that could be easily employed in certain circumstances and that could bear fruit providing sufficient safeguards were taken.

A potentially exciting area of work resides in the possibility of different encoding operations eventuating in different levels of accuracy at recall or recognition. In both the pure verbal memory and visual identification fields some research suggests that recognition can vary as a function of the type or depth of encoding performed on the to-be-remembered stimulus when it is initially presented (Bower & Karlin, 1974; Clifford & Prior, 1980; Patterson & Baddeley, 1977). Broadly speaking the more meaningful (deep) the processing of the stimulus at presentation the better the eventual recognition or recall is found to be (we should note, however, Winograd's [1978] comments on this). Once again, no comparable studies into depth of processing with voices exist in the literature, although we have carried out several such studies, two of which will be reported here.

In one study, Clifford and McCardle (in press) presented 10 voices to 36 subjects who had been randomly allocated to one of six groups defined by the levels of processing to be performed on the target voices and which formed a (subjective) continuum from superficial to deep processing. Superficial processing tasks involved judging the age and sex of the talker; deeper processing involved assessments of the talker's character and emotional status. No significant effects were found.

In a second experiment we once again sought to find differential identification accuracy as a function of differential encoding, this time using 209 subjects randomly allocated to four levels of processing, again reflecting a continuum from superficial to deep. The actual levels used were "judge sex of speaker's voice," "judge speaker's age," "judge the warmth of the speaker," and "judge whether the voice reminds you of anyone." Once again, statistical analysis failed to reveal any significant difference between initial encoding modes on eventual identification accuracy.

These two null findings can be variously interpreted. One such interpretation could be that the levels-of-processing framework lacks an appropriate independent measure of depth and we have simply failed to employ appropriate superficial and deep encoding modes. This interpretation is not favored because of the wide range of encoding tasks used in the first experiment. A second possible interpretation is that different levels of voice processing do not have effects comparable to those found with words and facial photographs because there may be no enduring "semantic" structure in auditory memory, as there is in verbal and visual memory, to which a voice can be anchored or articulated. The overall performance in voice identification studies reported here and elsewhere possibly suggests that a semantic structure for voices is not available, although the fact of memory for a familiar voice still requires explanation.

In terms of the practical issue of trainability as assessed here by giving different subjects different ways of processing a to-be-remembered voice, we would have to conclude that at least as far as encoding processes are concerned, trainability does not seem very promising. Such training studies are still, however, in their infancy.

Witness confidence

An important question for research on voice identification that has great relevance for the legal system concerns the relationship between witness confidence and accuracy. It seems intuitively plausible that a person is more likely to be correct when he or she is certain of being correct. General memory research (e.g., Murdock, 1974) seems to support this intuition, but research on eyewitness testimony by no means clearly does so (see Chapter 8, by Wells & Murray, in this volume). In general our studies have consistently yielded significant relationships between confidence and accuracy (see Clifford, 1980b, for a review). The exception to this finding is the study using "open" and "closed" instructions (discussed later), wherein no relationship between confidence and accuracy was found for trials in which the target was not in the array. Whether or not a real-life lineup is a blank trial is, of course, not known at the time. This is a serious limitation on any general conclusions about confidence–accuracy relationships in voice recognition and points to the need for further research.

The nature and quality of the speech samples

In this section we shall examine the effects upon voice identification of the length of the speech samples heard and of the number of nontarget, distractor voices (or foils) in the test array. We shall examine the effects of voice disguise and note also whether hearing voices over the telephone affects their recognition.

The length of the speech sample

One of the few factors that has been examined more in earwitnessing than in eyewitnessing is that concerning the duration of exposure of the target to the witness. In eyewitness research, Laughery, Alexander, and Lane (1971) found in the laboratory setting that longer exposure to facial photographs led to better later recognition of them. In a field setting, Clifford and Richards (1977) found that policemen's recall of visual information about a target person was more accurate after long exposure (30 seconds) to the target than after short exposure (15 seconds), whereas that of civilians was not significantly influenced by target exposure duration. Given that target exposure duration was one of the factors the British Devlin Committee suggested that judges should draw to the attention of juries, more research on the effects of this factor on eyewitnesses is necessary (Bull, 1982).

An important consideration in estimating the likelihood of a witness's providing accurate voice identification in criminal cases would seem, therefore, to be how long the criminal talked or was "kept talking." Within the context of speaker recognition the effect of target exposure duration has received a fair amount of attention. A considerable proportion of this work has been concerned with voiceprints (or spectrograms) and other electromechanical methods of speaker identification, and such studies will not be discussed here. Readers interested in these methods of speaker identification may wish to consult some reviews of this topic, which suggest, among other things, that in several situations, even when a recording of the target voice was made during the commission of a crime, voiceprint speaker recognition is no more accurate than are human listeners (Bull, 1978, 1981).

In connection with speaker identification by human listeners Pollack, Pickett, and Sumby (1954) found that the larger the speech sample heard the more accurate were the identifications. This effect was due to the greater speech repertoire evidenced in the longer samples, they believe, because repetition of short samples did not increase the number of correct identifications. Bricker and Pruzansky (1966) also examined the effect of stimulus duration and content upon talker identification of the voices of people who worked together. They found 98% correct identification when spoken sentences were provided, 84% for syllables, and 56% for vowel excerpts. The number of different phonemes contained in the speech sample rather than its duration was found to provide a better explanation of the findings. Thus Bricker and Pruzansky concluded that the improvement in identification accuracy with sample duration was due to an increased sample of the talker's repertoire being provided.

Murray and Cort (1971) investigated the same issue, this time with children. They found that mere repetition of speech samples (a vowel, a sentence, or a paragraph) does not lead to any increase in identification accuracy, whereas increasing the speech repertoire to a sentence in length is sufficient for identification performance to reach an asymptote, and they conclude that for their subjects a 15-syllable sentence provided sufficient cues for voice identification. In this experiment, however, the children had been together in the same class for at least several months, thus the conclusions that can be drawn from this study are tentative, as are those from several of the other experiments mentioned for the situation wherein recognition is required of a stranger who provided only one speech sample.

Some studies suggest that accurate identifications and a number of judgments can be made on the basis of very brief speech samples. Compton (1963) showed that subjects were able to recognize familiar voices on the basis of a 25-millisecond speech sample at above chance level, and La Riviere (1972) found the same thing for single utterances of isolated vowels. Rousey and Holzman (1967) found that a 1-second speech did not lead to any poorer recognition of the listener's own voice than did a 5-second sample ($M = 38\%$). Likewise Doehring and Ross (1972) found that subjects could identify which of three strangers' voices speaking a nonsense syllable matched the speaker of a sample vowel. It appears that the sex of a speaker can also be assessed accurately from isolated voiceless fricatives (Ingemann, 1968; Schwartz, 1968). With speech samples of one syllable, C. Williams (1964) found that identification was 93% correct when subjects were required to identify whether two sequential speech samples were spoken by the same talker or by different talkers. In a comparative study of speech sample duration, Clarke, Becker, and Nixon (1966) found 89% correct recognition in a same–different decision for two samples comprising 3, 5, 7, 9, and 11 syllables. Thus in this study, voice identification was unaffected by increasing voice samples above 3 syllables. Goldstein et al. (1981) played to listeners a speaker uttering once just the single word *impossible*; in the test array there were four speakers and each uttered the same six-word sentence (which did not contain the word *impossible*). The mean recognition performance was 50% (guessing would result in only 25% accuracy).

In opposition to these examples of identification on the bases of extremely small speech samples, Stevens et al. (1968) and C. Williams (1964) have shown an appreciable decrease in error scores for identifications of a 2- or 3-syllable sample of speech compared with a 1-syllable sample. Additionally, repetition of an utterance has sometimes been shown to lead to a large improvement in performance (Haggard, 1973). Haggard and Summerfield (1982) found that speech samples of less than 2 seconds produced poor recognition accuracy and stated: "there is reason within the data... to believe that further valuable improvements would be possible beyond two seconds" (p. 17). This quality–quantity equation and its complexity is again raised in the study of Pollack et al. (1954), who found little improvement in recognition accuracy following increases in speech duration beyond 1 second but a very substantial increase following longer speech samples if the stimulus was a whispered message.

Given the vast range of speech sample size within which positive identification effects have been noted, we set out to investigate in several of our own studies whether speaker identification accuracy varied as a function of speech sample duration. The first experiment we performed on speech sample length involved 134 adult subjects who were randomly allocated to one of three conditions, the conditions being determined by the amount of speech initially heard. One group of subjects initially heard six target voices (one per trial) uttering a speech sample of four sentences in length; a second group heard the same voices uttering two of the four sentences; and a third group heard the target voices uttering one of the four sentences. Each voice in the test parade, which comprised the target and five distractors, was heard to utter the same sentence. In terms of results, across the three speech-sample length conditions the mean recognition accuracy performance was 78%, with one-sentence samples producing 75.2% correct identification; two-sentence samples, 77%; and four-sentence samples producing 81.6% correct identification. Statistical analyses revealed, however, a nonsignificant difference between any of the means.

In a second experiment, 132 subjects aged 12–16 years were again randomly allocated to one of three conditions: half-sentence, one-sentence, and two-sentence speech samples. The design was similar to that of the first experiment. The results of this experiment differed from those of the previous one. First, the accuracy scores were much lower (41%, 36%, and 49% for half-, one-, and two-sentence speech samples, respectively), which most probably reflects the different perceptual accuracy between children and adults. Second, in this experiment, unlike the previous one, there was a statistically significant difference among the three speech-sample conditions ($p < .025$), which is best accounted for by the difference between the one- and two-sentence speech-sample conditions ($p < .025$).

A third experiment in this series looked for a possible interaction between length of speech sample and the number of distractors employed at recognition by presenting independent groups of subjects with either one- or eight-word speech samples and testing for identification of target voices placed within either 5 or 11 distractors. The 124 adult subjects were randomly allocated to the four resulting cells, and a two-way analysis of variance was applied to the mean correct accuracy scores. This analysis revealed that the only significant main effect was size of speech sample initially heard, with identification being better for eight-word samples ($p < .01$). No interaction was obtained.

From this series of studies it would appear that support is offered, at least with adults, for the extant finding that the length of the speech sample initially heard makes little difference to later identification providing that at least one sentence is presented. With children, however, this does not seem to be the case; they seem to be able to benefit from more extended speech samples.

A few cautionary points should perhaps be made explicit before any hasty, applied implications are drawn. The accuracy levels were not impressive in any of our three studies reported here, despite the fact that memory was tested over very short time intervals. Thus, only further research can establish whether there is a general and genuine effect of speech sample size, and if so, what length of sample is required for optimum identification performance.

The number of voices in the test array

A factor concerning the construction of lineups that has been much discussed in the legal world is that concerning the number of nonsuspects that are present. The Devlin Committee (1976) among others, argued that the use of showups (i.e., a lineup containing only one person, the suspect) should be avoided. There has also been some discussion recently in the eyewitness literature concerning the effects of the number of nonsuspects in visual lineups, especially in terms of their functioning as suitable distractors (Lindsay & Wells, 1980; Loftus 1979; Malpass & Devine, 1982), and the issues raised may well apply also to earwitnessing. Although Wallace (1980) argues that "testing recognition memory without distractor items in the test is a viable laboratory procedure" (p. 696), it is doubtful whether showups will ever be as acceptable to the legal world as are lineups, even with their many weaknesses (Clifford & Bull, 1978). Few studies have, in fact, directly examined the effects of the number of distractors in a lineup, and similarly few have looked at the effects of the number of targets witnessed (e.g., for earwitnessing, McGehee [1937]; for eyewitnessing, Clifford & Hollin [1981]).

The effect of target location within the test array has received some attention. In a study of mug-shot searching, Laughery, Alexander, and Lane (1971) found that recognition performance was an inverse function of the position in the search list of the target face, this effect being found only when the nontarget faces were similar to the target face (Laughery et al., 1974).

Concerning earwitnessing, Doehring and Ross (1972) asked their listeners to indicate which of 3 voices speaking a nonsense syllable matched that of a previously heard speaker of a vowel. A significant though small effect of target position in the test array was noted in that when the target was in the first position, performance was 65%; when in the second, it was 62%; and when in the last position, it was 56%. Clarke and Becker (1969) observed a similar effect in their study in which listeners (of which there were only five) heard a target voice utter a few syllables and were then required to pick it out from an array of 4 speakers. They found that "the percentage correct responses declined almost linearly from 70% to 48% as the number of interpolated incorrect alternatives increased from zero to three" (p. 754). What these two studies suggest is that a voice parade consisting of only 4 (or fewer) speakers is not sufficiently large for performance to have "bottomed out," and thus voice parades of fewer than 5 speakers may not be employing enough distractors. A study by Carterette and Barnebey (1975) may shed a little light on this problem, though their experimental procedure was rather far removed from the holding of voice lineups. In their study subjects heard either 2, 3, 4, or 8 speakers saying "you all be," and in an immediate test consisting of 4, 6, 8, or 16 voices they were required to indicate which 50% of the voices they had heard previously. The results were expressed in terms of correct recognitions as a function of correct rejections. For 4, 6, 8, or 16 voices in the test array, mean performance on this measure was 79%, 72%, 64%, and 62%, respectively. Thus a monotonic decline in performance was observed as the size of the test array (and therefore the number of voices to be recognized) increased, but as Carterette and Barnebey point out, this was a "linear decline of less than 2% per voice" (p. 258). When they analyzed the data in more detail they found that "the hit rate ... appears to be almost independent of the number of voices in the recognition set whereas the false-alarm rate increases from 4 to 16 voices" (p. 259).

Overall, then, it seems that previous research is unable to answer the question, What is the minimum number of speakers that a voice lineup should contain for it to be seen to be fair regarding having a sufficient number of distractors among which to place the suspect's voice? This being so we decided to examine this question in our own studies.

Two of our studies had the effect of the number of distractors in the test array as a prime factor of interest, and these will be discussed once others have been briefly mentioned. In one of our studies of speech sample length (1 vs. 8 words) we also varied the number of foils in the test array (5 vs. 11) and found that this latter variable surprisingly had no significant effect upon performance. With the larger sample length, performance was 49% with 5 distractors and 53% with 11. Similarly, having more than double the number of distractors (i.e., 11 vs. 5) did not reduce performance with the 1-word speech samples (36% and 38%, respectively). Traditional studies of memory suggest that as the number of distractors increased, performance would decrease, and so these results surprised us somewhat. Still, if it could be determined that beyond a certain number of distractors performance did not progressively decrease, this would offer a guideline as to the number of nonsuspects to have in real-life voice lineups. The performance level we had observed for test arrays employing 11 distractors was considerably above chance level (i.e., 9%), suggesting that on some trials some earwitnesses can perform quite well on this task. Similar levels of performance were observed in our "short" and "long" delay studies (56% and 43%, respectively), which also used 11 distractors (in fact, 22 distractors, 11 of which were male and 11 female, there being 1 male and 1 female target per trial). In the first of our two studies that were specifically designed to examine the effect of number of distractors, we varied this number from 4 to 6 to 8. We chose the range 4 to 8 because the vast majority of real-life visual lineups employ this number of distractors. Few lineups contain more than 8 distractors, more because of the difficulty the police have in finding a larger number of suitable distractors than because of the results of any scientific studies. In our study we found that whereas there was a significant difference between 4- and 6-distractor lineups (68% and 48%, respectively), there was no difference between the 6- and 8-distractor conditions (48% for each). That we had almost by chance perhaps found the minimum number of distractors required in a "fair" lineup necessitated a replication of our study. In this replication we employed a within-subjects design rather than a between-subjects design as in the initial study. We did this because although it is not yet known why individuals differ in their earwitnessing ability (apart from a possible age effect), there is no doubt that some individuals are better at this kind of task than are others. Consequently, a lack of effect of a variable in a between-subjects design could be due to the variance caused by subjects. In our within-subjects replication we found the same result as in our initial study. That is, whereas there was a significant difference between the 4- and 6-distractor conditions (73% and 58%, respectively), there was no difference between the 6- and 8-distractor conditions (58% and 62%, respectively). (There was a significant difference between the 4- and 8-distractor conditions.) The slightly higher performance in the replication study could be due to the fact that the first study used as subjects adult members of the public of all ages, whereas the replication used undergraduates. The two studies are, however, in strong agreement that, in our testing situation at least (i.e., "immediate" testing involving little stress and speech samples of one sentence in length), 6 distractors are all that are required (given that these 6 voices bear some similarity to the suspect's and none has any speech impediment or strong accent). Unfortunately, the situation may not be as clear-cut as this; in our study of the effects of disguise (to be described in the next subsection), we found a significant monotonic decline in performance as the number of distractors increased from 4 to 6 to 8 (36%, 26%, and 17%, respectively).

We found no evidence that target location in the test array influences recognition performance except for those trials in which the target appeared as the first voice in the test array. When the target did appear first, we found in most of our studies that performance was significantly higher than (and sometimes almost double) that when the target was placed elsewhere in the test array. (Performance rates for locations other than the first did not differ from each other.) So here again, witness memory appears not to function precisely in the way that many studies of memory would have us believe.

The effects of voice disguise

It is generally accepted that crime commission is an anxiety arousing activity. This has implications for voice identification accuracy estimates, because it is also well known that physiological arousal or emotionality can create distortion in the way people speak – in cadence, pitch, intonation, and so on. Thus, over and above *intentional* disguise, it might be argued that voice identification always involves such considerations. The problem is exacerbated by the fact that physiologically determined voice changes may be different in important respects from intentionally distorted voice production. The dilemma for forensic psychologists is that whichever type of disguise may be operative, we know little or nothing about its effect upon later identification accuracy. Voiceprint research is, however, suggestive.

McGlone, Hollien, and Hollien (1977) have shown by means of spectral monitoring that the acoustical components of speech can be significantly altered by persons speaking with a freely chosen disguised voice. Using visual inspection of voiceprints, Hollien and McGlone (1976) showed identification of freely disguised voices to be only 23.3% correct. Using a similar procedure, Reich, Moll, and Curtis (1976) compared normal voice identification with identification of disguised voices. Identification dropped from 56.66% correct spectral matching with normal voices to 21.6% correct matching for disguised voices. The weight of this evidence, then, suggests that recognition following disguise manipulations is considerably less accurate than with nondisguised voices.

Pollack et al. (1954) used 16 familiar talkers yet obtained only 30% accurate identification when these talkers were heard whispering, compared with 95% correct identification for 1 second of normal speech. Pollack and colleagues, in fact, found that the sample of whispered speech needed to be heard for three times as long as normal speech before comparable identification levels were achieved. Saslove and Yarmey (1980) altered the tone of a heard voice between initial hearing and later identifying. This manipulation can be construed as a disguise effect in that alterations along a number of speech dimensions would result from altering a voice from, for example, an angry to a normal tone (as Saslove and Yarmey did). As predicted, these researchers found a strong and reliable effect of this change in voice tone, identification accuracy dropping from a mean of 5.15 correct identifications out of a maximum of 6 under no-tone-change conditions to a mean of 2.36 correct identifications under tone-change conditions. Therefore it appears that even a relatively simple change in the voice can cause a substantial decrement in the recognition accuracy of human listeners. Interestingly, the authors do point out that some voices were so distinctive that they were recognized even though the tone was altered, although these were in the minority. Recognition in these cases would seem to be due to certain features of the voice being so prominent that a simple change in voice along one dimension (such as tone of voice) is unable to conceal the true identity of the speaker.

In 1979, Reich and Duke investigated the effect of six different "voice mode disguises" (normal, aged, hoarse, hypernasal, slow, and free disguise) upon speaker identification by human listeners. The subjects were instructed to decide whether two taped voice samples, the first of which was undisguised, the other either disguised or not, were uttered by the same or different speakers. For naive listeners the nasal and free disguise were the most effective modes of disguise in reducing performance (59.4% and 61.3% correct, respectively), whereas the undisguised condition led to significantly higher accuracy (92.3%) than any of the other conditions. The different disguises may have produced varying degrees of accuracy because of the varying ability of each disguise to hide the most salient vocal or speech features employed in voice recognition.

Thus it would appear from the limited literature available that voice disguise may adversely affect speaker recognition whether machine or human based. The main emphasis of our own study was to investigate further the extent of the effect of voice disguise on listeners' recognition ability, correcting for artificiality and ecological validity.

A total of 216 members of the general public took part in the experiment, being divided into 3 groups by age (16–20, 21–40, and 41–70 years), with equal numbers of males and females in each group. Half the subjects in each group received disguised voices, half received the same persons talking in their natural voices. The basic procedure was to have subjects hear a target voice, either disguised or not, and then have them attempt to identify that voice, undisguised, in a recognition set of 4, 6, or 8 distractor voices. The target voice was always present in these recognition sets, and recognition sets were carefully controlled and compiled to have a very high degree of similarity (as assessed by nonexperimental subject raters). The targets and distractors had no strong accents or speech defects.

Six trials were given to each subject with three of the trials involving female target voices and three involving male voices. Naturally the voices in the recognition set were of the same sex as the target. The recognition phase of each trial began 10 seconds after the offset of the target voice, and both the target and the distractor voice were heard to utter the same 13-word sentences. The disguised targets were instructed to disguise their voices any way they chose. The results were clear. Recognition accuracy for a disguised voice was much lower than that for a nondisguised target voice ($p < .001$).

Our finding thus supports those of the voiceprint work and other work in auditory memory, and it parallels the effects of disguise in visual memory (Patterson & Baddeley, 1977). The conclusion is fairly clear: If there is reason to believe that voice disguise was employed by a crime perpetrator, then estimation of accuracy of listener identification should assume a low value.

This somewhat pessimistic conclusion is supported by an experiment conducted by Clifford and Denot (1982). In a simulated real-life situation, subjects were seated quietly at a number of galvanic skin response (GSR) machines, having been told that they were taking part in a psychophysiological experiment. On a prearranged signal a stooge entered the experimental room (quietly or noisily), interacted verbally and physically with the experimenter (violently or nonviolently), and then left the room (quietly or noisily). Under both conditions (violent and nonviolent) the experimenter then apologized for the disruption and asked the subjects to continue with the (fictional) experiment. Incidental voice memory, as indicated by correct identification of the stooge's voice from a voice parade comprising 10 voices, was then tested. Subjects either heard and were tested on an angry or a quiet voice (unchanged condition) or heard an angry voice but were tested on a normal (changed) voice.

Those who had to recognize under the changed-voice condition were accurate 33% of the time, whereas those who were presented with an unchanged voice recorded a 50% accurate identification. The overall low rate of correct identification could be explained by the incidental and/or real-life arousal nature of the experiment (Clifford, 1980a), but for our purposes here it should be noted that (a) this study has a close affinity to the Saslove and Yarmey (1980) study cited earlier, and (b) if we can equate voice change with disguise manipulations, then further evidence has been provided for the belief that disguise influences earwitness accuracy.

Earwitnessing involving the telephone

As part of our report to the British Home Office we were asked to conduct a survey of past criminal cases in which voice identification played a part (Clifford, Bull, & Rathborn, 1980). It became apparent from this survey that a sizable proportion of such cases had involved the telephone. At present, when a suspect is picked up on a charge relating to a crime that involves the identification of a voice heard initially over the telephone, it is common practice for the police to request the suspect to telephone the victim and repeat the same phrases the criminal had spoken. This procedure suggests that the police share the commonsense belief that voice recognition will be enhanced if the test takes place under the same circumstances as the initial hearing of the voice. This assumption is supported by D. Smith (1977) but to our knowledge has never been directly tested experimentally in the earwitness field (although there is a large literature in general memory research of context effects on memory performance).

Tosi (1978) noted that telephone lines restrict frequencies in complex ways and therefore believes that to obtain as close a comparison as possible between the criminal's voice and that of the suspect, samples of the latter must be obtained through channels as similar as possible to the criminal's. Most studies on this topic have not actually employed telephonic communication but instead have passed voices through filters that to a certain degree simulate the effects of the telephone.

A minor part of Nerbonne's (1968) study was a comparison of the effect on identification accuracy of directly recorded speech as opposed to speech recorded over the telephone. Judgments of the physical size of speakers were more accurately made from directly recorded speech samples than from samples recorded over the telephone, whereas judgments of speaker's age and dialect were more accurate over the telephone. In a comparison of voice identifications made with speech recorded directly into a tape recorder and via a filtering apparatus that simulated the effects of the telephone, Rothman (1977) found that performance was consistently poorer under the latter condition, although the numerical difference in performance between the two conditions was only of the order of 3% (the overall accuracy being approximately 60%). Pollack et al. (1954) also investigated the effects on voice recognition of low- and high-pass filtering. They concluded that "over a fairly wide frequency range, the identification performance is resistant to a selective frequency emphasis of this type. This result suggests that the identification of a speaker's voice is not critically dependent upon the delicate balance of different frequency components in any single portion of the speech frequency spectrum." Still, it should be noted that their conclusion was based on the use of monosyllabic word series. R. Peters (1956), on the other hand, used longer speech samples and he found that compared with the nonfilter condition all of the filtering conditions led to decreases in performance. Peters's results seem to support Tosi's belief that voices that are to be compared should, ideally, be recorded across similar mediums, and it seems to be the belief of laymen (e.g., jurors), the police, and the legal world that if during a crime the criminal's voice is heard over the telephone, then testing for voice recognition without using a telephone is inappropriate and error prone. We conducted a study to examine this notion (Rathborn, Bull, & Clifford 1981).

The subjects ($n = 134$) were randomly assigned to one of four groups. For one group the target voice and the recognition set were taped directly into the tape recorder. For the second group the target voice was taped directly, but the recognition set was recorded over the telephone. For the third group the target voice was taped over the telephone, and the recognition set was taped directly; and for the fourth group both the target voice and the recognition set were taped over the telephone. All four conditions employed the same speakers uttering the same sentence. There were six trials (each employing different voices) in each condition. The mean voice identification scores were 63%, 42%, 45%, and 45% for the four groups, respectively. Thus the three conditions that involved voices heard over the telephone all resulted in a similar level of performance, significantly below that of the no-telephone condition.

From these results it appears that the use of the telephone is likely to reduce somewhat voice identification accuracy (but not down to chance level, which was 17%) even when at recognition test the suspect's voice is again heard over the telephone. Thus, if during the commission of a crime the criminal's voice is heard over the telephone, testing for recognition using the telephone will not result in greater accuracy. This is an important finding for police practice because it negates the need to persuade a suspect to speak to a witness over the telephone (or to use more devious means to achieve this) if the witness initially heard the criminal's voice via that medium.

The effects of delay on earwitnessing

Several key criminal cases, usually described from a visual identification point of view, have served to raise the whole issue of the value and validity of witness testimony and identification. What is not well known (Clifford, 1980b, 1983) is that voice identification was also crucially involved in these causes célèbres. Further, a chief factor was that the voice identification was attempted after a long delay interval. Two questions naturally arise: Does this delay have an effect upon accuracy of identification? Is there some critical cut-off point after which no credence at all should be placed in proffered identification?

Once again, we do not know. An early study by McGehee (1937) specifically manipulated time intervals. Groups of students listened to an adult stranger reading a paragraph of 56 words from behind a screen and were tested for voice recognition after time intervals ranging from 1 day to 5 months. In the recognition situation the listeners were required to indicate which of five readers they had heard previously. For listeners who initially heard only one reader, McGehee observed 83%, 83%, 81%, and 81% accuracy for time intervals of 1, 2, 3, and 7 days, respectively, After an interval of 2 weeks, performance dropped to 69%, and after a further week to 51%. Intervals of 3 and 5 months led to accuracy scores of 35% and 13%, respectively. Thus, it was concluded that with the passage of time, "there is a general trend towards a decrease in percentage of listeners who were able to correctly recognize a voice the second time it is heard" (p. 262).

Since live and not recorded voices were used it is possible (though perhaps unlikely) that the observed decrease in recognition accuracy with increased delay intervals was due to the target voice having changed somewhat between the witnesses' first and second hearing of it. Thus, the decreases in performance may not have been entirely a result of the effects of delay upon witness memory. In a subsequent experiment, McGehee (1944) obviated this possibility by using recorded voices reading out a few sentences. With a

2-day interval between the subjects' initially hearing the target voice and later trying to pick it out, recognition accuracy was found to be 85% (there being no test of the accuracy of "immediate" recall). With a delay interval of 2 weeks, performance dropped to 48%, falling not much further for the longer delays of 4 weeks (47% accuracy) and 8 weeks (45%). Thus, in this study, recognition performance was not found to deteriorate with the longer increases (2 to 4 to 8 weeks) in delay interval, as found in McGehee's earlier (1937) study. A similar decrease in performance between delays of 2 days and 2 weeks, however, was observed in the two studies.

Saslove and Yarmey (1980) examined the effects of a shorter delay interval (24 hours) upon voice recognition accuracy. The listeners initially heard a voice uttering a 10-second sentence and were then required to pick out that voice from among four others. Some listeners were tested immediately, whereas others were tested after a delay of 24 hours. For those listeners tested immediately recognition performance was 60% accurate, and for those tested after a delay of 24 hours it was 70%. Thus, a 24-hour delay had no deleterious effect on performance. This noneffect of delay was found to apply both when subjects were informed and when they were not informed as to the fact that their recognition accuracy would be tested; it also applied when the target voice changed and when it did not change in tone between the initial hearing and later recognizing phases. Surprisingly, though Saslove and Yarmey did not investigate the effects of delays greater than 24 hours, they stated: "It is suggested that long-term speaker identification must be treated by the criminal justice system with suspicion and caution" (p. 111).

The three studies just reviewed seem to contradict each other on the effects of both short (e.g., 24 hours) and long (e.g., 4 weeks) delay intervals upon voice recognition accuracy. Partly as an attempt to resolve this issue Clifford and Denot (1982) had subjects witness a live incident in which a stooge entered a room, had a brief (aggressive or neutral) conversation with the experimenter, and then left. After 1, 2, or 3 weeks the witnesses' abilities to recognize voice and face were tested. For voice recognition, after a delay of 1 week correct identification performance was 50%, after 2 weeks it was 43%, and after 3 weeks it was at the chance level of 9%. Statistical analysis of these data revealed that there was no difference in performance between delays of 1 and 2 weeks, but there was a significant drop in performance with a 3-week delay.

To summarize these studies so far, little or no decrement appears to occur in voice identification over a 24-hour delay period, but after 2 to 4 weeks, accuracy may drop. Because of the importance of this topic to real-life criminal issues and because previous research by no means offers a clear prediction concerning the effects of either short (e.g., hours) or long (e.g., days and weeks) delay intervals upon voice identification accuracy, we undertook a series of studies into delay effects, two of which are reported here.

Sixty-four female subjects were presented with tape-recorded male and female target voices that could be objectively defined from previous experimentation as either "high-recognition voices" or "low-recognition voices" (i.e., voices that had in previous studies been found to lead to high- or low-recognition scores). They were then tested for identification of these target voices among a number of distractor voices after an interval of either 10, 40, 100, or 130 minutes. The recognition set comprised 22 voices of which 20 were distractors and 2 were targets (1 male, 1 female). The recognition set contained equal numbers of male and female voices, and the target and distractor voices were randomly allocated to serial position in the set. The order of male and female target voices in the learning set was counterbalanced within and across conditions.

The distractors and targets were selected from a large pool of voices in such a way that a fairly high degree of similarity within the recognition sets was obtained (as confirmed by independent raters). Voices were selected so as to have no marked accents or unusual vocal characteristics. All target voices uttered a semantically identical one-sentence speech sample, as did the distractors. A between-subjects design was employed such that each subject performed under only one testing delay and type of voice ("high recognition" or "low recognition") treatment combination.

The results indicated that identification accuracy was better at 10 minutes delay ($M = 56\%$) than at all other delays ($p < .025$), which did not differ significantly among themselves ($M = 42\%$). The low- and high-recognition voice factor did not interact with delay, indicating that well-recognized voices were as much affected by delay as were objectively defined poorly recognized voices. For a fuller discussion of this experiment see Clifford, Rathborn, and Bull (1981). Overall, then, these results suggest that although delay does have an effect, it is not massive. The relatively short durations tested in this experiment, however, render any firm conclusions extremely tentative, given the usual time lapse between hearing or seeing a criminal and later trying to identify him (see Devlin, 1976, for United Kingdom estimates of delay in real cases). The next experiment to be reported here took ecological validity into account and ran basically the same design but this time with intervals of 10 minutes, 24 hours, 7 days, and 14 days.

Each of the subjects, 112 trainee nurses, performed under only one Delay x Type of Voice (well or poorly recognized) treatment condition. The only significant effect was for delay interval, with 10 minutes leading to better identification ($p < .025$) than any of the other delays, which themselves did not differ, the mean percentage correct being 55%, 32%, 30%, and 37%, respectively. Although not significant, the well-recognized and poorly recognized voices did behave differently under different delay conditions: Whereas recognition of the former type of voice was best at 1 and 7 days delay and poorest at 10 minutes and 14 days, recognition of the latter type of voice steadily declined in accuracy as the delay interval increased. Possible reasons for the bowed curve for well-recognized voices under delay manipulation have been discussed elsewhere (Clifford, Rathborn, & Bull, 1981), but for the moment the safest, most valid conclusion is perhaps that although delay does have a detrimental effect, that effect is far from catastrophic. A definitive statement on delay and accuracy thus awaits further research.

Earwitnessing preparedness and expectancy

One of the issues raised by Clifford (1978, 1981), in a general critique of the relevance to real-life criminal procedures of laboratory research on eyewitness testimony was that of preparedness. In the laboratory, it was argued, for witnesses to be forewarned of what was expected of them eventuated in a positive cognitive set encompassing maximally efficient processing and encoding strategies that may or may not faithfully reflect those strategies employed in real-life witnessing situations (which may be generally characterized as dynamic, rapid, unexpected, and of sudden onset and offset). If there is a disjunction between the two sets of strategies employed in the respective situations, then perhaps we should not expect a concordance between the indices of accuracy recorded in each. This certainly seems to be true of the eyewitness situation. Is it also true of the earwitness situation?

In an experiment design somewhat analogous to real-life criminal situations, which has already been referred to, Saslove and Yarmey (1980) looked at voice identification under conditions where the subjects were not warned of a subsequent voice memory test. All subjects were given a cover task of clairvoyance, but those in one group were also told that they would be tested on their ability to recognize a taped voice of someone answering a telephone, which they would hear while performing the clairvoyance task. A second group was not warned of either the onset of a voice or the voice identification test. Saslove and Yarmey found that there was a highly significant difference between the two groups in accuracy of later voice recognition, with the informed group performing better than the uninformed group (70% and 62%, respectively).

In our own research projects into voice memory, Clifford and Denot

(1982) also looked at voice memory under incidental conditions as part of a larger experiment into eyewitness memory under a simulated real-life incident situation. Here witnesses were exposed to a stooge who behaved in an aggressive or a friendly manner toward an experimenter and were then required to offer testimony and identification on visual, verbal, and action aspects of the staged events. They were totally unaware of the true nature of the experiment or that an unannounced testimony session would be conducted. Thus, we had a setup where students were unprepared for what was to happen, this being analogous to many real-life criminal episodes. Correct identification of the incidentally heard voice was 49% at 1 week, 41% at 2 weeks, and 8% at 3 weeks.

Most of our experimentation (see Clifford, Bull, & Rathborn, 1981, and elsewhere in this chapter) has been concerned to date with baseline performance of earwitnesses under optimal conditions of hearing and testing and an overall estimate has been arrived at of about 60%–70% correct detection. Therefore the results from Clifford and Denot strongly suggest that voice identification accuracy under incidental (unprepared) conditions is much lower. This is strengthened by the fact that in the Clifford and Denot study the witness heard a rather extensive speech sample being delivered in a nearly unique accented voice, and the recognition set comprised a heterogeneous set of accented voices that eventuated in a functional lineup size of only three.

In another study, conducted by Clifford and Fleming (in press), the major interest was in voice and face identification by shopkeepers and bank clerks following a low-key innocuous interaction sequence such as would occur in counterfeit situations. A stooge entered either banks or shops, approached the clerks or shopkeepers and introduced himself, explained that he had lost a check card and sought clarification of the correct procedure to be followed in such situations. Voice identification was attempted either immediately, 1 hour, 4 hours, or 24 hours later. After it was established that the witness actually remembered the incident, he or she was then asked to identify the stooge's voice, said to be definitely present, in a taped voice parade comprising nine distractors and the target voice. Overall performance declined over time with correct identification being 50%, 33%, 17%, and chance, at immediate, 1 hour, 4 hours, and 24 hours, respectively. Females proved much better at voice recognition than males, scoring approximately twice as many hits. The fact that bank clerks scored numerically better than shopkeepers (but not significantly so) rules out one possible objection to the validity of these results. Because it may be assumed (wrongly) that bank employees are asked about check card losses much more often than shopkeepers, it could be argued that the salience of the task may have been different for the two groups, with the "routine" nature of the query leading to poor processing by the clerks. Such seems not to be the case.

This study, then, corroborates the previous findings in suggesting that when voice identification is sought following incidental exposure, accuracy is unlikely to be high, and, further, what accuracy there is is likely to decrease rapidly over time. Just how rapidly and over what time scale, however, remain problematic.

We have argued elsewhere (Clifford & Bull, 1978) that at real-life lineups there may frequently be considerable pressure on the witness to pick out somebody from the parade. This pressure may be more due to the witness than to any untoward behavior by the police. The witness will be of the opinion that there *is* a police suspect in the lineup (otherwise why would the witness be there?) and that the police are often efficient in that their suspect is, in fact, the true criminal. In most countries the police are required to inform the witness that the lineup may not contain the criminal. Typically, however, little emphasis is given by the police to this instruction, and witnesses may well ignore it. Hecker (1971) suggested that in a voice identification situation, "the listener carries out two tasks in succession; first he decides which reference sample is most similar to the test sample, and then he decides whether the two samples are similar enough to have been produced by the same speaker" (p. 13). The second stage of Hecker's decision-making model may well be where a strong effect could be found of a witness's belief about the likelihood of the target's being in the test array. If a witness believes that the target is very likely to be present in the test array, he or she may give little or no consideration to the second stage of Hecker's model. A study by Warnick and Sanders (1980) may be considered relevant here. They found that providing an explicit option for eyewitnesses to respond "don't know" and also permitting the response "not present" led to somewhat of an increase in correct identifications and a considerable decrease in false identifications. Unfortunately, Warnick and Sanders did not go as far as they might have in their study, because all their trials did have the target present in the test array. The effect of emphasizing that the target may not be present also needs to be investigated for situations in which the target is absent from the test array.

In a study of voiceprint matching, Tosi et al. (1972) informed the voice-print examiners that on some trials a match would exist ("closed" trials) and on some it would not ("open" trials), the examiners not being told for each trial whether it was "open" or "closed." Tosi and colleagues found that emphasizing in this way the possibility that a target may not be present in the test array led to a considerable increase in errors (i.e., whereas false positive errors decreased from "closed" to "open" trials, false eliminations, not surprisingly, increased). Malpass and Devine (1981a) also employed some trials in which the target was not present in the test array. For such "open" trials they found that "biased instructions" that implied that the witnesses were to choose someone from the lineup led to 78% false positive choices, whereas without such a bias the false positive rate was 33%. With "closed" trials the biased instructions led to all the errors being false positives, whereas with unbiased instructions all the errors were incorrect decisions of "not present." Lindsay and Wells (1980) also found photo arrays that did not contain the target to lead to a considerable number of false positives. Now, although false positives may at first glance appear not to be a major problem for the police, one of the primary reasons for the Devlin (1976) inquiry in Britain was the number of people who had been wrongly imprisoned because of witnesses' false positive choices in identification parades.

In our own program of research on earwitnessing we conducted a study to investigate concomitantly the effects of biased as opposed to nonbiased instructions ("target will always be present in the test array" vs. "target may or may not be present in each test array") and of whether the target, in fact, was or was not in the test array ("closed" vs. "open" trials). For the closed trials, we found, as one might expect, that whether the instructions were biased or not had little effect on correct recognitions (64% vs. 57%). In the open trials, however, where one might have expected a sizable difference between the effects of the two sorts of instruction, there was little. In open trials, correct responding (i.e., saying "not present") with unbiased instructions occurred in 12% of the trials and with biased instructions in 6% of the trials. Although the use of unbiased instructions with the target absent doubled the rate of correct responding, over 87% of the responses in this condition were false positives. Such a high rate of false positives cannot merely be due to any difficulty the listeners may have had in discriminating among the voices, because when the target was present, correct performance was much higher than chance (60% vs. 17%). Further, in the unbiased condition it was not the case that the subjects were unaware that they could use the "not present" response, because 50% of them indicated "not present" on at least one of the six (open) trials that they underwent. (For a fuller discussion of this study, see Clifford, Bull, & Rathborn, 1980.)

Brigham (1980) suggests that it would be worthwhile examining the relationship between witnesses' confidence in their decision "not present" and their accuracy. Because the correct response of "not present" occurred so rarely in our study this was not directly possible. As noted in this chapter's section on witness confidence, however, it was only in the target-not-present condition that we did not find a significant relationship between confidence and accuracy.

Conclusions

Our studies of the effects of the presence and absence of the target voice from the test array, together with the effects of instructions on this matter, go a little way toward making earwitness research more ecologically valid. As with most eyewitness research, the majority of (the relatively few) studies of earwitnessing bear little resemblance to real-life witnessing circumstances. Most have used nonstressful situations with prepared subjects participating in laboratory situations. Only in recent months have some earwitnessing studies come to resemble real life (e.g., Clifford & Fleming, in press) but even these have not contained much fear or stress.

However contrived or realistic future earwitnessing studies are, they will need to contain more ecological validity. The research reported in this chapter has shown that although under *ideal* conditions maximal earwitness performance can be quite high (but rarely as high as optimal eyewitness performance), such factors as delay and disguise can substantially reduce earwitness accuracy (perhaps right down to chance level). Until future, more realistic studies argue to the contrary we would recommend that prosecutions based solely on a witness's identification of a suspect's voice (if the suspect is a stranger) ought not proceed, or if they do proceed they should fail. We say this because, even though the topic of earwitnessing presently lacks any theoretical underpinnings, we are of the opinion that earwitnessing and eyewitnessing are similarly and considerably error prone. This is not to say that voice identification should not be used as an aid to the prosecution or the defense, but it should not form any major part of the evidence presented in court.

6   Postevent information and changes in recollection for a natural event

David F. Hall, Elizabeth F. Loftus, and James P. Tousignant

The testimony of an eyewitness in a courtroom is not an isolated event; rather, it is the culmination of a series of events. This testimony can easily be conceived as the final trial in a series of trials of recollection. Initially a witness has an opportunity to view an incident as it occurs. This is analogous to an initial learning trial. Then, typically, the witness is interviewed by police or by lawyers. If it is a criminal case, the interview may involve the viewing of mug shots or lineups. Such interviews are analogous to a series of cued or uncued rehearsal trials. At last, in court, there is a final test in which a witness attempts to answer specific questions about the original incident (a cued recall test) or attempts to make an accurate identification of the suspect (a recognition test). A considerable body of psychological research, some of which will be reviewed here, seems to indicate that under certain circumstances rehearsal of information can interfere with, rather than enhance, recollection. In particular, interference is likely to occur if rehearsal trials include exposure to new, potentially misleading information.

Does information that the witness acquires after the crime, perhaps in the course of interviews with the police, or while viewing mug shots, bring about changes in the witness's recollection of the crime or of the suspect? The case of Robert Dillen, a young free-lance photographer from Dormont, Pennsylvania, suggests that the answer may be yes (Tomsho, 1981). Dillen's initial arrest was little more than a misunderstanding. What is significant is the fact that the arrest resulted in a mug-shot photograph of Robert Dillen in the files of the Dormont police. By chance, one investigating officer thought he noticed an uncanny resemblance between Dillen and a composite

The writing of this chapter was supported by a grant from the National Science Foundation, and a supplement to that grant enabled David Hall to spend a sabbatical year at the University of Washington. We are grateful for support provided for David Hall by Thiel College. We wish to thank Pamela Tousignant for editorial assistance.

sketch made by a holdup victim, Diane Jones. Several weeks after the holdup, Diane Jones was asked to look at a set of ten mug-shot photographs, one of which was Dillen's. It was Dillen's that she identified.

Copies of Dillen's photograph were then sent to other police departments, where they were identified by the witnesses and victims of 13 different crimes, leading subsequently to the identification of Dillen in a live lineup by several witnesses and finally to an identification in court by a 16-year-old victim of rape and abduction. Dillen was eventually proved innocent. Our main concern here is with the series of events that led to Dillen's having been falsely identified by a score of witnesses, some of whom had observed the real criminal for several hours at the time of the crime.

It appears that these witnesses encountered new information during the course of initial interviews with police and while attempting initial descriptions and initial identifications. Such information may have altered the witnesses' recollections of the real criminal's actual appearance, leading to the false identification of Dillen as the criminal.

In this chapter, we will review literature pertaining to the effects on a subject's memory of information that he or she receives subsequent to an event. We will consider the issue of the permanence of memory, that is, the issue of whether postevent information actually brings about changes in underlying memory (as evidenced by changes in the subject's recollection of an event) or merely makes the process of retrieval more difficult. We will offer a strong interpretation of changes in recollection, that is, an interpretation of such changes as indicative of an underlying change in the content of memory. We will also point out reasons why this issue remains controversial.

We will review experimental evidence that seems, in fact, to indicate that postevent information can, in specifiable circumstances, bring about changes in a person's recollections, including recollection of faces. We hope to be able to specify, with as much precision as current research allows, the circumstances under which postevent information is likely to affect such recollections. This knowledge will make it possible for us to offer, in our conclusion, a framework for understanding the existing experimental data on changes in recollection and, we hope, for guiding new experimental work. We intend to outline, as part of this concluding framework, some general principles that seem to govern the alteration of human recollections for complex events.

This research evidence has practical implications for criminal investigations. Research indicates that certain investigative procedures are likely to bring about changes in a witness's recollections of details of a crime, including recollection of a suspect's appearance. Common misconceptions about the reliability of human memory are likely to lead police, lawyers, and jurors to overlook the very real possibility of changes in witnesses' recollections. We hope that the research reviewed in this chapter will prove useful in bringing about improvements in the way in which eyewitness testimony is treated in criminal investigations and in criminal trials.

A paradigm for changes in recollection

Loftus (1979) has developed an experimental paradigm for studying changes in recollections of complex events. Typically, subjects view a film of a complex event and immediately afterward are asked a series of questions. For some subjects, some of the questions are designed to present misleading information – for example, to suggest the existence of an object that did not exist. Thus, in one study some subjects who had just watched a film of an automobile accident were asked, "How fast was the white sports car going when it passed the barn while traveling along the country road?" No barn existed. Other subjects were asked a control question such as, "How fast was the white sports car going while traveling along the country road?" All subjects were asked whether they had seen a barn.

It was found that misleading questions increased by a factor of six the likelihood that the subject would later report having seen the nonexistent barn. Based on these and similar results, Loftus advanced the argument that the questions are effective because they contain information – in this case, false information – that becomes integrated into the person's recollection of the event, thereby supplementing that memory. In other studies, Loftus and her co-workers have shown that new information can do more than simply supplement a recollection. It can actually alter or transform a recollection. Thus, in one study subjects saw a series of color slides depicting successive stages in an accident involving an automobile and a pedestrian. In the midst of the series, the auto, a red Datsun, was seen traveling along a street toward an intersection at which half the subjects were shown a stop sign and the remaining subjects a yield sign. Some subjects then received a question containing a piece of misinformation. For example, the question "Did another car pass the red Datsun while it was stopped at the stop sign?" contains misinformation when it is asked of subjects who actually saw the yield sign. Finally, the subjects were tested for their recollection of the sign. Depending on the time intervals that occurred between the slides, the intervening questions, and the final recollection, up to 80% of the subjects indicated that their recollections were influenced by the misinformation. That is, they remembered a yield sign, when a stop sign had actually been seen in the slide, or a stop sign when a yield sign had been seen. These results were interpreted as indicating that new, misleading information is not only added to memory, it actually alters the content of what the subject is able to remember.

Our experimental paradigm can easily be described in terms of three essential stages:

1. Acquisition: A witness views an initial complex event, which might also include viewing one or more faces.
2. Retention and change: A witness encounters new information subsequent to the initial event. The source of new information might include biasing suggestions, viewing photographs, a combination of pictures and messages, or even rehearsal of the original event. Whatever the source, postevent experiences make possible changes in recollections. New information can be added, old information altered, or perhaps even erased.
3. Retrieval: A test of memory for the original event reveals that postevent experiences have produced substantial changes in recollection. Indeed, the witness reacts as if original memory and postevent information have been inextricably integrated.

The circumstances of change in recollection for a complex event

It is well known that a number of factors influence the retention of memory for an event. Ebbinghaus's (1885/1964) description of forgetting as a function of the interval between training and testing is well supported by modern research on memory for complex events (e.g., Lipton, 1977). Memory for human faces fades as well, although the time course may be somewhat different (e.g., Shepherd & Ellis, 1973; Ellis, Shepherd, & Davies, 1980).

Experiences and activities that occur subsequent to the initial acquisition of memory have an even more radical effect than does the mere passage of time. Time causes memory to fade, but experiences and activities seem to bring about changes in the actual content of recollections. Research by Loftus and her colleagues, and similar work by other investigators, has been concerned with specifying some of the circumstances in which changes in recollections are likely to occur.

Effects of mug shots, composite reconstruction, and police sketch artists

Many experiments demonstrate interference from a wide range of postevent activities, some corresponding closely to activities that are likely to be engaged in by witnesses to real crimes, especially in the course of interrogation by the police. One such activity is the viewing of mug shots.

In one study, subjects viewed a videorecording of three men whom they would later try to identify (Davies, Shepherd, & Ellis, 1979a). Those who searched through a sequence of 100 mug shots to identify the targets made many more errors on a subsequent test than did control subjects, who had not viewed the intervening mug shots. Unfortunately, Davies et al. (1979a) did not report their results in a form that allows a clear discrimination between a change in the amount of information contained in a subject's recollections (i.e., a change in the value of d', Swets, 1973), as opposed to a mere change in the witness's guessing strategy or response criterion (i.e., a change in the value of Beta).

Even more definitive are studies by Brown, Deffenbacher, and Sturgill (1977) and by Gorenstein and Ellsworth (1980). These studies strongly suggest that viewing mug shots alters a subject's capacity to recognize faces that were viewed prior to the mug shots.

In the experiments reported by Brown and colleagues, subjects initially viewed a number of live "criminals." In one experiment, subjects were actually instructed to scrutinize the "criminals" in anticipation of a recognition test. In a second experiment, subjects were not told to expect a recognition test but were given ample opportunity to casually observe the "criminals" in a classroom setting.

After an interval (between experiments) ranging from hours to days, subjects were asked to view a mug-shot montage. The montage included facial photographs of the "criminals" together with photographs of "innocent suspects."

Finally, 4 days to a week after viewing the mug shots, subjects were asked to view live lineups. For each person in the lineup, subjects decided whether or not the person had been seen in the original "crime." The lineups included, of course, three sets of stimulus persons: criminals, innocent suspects from the mug-shot montage, and totally unfamiliar foils. The results indicate that subjects were quite proficient in discriminating the unfamiliar foils from both the criminals and the innocent suspects in the mug-shot montage. Subjects were totally unable, however, to discriminate the criminals from the innocent suspects whose faces had been viewed in photographs. In other words, subjects detected familiar faces but did not know how or when the faces had come to be familiar. Apparently, any familiar face in a lineup is likely to be identified, often with a high degree of false confidence, as a criminal suspect. In terms of our research paradigm, Brown et al.'s study shows that faces viewed in mug shots are added to the same memory store as faces viewed at the time of the initial event. As a result of this process of incorporation, memory for each set of faces can no longer be discriminated.

The results of Gorenstein and Ellsworth's (1980) research are perhaps even more dramatic. These researchers have shown that there seems to be a "commitment" effect when a witness makes identifications from photographs. Making the initial, tentative decision that a face viewed in a photograph might be the criminal's face seems to lead to increasing confidence in that decision. As this apparent increase in confidence is occurring, the witness seems to incorporate the photographic face into memory, overriding, and perhaps even replacing, memory for the original face.

If witnesses retain memory for the original face, then we would expect witnesses to reverse their original error when they encounter the real criminal in a lineup. In Gorenstein and Ellsworth's experiment, this result did not occur. Subjects who made false identifications from photographs subsequently performed no better than chance when they encountered the real criminal in a lineup. They continued, however, to identify their photographic choice in the lineup. Apparently, under these circumstances, new information from the photograph supplanted original memory for the suspect's face.

It is clear that viewing mug shots interferes with memory for faces. What is not so clear is why this should be so. Not enough studies have been done to allow us to delineate a process. Still, a few experiments, involving composite identification kits (Mauldin & Laughery, 1981) and police artists (Hall, 1976), suggest that active reconstruction can be a critical factor in memory for faces.

Mauldin and Laughery found that reconstructing the suspect's face with a composite identification kit facilitated subjects' recognition of the suspect's face. Hall (1976), however, found that subjects who directed an artist's efforts to sketch the suspect's face were subsequently unable to identify the suspect in a lineup at better than a chance level of performance. Subjects in a control group, by contrast, performed at a level significantly better than would be expected by chance. Both Mauldin and Laughery's enhancement effect and Hall's interfering effect suggest that a witness's active reconstruction of a face alters a subject's ability to recognize the face.

Why one procedure brought about a positive effect and the other a negative effect is not clear at the present time. Also, whether a similar active reconstruction process occurs when subjects are asked to view mug shots remains to be shown by further study. Certainly, experimental study of the effects of postevent experiences on recognition of faces leaves a number of interesting questions unanswered. In any case, we must turn now to a consideration of the general circumstances that seem to bring about changes in recollection for details of natural events.

Effects of misleading questions and suggestions

Many experiments have shown that recollections can be changed, under some circumstances, by misleading messages or questions. Several factors have been found to moderate the effectiveness of misleading messages, including: (a) the intervals between an event, a subsequent misleading message, and a final test of recollection, (b) warnings, and (c) the syntactic form of questions and messages.

The intervals between an event, a subsequent misleading message, and a final test of recollection. The intervals between the major procedural steps in our experimental paradigm have been found to be critically important (Loftus, Miller, & Burns, 1978). Loftus et al. found that changes in recollection are prompted by two factors: First, the effect of a misleading message is greater if the interval between the original event and the misleading message is longer, rather than shorter; and, second, the effect of a misleading message is greater if the interval between the misleading message and the final test of memory is shorter, rather than longer. Apparently a misleading postevent message is most effective if memory for the original event has been allowed to fade with time. As a complementary principle, the misleading message is most effective if it is recent, and therefore readily retrieved, at the time that memory is tested.

Warnings. Can change in recollection be prevented by warning subjects that they might find contradictions between an original event and a subsequent misleading message? Research by Greene, Flynne, and Loftus (1982) indicates that the answer to that question is a provisional yes.

In four experiments, subjects first viewed a slide sequence depicting a wallet snatching, and 5 minutes later read a short paragraph describing the event. For some subjects, the paragraph contained misleading information. Some subjects were warned that they might find contradictions between the original event and the account given in the short descriptive paragraph. Such warnings were given at different times: before the slide sequence, immediately after the slide sequence, immediately before the misleading paragraph, or immediately before the final test of recollection. The final test included 20 multiple-choice items, 4 of which tested recollection of critical details about which subjects had been given misinformation.

The results indicated that a warning given immediately prior to the misleading paragraph increased resistance to changes in recollection. Warnings given at other times had no apparent effect. One other finding helps to explain these results. That is, subjects warned just prior to reading the misleading paragraph read the paragraph more slowly than did subjects warned at other times. Apparently, the warning worked by causing greater scrutiny of the postevent information while it was being processed. Increased scrutiny, however, seems to have occurred only if subjects had been prompted virtually at the very moment that such scrutiny was needed.

In brief, there is just one point at which warnings appear to be effective, and that is immediately before the misleading message itself.

The syntactic form of misleading questions. Research indicates that fairly subtle aspects of the way in which questions are worded can have profound effects on a subject's recollection of details of an event.

In one experiment (Loftus, 1981a; Loftus & Greene, 1980), students attending a lecture witnessed an intruder who abruptly entered the classroom, argued with the professor, and then just as abruptly departed. Students were then given a 15-item test on details of the incident, which included 1 misleading question. Two versions of the misleading question were prepared. Each version presented the same false presupposition, that is, that the intruder had a mustache. One version, however, consisted of a simple interrogative sentence: "Was the mustache worn by the tall intruder light or dark brown?" The second version offered the presupposition in a complex interrogative sentence: "Did the intruder who was tall and had a mustache say anything to the professor?"

Subjects were tested a day later for recollection of the incident, including recollection of the nonexistent mustache. Subjects were also asked to indicate whether they remembered having read about a mustache in the postevent questionnaire.

Results indicated that misinformation embedded in a complex question was more likely to alter recollection than was the same misinformation embedded in a simple question. Furthermore, subjects were less likely to remember having read about the mustache if they had read the complex version of the question than if they had read the simple version.

One explanation of these results is the following: A complex question draws the subject's attention to something other than the misinformation. In other words, it is attention distracting. Thus, the misinformation does not receive careful scrutiny. Just enough attention is given, however, to allow the misinformation to be placed in memory, perhaps uncritically or, in some sense, unthinkingly. Later, the misinformation is retrieved from memory with no indication of when or where it had actually been acquired. Apparently, the subject simply attributes the source to the original event, rather than to the postevent questions.

In summary, we have reviewed a body of literature that demonstrates that recollection of complex events can be altered, after the event, by exposure to misinformation. We have specified some circumstances that have been shown to be sufficient for change in recollections to occur.

Recollections are, we must presume, based on memory. If recollections have been shown to change, does that mean that memory changes?

Does memory really change?

Although an impressive amount of research has been conducted showing that a subject's recollections are readily altered by exposure to postevent information, debate continues over what happens to the underlying memory trace. Has the underlying memory trace actually been changed, beyond all possibility of recovery? Or has the trace merely been rendered relatively inaccessible but still potentially retrievable given optimal conditions? Loftus and Loftus (1980) have taken the position that some memories undergo irreversible transformations, but other researchers continue to look for evidence supporting the permanence of underlying memory traces (Mand & Shaughnessy, 1981; Morton, Hammersly, & Bekerian, 1981). Morton et al. have presented a "headed-records theory." Headed-records theory proposes that for each distinct experiential episode a person creates a separate record, or file, in memory. Hereafter, the terms *headed record* and *file* will be used interchangeably.

According to Morton et al., each time an episode is retrieved from memory, a new file is created, presumably by recopying the original file. The new, recopied file may differ from the original file. In particular, new details can be added and original details deleted in the recopying process. Thereafter, the recopied file may be retrieved from memory, rather than the original file. Presumably, each incident of retrieval results in yet another file, each progressively more distant in content from the original. This progression of later files is likely to make recovery of the original increasingly difficult. Yet, recovery of the original is never, according to Morton et al., totally impossible. Given some set of optimal cues, the original file should be recoverable.

In a similar vein, Mand and Shaughnessy (1981) have reinterpreted the Loftus memory change paradigm in terms of Underwood's (1971) frequency theory of recognition memory. According to this interpretation, the subject's ability to recognize a target stimulus is a function of the number of presentations of the target relative to the number of presentations of distractor items, with allowance made for other factors, such as the order and recency of presentation of each item. Recognition of the target stimulus is facilitated by each successive presentation. Thus, an experiment could be designed to demonstrate a residual facilitating effect of the initial presentation of a target stimulus, even though subsequent presentation of distractors had at some point given apparent ascendancy to the distractors. Methodological problems in Mand and Shaughnessy's single experiment make interpretation a little difficult. Still, their theoretical point is interesting and suggests a potentially enlightening experiment. Future experiments in our laboratory will incorporate repeated presentations of information and repeated tests both of memory for the original event and of memory for postevent information, as suggested by Mand and Shaughnessy.

In short, both headed-records theory and frequency theory seem to be in line with a coexistence hypothesis. According to this hypothesis, memory has not been changed; rather, original memory coexists with, and competes for retrieval with, more recent information.

It is difficult to disprove the coexistence hypothesis. After all, one can always argue that something, let us say item *x*, is present in memory but just exceptionally well hidden. Now, prove that item *x* does not exist!

Perhaps then, it is impossible to prove that any given bit of information no longer exists in memory. Nonetheless, techniques have been devised to coax an appearance from reluctant memory traces. Such techniques include (a) the method of multiple probes' employing different question forms and using recognition as well as recall; (b) use of the postexperiment debriefing period as an occasion for a final, introspective memory probe (Loftus, Miller, & Burns, 1978, Exp. 2); (c) monetary incentives for correct responding (Loftus, 1979); (d) the second-guess technique (Loftus, 1979); and, finally, (e) hypnosis (Putnam, 1979).

These methods for detecting weak but lingering memory traces are discussed in detail by Loftus and Loftus (1980). It is sufficient for present purposes to note that sometimes, in some circumstances, these techniques have been used successfully to uncover the existence of otherwise surprisingly intractable memories. Within the context of the experimental paradigm that we have been considering, however, these techniques have usually failed to resurrect lost memories, in spite of every reasonable effort to make them do so. In many experiments, memory which would have been demonstrably present had subjects not encountered a misleading postevent experience seems to have vanished as if it had never existed. At some point, depending on one's personal criterion, one might begin to suspect that something that cannot be found does not exist.

One experiment (Bekerian & Bowers, in press), however, has been offered as evidence for the continued existence of displaced memory traces. Subjects began by viewing a sequence of slides depicting a complex event, and afterward some subjects received misleading information. There were two versions of the final memory test. Half the subjects received the test slides in a random order, which is also the typical procedure in experiments reported by Loftus and her colleagues. The other half received test slides in a carefully constructed sequence corresponding to the sequence of the original event.

Bekerian and Bowers found strong testing effects. Misleading information had a large effect when subjects were tested in random order, replicating the original work of Loftus. Sequential testing, however, effectively neutralized the impact of misleading postevent information. In fact, subjects given sequential test items responded as accurately as subjects who had encountered no misleading information.

Bekerian and Bowers concluded that the difficulty of retrieval, not the loss of the original memory trace, explains the apparent inability of some subjects to remember details of a complex event. According to this interpretation, the sequential order of test items provided sufficient cues to overcome the usual difficulty in retrieving original memory traces. Another interpretation is possible, however, an interpretation that requires no assumptions about the permanence, or impermanence, of memory traces.

There seems to be no reason, empirical or theoretical, to expect that the process of changing recollections must have reached completion within seconds after exposure to a misleading message, or within minutes, or within any particular span of time. Perhaps a subject maintains for a while two inconsistent recollections of an event. As long as neither of these recollections has been retrieved from memory, both are presumably held in a state of independent coexistence. Each recollection presumably fades gradually and independently, as would any information in memory.

To continue our interpretation, each alternative recollection is accessible to a somewhat different but overlapping set of retrieval cues. Thus, at any moment following an initial event in the presence of certain cues, one alternative recollection is more readily obtained than another. Any theory of memory is obliged, by experimental fact, to state that information that has been successfully retrieved from memory is thereafter, in some sense, more accessible.

More puzzling is the fate of a recollection that has never been retrieved and that has apparently been replaced by a more accessible recollection. Existing experimental data do not provide an answer.

In summary, Bekerian and Bowers's data are consistent with the notion that the process of change in recollections occurs gradually. The process of change begins when original memory for an event is reactivated and new information is added by a postevent experience. The process of change is delayed while alternative recollections coexist in long-term store, and it finally reaches its culmination when one recollection of an event is activated and alternative recollections are not. The fate of unretrieved, unactivated recollections cannot be determined from existing data.

What is needed at this point is a conceptual framework within which to think coherently about problems of memory change and about the relevant experimental data. In the next section we will present a general framework for understanding changes in recollections for complex natural events.

A framework for understanding changes in recollection

We have discussed some of the particular circumstances under which recollections appear to have been changed by postevent information. We now offer two general principles that we hope will constitute the beginnings, at least, of a framework for discussing when and how changes in recollections occur.

1. Recollections can change only if the subject does not immediately detect discrepancies between postevent information and memory for the original event.

Detecting discrepancies leads subjects to treat postevent information in one of two ways, both of which have the common effect of preventing such information from replacing or changing original memory. First, subjects may suddenly discontinue giving even minimal attention to a source of information that because of discrepancies has been discredited. Thus, parts of the postevent information may be totally ignored. Second, even if a source of discrepant information continues to receive some degree of attention, there is no integration or association of the discredited information with memory for the original event. Rather, it is perceived and encoded in memory as belonging to a distinct postevent experience. Memory for the postevent experience is thereafter easily discriminated from memory for the original event.

The first principle of change in recollection is supported by the results of many different experiments, representing different procedures, materials, and retention intervals. Some of these experiments have already been discussed but can be quickly reconsidered.

For example, it has been shown that recollections of peripheral details of a complex event are more likely to be altered by postevent experiences than are recollections of salient or central aspects of the original event (Dristas & Hamilton, 1977; Marquis, Marshall, & Oskamp, 1972; Marshall, 1966). In the experiments reported by Marshall and his colleagues, subjects viewed a film depicting a crime. The film was, of course, rather complex, and included elements that were judged to be salient (likely to be noticed and recalled with accuracy) and peripheral (likely to be overlooked and difficult to recall). After viewing the film, subjects underwent a misleading interrogation, which was rather similar to the misleading questions and messages encountered by subjects in most of the Loftus studies.

Marshall and his co-workers found that misleading interrogation reduced accuracy of recall for peripheral elements but not for salient elements of the original event. In a similar study, Dristas and Hamilton found that recollections of peripheral details in a film about machine shop accidents could be readily altered by misleading questions. Recollections of central details, however, were not so readily altered.

One explanation for these results can be rejected. It might have been argued, if the evidence were otherwise, that "changes" in recollection are observed because peripheral details are, by definition, details for which little or no information has been committed to memory in the first place. Fortunately, other studies strongly indicate the rejection of that hypothesis. For example, Loftus, Miller, and Burns (1978) showed that in the absence of misleading messages, there is a significant amount of information recalled about seemingly minor elements of the original event. Only after encountering a misleading message does that information appear to have been lost. Thus, there is initially a measurable amount of information about peripheral details, but that information, more than information about salient details, seems vulnerable to misleading questions.

We must seek another explanation. It seems reasonable that a discrepancy between a peripheral detail of an original event and a corresponding detail of a postevent experience is likely to pass unnoticed. It would seem to be the nature of peripheral details that they are given some minimal attention but not critical, scrutinizing attention. Thus, in terms of our first principle of change in recollections, recollections of peripheral details are vulnerable to alteration by postevent information because subjects often fail to attend to discrepancies concerning such peripheral details.

The results of studies of the effectiveness of warnings also strongly support the first principle of change in recollection. As noted before, subjects who have been warned about possible discrepancies between an event and a subsequent misleading message are resistant to changes in recollection. The implication of this finding is straightforward. A warning effectively instructs the subject to search for discrepancies. Clearly, if the first principle is valid, such forewarned subjects ought to be resistant to changes in recollection, which is exactly the result obtained.

In addition to warnings, another factor, the syntax of a misleading message, also seems to affect the likelihood of a change in recollection. As noted earlier, misleading information embedded in a peripheral clause of a complex sentence has been found to be highly effective in changing recollections. By contrast, misleading information presented in a simple sentence is much less effective.

Perhaps subjects attend more carefully to the central point of a simple sentence than to a seemingly minor assumption contained in a complex sentence. If so, it seems likely that a discrepancy between an original event and a subsequent simple message would be noticed. In terms of our first principle of change in recollections, such attention to discrepancy is sufficient to prevent change. A discrepancy between an event and a subsequent complex message, however, is more likely to pass unnoticed. Such an oversight is, in terms of our first principle, a necessary condition for a change in recollection.

In summary, experiments that support the first principle of change in recollections include studies of memory for peripheral as opposed to central details, studies of the effects of warnings, and studies of the syntactic form of misleading messages. Implicit in the first principle of change in recollections is the assumption that noticeably discrepant information can be stored separately, perhaps in independent, discriminable files, as suggested by Morton et al. (1981). Given independent storage, change in recollection is avoided. The second principle of change in recollections offers another strategy for avoiding change, that is, keeping recollections out of active memory.

2. Change in recollections for an original natural event occurs only if a postevent experience restores memory for the original event to an active status.

Lewis (1979) has made a distinction between active memory and inactive memory. According to this distinction, inactive memory includes information that has been committed to long-term storage but that has not recently been retrieved for active problem solving. Active memory, by contrast, includes newly formed memories and memories that have been recently retrieved from storage for active problem solving. A body of evidence in animal memory literature suggests that when called into the active status, memories become highly susceptible to interference. This research also suggests that as long as a memory is not used, it is, for the most part, invulnerable to the effects of intervening experience.

This animal research supports our own view that postevent experiences induce subjects to retrieve original recollections from memory. Once retrieved, those recollections can be changed by adding, deleting, or reworking some of the details. By contrast, it is a commonplace finding that irrelevant filler tasks assigned during the interval between training and testing are adequate to prevent changes in recollection. Such filler tasks are effective in preserving recollections, presumably because they do not evoke memory for the event. Virtually all of the research we have discussed suggests that postevent experiences change recollections only if such experiences are capable of activating original memory. In short, the second principle of change is consistent with a large body of experimental evidence.

Conclusions

We have reviewed some of the major studies of the effects of postevent information on recollection for details of complex natural events. Two general principles have been suggested as a framework in which to organize this knowledge. Just as important, an effort has been made to summarize some major questions that remain unanswered.

One question that remains to be answered is this: What happens to original underlying memory after a change in recollection has been observed? Some fairly serious practical problems could be more readily solved if there were an answer to that question. In criminal investigations, for example, considerable effort has sometimes been expended in an effort to coax memory for fine details of an event from witnesses. Hypnosis, lengthy and detailed verbal reconstruction of events, and the use of aids to recollection such as sketches, photographs, and composite facial identification kits are all used in an effort to maximize the amount of information obtained from witnesses. The presumed permanence of memory might, perhaps, provide a justification for such heroic efforts to retrieve intractable recollections. If actual change in memory traces could be demonstrated, however, then police might be more firmly advised to regard such overworked recollections with appropriate skepticism.

We have offered two general principles that seem to govern changes in recollection. These principles can be restated, slightly paraphrased:

1. For change to occur, the subject must not notice discrepancies between an original event and the misinformation that follows.
2. For change to occur, memory for an original event must be activated, and thus rendered accessible to the influence of postevent experiences.

It thus becomes apparent that what we know about changes in recollection constitutes, for the most part, a set of necessary conditions. At this point, we can only speculate about sufficient conditions.

Recent speculations by other theorists may aid in the specification of these necessary or sufficient conditions. Johnson and Raye (1981), for example, recently proposed that memories are tagged differently for internal as opposed to external events, allowing discrimination of past perceptions (reality) from past acts of imagination (fantasy). It would therefore seem reasonable to speculate that changes in recollection occur when internal or external discrimination fails.

Of course, many items of misleading information come from external sources as well. Thus, the failure of discrimination in this case is actually between memories derived from different external sources (one's own perception as opposed to that imposed by some other external source).

Other models of interest are those suggested by Medin and Shaffer (1978) and Lehnert, Robertson, and Black (in press). These researchers have proposed that information in memory is integrated, sometimes beyond the point of accurate discriminability, by combining cue dimensions "in some context...in an interactive, specifically multiplicative manner" (Medin & Shaffer, 1978, p. 212) or through a "ripple effect" (Lehnert et al., in press). The basic idea is that memories that share a large number of common attributes undergo considerable integration and redefinition, especially at the time of retrieval. Thus, the boundaries between memories can dissolve, depending on the number of common attributes and on the specific retrieval cues available. These ideas hint that underlying memory really changes.

The idea that underlying memory really changes is also supported by the interesting phenomenon of compromise memories. Compromise memories are perhaps best demonstrated in studies of change in recollection for colors (Bornstein, 1976; Loftus, 1977; Thomas et al., 1968). In Loftus's (1977) study, subjects who had witnessed an automobile accident involving a green car were afterward asked a question that included a misleading reference to "the blue car." On a subsequent color recognition test, subjects who had been exposed to the misleading question tended to shift their color selection in the direction of the misleading information. The color selected in the recognition test, however, was influenced not only by the postevent misinformation (blue) but also by the original perceived color (green). In fact, many subjects selected a blue-green color that seemed to represent a compromise between the two sources of information. Thomas et al. (1968), Bornstein (1976), and others have reported similar results, indicating a compromise in memory between information derived from verbal cues (labels) and visual cues (colors). The phenomenon of compromise memories creates a paradox for theories that do not allow for changes in underlying memory traces. The problem that compromise memory creates for interference theory can serve to illustrate the issue.

Interference theory is one of the oldest and most widely held explanations of forgetting and is based on the assumption that people forget an event because something else they have learned prevents the event from being remembered. The theory includes several paradigms, the most relevant of which for the present discussion is retroactive interference, which refers to the fact that something learned during a retention interval produces forgetting of previously learned material (Postman & Underwood, 1973). To be more explicit, both an experimental group and a control group learn that the response "green" is associated with a cue "the passing automobile." In addition, during a subsequent retention interval, the experimental group learns that the response "blue" is associated with the cue "the passing automobile," whereas the control group does not. Finally, at some later time, both groups are asked to recall the true color. The control group can be expected to recall or recognize "green" as the color of the automobile, but the experimental group, or at least some portion of the subjects in this group, can be expected to recall or recognize "blue." Different versions of interference theory explain retroactive interference in terms of extinction and unlearning (Adams, 1976; Pavlov, 1927) or in terms of response competition (McGeoch, 1942) or response-set interference (Postman, Stark, & Fraser, 1968). What all of these various explanations have in common is the basic assumption that at the time of testing one particular response, perhaps the response "blue," will be strongest, or most closely bonded to external cues, whereas other responses, such as the response "green," will be weaker, or less closely bonded to external cues. Thus, the subject can be expected to emit the response "blue," not "green."

The difficulty for interference theory arises when a subject's response ("blue-green") is a novel blending of these previously learned responses. One might argue that the notion of stimulus or response generalization is adequate to explain a certain latitude of error in a subject's selection of a green or a blue color in the color recognition test. Indeed, Loftus (1977) found a certain latitude of generalization in the selection of colors, even by subjects in the control group. Such spontaneous variance in subjects' selection of colors, however, is not adequate to explain the fact that the modal response for subjects in the experimental group was an apparent compromise between "blue" and "green." In fact, interference theory simply does not provide a framework in which such a phenomenon can even be discussed.

In short, compromise memory is a puzzling phenomenon. We suspect that compromise memory, as well as some other instances of change in recollection, may best be explained in terms of changes in underlying memory traces. Our present framework is a step toward accommodating the phenomenon.

One point of potential concern is the consistency of compromise memory with the first principle of change in recollections. One might wonder how a person could reach a compromise between two, somewhat discrepant memory traces without, in the process, noticing the discrepancies. If discrepancies were detected, then, according to our first principle, memory change would not be likely to occur. In answer to this potential objection, it can be argued that there is no reason to believe, a priori, that the process of "bringing memory traces together" necessarily highlights the discrepancies. Perhaps, differences between memory traces are inconspicuously or unconsciously neutralized as the information in the traces is integrated. To resolve this issue, an experiment could be designed to include measures of both change in recollection and detection of discrepancy. In any case, the present chapter provides a framework in which we can at least discuss the existing experimental data on compromise memories, as well as plan future research.

To reiterate, changes in recollection have been demonstrated for many different aspects of complex events. The changes have occurred in an impressive number of experiments, some closely modeling real-life occurrences. Still, the general validity and robustness of the phenomenon remains a matter of some controversy. The limits of memory change have not yet been determined.

7   Age as a factor in eyewitness memory

A. Daniel Yarmey

Individual differences of age, sex, race, cognitive style, and personality factors have received relatively little attention from researchers of eyewitness testimony (see Clifford & Bull, 1978; Loftus 1979; Yarmey, 1979). Although most experimental psychologists are uninterested in individual differences and treat these variables as part of the error term in research designs (see Eysenck, 1977), the courts are highly concerned with the influence of such factors, especially with the effects of age on testimony (see Melton, 1981; Stafford, 1962; J. Wilson, 1980). This chapter will focus on the extremities of the age continuum, specifically, on the child and on the elderly as witnesses.

The courts have to be concerned with the accuracy and completeness of reports and the credibility of witnesses. In particular, this concern is heightened by witnesses who may have unreliable memory because of incomplete development or advancing degeneration associated with aging. Prosecuting attorneys and lawyers for the defense are not, of course, totally free to pick their witnesses; instead, they must for the most part accept them as they find them. Elderly people and young children may be either bystander witnesses to crime or victim witnesses. Furthermore, they may be the only witnesses available to the state in prosecuting the accused. An important question is whether the testimony of children and the elderly is as unreliable as is generally believed. Before reviewing the limited but growing research evidence that attempts to answer this question, a brief examination of the major concerns and decisions of the courts toward the child as a witness will be presented.

Children as eyewitnesses

Legal consideration on the child as a witness

English law recognized as early as 1779 that children could be competent

Preparation of this paper was facilitated by a Social Sciences and Humanities Research Council of Canada grant, no. 492-80-0016.

witnesses in criminal trials provided they understood the nat
sequences of an oath (*Rex* v. *Brasier*, 1779). In 1895 the U
Supreme Court held:

[T]he boy was not by reason of his youth, as a matter of law, absolute
as a witness . . . . While no one would think of calling as a witness an i
or three years old, there is no precise age which determines the question of competency. This depends upon the capacity and intelligence of the child, his appreciation
of the difference between truth and falsehood, as well as of his duty to tell the former. The decision of this question rests primarily with the trial judge, who sees the
proposed witness, notices his manner, his apparent possession or lack of intelligence,
and may resort to any examination which will tend to disclose his capacity and intelligence, as well as his understanding of the obligations of an oath. (*Wheeler* v. *United
States*, 1895)

The absolute minimum age that the appellate courts of most states will consider a child as competent to testify is four years. (See, e.g., *Jackson* v.
State, 1940; *State* v. *Juneau*, 1894.) According to Stafford (1962):

[T]he test of a child's competency involves four fundamental elements: (1) present
understanding or intelligence to understand, on instruction, an obligation to speak
the truth; (2) mental capacity at the time of the occurrence in question to observe and
register such occurrence; (3) memory sufficient to retain an independent recollection
of the observations made; and (4) capacity truly to translate into words the memory
of such observations. (pp. 313–314)

Competency of a child also is dependent upon his or her understanding of
the significance of the oath and general understanding that it is his or her
duty to tell the truth. Although Stafford cautions the courts about the dangers of using leading questions with children because of their high suggestibility, he admits that on occasion the courts find it necessary to do so.

Early studies of eyewitness testimony and children

Much of the early history of children's testimony, especially the contributions made by non-English-speaking European psychologists, is available
from a series of reviews published between 1909 and 1917 by Guy Whipple.
In his 1911 article, Whipple cites the writings of two German physicians,
Babinsky (1910) and Duprée (1910), who flatly declared that children are
the most dangerous of all witnesses. They proposed that, wherever possible,
testimony by children should be disallowed in court. These demands did not
go unchallenged. Gross (1910), a criminologist and jurist, criticized these
views as biased because they were based on observations of sick children. In
contrast, Gross felt that healthy children are the best possible witnesses for
simple events, and any errors in their testimony are comparable and equal
to similar errors in the testimony of adults. Furthermore, Gross hypothe-

sized that children in some respects may be superior to adults in accuracy of reports because they are less prejudiced, are not troubled by interpretations of blame and responsibility, are more in control of their emotions, and do not get intoxicated.

Two other researchers who significantly contributed to an understanding of children's abilities as eyewitnesses were Alfred Binet (1900, 1911) and L. Wilhelm Stern (1910, 1939). Binet was the first psychologist to investigate visual memory by constructing a "description-of-pictures test." Subjects were shown a complex picture for 2 minutes and were given 10 minutes to write a description of the picture solely from memory. Binet found that for both children and adults, individual differences of intelligence, rather than the pictorial target, were more important in determining report selection. The suggestion of relationships among recognition ability, accurate reporting, and intelligence that was developed from this work is still evident in the modern use of the Stanford-Binet Intelligence Scale.

Beginning in 1901, Stern used picture tests of memory and later investigated more realistic events of simulated crimes to study the psychology of testimony. Subjects inspected pictures for 45 seconds each and then immediately reported on their content. They were told to describe only those pictorial items they remembered with certainty. Results yielded a small average error rate of 5.5% for incorrect statements. Some weeks later, an unexpected recall test was given and the error rate increased slightly to 10%. Stern noticed that time altered the quality of memory, as revealed by intrusions of imagination and errors of confusion, as opposed to the quantity of memory reports. Still later a third test was given and each subject made on the average one or two serious errors, even those subjects who were absolutely certain and would swear under oath to the accuracy of their testimony.

Stern carried out his studies with both children and adults. In one study, children of both sexes aged 7, 11, and 13 and boys between 16 and 18 years were tested by free recall and leading questions in cross-examination. Free narration produced an average error score of 5% to 10%, whereas the use of leading questions resulted in an average error of 25% to 30%. Stern (1910) concluded that "the power of the 'suggestive' question showed itself to be dependent in large measure on age" (p. 272). Younger children proved to be much more suggestible than older children, but even adults were influenced by suggestion. Stern (1939) believed that the courts must use child psychologists as experts in interviewing child witnesses because children are predisposed to distort and give false testimony.

Perhaps the most dramatic historical example of the use in criminal court of scientific evidence (as opposed to clinical insight) on matters of children and eyewitness testimony was the work of Varendonck (1911, reviewed in

Rouke, 1957; Whipple, 1913). In an attempt to evaluate whether or not the testimony of two young girls, aged 8 and 10, could have been unduly influenced by suggestive questions, Varendonck conducted a series of experiments on young children incorporating questions similar to those put to the two actual witnesses. For example, 18 children were asked to name the color of the beard of one of the teachers, and 16 responded "black." The teacher did not have a beard. Results of these investigations convinced Varendonck that young children are easily led by suggestive questioning and that the two young girls may have falsely accused the suspect because of the pressure of intense suggestion. Varendonck presented these observations and conclusions in a Belgian court as an expert witness and contributed to the jury's decision to acquit.

In 1912, Whipple reported on the work of other European psychologists, such as Marbe (1913), Mehl (1912), and Dauber (1912), each of whom showed that the testimony of young children was unreliable because of the influence of rumor, suggestion, or imagination. In addition, Dauber (1912) showed that young children and adults can make the same identical group error. For example, 27 of 38 boys in one class gave the *same* incorrect answer to a question asked about a familiar city landmark. Thus, witnesses can independently make group errors by responding with common but false answers.

In sum, early European researchers concluded that younger children were more suggestible and less reliable as witnesses than older children and adults (see also M. R. Brown, 1926; Lipmann, 1911; McCarty, 1929).

Contemporary research on children as eyewitnesses

Researchers have tested children under a variety of eyewitness circumstances for the accuracy of their verbal reports, visual identification, speaker recognition, and their susceptibility to suggestion.

Questioning child witnesses. The credibility of a witness's statement depends upon two factors – the capacity to report a past event accurately and completely and the willingness to tell the truth. Unlike contemporary European psychologists, such as Udo Undeutsch (1982) and Arne Trankell (1972), who focus on the veracity of witness's reports, British and North American researchers have emphasized the experimental investigation of the capacity of eyewitnesses. We will follow the Anglo-American tradition and limit our review to the child's capacity as an eyewitness. Still, contrary to the simple view held by some police officers that "young children are 'innocents' who have no cause to lie, and will, therefore, give accurate evidence" (Dent, 1978, p. 237), it must be acknowledged that children can and do distort their testimony for a number of reasons, including deceit.

Does the type of question asked influence the eyewitness testimony of young children? Dale, Loftus, and Rathbun (1978) interrogated 32 preschool children after showing them four short films. The form of the questions was varied to test, among other things, the variables of affirmation and negation (i.e., "Did you see some bears?" and "Didn't you see some bears?"); and presence or absence of entities (i.e., events actually presented vs. events not presented in the films). The results were quite clear. Young children proved to be highly suggestible. Leading questions asked about objects that were not present in the film yielded a high probability that a child would incorrectly respond yes. The form of the question, however, did not reliably influence answers about entities that were present in the film. Dale and colleagues concluded their article with the valuable observation that the courts (see Rules of evidence, 1973) recognize that leading questions are undesirable, but they make an exception in the case of children. It is children, however, who are probably most easily misled by suggestive questions.

Shortly after the publication of the article by Dale et al. (1978), two other articles appeared that also addressed the question of the susceptibility of child witnesses to suggestive questioning. In the first study, Marin et al. (1979) tested 12 male and 12 female subjects each from kindergarten and first grade, third and fourth grades, seventh and eighth grades, and at university level. Subjects were exposed unexpectedly to an argument between a male confederate and the male experimenter. Subjects were tested 10 or 30 minutes later for their memory of the event by free recall, objective questions (e.g., "Was the man wearing brown pants?"), including one leading question (e.g., "Did the man slam the door as he closed it?"), and photo identification. Two weeks later, subjects were retested but this time with the leading question in nonleading form (e.g., "Did the man close the door as he left?"). Analyses revealed that the suggestive question produced a significant increase in false positive answers. Participants doubled the number of false positive responses to the nonleading question 2 weeks later if they had earlier received a leading question. There were, however, no reliable age differences in susceptibility to the leading question. Before accepting the conclusion of Marin and colleagues that children "are no more easily swayed [than adults] into incorrect answers by leading questions" (p. 304), a more rigorous series of investigations involving more than one leading question under a variety of circumstances must be completed. Furthermore, the vast majority of the literature on suggestibility shows that young children (age 7) are very susceptible to an experimenter's suggestion and that resistance to suggestion increases with age (see Messerschmidt, 1933; Sah, 1973). One negative finding does not disprove the results of other investigators but, instead, suggests that eyewitness researchers should be attentive to the question of the limits of their research.

In this vein, Cohen and Harnick (1980) investigated the effect of suggestion on memory in children aged 9 and 12 years and in college students. Subjects were shown a 12-minute film depicting two detailed episodes of petty crime and then were asked 22 questions. The questions tested recollection for events that were clearly presented in the film. Each subject was asked 11 suggestive questions (e.g., "The young woman was carrying a newspaper when she entered the bus, wasn't she?" – she actually carried a shopping bag) and 11 nonsuggestive questions (e.g., "What was the young woman carrying when she entered the bus?"). Performance scores indicated that the youngest children agreed with the false suggestions significantly more frequently than did subjects in the other two groups. There was no difference in susceptibility between the 12-year-olds and the college students, although both groups were influenced to some extent. These results imply that a 12-year-old child is as capable of resisting leading questions in some eyewitness situations as a young adult.

Accuracy and completeness of recall. A consistent finding in memory research is an improvement in verbal recall consonant with an increase in age from childhood to young adulthood (see Brown, 1975). Similarly, eyewitness researchers have found that young children are inferior to older children and young adults in free recall of "criminal" details (Cohen & Harnick, 1980; Marin et al., 1979) but do not differ on yes or no objective questions (Marin et al., 1979). In contrast, Dent and Stephenson (1979) discovered that 10- and 11-year-old children shown a short, exciting film of a theft and chase of a robber were more accurate, although less complete, in free recall than in answers given to general and specific questions. Furthermore, young children displayed very inaccurate recollections of the appearance of people relative to their more satisfactory descriptions of the course of events.

Visual identification. Laboratory studies of face recognition, with one exception (Cross, Cross, & Daly, 1971), have shown an improvement in performance with age. Seventeen-year-olds are superior to 12-year-olds (Ellis, Shepherd, & Bruce, 1973), and older children are superior to younger children over the age range 5 to 14 years (Goldstein & Chance, 1964). Similarly, a study by Blaney and Winograd (1978) found a clear improvement in children's recognition memory for adult male faces from the ages of 6 to 8 years and 8 to 10 years.

Of potential critical importance to the law are the recent findings of a developmental trend in improved facial recognition for unfamiliar faces between the ages of 6 and 10 (Diamond & Carey, 1977), then little or no improvement, or even a decline in performance, and finally improvement again about the age of 16 (Carey, Diamond, & Woods, 1980). Consistent with these results are the findings of Flin (1980), who found a steady improvement in recognition memory for unfamiliar faces in children between 6 and 10 years, a slight drop in performance at 11 and 12 years, and higher performance again with 13-, 14-, and 15-year-olds. Carey et al. (1980) attribute these age-related differences to maturational factors, particularly to maturational changes in the functioning of the right hemisphere of the brain. It is possible that the temporary leveling or dip in performance after the age of 10 is due to hormonal changes associated with the onset of puberty, which influences the processing of facial stimuli by the right hemisphere (see Carey & Diamond, 1980).

Very few investigators have used children as subjects in more realistic eyewitness tasks. Marin et al. (1979), in the study mentioned earlier, presented subjects with a six-person photo identification test. Overall, 57% of the subjects correctly identified the target. There were, however, no significant age-related differences among the four age categories ranging from kindergarten to university students. Unfortunately, the false-alarm rate and omission scores were not reported and, as other studies show, younger children tend to guess more frequently when uncertain than do older children (see Ellis et al., 1973).

Dent (1977) tested 220 children aged 10 and 11 on their ability to identify a workman 1 week after seeing him in their class for a period of 2 minutes. Identification was made from a nine-person corporeal lineup or from nine color slides. The children were told that the target might or might not be present and were asked to identify someone only if they were very confident in their selection. In the slide presentation, 29% of the identifications were correct, and in the lineup, only 12% were correct, which is not significantly better than chance (11%). On the slides, 31% of the identifications were incorrect, and on the lineup, 32% were incorrect. No identification was made by 40% of the children with color slides, and 51% failed to identify anyone from the lineup. The children found the live lineup particularly stressful, probably because they feared possible repercussions from the suspect. This factor may be highly relevant in England, where witnesses confront the accused directly and indicate their choice by tapping him or her on the shoulder.

Voice identification. The same types of problems inherent in eyewitness identification also are found in earwitness identification. Furthermore, the development of voice recognition with age has parallels with face recognition. Mann, Diamond, and Carey (1979) tested 20 college students and 20 children each at the age of 6, 8, 10, 11, 12, 13, 14, and 16 in immediate recognition of one or two unfamiliar voices. Collapsing performance with the number of targets, 6-year-olds performed at the level of chance (50%), whereas all others performed above chance level (between 60% and 75% correct). Performance steadily improved between ages 6 and 10, with 10-year-olds approaching adult levels. Accuracy declined between ages 11 and 13 but returned to the adult level by age 14. Age-related performance was generally the same for recognition of one or two speakers and for utterances being the same or changed from original listening to the test for recognition. Performance was superior for all age groups, however, in the easiest condition, the one-target–same-utterance condition, with 6-year-olds performing at better than chance (60% accuracy). All groups, including adults, performed poorly with the most difficult condition, the two-target different-utterance condition.

Clifford, Bull, and Rathborn (1980) tested 107 schoolchildren aged 12–13 years, 13–14 years, and 16 years and over. Recognition memory for a target voice mixed with five distractor voices showed considerable improvement with age. Mean percent correct recognitions for each group were 28, 47, and 67, respectively (see also Clifford, 1980b).

As a general rule, the court considers any child under the age of 14 to be of "tender years," and judges will warn the jury not to convict on the uncorroborated evidence of a child and to weigh the evidence, even that given under oath, with extreme caution (Cartwright, 1963; Wilson, 1980). The experimental evidence on juvenile person and voice identifications supports the caution that the courts use in dealing with the child witness.

The elderly as eyewitnesses

Just as mock jurors will disregard the testimony of a child when given a choice between believing an adult or a child (Goodman & Michelli, 1981), real jurors may not accept the eyewitness accounts of elderly witnesses. In a recent study completed in our laboratory (Yarmey, Rashid, & Jones, 1981), young adults in a mock jury perceived the older person as ineffective, highly dependent, and personally unacceptable. Young people have low expectations of elderly persons because of judgments of diminished competence (Rodin & Langer, 1980). Stereotypes about the elderly are readily available in the mass media, magazines, and cartoons. Most typically, the elderly are portrayed as rigid, ultraconservative people. A common prototypic representation of their physical and personal characteristics pictures them as thin, wrinkled, and stooped, which is associated with the belief that they are highly dependent, psychologically helpless, and intellectually inferior. To the extent that this stereotype is held by judges and juries, the credibility of the elderly witness will be low.

Few people would disagree with the observation that memory fades with advanced age. The elderly often are embarrassed by their memory failures, and complaints about poor memory are common (see Thompson, 1980). Older persons show poorer memory performance than young adults on episodic memory tasks of paired-associate learning, serial recall, and free recall of words (Craik, 1977; Walsh, 1975). These differences are found whether memory is tested by recall or recognition, although some improvement is apparent with recognition measures (Craik, 1977; Erber, 1974; Schonfield & Robertson, 1966). Age-related differences in short-term retention are minimal with one exception: The elderly have greater difficulty when their attention is divided during encoding, or where the verbal material must be manipulated during storage (Craik, 1971). These results suggest an attentional deficit in which verbal information is insufficiently processed at input. Age-related declines in visual memory also have been reported for both simple and complex stimulus patterns (Adamowicz, 1976). These deficits are attributed to encoding inaccuracy rather than to storage or retrieval problems (Adamowicz, 1976; Charness, 1981).

Explanations for age-related differences in memory have focused on four theoretical issues: (a) high susceptibility to the effects of interference (Arenberg, 1973; Botwinick, 1973); (b) excessive cautiousness (Okun, Seigler, & George, 1978); (c) difficulties in reorganization of information (Craik, 1977); and (d) disabilities with perceptual organization (Clay, 1956; Heath & Orbach, 1963). It is beyond the scope of this chapter, however, to discuss each of these theoretical positions and their relationship to eyewitness testimony.

Accuracy and completeness of recall of elderly eyewitnesses

Tadashi Uematsu (1982), a Japanese psychologist, first investigated the effectiveness of the elderly as eyewitnesses in 1940. Following the inspection of still pictures, subject-witnesses were immediately questioned. Elderly witnesses, in contrast to 17- and 18-year-olds, were shown to be unreliable both in terms of their verbal recall and their high suggestibility to leading questions.

Relative to the interest over the years given to children and young adults as eyewitnesses, little experimental evidence is available on the elderly eye-witness. Sociologists and criminologists have made the usual general state-ments that older persons are unlikely to be good witnesses (Groth, 1979) or that they could be reliable witnesses providing the police are patient when conducting investigations (Hoyer, 1979). Recently, Judy Kent and I (Yarmey & Kent, 1980) tested 40 young males and females (mean age of 19 years) and 40 elderly males and females (mean age of 73 years) as eyewit-nesses to a simulated crime. Subjects were shown a series of slides of an assault and theft of a wallet by a male assailant on a male victim. Two other people also were present in the criminal scenario, a female friend of the vic-tim, and a female bystander. Each character was spotlighted with a close full-front facial view for 10 seconds each.

One of our primary interests was to test whether subjects, and in particu-lar the elderly, are unduly influenced by stereotypic conceptions of what criminals should look like. The demeanor of the assailant and the victim was controlled and subjects saw one of four different combinations of inno-cent- and guilty-looking assailants, and innocent- and guilty-looking vic-tims. Verbal memory was assessed by a 40-item questionnaire consisting of declarative sentences requiring a word or a phrase to be completed (i.e., "The assailant wore: (a) dark brown pants; (b) light blue pants; (c) blue jeans; (d) light brown pants"). Approximately 30 minutes after the recall test, subjects were given a recognition memory test for the four principal characters. Results of the identification test will be given in the next section. Young adults were reliably ($p < .01$) superior to the elderly in their overall verbal recall of the mugging scenario, with the young correct on 81% of their responses compared with 71% for the elderly. Young subjects were significantly superior in recall of person attributes (81% vs. 71%), nonper-son items (80% vs. 65%), assailant characteristics (80% vs. 69%), and vic-tim characteristics (87% vs. 77%). There were no significant differences in recall for males and females or for the interaction of age and sex; neither did subjects differ in their recall of details as a function of the demeanor of either the assailant or the victim.

Visual identification. Bahrick, Bahrick, and Wittlinger (1975) found that elderly persons' very-long-term memory for familiar faces and names can be quite good. Individuals who had been away from high school for 35 years accurately identified 90% of their classmates' photographs. People in their late 50s and 60s correctly identified 75% of their classmates. These results suggest that recognition memory is impressive. Nevertheless, old memories of 30 years or so of well-known faces do decline with increasing age in nor-mal subjects aged from 40 to 89 (Warrington & Sanders, 1971).

Experiments on face recognition confirm the results of Adamowicz (1976) and others showing a deficit in elderly persons' visual memory. Smith and Winograd (1978) found that young adults (18–25 years) were superior to older adults (50–80 years) in memory for faces when recognition was measured with d' scores based on signal detection analyses. Older subjects also had a higher false-alarm rate, indicating that they operated with a looser criterion or were more willing to classify a distractor face as "old" when uncertain. Brigham and Williamson (1979) also found that recognition accuracy for faces was reliably lower for elderly subjects than for young adults. Finally, Ferris et al. (1980) discovered that elderly normals and elderly senile dementia patients were inferior to young normal adults in recognition memory for faces but did not differ from each other. These results were interpreted as suggesting a deficit in visual encoding and storage due to normal aging. No evidence was found, however, for the hypothesis that the elderly are more cautious in recognition memory.

The Yarmey and Kent (1980) study, mentioned earlier, found no reliable differences between the two age categories in recognition (hits) of the assailant, the victim, or female companion. Young people were superior to the elderly only in their recognition of the most peripheral figure in the crime scenario, the female bystander. Recognition memory was analyzed in this study in terms of "pure" hit–miss scores, "pure" false-alarm–correct-rejection scores, and a combination of these two indices with subjective confidence levels. There were no reliable differences as a function of age in the analysis of "pure" false alarms and correct rejections. When confidence scores were combined with false alarms, however, young subjects were superior to the elderly in correct rejection of distractors. These results suggest that the elderly are less confident than the young regarding decisions concerning the foils. Recognition performance scores also showed that the elderly and the young are not directly influenced by the criminal or innocent demeanor of either assailants or victims. Identification of the assailant, however, was influenced by complex interactions of facial demeanor of the assailant and the victim, as well as the sex and age of the witnesses. For example, elderly males and young females were particularly attentive to guilty-looking assailants, whereas elderly females were most accurate in their recognition of innocent-looking assailants.

The final study I wish to report on is an investigation by Yarmey and Rashid (1981; also see Yarmey, 1982). Elderly adults and young adults observed a simulated assault and theft of a wallet from a young adult male victim by either one, three, or five male assailants. A young adult male bystander was also seen during the criminal episode. Back views of the characters were presented except that each person turned to face the camera for

2 seconds, showing his full face. The demeanors of both the victim and his assailants were prerated as neutral in terms of their criminalistic or normal appearance. Half of the subjects, however, saw a "criminal-looking" bystander, and the remainder saw an "inoffensive-looking" bystander. Subjects were given two photo lineups, one of which contained the assailants (valid display) and the other of which did not but did contain a photograph of the bystander (blank display).

A summary of the major results are as follows:

1. The elderly and the young were equally accurate in recognizing the assailants (hits) on each of the three types of assailant conditions.
2. There were no reliable age differences in false alarms.
3. The elderly were less confident in their rejection of foils.
4. The elderly made significantly more errors of omission on both the valid and blank photo displays, suggesting increased cautiousness on their part.
5. There were no reliable differences in response bias, indicating that the elderly were no less likely to guess than were the young.
6. d' scores indicated that the elderly showed deficits in facial recognition relative to the young on the three-assailant and five-assailant conditions.
7. Recognition performance declined substantially with an increase in the number of assailants for both the young and the elderly.
8. Significantly more elderly subjects (38%) than young subjects (22%) misidentified the bystander as the criminal suspect ($p < .01$).

Moreover, twice as many elderly subjects misidentified the bystander as the assailant when he was "criminal-looking" as opposed to having an "inoffensive" appearance ($p < .01$). Demeanor of the bystander was not a factor in the misidentifications by the young.

These findings, along with the results of previous investigations, suggest that the criminal justice system has to be somewhat skeptical of the eyewitness testimony of elderly witnesses compared with that of young adults (see Yarmey, Jones, & Rashid, in press). Older persons may be more susceptible to such things as unconscious transference and negative stereotypes, which are more likely to influence their misidentification of peripheral figures, such as innocent bystanders. This may be especially true when the observational conditions are ambiguous and short in duration. Unconscious transference occurs when a person observed in a certain context is confused with or recalled as another person seen in the same context but committing a different act (see Loftus, 1976). In addition, verbal descriptions given by the elderly are definitely poorer than those given by the young, and their visual identifications, although equal to those of the young in terms of hits, are not as accurate on the average if measures of signal detection theory are employed. Thus, the credibility of the elderly as witnesses may be low. Finally, because of their tendency to make a relatively high number of omission errors, the elderly are likely to fail to identify a suspect when he or she truly is the wanted person. Future research on the elderly has to concentrate on those system variables (Wells, 1978) that, in particular, can improve the performance of the elderly as eyewitnesses.

8   Eyewitness confidence

Gary L. Wells and Donna M. Murray

"I have no doubt, I mean that I am sure that . . . when I first laid eyes on him, I knew it was the individual."

The above statement is an in-court quotation from an eyewitness in the case of *Neil* v. *Biggers* (1972). This was an important case as it resulted in the U.S. Supreme Court's offering guidelines in the interpretation of eyewitness identification evidence. The court identified five factors: The witness's opportunity to view the criminal at the time of the crime; the witness's degree of attention; accuracy of the witness's prior description of the criminal; the amount of time between the crime and confrontation; and the level of certainty demonstrated at the confrontation. Although questions can be raised regarding each of these factors,[1] eyewitness certainty has been of particular import to eyewitness researchers in the last few years.

Several studies have shown that an eyewitness's expressed certainty strongly affects how people perceive the credibility of the eyewitness under cross-examination (e.g., Wells, Lindsay, & Ferguson, 1979; Wells, Ferguson & Lindsay, 1981). An eyewitness's certainty most likely affects processes at even earlier points. The voracity with which police investigators search for corroborative evidence, for example, is likely to be affected by the certainty with which an eyewitness chooses a suspect from a lineup or picture array. Eyewitness certainty could also affect a prosecutor's decision about the sufficiency of evidence, and in turn whether and how to prosecute a suspect. Should eyewitness certainty be used in these ways?

Eyewitness confidence or certainty is a belief in the accuracy of one's memory report. (The terms *certainty* and *confidence* will be used interchangeably in this chapter.) Confidence can be measured in a variety of ways. A person's confidence can be measured, for example, by having the person indicate the subjective probability that the statement is true (e.g.,

The research and writing for portions of this chapter were assisted in part by grant no. 410-81-0400-R1 from the Social Sciences and Humanities Research Council of Canada to the first author.

155

..oriat, Lichtenstein, & Fischhoff, 1980). Eyewitness researchers more commonly measure confidence using Likert-type scales with anywhere from 3 to 11 points. End points typically are labeled "not at all confident" and "totally confident" or "completely uncertain" and "completely certain." Alternative approaches to the measurement of confidence include recording open-ended responses that are later scaled by experimenters on a unitary continuum (e.g., Murray & Wells, 1982) and having subject-jurors estimate the confidence of an eyewitness after viewing a cross-examination of the eyewitness (e.g., Wells, Lindsay, & Ferguson, 1979).

There are several related questions concerning eyewitness confidence that have strong implications for criminal justice proceedings. Obviously it is important that we determine whether or not the credibility accorded to eyewitness confidence is warranted. To do this we must examine empirically the reliability and validity of eyewitness confidence. *Reliability* refers to the consistency of eyewitness confidence scores as measured in various ways. If eyewitness confidence cannot be reliably measured, then it cannot be used *validly*. In this context, validity refers to whether or not eyewitness confidence is a predictor of eyewitness accuracy (sometimes called predictive validity or concurrent validity.) This chapter addresses both the reliability and validity of eyewitness confidence. This chapter also describes four conceptual accounts of the confidence–accuracy issue. Finally, this chapter draws conclusions about the utility of eyewitness confidence and how it should be treated in the criminal justice process.

Reliability of eyewitness confidence measures

One of the most basic tests of reliability involves the use of *parallel measures*. This involves giving people (in this case, eyewitnesses) two measures of confidence that are functionally equivalent and correlating scores on the two measures. Although eyewitness research has not examined parallel measures of confidence per se, a recent experiment examined relationships among several related measures of confidence. Murray and Wells (1982) used a staged theft to generate eyewitnesses who later attempted identifications of the thief from a photo array. The eyewitnesses were asked to indicate (prior to identification) whether they thought that they could make an identification, how confident they were (after the identification or non-identification) that they had made the correct decision, whether they would be willing to sign a sworn statement that the identified person was the thief (given that an identification was made), and whether they would be willing to go downtown to view a live lineup. The resultant correlations among these measures are presented in Table 8.1. These data show that some

Table 8.1. *Intercorrelations among eyewitness confidence measures*

		1	2	3	4
1	Predecision confidence that an identification could be made	—	.35*	.10	.03
2	Postdecision confidence that correct decision was made	—	—	.40*	.33*
3	Willingness to sign an identification statement	—	—	—	.58*
4	Willingness to view a live lineup	—	—	—	—

*$p < .01$.
Source: Murray and Wells (1982).

measures of eyewitness confidence are reasonably correlated to each other (e.g., postdecision confidence that a correct decision was made and willingness to sign a statement to that effect). Other measures are not correlated, however, and should not be considered redundant (e.g., predecision confidence that a lineup identification can be made and later willingness to sign an identification statement). They tell us that it may be desirable to use more than one measure of eyewitness confidence in attempting to predict accuracy. Such an attempt is described later in this chapter.

A more common test of reliability is the test–retest procedure, wherein the same measure is administered twice at different times to the same people. There are three staged-crime studies in which eyewitness confidence was measured with Likert-type scales immediately after lineup identifications and again following cross-examination of the eyewitnesses (Lindsay, Wells, & Rumpel, 1981; Wells & Leippe, 1981; Wells, Lindsay, & Ferguson, 1979). These studies showed average correlations of .91 between the two administrations of the measure.

Interjudge reliability is another method of assessing reliability. This method measures the extent of agreement between two or more individuals who independently assign scores to target cases. Agreement between subject-jurors in judging the confidence of eyewitnesses is an important measure of interjudge reliability because it holds a statistical relationship to the question of how much impact eyewitness confidence can have on jurors' verdicts. That is, lack of interjudge reliability among jurors means that the average for jurors' perceptions of witnesses' confidence does not discriminate among witnesses. Therefore, this average cannot be related to any differential weighting of witnesses' testimony. Conversely, high interjudge reliability means that the subject-jurors as a group are discriminating reliably between eyewitnesses on the basis of perceived witness confidence. This latter statement about high interjudge reliability should not be taken to mean that the subject-jurors are assigning confidence to eyewitnesses in a *meaningful* much less a *useful* way; it only means that subject-jurors are in agreement in the perceptions of witnesses' confidence. It is possible to have reliable but not useful discriminations, because agreement does not imply that jurors are accurately perceiving witness confidence nor does it imply that witness confidence reflects witness accuracy. Agreement in jurors' perceptions of witness confidence, however, does provide the first step toward meaningful and useful group discrimination.

In a series of studies, subject-jurors observed cross-examinations of eyewitnesses of varying levels of confidence. It was found that agreement among subject-jurors in ascribing confidence to eyewitnesses was extremely high (correlations averaging over .80, e.g., Lindsay et al., 1981; Wells et al., 1981; Wells & Leippe, 1981; Wells, Lindsay, & Ferguson, 1979). High interjudge correlations also have been reported in the coding of open-ended statements made by eyewitnesses. The statements are eyewitnesses' responses to such questions as "How sure are you that you have identified the correct person?" (Murray & Wells, 1982). Thus, there seems to be little ambiguity in observers' perceptions of eyewitness confidence.

Interjudge agreement in estimating eyewitness confidence is not as high, however, when one of the judges is the eyewitness and the other is an observer (e.g., juror). In general, observers' ratings of eyewitness confidence seem to "regress" on the eyewitness's self-rated confidence. That is, eyewitnesses who rate themselves as either extremely high or extremely low in confidence will have less extreme confidence ratings ascribed to them by subject-jurors. As a result, the correlation between eyewitnesses' self-rated confidence and jurors' ascriptions of confidence is only in the range of .55 (see Wells, Lindsay, & Ferguson, 1979). If we assume that eyewitnesses' self-rated confidence is more valid (as discussed in the next section) than are jurors' ratings, this modest correlation is problematic for the courtroom. It suggests that the utility of eyewitnesses' self-rated confidence in predicting accuracy (discussed in the next section) will not get used effectively by jurors because jurors' estimates of eyewitnesses' confidence are only moderately related to eyewitnesses' self-rated confidence. In general, one must have high correlations between one predictor variable (e.g., jurors' ascriptions of confidence) and another predictor variable (eyewitnesses self-rated confidence) in order to use the first predictor as a substitute for the second predictor.

A study by Brown, Deffenbacher, and Sturgill (1977) showed people multiple pictures of faces and measured identification accuracy and confidence for each picture. The results showed that an eyewitness's confidence when correct is highly correlated to the eyewitness's confidence when incorrect. This relationship is neither test–retest reliability nor interjudge reliability in any simple sense. Nevertheless, it suggests that eyewitness confidence may be a relatively stable characteristic of the eyewitness (although, as outlined later, confidence may be tractable given certain events). If this is true, then the relationship between confidence and accuracy (i.e., the validity issue) could not be robust unless there were also stable individual differences in eyewitness accuracy.

Validity of eyewitness confidence

The majority of the empirical studies dealing with eyewitness confidence bear on the question of validity. Unlike reliability, questions of validity require the identification of a criterion. The criterion for judging the validity of eyewitness confidence is the accuracy of the eyewitness.[2] One way to assess validity is to see if the confidence measure appears, on the face of it, to be "relevant" to witness accuracy. This type of validity, called *face validity*, is undoubtedly high. A number of researchers using a variety of methods have found that people intuitively believe that eyewitness confidence is a valid predictor of eyewitness accuracy (e.g., Brigham & Wolfskiel, 1982; Deffenbacher & Loftus, 1982; Rahaim & Brodsky, 1981; Wells, Lindsay, & Ferguson, 1979; Yarmey & Jones, 1983).

Predictive validity

Although reliability and face validity address possible problems regarding the use of witness confidence, predictive validity is the ultimate measure of interest. Predictive validity is measured by calculating the correlation between eyewitness accuracy and eyewitness confidence. The Court was assuming predictive validity when it suggested that an eyewitness's certainty at the time of identifying a defendant is reflective of identification accuracy.

Perhaps the first empirical test of the relationship between eyewitness confidence and accuracy was a study conducted by Munsterberg (1908). Munsterberg had children examine pictures for 15 seconds and then write a report of everything they could remember. Subsequently they were required to underline those parts of their report of which they were absolutely certain. Although we are not blessed with statistical summaries in this early work, Munsterberg reported that "there were almost as many mistakes in the underlined sentences as in the rest." Thus, there was only trivial predictive validity of knowing whether a statement was made with enough confidence to underline it.

Two other early studies (one by Stern and one by Borst) were reported by Whipple (1909). Stern and Borst's subjects observed complex stimuli and then gave testimony about their observations under conditions where they were asked to swear to the truth of the testimony or not. Stern found that the accuracy of sworn testimony was 89%, whereas unsworn testimony yielded 80% accuracy. Borst found comparable figures of 91.8% and 85.5% for sworn and unsworn testimony, respectively. These results could be considered to be either substantial or trivial, depending on how one emphasizes the data. Deffenbacher (1980), for instance, argued that the difference between sworn and unsworn testimony was substantial because the error rate for unsworn testimony was almost twice that of sworn testimony (20% and 14.5% vs. 11% and 8.2%). On the other hand, one could argue that the accuracy rate for sworn testimony was only 6.3% and 9% (in Borst's study and Stern's study, respectively) more accurate than unsworn testimony. Indeed, over 35% of all false testimony was believed strongly enough by the witnesses that they were willing to take an oath as to its truth.

These early studies should have led researchers to explore whether or not and when eyewitness accuracy and eyewitness certainty are related. Instead the published literature shows no indication that there was any empirical interest in this issue until almost 65 years later. Since 1974, however, the empirical evidence has grown remarkably.

It is not the purpose of this chapter to describe each and every study that has examined the relationship between eyewitness confidence and eyewitness acuracy in the last few years. Nevertheless, Table 8.2 is a relatively complete summary of the relevant modern studies on this issue. In this list of 31 separate investigations, 13 report positive accuracy–confidence correlations that are statistically significant and the remaining 18 report nonsignificant correlations.

At this point we must remind the reader that statistical significance simply means that the correlation is not likely to be attributable to chance. Statistical significance does not mean that the correlation is useful or socially significant. In fact, the average correlation among all those that are significant in Table 8.2 is approximately .31. The median correlation among those that are significant is .23. Thus, even if we bias our estimate of the confidence–accuracy correlation so as to focus only on those studies that found statistically significant correlations, the estimate is impressively low: A .31 correlation is interpreted generically in this context as meaning that approximately 9% of the variation in eyewitness accuracy is accounted for by eyewitness confidence.

One could argue that 9% of the variance is a reasonable level in order to

Table 8.2. *Studies reporting the relationship between eyewitness confidence and eyewitness accuracy*

Study	Statistical significance[a]
Brigham et al. (1981)	Significant
Brigham et al. (1982)	Significant
Brown et al. (1977)	Not significant
Buckhout et al. (1974)	Not significant
Buckhout, Figueroa, & Hoff (1975)	Not significant
Clifford & Scott (1978)	Not significant
Clifford & Hollin (1981)	Not significant
Courtois & Mueller (1981)	Significant
Davies, Ellis, & Shepherd (1978b)	Not significant
Deffenbacher, Brown, & Sturgill (1978)	Not significant
Hilgendorf & Irving (1978b)	Significant
Hosch & Cooper (in press)	Not significant
Hosch, Leippe, Marchoni, & Cooper (1982)	Not significant
Leippe, Wells, & Ostrom (1978)	Not significant
Lindsay & Wells (1980)	Not significant
Lindsay, Wells, & Rumpel (1981)	Significant
Lipton (1977)	Significant
Loftus, Miller, & Burns (1978)	Significant
Maas & Brigham (1982)	Significant
Malpass & Devine (1981a)	Not significant
Malpass & Devine (1981b)	Significant
Murray & Wells (1982)	Significant
Ruback, Greenberg, & Westcott (1982)	Not significant
Sanders & Warnick (1981a)	Significant
Sanders & Warnick (1981b)	Not significant
Saslove & Yarmey (1980)	Significant
Sturgill (cited in Deffenbacher, et al., 1978)	Not significant
Wells, Ferguson, & Lindsay (1981)	Not significant
Wells & Leippe (1981)	Not significant
Wells, Lindsay, & Ferguson (1979)	Significant
Yarmey (1979b)	Not significant

Note: This table represents "overall" results. As indicated in the text, some studies report more than one correlation between accuracy and confidence because there were multiple conditions. In those cases statistical significance is based on a combination of the correlations (see text).

[a]Statistical probability that such relationships could occur by chance is 1 in 20. Average correlation of those that are statistically significant $\simeq .33$. Across all studies, the average estimated correlation is $\simeq .08$.

judge eyewitness confidence to be useful. In all fairness, however, we cannot assume that the studies indicate that the real-world correlation between witness confidence and witness accuracy is in the order of .31. For one thing, an overall analysis of Table 8.2 (not just an analysis of the studies showing statistical significance) indicates an estimated correlation of only .07. A correlation of such magnitude is relatively useless in any applied sense.

We feel that any simplistic combination of the data in these 31 studies might be misleading. Some studies found a statistically significant relationship (albeit usually of trivial magnitudes), whereas others did not. It might make more sense to ask *why* the relationship sometimes occurs and sometimes does not occur. Unfortunately, the differences between studies are too numerous to discern why one study found a confidence–accuracy relationship and another study did not. Within studies, however, there is sometimes variation in the confidence–accuracy relationship. These within-studies comparisons can provide valuable insight regarding why the confidence–accuracy relationship sometimes occurs and sometimes does not. Three studies are of particular import in this regard. In each of these studies there were significant accuracy–confidence correlations in some experimental conditions and either negative or null correlations in other conditions. We will give special attention to these three studies in an attempt to ascertain why some studies yield statistically significant relationships.

Malpass and Devine, 1981a. This study calls into question the significant correlations obtained in such studies as Brigham (1980), Brigham et al. (1981), Lindsay et al. (1981), Maas and Brigham (1982), Malpass and Devine (1981b), and Wells, Lindsay, and Ferguson (1979) because these eyewitness identification studies used only perpetrator-present lineups. Malpass and Devine's (1981a) study used a staged vandalism in which eyewitnesses later attempted to identify the vandal from a lineup that either did or did not contain the vandal. When the lineup contained the vandal, there was a highly significant and positive correlation between eyewitnesses' accuracy of choice and their confidence. When the lineup did not contain the vandal, however, there was a negative correlation between confidence and accuracy (i.e., the more confident the eyewitness the more likely it was that he or she was wrong). Across both types of lineups there was no significant correlation (i.e., the positive and negative correlations cancelled each other). This pattern of data apparently is due to the strong relationship between choice and confidence. That is, Malpass and Devine (1981a) found that eyewitnesses who made a choice were far more confident in their decision than were eyewitnesses who made no choice. Note that eyewitnesses who make a choice in perpetrator-absent lineups are necessarily incorrect, whereas those who do not make a choice in perpetrator-absent lineups are necessarily correct. Because choosers were more confident than were nonchoosers, Malpass and Devine found a negative confidence–accuracy correlation with perpetrator-absent lineups. This suggests that any positive relationship between confidence and accuracy with perpetrator-present lineups may be cancelled by a negative relationship that obtains with perpetrator-absent lineups! It seems probable that the studies by Brigham (1980), Brigham et al. (1981), Lindsay et al. (1981), Maas and Brigham (1982), Malpass and Devine (1981b), and Wells, Lindsay, and Ferguson (1979) would have obtained much smaller and possibly even nil confidence–accuracy correlations had they also included perpetrator-absent lineups in their designs.

Similar results to those of Malpass and Devine (1981a) have been demonstrated in the study of voice recognition. Specifically, the research of Clifford and Bull (see Chapter 5 in this volume) indicates that voice recognition accuracy and earwitness confidence are significantly related when the correct target voice is present in the array of voices, but no such relationship obtains when the correct voice is absent from the target array.

Note that the inclusion of perpetrator-absent lineups is an important real-world factor. Practically speaking it does us no good to know that confidence–accuracy correlations are positive only when the perpetrator is present in the lineup. In real-world cases we do not know whether the lineup contains the perpetrator or not and it is, therefore, the overall correlation that is important. As long as this overall correlation is nil we have no applicable value from knowledge of eyewitness confidence.

Wells, Ferguson, and Lindsay, 1981. This is another study where the confidence-accuracy correlation is significant under some conditions and not significant under other conditions. Using a staged theft, Wells and his colleagues found a significant positive correlation between eyewitnesses' confidence and their accuracy in identifying the thief from a picture array (correlation = .30, or 9% of the variance) in their control groups. Prior to stating their confidence, however, half of the eyewitnesses were given a "briefing" that warned them of the fact that they would be cross-examined about their previous identification. They were also told which types of questions to expect. The witnesses who were briefed showed a significant elevation in their confidence. This elevation in confidence was most pronounced for witnesses whose confidence was initially low. As a result of this, the relationship between confidence and accuracy was eliminated. This result is important because such briefings are common in actual criminal cases. Thus, even if there is an accuracy–confidence correlation at one point in time, real-world experiences can obliterate the accuracy–confidence correlation prior to the witnesses' courtroom testimony.

Recent data also suggest that the passage of time per se can harm accuracy–confidence correlations in eyewitness identifications. Ruback, Greenberg, and Westcott (1982) found that eyewitness identifications by staged theft victims yielded statistically significant (albeit trivial) confidence–accuracy correlations at delays of 2 months (correlation = .09) but negative correlations at 15 months (correlation = −.11). Thus, even if attorneys and others do not intervene to brief eyewitnesses, it appears that eyewitness confidence can be a profoundly misleading form of information for triers of fact. Because almost all eyewitness studies reported in Table 8.2 used extremely short witness–test intervals, there may be a general tendency for these studies to be overestimates of the level of accuracy–confidence correlations obtained in real-world settings.

Murray and Wells, 1982. This study suggests that the literature generally overestimates the magnitude of the confidence–accuracy relationship that could be expected to occur in actual criminal cases. Murray and Wells (1982) staged repeated thefts and found that the accuracy–confidence relationship for eyewitnesses was statistically significant only when the eyewitnesses knew (at the time of their identification and confidence measurement) that the crime was staged. For the most part it is standard procedure in eyewitness research to inform subjects that the crime was staged prior to any identification attempt. Thus, it is important to note that eyewitnesses who believed that the crime was real (at the time that they made their identifications and stated their confidence) showed no significant accuracy–confidence correlation ($r = -.004$). It may be that the anxiety that people experience when they believe that their identification will have profound consequences serves to destroy any accuracy–confidence relationship. Thus, we suggest that real-world eyewitnesses may show even less correspondence between their confidence and their accuracy than the general literature suggests.

A similar argument can be made from a study by Clifford and Hollin (1981). These researchers found that confidence and accuracy were significantly related for witnesses who viewed a nonviolent videotape; in contrast, a violent videotaped scene produced no correlation between confidence and accuracy. Such an effect might occur for a number of reasons, but whatever the reason, it suggests that confidence and accuracy are more poorly related in realistic, anxiety-producing situations than in more trivial, typical laboratory situations.

The idea that realism and consequences for eyewitnesses' identifications serves to lower the accuracy–confidence relationship is in contrast to the suggestions of Brigham et al. (1982). Brigham and colleagues used as subjects convenience-store clerks who had witnessed mildly unusual behavior by a customer. Later, they were asked to identify the customer from a photospread. Brigham and colleagues made a reasonable argument that their convenience-store clerks assumed that the task had important consequences (unlike many laboratory experiments) and that this may account for why they obtained a high confidence–accuracy correlation. Unlike Murray and Wells (1982), however, Brigham and colleagues did not have a trivial-consequences condition with which to compare their results. Furthermore, Brigham and colleagues used only criminal-present photo arrays, the problems of which have already been discussed in this chapter and that by Malpass and Devine (Chapter 4, in this book).

The Murray and Wells (1982) study also addressed another question in the confidence–accuracy issue, namely, Is any one measure of eyewitness confidence better than some other measure in predicting eyewitness accuracy? As we described earlier in this chapter, Murray and Wells obtained four measures of confidence for eyewitnesses: whether they thought they could make an identification (predecision confidence), whether they thought they had made a correct decision (postdecision confidence), willingness to view a live lineup, and willingness to sign a sworn statement of identification. None of these measures was significantly different from any other in its ability to predict accuracy.

Why should eyewitness confidence and accuracy be so poorly related?

We submit that the eyewitness accuracy–confidence relationship is weak under good laboratory conditions and functionally useless in forensically representative settings. Forensically representative factors include the use of both perpetrator-present *and* perpetrator-absent lineups or picture arrays, the allowance for attorney "briefings" of witnesses, and the anxiety and other relevant accompaniments of knowing that the identification and testimony have real consequences. Studies that include these factors do not find accuracy–confidence correlations.

Yet, intuitively it seems implausible that confidence and accuracy should be unrelated. Even when we consider these forensically relevant factors, our intuition suggests that a useful amount of information about the likely accuracy of an eyewitness's memory should be obtainable from the eyewitness's stated confidence in that memory. After all, people generally know when their memories are vague on some issue, and they indicate this by expressing low levels of certainty about that memory. What makes eyewitness identifications special in producing noncorrespondence between confidence and accuracy?

There is probably no single factor responsible for the poor correspondence between confidence and accuracy in eyewitness accounts. As with most phenomena, there are probably multiple causes. In the published eyewitness literature, four explanations have been offered.

Experience. Wells, Lindsay, and Ferguson (1979) argued that people's daily encounters with others do not provide proper experiences for establishing good correspondence between certainty and accuracy in person identification. Wells and his colleagues note:

We often see someone in a hallway, on the street, or at a party who we believe we recognize, but, not knowing the person well, we simply smile or make some ambiguous gesture of recognition. Such gestures are almost always reciprocated and, thus, we consider our belief (i.e., that we made a correct recognition) to be confirmed. However, in signal detection terms, we have failed to distinguish between a "hit" and a "false alarm," with the verdict almost always being that it was a hit. Our perceptual set has led us to think of such events as confirmations. Of course, in some cases we do get feedback. For example, at a social gathering a third party might take initiative of the form, "Have you and John met?" However, the nature of social intercourse usually takes the form of a pause following such a question so that if one person says "yes," the other person will be able to avoid an embarrassing "no" response. Indeed, there seems to be a general belief that if one person says "yes" both individuals believe that they have previously met; the remainder of the conversation is to determine where or when they met. While this may provide the person who says "no" with a disconfirmation, the overall nature of daily experience is that *if one believes that he or she recognizes another person it is practically disconfirmable.* Thus, people's daily experiences may lead them to believe that if they make a recognition, they are correct. Because they lack veridical feedback experience, people fail to be sensitive to factors leading to correct and incorrect recognitions which, in turn, leads to eyewitnesses' poor accuracy–confidence calibration. (Wells, Lindsay, & Ferguson, 1979, pp. 446–447)

Although Wells, Lindsay, and Ferguson's "feedback experience" hypothesis remains plausible, there is as yet no empirical evidence showing that feedback training improves the accuracy–confidence correlation for eyewitnesses.

Optimality. Deffenbacher (1980) argued that the low or nonexistent relationship between confidence and accuracy for eyewitnesses is due to the low levels of accuracy obtained in eyewitness studies. In general, Deffenbacher argued that the correlation between accuracy and certainty should be a function of the "optimality" of the witnessing and testing conditions. Deffenbacher suggests that optimality is measurable by examining the level of accuracy obtained in a study. The eyewitness literature is not highly supportive of this hypothesis. One example that could be said to conflict with the optimality hypothesis is a study by Lindsay et al. (1981). Lindsay and his colleagues varied the witnessing conditions of a staged crime so as to yield lineup identification accuracy rates of 33%, 50%, and 74%. The accuracy–confidence correlations were as poor in the 74% accurate conditions (high optimality) as they were in the 33% accurate conditions (low optimality). Other exceptions to the optimality hypothesis include studies showing that the relationship between certainty and accuracy can vary within a given level of accuracy (e.g., Wells et al., 1981).

Nevertheless, in one respect the optimality hypothesis has a *statistical* truth to it. Statistically it is impossible to find a confidence–accuracy correlation if accuracy is at a level expected by chance. (By definition, chance occurrences represent random patterns that will not correlate with other measures.) Thus, if we consider chance to be .16⅔ in a six-person lineup,[3] we should find accuracy to be uncorrelated with anything if accuracy rates are .16⅔. As the accuracy rate increases, proportionately less of the variance in accuracy is due to chance, thereby allowing more "reliable variance" for obtaining a correlation. This does not mean that higher levels of accuracy necessarily produce higher confidence–accuracy correlations. If confidence and accuracy are correlated, however, then statistical considerations would lead us to expect the level of the confidence–accuracy correlation to be partly related to the level of accuracy.

Self-attributions. Leippe (1980) has argued that eyewitness confidence could be construed as a self-inference made by the witness. The inference, or attribution, is based on the witness's action and the context of the action. This viewpoint, drawn from Bem's (1967) theory of self-persuasion, predicts no differences in the certainty of those who choose someone from the lineup regardless of accuracy, as long as internal cues (i.e., some internal knowledge of accuracy) are weak. This is because the action (i.e., choosing someone in the lineup) and the context of the action (free choice) are identical for accurate and inaccurate witnesses. In effect the witness is construed to be engaged in a thought process akin to "I chose this person under conditions where I wasn't forced to choose. . .therefore, I must be fairly confident that he is the culprit." There is virtually no research evaluating this self-attribution version of the confidence–accuracy issue. Extant theory and data suggest, however, that the viability of the self-attribution explanation could be tested by varying the witnesses' perception of how much pressure they are under to choose someone from the lineup (see Bem, 1972).

Selective cognitive search. Research in other cognitive domains shows that when reviewing evidence about their own choices, people bias the review by searching for evidence supporting a tentatively preferred choice (e.g., see Koriat et al., 1980). In the eyewitness domain, Wells et al. (1981) argued that people will naturally bolster their certainty in their memories up to a point where they feel sufficiently confident to identify a target or testify about their recall. Wells and his colleagues further argued that the process is selective (i.e., information not supportive of their memory is largely ignored). As a result, virtually every witness is able to reach this level of sufficiency (i.e., even those who have false memories). Wells and colleagues found that telling witnesses that they were going to have to testify regarding their lineup identification served to inflate witnesses' confidence. The increased thought purportedly generated by this witness-briefing eliminated the already-small correlation between eyewitness confidence and eyewitness accuracy. Thus, the accuracy–confidence relationship might be made poorer, rather than better, by the way an eyewitness prepares or is prepared for testimony.

Regardless of the precise explanation for poor confidence–accuracy correlations, we believe that there are many variables that affect eyewitness certainty that do not effect eyewitness accuracy (see Leippe, 1980). In actual cases it is common for an eyewitness to gain confidence-inflating information after identifying a suspect from a lineup. The eyewitness may learn, for example, that the suspect was found in possession of stolen goods that are linked to the case. Such information is bound to increase the eyewitness's certainty that he or she made an accurate identification, but, of course, such information does nothing to increase accuracy. Indeed, an eyewitness's subjective certainty is probably increased simply through the fact of their being subsequently called into court as a witness, because it is clear by that time that she or he must have identified the person suspected by the police. It has been demonstrated already that the use of leading questions (Loftus, Miller, & Burns, 1978), repeated questioning of the eyewitness (Hastie, Landsman, & Loftus, 1978), and eyewitness briefings (Wells et al., 1981) affect eyewitness certainty without corresponding effects on eyewitness accuracy. As Leippe (1980) noted, "as social influences increase, the correspondence of accuracy and confidence should decrease" and "as reconstructive [memory] processes become more extensive, the accuracy–confidence relationship should become ... smaller" (p. 264). We believe that the variables researched thus far are only the tip of a larger domain of variables that produce confidence shifts by eyewitnesses without altering the witnesses' accuracy and vice versa. The elusive presence and absence of these variables across eyewitness cases simply contribute to the noncorrespondence between confidence and accuracy.

Conclusions

An eyewitness's confidence in his or her identification of a perpetrator or in other forms of testimony is an intuitively appealing heuristic for ascribing accuracy to the eyewitness. Indeed, there is evidence that eyewitness confidence can be reliably and easily measured. Yet, the empirical evidence does not support the idea that eyewitness confidence is a valid measure of eyewitness accuracy under ecologically valid conditions. Although no single experiment is necessarily perfect, the studies as a whole faithfully represent the crucial elements of the hypothesis regarding the utility of eyewitness confidence for predicting eyewitness accuracy. Indeed, the closer the studies come to representing real-world factors (e.g., presence or absence of perpetrator in lineup, interactions of witness and attorney, realistically staged crime properties), the clearer the evidence becomes that eyewitness confidence is not useful as a predictor of eyewitness accuracy in actual criminal cases.

If eyewitness confidence is not meaningfully related to eyewitness accuracy, then has this not been noted by criminal justice persons over the many years in which they have been exposed to eyewitness testimony? That is, perhaps, a question that has too complex an answer to be addressed fully here. Still, three points seem worth noting at this time. First, not all people in the criminal justice system believe that eyewitness confidence is a meaningful cue to eyewitness accuracy. Many justices and lineup investigators show some reservations on this point. Indeed, a recent study by Brigham and Wolfskiel (1982) showed that older, more experienced police investigators were more likely to indicate that eyewitness certainty is poorly related to eyewitness accuracy than were their younger, less experienced counterparts. Second, a full set of data does not reach the court. Courts generally do not find out, for example, about eyewitnesses who identify with great confidence a police detective or some other known-innocent foil from a police lineup. That is, an eyewitness's false but certain testimony is often never given in court because it can be discounted for other reasons (e.g., an iron-clad alibi). Perhaps this is why police investigators who have conducted large numbers of lineups are more likely to see eyewitness confidence as poorly related to eyewitness accuracy than are other criminal justice personnel (Brigham & Wolfskiel, 1982). These same police investigators, however, are unlikely to belabor that important fact when the eyewitness happens to choose their suspect instead of choosing a foil. Finally, how is a trial judge to know that an eyewitness who was highly confident was wrong? In order to observe such occurrences in court there must be some persuasive exonerating evidence. If there were such evidence, however, the matter is most likely to have been resolved in precourt investigations by police. Thus, we see the trial judge as one who is neatly protected from learning that the confidence of an eyewitness bears no useful relationship to the accuracy of an eyewitness.

We agree with Deffenbacher (1980) and Leippe (1980) that the Court's recommendation regarding eyewitness certainty is in dire need of review.

Intuition regarding the certainty–accuracy link should not prevail in light of existing scientific data.

Notes

1 For example, opportunity to view the criminal is often defined in terms of the length of time that the criminal was in view. This kind of information must come from the witness, whereas research shows that witnesses consistently overestimate short temporal durations (e.g., Schiffman & Bobko, 1974). Also, the accuracy of a facial description has an ambiguous referent. One cannot actually measure the *accuracy* of a witness's description unless one knows that the accused is the original perpetrator. If the accused is innocent, then the match between the witness's prior description of the perpetrator and the accused is simply *agreement*. Thus, the court must presume that the accused is guilty in order to refer to the "accuracy" of the witness's prior description.

2 This is not the only possible criterion for judging the validity of eyewitness confidence. A prosecutor, for example, might want to know whether eyewitness confidence is a valid measure of jurors' willingness to believe the eyewitness. In this case, juror belief is the criterion.

3 Chance in a six-person lineup is not necessarily .16⅔ (i.e., 1 out of 6). One must consider several factors, including the prior probability that the suspect is guilty (see Wells & Lindsay, 1980), the number of suspects in the lineup, and the *functional* (cf. nominal) size of the lineup (e.g., Wells, Leippe, & Ostrom, 1979).

9   Hypnotically induced testimony

Martin T. Orne, David A. Soskis,
David F. Dinges, and Emily Carota Orne

The recollections and reports of victims and witnesses of crimes form the basis of most criminal investigation and subsequent courtroom testimony. Given the importance of remembered events within the criminal justice system, it is hardly surprising that law enforcement officials are eager to discover techniques that will increase the reliability and usefulness of victim and witness recollections. Thus, when hypnosis was introduced as a method to aid recall, it was enthusiastically adopted by many law enforcement officials and hailed as a major breakthrough in police investigation. The promise of hypnosis as a memory aid in forensic settings was heralded in large part by its use in a number of celebrated cases, such as the Chowchilla kidnapping and the Boston strangler case, where the technique served to provide information that led to incontrovertible physical evidence and facilitated apprehension of the individuals responsible for the crimes.

While this use of hypnosis – as a technique for increasing leads to physical evidence – has continued within the criminal justice system, problems have arisen in cases where sworn courtroom testimony was based solely on recall following hypnosis. Lacking physical proof to corroborate fully the vague, fragmented, inconsistent, or uncertain recollections of victims, witnesses,

This chapter is a modified version of a policy brief prepared for the National Institute of Justice. The review and evaluation upon which the substantive theoretical outlook presented in this chapter is based was supported in part by grant no. MH 19156 from the National Institute of Mental Health, U.S. Public Health Service, in part by grant no. 82-IJ-CX-0007 from the National Institute of Justice, U.S. Department of Justice, and in part by a grant from the Institute for Experimental Psychiatry. This work was conducted at the Unit for Experimental Psychiatry, the Institute of Pennsylvania Hospital, and the Department of Psychiatry, the University of Pennsylvania. We are especially grateful to Carole W. Soskis for her review of the legal cases, to Matthew H. Erdelyi for his substantive contributions, to Campbell Perry, Michael Barnes, Diane L. Dintruff, and Challenger A. Vought for their comments on an earlier version of this chapter, and to Mae C. Weglarski, Stephen R. Fairbrother, Mary Fleming Auxier, Barbara R. Barras, and Lani Pyles MacAniff for help in researching, formatting, and preparing the manuscript.

or even defendants, law enforcement officials have tended to use hypnosis to aid memory for testimony to the events in question. In the absence of corroborating evidence, however, this application of hypnosis focuses debate on whether the technique produces bona fide remembering of forgotten events or whether it alters memories – and therefore, evidence – in ways that undermine the effectiveness of cross-examination.

These issues have been the subject of considerable legal concern within the criminal justice system, and expert testimony based on forensic, clinical, and scientific evidence has been influential in this controversy. In recognition of these issues different approaches have been taken by different courts to testimony based upon hypnotically induced recall. Each legal approach has had a profound impact upon subsequent adjudications of the matter.

The major legal precedent for introducing hypnotically induced recall as testimony was set by the Maryland Special Court of Appeals in *Harding* v. *State* (1968). Acknowledging some potential problems, the court ruled that the witness may give "hypnotically refreshed" testimony to judge or jury. The legal approach taken in this case was that the difficulties that hypnosis might cause should go to the weight of the evidence and that the judge or jury as trier of fact was capable of making the ultimate decision. Following this favorable ruling, the forensic use of hypnosis increased dramatically, and a number of other courts ruled that witnesses' recollections "refreshed" by hypnosis could be presented to juries.

These rulings and the widespread forensic application of hypnosis that prompted them led to a reexamination of the reliability of hypnotically induced testimony. In 1980 the Minnesota Supreme Court ruled in *State* v. *Mack* (1980) that "hypnotically refreshed" recall was sufficiently unreliable that it must be excluded from testimony as a matter of law. This ruling was radically opposed to that of the earlier *Harding* v. *State* (1968) and its legal progeny, for it held that a witness who had been hypnotized to enhance recall could not be allowed to testify because the probative value of the testimony was less than the inherent risk of distorting recollections or of increasing the witness's confidence without increasing recall. Since the Minnesota ruling, a considerable number of state supreme courts that have ruled on the matter have taken similar positions.

Between the two extreme positions of Maryland (1968) and Minnesota (1980), a third legal approach to the problem has been taken by the New Jersey Supreme Court in *State* v. *Hurd* (1981). Here the court decided that "hypnotically refreshed" recall may be considered as testimony provided that certain procedural guidelines are followed. These guidelines or safeguards were intended to make it possible for independent experts to evaluate precisely what was done during a forensic application of hypnosis, in order to assess the likelihood of explicit or implicit suggestions altering the subject's recall and subsequent testimony. Rather than include or exclude all "hypnotically refreshed" testimony as a matter of law, the New Jersey decision relegated the issue to a case-by-case consideration based upon what specifically had been done.

The three legal approaches taken by the courts thus far highlight the basic scientific issues at the heart of the controversy concerning the forensic use of hypnosis. This chapter seeks to evaluate the empirical evidence relevant to the questions that have concerned the courts in this matter. These include the following:

1. The reliability of information obtained through hypnosis
2. Whether hypnosis increases the likelihood of pseudomemories
3. Whether hypnosis makes the individual's recollections more susceptible to alteration due to subtle cues or expectations
4. Who should carry out the hypnotic procedures
5. Whether hypnosis alters the certitude of what can be remembered, independent of the accuracy of memories
6. Whether one technique for recall in hypnosis is more or less effective than another in either enhancing or distorting recollections
7. Whether there are procedures that might increase the probative value of "hypnotically refreshed" recall relative to the risk of distorting memory
8. Whether a jury is likely to be unduly affected by knowing that testimony is based upon "hypnotically refreshed" recall

After considering the scientific data and its implications for the forensic use of hypnosis, we will review major legal decisions that have reflected the impact of expert testimony stemming from these data and will present expanded guidelines for the investigative use of hypnosis for "refreshing" memory. In this area particularly, the courts have looked to the scientific community to help clarify appropriate legal approaches to how and when hypnosis may or may not be used within the criminal justice system.

Aspects of hypnosis relevant to its forensic application

To clarify why concern has been expressed over the forensic use of hypnosis, we will briefly review what is known about hypnosis as a result of extensive experimental and clinical investigation of the phenomenon during the past 50 years and how this information relates to the forensic use of hypnosis to "refresh" memory.

Experience and critical judgment in hypnosis

Hypnosis is characterized by a subject's increased responsiveness to suggestions (Hull, 1933). Typically these suggestions involve the person's ability to experience alterations of perception, memory, or mood (Orne, 1977). Regardless of whether the phenomenon is conceptualized as an altered state of consciousness, believed-in imagining, role enactment, fantasy absorption, or focused attention, hypnosis is a real experience in the sense that the hypnotically responsive individual believes in it and is not merely acting as if he or she did.

By allowing the hypnotist to define what is to be experienced, the hypnotized individual forgoes evaluation both of the nature of the suggestion and his or her reaction to it. Given a suggestion that is acceptable within the hypnotic context, subjects will attempt to respond without concern for whether the suggestion is logical or meaningful. Their increased willingness to accept suggestions in hypnosis inevitably requires that for the time they suspend critical judgment.

Although nearly all individuals can voluntarily forgo some aspects of their reality orientation in an attempt to experience hypnosis, not all are equally capable of responding to hypnotic suggestions. The ability to experience suggestions is called hypnotizability and is a fairly stable attribute of the person (Morgan, Johnson, & Hilgard, 1974). Though hypnotizability varies considerably among individuals, it is not the same as acquiescence, gullibility, or neuroticism (Bowers, 1976).

Despite considerable theoretical controversy over whether hypnosis is a unique state and the role that social psychological factors play in accounting for its effects, there is general consensus that more highly hypnotizable individuals are profoundly affected by the hypnotic process. Further, even persons with only moderate hypnotizability also usually experience changes in their subjective response to hypnotic suggestions, as well as in their relationship with the hypnotist. For most individuals, therefore, hypnotic suggestions administered in a cooperative setting can be used to alter private experience in a manner that is uncritically accepted by the person. The use of hypnosis in forensic settings is no exception.

When hypnosis is used to "refresh" memory for events that might have been observed, it involves – implicitly or explicitly – the suggestion that this process will result in additional, accurate recollections. Regardless of how the suggestions of enhanced recall are phrased (e.g., watching the events on an imaginary television screen, or actually reliving the events), the subject will typically accept the hypnotically created recollections – accurate and inaccurate – as actual memories. This uncritical acceptance of the material brought forth during hypnosis, regardless of its veracity, is further affected by the hypnotized individual's expectations about the efficacy of hypnosis to aid memory, by a desire to please the hypnotist, and by the nature of the suggestions given to the subject.

Induction, expectations, and the nature of suggestions

Hypnosis is typically induced in the context of a voluntary social interaction. The hypnotist begins by establishing rapport (i.e., a trusting relationship with the subject), by discussing the purpose for using hypnosis in a given situation (e.g., to aid in recall of events), and by clarifying that it is the subject's wish to enter hypnosis. There are a large number of induction procedures, but most include instructing the individual to focus attention, to concentrate on the hypnotist's voice, to relax, and eventually to close the eyes and imagine what the hypnotist is suggesting.

The apparent trivial nature of the hypnotic induction juxtaposed with the dramatic effects subsequent suggestions can have upon some subjects' experiences has spawned much of the controversy surrounding hypnosis and its effects. Though hypnotic induction may serve to accentuate the response of hypnotizable individuals to certain hypnotic suggestions, it is not a necessary condition for these effects (Orne, 1980). Nevertheless, in practical applications of hypnosis, such as within the criminal justice system, it is heuristically useful to assume that hypnosis has taken place if a hypnotic procedure has been carried out with a cooperative subject who appears to respond to suggestions.[1]

Following the hypnotic induction, the subject's attention is intensely focused on the hypnotist, and there is an increased tendency to please the hypnotist and to comply with both explicit and implicit demands in the hypnotic context (Orne, 1962, 1981a). This cooperativeness and compliance is largely determined by the subject's expectations about hypnosis and its effects, as well as by the hypnotist's behavior.

Subjects inevitably bring with them to the hypnotic situation expectations and preconceptions about hypnosis. These vary greatly in their accuracy and generally reflect hypnosis as it is portrayed in films, novels, and the media. For example, in terms of the forensic use of hypnosis, we recently found that the vast majority (96%) of 167 college students surveyed believed that hypnosis could help a person remember things that were not remembered without it.

These prehypnosis beliefs can greatly enhance the impact of the hypnotic situation on the subject's willingness to produce the desired and expected effects (e.g., Zamansky, Scharf, & Brightbill, 1964). Further, the subject's beliefs or expectations can serve as an effective prehypnotic suggestion (see Alexander, 1971). That is, preconceptions about what will occur during hypnosis can produce specific hypnotic effects when the subject is hypnotized, without any additional suggestion at that time (see Orne, 1959). Thus, the hypnotic situation not only can bring about strong expectations that hypnosis will, for example, facilitate recall, but also may provide implicit suggestions that the recall in hypnosis must somehow be different (i.e., more accurate or more certain) than nonhypnotic recall. In an effort to comply with this prehypnotic suggestion, the hypnotized individual may alter his or her recall in ways that seem consistent with the suggestion. These changes may or may not involve increases in accurate information.

Implicit suggestions and unwitting cues that direct the subject's response and experience during the session can also occur within the hypnotic interaction (Orne, 1981a). Subjects in the hypnotic situation feel relaxed and less responsible for what they say because they believe that the hypnotist is an expert and somehow in control. The hypnotist in turn makes certain that subjects cannot "fail." Hypnotic technique involves the extensive use of reinforcers through frequent verbalizations, such as, "Good," "Fine," "You are doing well," and so on, which are both satisfying and reassuring to the subject. Not surprisingly, subjects want to maintain this level of approbation; consequently, when the hypnotist stops the expressions of approval (simply by not saying "Good"), he or she clearly communicates that something else or something more is wanted. It requires only a modest decrease in the level of support to alter subjects' behavior, after which there is a return to the previous frequent level of reassurance. Similarly, once a series of details is reported by the subject and accepted as valid by the hypnotist, that very fact can serve to persuade the subject to accept these "recollections" as accurate – memories that might previously have been extremely tentative and about which the subject had little or no subjective conviction, or memories that might have been created during hypnosis.

Moreover, in the relaxed context of hypnosis, subjects are generally less anxious and less critical, allowing themselves to say things about which they are uncertain – information that would not be forthcoming in contexts where the subjects are made to feel responsible for their memories and challenged about their consistency. Thus, the hypnotic situation itself may serve to increase the amount of information – both accurate and inaccurate – produced by the subject.

Finally, posthypnotic suggestions given during hypnosis can influence a subject's response following hypnosis. Implicit posthypnotic suggestions can be as effective as, or even more effective than, explicit posthypnotic suggestions. For example, if a hypnotist suggests to a subject that he or she will relive the events in question, and the subject appears to do so, the hypnotist may say prior to the subject's awakening that he or she will later recall everything that has happened, including the event in question – thus implicitly giving a posthypnotic suggestion that what the subject relived is what actually happened and will subsequently be remembered as such. These effects are likely to persist after the hypnotic intervention, regardless of the veracity of the information reported, and the subject may be unaware of the source of the recollection when he or she later recalls or testifies about the event in question.

Lying and simulation versus fantasy and confabulation

The views widely held by a substantial portion of the public (and fostered by fiction writers) that deeply hypnotized individuals will commit acts that they would not commit in other circumstances, that they will be compelled to tell the truth in hypnosis, and that hypnosis cannot be faked, are simply not consistent with scientific evidence. Though the effects of hypnosis on experience can be dramatic, the process is generally not effective for control or modification of voluntary behavior (see Wadden & Anderton, 1982, for a review). Regardless of ability to respond to suggestions, subjects can resist specific suggestions if they choose to do so (cf. Erickson, 1939). It is not surprising, therefore, that an individual can purposively lie even though deeply hypnotized, especially when this would serve the individual's interest (Orne, 1961).

Though possible, conscious lies in hypnosis are rarely a major problem. Because the hypnotic procedure often involves encouraging the subject to experience suggested alterations of perception, memory, or mood, the hypnotized individual may honestly report these distortions or hallucinations as real. For example, a hypnotized subject given a suggestion that a white wall is actually blue will report seeing a blue wall. This is not a lie in the sense of purposeful deception but, rather, can be an honest report of a distorted perception.

Similarly, if during hypnosis, an individual is asked to "look at" an event 100 yards away using hallucinated binoculars he or she may describe in detail the pattern on the necktie of a participant in that event, despite the fact that such a "perception" exceeds the limits of visual acuity. Needless to say, the pattern may have nothing to do with the individual's necktie unless the hypnotized person had an opportunity to see it previously. Without prior information of such details, the hypnotized subject will nonetheless respond to the suggestion to observe with binoculars by hallucinating or imagining details of the event. This kind of filling in or fantasizing of information that seems plausible is called confabulation.

A pseudoperception of this sort will tend to be accepted by the hypnotized subject as a factually accurate perception if, as previously noted, there are explicit or implicit demands in the hypnotic situation that suggest it should be accepted as accurate. Analogous distortions when remembering events, and confusions between fact and fantasy in reporting the events, may occur for hypnotized subjects.

A problem rarely encountered in clinical practice but potentially highly significant in some forensic contexts involves the ability of individuals to fake being hypnotized. Contrary to popular assumption, it is possible for untrained, naive subjects to simulate hypnosis and fool even a very experienced hypnotist by behaving in ways that they think a hypnotized subject would behave and by complying with what they think the hypnotist wants (Orne, 1971). Because purposive simulation poses no significant problem in clinical practice with hypnosis, some clinicians are convinced that they could easily identify a subject feigning being hypnotized. Simulation has, however, been extensively researched (see Sheehan & Perry, 1976), and the evidence clearly indicates that without specially designed procedures, blind observation over time, and subsequent feedback as to real or simulating status, highly trained clinicians and researchers cannot accurately identify individuals who are feigning hypnosis (see Orne, 1977). Simulation is a real problem in forensic uses of hypnosis, particularly with a defendant, where there is a vested interest in persuading the authorities to accept one's version of the events in question (see Orne, 1981b; Orne, Dinges, & Orne, in press).

In summary, hypnosis involves a capacity to experience suggested changes in perception, memory, or mood. Beyond this, however, expectation and the hypnotic situation also contribute importantly to the nature of these experiential changes and the manner in which they are expressed. It is difficult to distinguish between the bona fide effects of hypnosis on experience and thought processes and the desire of the subject to provide responses consistent with explicit or implicit suggestions about what is wanted. Moreover, a subject can fantasize, hallucinate, and confabulate with conviction in hypnosis. It is also possible to lie purposively, or even feign hypnotic behavior, without the hypnotist's awareness. Acknowledgment of these problems would seem an essential prerequisite to the use of hypnosis in any applied area, but especially in its use within the criminal justice system as a means of "refreshing" recall that later forms the basis of courtroom testimony. Whether or not hypnosis should be applied at all within the forensic arena, however, depends upon what is known about its effectiveness as an aid to memory.

The effects of hypnosis on memory, belief, and certitude

Though claims for the forensic use of hypnosis in law enforcement were made by Bryan (1962) and by Arons (1967) approximately 20 years ago, application of the technique has increased sharply during the past decade, owing to the establishment of a number of training programs for police officers (see Hibbard & Worring, 1981; Reiser, 1980). During this time, survey and field studies of criminal cases in which hypnosis was used have been reported in an effort to document the effectiveness of the technique (Block, 1976; Kroger & Doucé, 1979; Reiser, 1976; Schafer & Rubio, 1978; Stratton, 1977). These reports consistently claim that hypnosis helped to provide new information or valuable leads in 60% to 90% of the cases in which it was employed.

Such figures make it easy to understand why there would be considerable enthusiasm for using hypnosis to aid memory in criminal investigations. These figures, however, do not pertain to the accuracy of recall elicited during hypnosis. Rather, as Timm (1982) has noted, "These field studies are more a reflection of the benefits perceived by those administering the procedure than a more objective evaluation requiring documented corroboration of these new leads" (p. 3). Further, though such reports suggest that hypnosis may be helpful for investigative purposes, they do not deal with the more problematic issues at the heart of introducing "hypnotically refreshed" recall as testimony – where inaccuracies can have far more serious consequences than in the investigative stage of the criminal justice process.

In order to consider the question of hypnotically induced memory as testimony in court, critical evidence is needed on the extent to which hypnosis facilitates recall of accurate (more than inaccurate) information, on the degree to which individuals can be biased or influenced when recalling in hypnosis, and on the effects of hypnosis on confidence of recall versus accuracy of recall. Such data have begun to appear in the scientific literature, especially in the past decade. Prior to this work, however, there was a long history within psychiatry of using hypnosis to aid recall for emotionally charged memories. Much has been learned from this endeavor, and an examination of empirical evidence begins here, because hypnosis is often believed to be uniquely suited to facilitate recall of traumatic or emotionally blocked events (e.g., Dorcus, 1960; MacHovec, 1981).

Hypnotic age regression and recall of traumatic events

In the late 19th century, Sigmund Freud, working with Josef Breuer, used hypnosis to help adult patients suffering from psychological symptoms relive traumatic childhood events that were related to these symptoms (Breuer & Freud, 1895/1955). During this work Freud observed several compelling phenomena that lent credence to the presumed historical accuracy of the events "remembered" in hypnosis. First, in hypnotic age regression, patients often experienced extremely powerful emotional reactions while reliving the traumatic childhood event. Second, they often spontaneously reported minute details, such as scratches on furniture or defects in the wall covering, which gave the appearance of being accessible only to a person who had actually experienced the event. Finally, patients often achieved dramatic relief of their symptoms after the reliving in hypnosis of experiences relevant to the symptoms.

Freud used these observations, gathered during the development and application of the cathartic technique, to formulate his early theories concerning the sexual etiology of hysteria. He eventually realized, however, that much of what was relived or "remembered" in the treatment reflected the patient's sexual feelings and fantasies without necessarily being historically accurate (cf. Freud, 1905/1953, p. 274). Often the "recalled" traumatic episode involved confabulation – actual events combined with fantasies.

The development of psychoanalysis by Freud took into account the lack of historical accuracy for these "recalled" traumas (see Ellenberger, 1970), and hypnotic age regression continued to be used (though not by Freud) to aid in the recollection of emotionally charged events, such as wartime traumatic neuroses arising from combat experiences (see Kolb, 1982). This use of hypnosis by therapists was concerned only with helping the patient gain relief from a psychological symptom. Whether aspects of the "remembered" traumatic event were truth, fantasy, or confabulation, the "recollection" was accepted as valid within the treatment context if the patient improved following the emotional reexperiencing of the event.

Given this orientation, much of the research on hypnotic age regression has been directed at the extent to which age-regressed individuals actually relived earlier stages of development and both psychologically and physiologically responded as though they were regressed to an earlier age. Efforts were made to show that subjects who age regressed to 6 months of age displayed the kind of positive Babinski sign typically seen in neonates (Gidro-Frank & Bowers-Buch, 1948). The assertion was also made that age regression resulted in a functional ablation of memories subsequent to the suggested age (Spiegel, Shor, & Fischman, 1945). In addition to these rather exotic claims, there were some anecdotal efforts to show that age regression led to accurate recall of the events relived (e.g., Young, 1926). More systematic studies of these issues, however, failed to support either the neurophysiological claims (cf. McCranie, Crasilneck, & Teter, 1955), or the assertions concerning childlike functioning in age regression (cf. Orne, 1951; Young, 1940).

In the early 1960s, critical reviews of the empirical work concerning the issue of reliving versus role playing and that of increased recall versus confabulation concluded that the evidence for reliving, or for more accurately remembering, events in hypnotic age regression was scant at best (see Barber, 1962; Gebhard, 1961; Yates, 1961). Similarly, a more recent, careful replication and extension by O'Connell, Shor, and Orne (1970) of one of the key studies that reported positive findings (Reiff & Scheerer, 1959) discovered that many of the positive results were due to unwitting experimenter bias; more important, no evidence was found of bona fide hypnotic hypermnesia (memory enhancement) when appropriate experimental controls were instituted (see also Cohen, 1972). Instead, as Freud had observed with recall of traumatic childhood events, the modest increase in recall during hypnotic age regression to childhood was accompanied by increased confabulation.[2]

Thus, in reviewing the hypnotic age-regression studies, we have concluded the following:

The hypnotic suggestion to relive a past event, particularly when accompanied by questions about specific details, puts pressure on the subject to provide information for which few, if any, actual memories are available. This situation may jog the subject's memory and produce some increased recall, but it will also cause the subject to fill in details that are plausible but consist of memories or fantasies from other times. It is extremely difficult to know which aspects of hypnotically aided recall are historically accurate and which aspects have been confabulated. The details of material that is confabulated depend upon the subject's total past experience and all available cues relevant to the hypnotic task. Subjects will use prior information and cues in an inconsistent and unpredictable fashion; in some instances such information is incorporated in what is confabulated, while in others the hypnotic recall may be virtually unaffected. (Orne, 1981b, p. 72)

It is not possible here to review the extensive literature on age regression or to discuss how the observation of apparent physiological changes during age regression is misleading (see Barber, 1962). It would seem useful, however, to consider a particularly ingenious study that appears to document a profound increase in recall with hypnotic age regression.

True (1949) found that subjects who were age regressed to their 10th birthday accurately reported the day of the week in 93% of the cases. When age regressed to their 7th birthday, subjects were 82% accurate, and when age regressed to their 4th birthday, they were still 69% accurate. Because almost no one can recall, without hypnosis, the day of the week of even their 10th birthday, this appeared to be a simple and compelling demonstration of hypnotic hypermnesia. When several laboratories tried to replicate the finding, however, they were unable to do so.

When Dr. True was asked why there was difficulty in replicating the result, he explained that *Science* (the journal that published the paper) had deleted a crucial part of the procedure; that is, one does not ask the day of the week, but rather, "Was it Monday? Was it Tuesday? Was it Wednesday?" (see O'Connell et al., 1970, p. 2). The subject stops the investigator on a particular day. True (1962) acknowledged that a perpetual calendar was available to the investigator during the procedure.

In our view, True's (1949) findings can best be understood as the consequence of unwitting bias that communicated the correct answer to the hypnotized subject. It may seem presumptuous to draw such a conclusion, because it could be argued that True was a more effective hypnotist, or had better subjects, or for some other reason could elicit a phenomenon that eluded other investigators. Fortunately, independent evidence is available on this point; specifically, in the O'Connell et al. (1970) study that used actual 4-year-olds as a control group, none of the 10 children was able to identify the day of the week. Because bright 4-year-old children do not know the day of the week, the 69% accuracy report found by True (1949) for adults hypnotically regressed to this age cannot be explained as a recollection.

It would appear that hypnotic age regression for the purpose of reinstating full and accurate recall of either traumatic or nontraumatic events from childhood is not reliably effective, despite its compelling appearance. Though there is no reason to assume that the process of hypnotic age regression to childhood is any different from that involved in regression to a year or a month ago, it is worth reviewing the few studies concerning the effect of hypnosis on recall of relatively recent, emotionally charged events.

Investigators have attempted to vary the emotional arousal of subjects when observing stimuli or an event, and then (a few minutes, hours, or days later) test for increased recall with hypnosis. In these studies, emphasis was placed on encouraging relaxation and calmness – to overcome the memory blocking that may have resulted from the emotional nature of the situation. Though the initial investigation by Rosenthal (1944) found that hypnosis improved recall (beyond nonhypnotic recall) of material learned in an anxious state, more recent studies using recognition and/or recall have not confirmed this finding (Burch, 1974; DePiano & Salzberg, 1981; Helwig, 1978; Shaul, 1978).

Given the paucity of studies and the differences among them in the manner in which arousal or emotionality was manipulated and verified, it is not possible to draw any firm conclusions regarding the efficacy of hypnotic age regression for aiding recall of *recently* witnessed traumatic events, though initial impressions are negative. More work is needed, however, to determine whether hypnosis can overcome the effect of circumstances that block recall, as well as to evaluate different techniques that might be useful for this purpose.

Hypnosis to improve memory for verifiable facts

Perhaps the most fundamental issue underlying the controversy surrounding hypnotically induced recall in the criminal justice system is the extent to which hypnosis can serve to improve memory over and above that possible from attempting to remember without the aid of hypnosis. The basic question concerning the existence of hypnotic hypermnesia has been the focus of some two dozen scientific experiments during the past 50 years. Although space does not permit critical review of each of these studies, the general conclusions as well as conceptual limitations will be discussed.

Despite considerable variation in methodological sophistication, these studies have a number of characteristics in common: (a) hypnotic recall is compared with nonhypnotic (wake) recall for information originally observed any time from a few minutes to a few weeks earlier in a nonhypnotic state; (b) stimulus materials are not emotionally charged and are well controlled and verifiable so that there is no doubt about documenting the accuracy of recall; and (c) recall results are quantified and statistically analyzed to avoid impressionistic conclusions.

There are differences among the studies in critical areas such as experimental design, aspects of the treatment condition, assessment and makeup of subject groups, and type of stimulus materials used. Nevertheless, there is a remarkable consistency – emphasized by Weitzenhoffer (1955) and also noted by other researchers – in the results of these investigations when they are separated according to the meaningfulness of the material to be recalled. Thus, if the material to be remembered is not particularly meaningful, hypnosis does not aid recall beyond normal nonhypnotic recall levels. But if the to-be-remembered material is contextually meaningful, hypnosis appears to provide a way of obtaining increased recall performance, at least from some individuals in some situations.

More than 40 years ago, White, Fox, and Harris (1940) found that hypnosis improved the recall of contextually meaningful material, such as pictures and poetry, beyond nonhypnotic remembering but had no differential impact on nonsense syllables. Shortly thereafter, Rosenthal (1944) published a similar result; and more recently Dhanens and Lundy (1975) observed the same differential effect for biographical prose passages compared with nonsense syllables.[3]

In fact, nearly every study that has used nonsense syllables as memory stimuli has reported no effect from a hypnotic intervention (Barber & Calverley, 1966; Dhanens, 1973; Eysenck, 1941; Huse, 1930; Mitchell, 1932; Rosenhan & London, 1963). Similar negative results have been reported for stimuli comprised of single or paired words that were not meaningfully connected (Das, 1961; Rosenthal, 1944; Salzberg & DePiano, 1980; Young, 1925). The few exceptions to these negative results come from Rosenthal (1944) for words learned under stress (discussed earlier) and from Augustynek (1978, 1979), who reported that hypnosis improved recall of all types of material, ranging from nonsense words to complex passages from textbooks.

In contrast to the lack of evidence for hypnotic hypermnesia for nonsense materials and contextually nonmeaningful word lists, and consistent with the observations of White et al. (1940), Rosenthal (1944), and Dhanens and Lundy (1975), most studies that have used contextually meaningful stimulus materials (e.g., poems, pictures, stories, films) have observed an apparently significant degree of improvement in recall aided by hypnosis (DePiano & Salzberg, 1981; Gheorghiu, 1972; Hagedorn, 1970; Sears, 1954; Stager, 1974; Stalnaker & Riddle, 1932). However, not every study of meaningful materials has found positive results, particularly when hypnosis was tested against instructions for increased motivation (cf. Cohen, 1972; Cooper & London, 1973; Shaul, 1978; Wall & Lieberman, 1976). Furthermore, in experiments where hypnosis was compared with motivating instructions and found to be more effective, the results were confined to hypnotizable individuals (cf. Dhanens & Lundy, 1975; Stager, 1974).

More problematic than the possibility that motivational variables account for some of the positive effects of hypnosis are negative results from recent investigations of hypnotic hypermnesia for simulated accidents or mock crimes. Though Griffin (1980) reported that hypnosis substantially improved accurate remembering of witnessed mock crimes, other, better-controlled experiments on remembering of witnessed accidents (Putnam, 1979; Sturm, 1982; Zelig & Beidleman, 1981), of witnessed mock crimes (McEwan & Yuille, 1982; Sheehan & Tilden, 1983; Timm, 1981), of facial recognition (Wagstaff, 1982a; Wagstaff, Traverse, & Milner, 1982), and of victim-reported mock crimes (Timm, 1982) have not supported this view.[4]

The lack of demonstrated hypnotic hypermnesia in these simulated crime or accident studies cannot be due to the stimulus materials, because these were clearly meaningful. One possible explanation for the lack of effect is the manner in which memory was measured in the studies that used accident or mock crime scenarios. In nearly all cases where a negative result was obtained, the format for remembering was structured in some way, rather than permitting an open-ended free recall. This type of structuring or putting even mild pressure on the subject to remember details of an event was also done in much of the hypnotic age-regression research, where increased confabulation rather than hypermnesia was found.[5] Thus, whatever benefits for more accurate recall can be gained with the use of hypnosis, they are apparently lost when the manner in which the subject is required to respond is structured to meet the needs of the interviewer.

On the other hand, the use of a free narrative recall in hypnosis is not without potential problems with regard to assessing the extent to which hypnosis genuinely increases the ability to remember. In the studies already cited, when free narrative recall was used to document hypnotic hypermnesia, the emphasis was typically only on recall of accurate information. In the Stalnaker and Riddle (1932) study with poetry and prose, for example, conclusions supporting hypnotic hypermnesia were based on the amount of accurate information remembered with no regard for potential increases in inaccurate information. Yet they noted that subjects in their study appeared to produce more recalled information when hypnotized than when not hypnotized.

Clearly, if subjects are more productive when hypnotized, the fact that they show some increase in accurate information recalled does not necessarily mean that an enhancement of memory has occurred. Rather, it may well be that subjects' reduced critical judgment in hypnosis results in their willingness to report more things about the to-be-remembered event – items that they would normally reject as too uncertain to report – and this results in an increase in *both* accurate and inaccurate information. Such increases are likely to be the result of changes in the subject's report criterion – specifically, a shift to a laxer criterion in hypnosis.

This issue has been recognized and techniques have been devised to control for it in studies of waking (nonhypnotic) hypermnesia (cf. Erdelyi, 1970; Erdelyi & Kleinbard, 1978), the solution to the problem being based upon the application of the Signal Detection Theory (Green & Swets, 1966). The problem has yet to be adequately dealt with, however, in hypnotic hypermnesia studies, particularly those using free recall or probed recall formats (see Klatzky & Erdelyi, 1983). Though recent investigations of hypnotic hypermnesia have evaluated both accurate and inaccurate recall, as well as total recall, response criterion shifts have not been either adequately measured or controlled. As Klatzky and Erdelyi (1983) have recently emphasized, the use of a measure such as the ratio of accurate to inaccurate information has intuitive appeal but does not satisfactorily address the problem of response criterion shifts versus a true increase in memory accuracy, because the significance of the ratio is different depending upon changes in productivity.

An important aspect of false recollections is that they are often experienced not as guesses but, rather, as contextually appropriate and meaningful memories. The individual may remember some fragments and create plausible details that fill in the gaps in the narrative. This filling in of the gaps is confabulation. This is a particularly troublesome problem with "hypnotically refreshed" recall, already observed and commented upon by Stalnaker and Riddle (1932). Though they reported that during hypnosis there was a modest increase in accurate recall of poetry originally learned in childhood, the actual amount of improvement was far less extensive than it appeared. Because in hypnosis subjects filled in the gaps with plausible though incorrect poetry segments, it seemed as though they were "remembering" a great deal more. For example, one of the subjects of Stalnaker and Riddle (1932) was unable to recall in the wake state the second stanza of Longfellow's *The Village Blacksmith*. When hypnotized, this subject "recalled" the following as the second stanza:

> The smithy whistles at his forge
> As he shapes the iron band;
> The smith is very happy
> As he owes not any man.

The actual second stanza is as follows:

> His hair is crisp, and black, and long,
>   His face is like the tan:
> His brow is wet with honest sweat,
>   He earns what e'er he can,
> And looks the whole world in the face,
>   For he owes not any man.

Although the last line remembered by the subject is nearly correct, the first three lines are not only incorrect but do not resemble any other lines in the poem. Nevertheless, without the actual poem for comparison, these three lines, confabulated in hypnosis, sound quite plausible. In the absence of verification the observer as well as the subject might readily have accepted the entire stanza as accurate.

In this case hypnosis resulted in the subject's reporting some additional accurate information that was not previously offered. Hypnosis also resulted, however, in the subject's confabulating a good deal more inaccurate information. There is no evidence that either subject or observer can distinguish between accurate recollection and such pseudomemories unless the facts can be verified. In life situations, where the material to be remembered is *not* known, there is a tendency to accept plausible recollections as veridical. Furthermore, if one is able to verify a portion of these recollections (such as the last line of the stanza), there is a tendency to uncritically infer that the entire memory report has been verified and is accurate. Thus, the problem is not merely the inaccuracy of the confabulations, but the fact that these are likely to be accepted as accurate by the hypnotized individual. Other such examples of confabulation of details in hypnosis during a free narrative recall have been mentioned in the age regression literature, and Timm (1981) presents an illustration of confabulated details "recalled" in hypnosis by a victim of a mock crime.

Though confabulation has been recognized as an important aspect that requires assessment in hypnotic hypermnesia studies, the broader problem of control or assessment of response criterion shifts has not been, as we noted earlier, adequately dealt with. Only very recently have investigators taken note of this problem and begun to apply the techniques to control it developed in waking hypermnesia studies. The only study, thus far, that attempted to compare waking hypermnesia procedures with the effect of hypnosis, using contextually meaningful material, was reported by Dywan and Bowers (1983). Using a form of the forced recall technique intended to control for response criterion shifts (Erdelyi & Kleinbard, 1978), they found that the hypnotic condition modestly increased accurate recall *but* also produced a much greater increase in inaccurate recall. Both of these increases were greater than those observed for nonhypnotic (task-motivated) remembering, especially for the more hypnotizable subjects.[6]

The implication of the Dywan and Bowers (1983) study is that hypnosis produces a response criterion shift and not an actual increase in memory. There is another study of hypnotic hypermnesia where the procedure introduced controls for productivity. Stager and Lundy (in press; see also Stager, 1974) used a probed recall procedure in order to elicit remembering of specific details from a film that subjects had viewed. They compared highly hypnotizable and low hypnotizable subjects both with and without hypnosis. They found an increase in correct recall in the highly hypnotizable subjects who were hypnotized, and no such increase in either highly hypnotizable subjects who were not hypnotized or low hypnotizable subjects (with and without hypnosis). In contrast to all other studies, however, they observed a concomitant decrease in errors for highly hypnotizable subjects who were hypnotized.

This study provides by far the strongest empirical evidence to date for true hypnotic hypermnesia. The nature of the probed recall format used in the investigation may, however, be crucial to an understanding of these findings. Unlike other experiments on hypnotic hypermnesia, the probed recall format not only assured a highly structured response set, but also provided extensive and accurate information about the circumstances to which the subject was required to add an additional detail. The positive findings for hypnotic hypermnesia that they noted were obtained by asking such questions as:

Immediately after the title of the film was shown, a young man carrying some books was shown walking along in front of several billboards. What was the *color* of his sports jacket? A few seconds later another figure was shown walking hurriedly down the street. Can you describe her? (Stager, 1974, p. 94)

Thus, the results of this study raise the intriguing possibility that hypnosis may have a differential effect on recall specifically in situations where extensive and accurate retrieval cues are provided. Unfortunately, from a practical perspective, it limits generalizability of the results, because numerous accurate retrieval cues are rarely if ever available in the real world.

In considering the question of increased recall due to hypnosis, several studies compare hypnosis with either task-motivated instructions (Barber & Calverley, 1962) or with other cognitive strategies designed to enhance recall. In these investigations, groups are typically matched in hypnotizability and receive instructions for the same cognitive strategy, the difference being that one group receives a short hypnotic induction prior to recall instructions whereas the other receives no formal induction. Recall results usually show little or no difference between the groups. In these experiments, however, subjects have typically been pretested for hypnotizability, realize that the experiment involves hypnosis, and are requested to use imagery and cognitive processes that are characteristic of hypnosis. Consequently, it is not always clear that hypnosis is being compared with no hypnosis in such paradigms. Both conditions may involve hypnosis, particularly for hypnotizable individuals.

More important from the standpoint of the forensic use of hypnosis to aid memory are the recall results when the hypnosis group and task-motivated or cognitive strategy group are compared with a no-treatment control group. For example, Shaul (1978) reports 86% correct recall when hypnotic induction and cognitive strategy are combined, 81% accurate recall with the cognitive strategy without hypnotic induction, and 71% correct recall in the no-treatment control group – differences that are statistically significant. It is problematic, however, to extrapolate these findings to a life situation, because the results are likely to be due to factors in the experimental situation other than hypnosis or recall strategy – factors concerned with what the experimenter expects to happen, and what he or she knows about the information to be remembered.

Subjects are not only generally responsive to subtle cues and beliefs of an experimenter (Orne, 1962), but this responsiveness is greatly heightened by hypnosis and hypnotic-like contexts. These subtle cues and beliefs may readily appear in the "recollections" of subjects in memory experiments that involve hypnosis. In Shaul's (1978) study, for example, the hypnotist-experimenter was aware of which stimulus film the subject witnessed, and the specific recollections that would be scored as accurate, as well as the group to which the subject was assigned. Consequently, it is not possible with such a design to disentangle the effects of hypnosis, cognitive strategy, and experimenter expectancy. What appears to be increased recall may well be an experimenter expectancy effect (Rosenthal, 1966). In a life situation, where truth is not known by the hypnotist, his or her assumptions about what occurred are not necessarily accurate, but these assumptions or beliefs will comprise the expectancies that may influence the subject's recall. These biasing difficulties will be discussed later.

In conclusion, there is some evidence that hypnosis may aid recall of accurate, meaningful information over and above nonhypnotic recall. This increase may or may not also include a concomitant increase in inaccurate information being reported. The extant evidence suggests that hypnosis does not help improve a subject's *recognition* memory for past events, whereas *recall* formats appear to increase the likelihood of apparent hypnotic hypermnesia.

Only two very recent studies (with opposite findings) have attempted the critical control of response productivity that is necessary for meaningful conclusions concerning the nature of hypnotic hypermnesia. Regardless of how the recall procedure is structured, however, when subjects are pressured to provide information, hypnosis increases the likelihood of confabulation.

The influence of subtle cues on hypnotic recall

The potentially positive gain (more correct recalls) as well as the negative consequences (confabulation or false alarms) of asking persons to remember events appear to be greater and occur more rapidly when recall is in hypnosis. This is likely due to the increased suggestibility, relaxation, cooperativeness, and lowered critical judgment of hypnotized subjects. All of these factors can serve to increase the desire of the hypnotized individual to provide what is wanted. This type of cooperativeness is especially troublesome when, in a forensic situation, the interviewer conveys (wittingly or unwittingly) a bias to the hypnotized individual concerning the events to be recalled.

Because an individual is typically more compliant in accepting suggestions from a hypnotist, less critical of the nature of suggestions, and more responsive to experiencing suggested events in hypnosis, the person is also likely to be cued or led by what the hypnotist wants. Even very subtle communications from the hypnotist can influence the subject without either the subject's or the hypnotist's being aware that this is happening (Orne, 1981a).

Of course, inadvertent influencing or biasing of the recollections of an individual who is attempting to report an event accurately can occur even without hypnosis, particularly when the interviewer wants the witness to comment upon specific details of the event (see Hilgard & Loftus, 1979; Loftus, 1979). A critical question concerning the use of hypnosis, however, is the extent to which the process significantly *increases* the impact of biasing procedures on the memories reported by the subject.

Putnam (1979) reported the first systematic investigation of this issue. After viewing a mock accident, his subjects were questioned about details of the event; half were interviewed in hypnosis and half in the wake state. All subjects received 6 of 15 questions in a leading format, designed to suggest a specific answer (cf. Loftus, 1975).[7] Hypnotized subjects were found not to be more accurate or more inaccurate than nonhypnotized subjects in their answers to nonleading questions (i.e., no evidence for hypnotic hypermnesia). Hypnotized subjects, however, made significantly more errors on leading questions, in the sense that they were more likely to accept (and later, in the wake state, report as memories) inaccurate information conveyed through leading questions. Thus, hypnosis served to increase substantially the witness's responsiveness to inaccurate information conveyed through subtle cues.

Zelig and Beidleman (1981) attempted a replication of this finding using a more emotionally involving accident as a stimulus. Their results were virtually identical to those of Putnam (1979). Though there were no differences between hypnotic and nonhypnotic reports of accurate or inaccurate information requested with nonleading questions, hypnosis resulted in significantly more errors when leading questions were used.

In criticizing the Putnam (1979) study, Reiser (1979) argued that in real-life situations trained investigators avoid leading questions, and thus such studies are not relevant to the forensic use of hypnosis. Although law enforcement officials avoid obvious leading questions, it is extremely difficult and perhaps impossible to avoid all leading questions in actual practice. For example, the question, "Was the man behind, in front, to the left, or to the right of the blue car?" would be appropriate only if there was a man and there was a blue car. It would be better, therefore, to ask, "Was the person behind, in front, to the left, or to the right of the car?" This still assumes, however, that there was a car. Perhaps it was a jeep or a light truck. It is, therefore, better to ask, "Was the person behind, in front, to the left, or to the right of the vehicle?" Even this question assumes that there was a person and a vehicle. If either of these was not involved, what sounds like a very objective question is in fact a leading question insofar as it implies an inaccurate answer. In other words, it is not possible to determine whether a question is leading without knowing the accurate facts in advance – a circumstance that rarely if ever obtains in the real world.

Very recently, another study was reported on the potential of hypnosis for increasing the effect of bias on memory reports using the leading question technique (Sheehan & Tilden, 1983). This investigation involved primarily recognition memory. In contrast to the results from the studies of Putnam (1979) and of Zelig and Beidleman (1981), hypnosis did not yield increased acceptance (above nonhypnotic recall) of inaccurate information conveyed through leading questions for recognition memory. There was, however, a profound effect of hypnosis on individuals' confidence in their recollections and certitude about the veridicality of what they reported – the procedure made witnesses more confident and certain of their memories without actually helping them remember.

Although a study by Sturm (1982) also included some leading questions, she reported no differential negative effects of hypnosis on either susceptibility to leading questions or on confidence. She also observed no increase in accurate information with hypnosis. The reason for her partially discrepant findings remains to be clarified.

Quite a different kind of biasing effect brought about by hypnosis was demonstrated in a recent study by Laurence (1982; see also Laurence & Perry, in press). As part of a larger investigation, he determined that subjects had slept through a particular night, and then during hypnosis had them relive the night in question. As the deeply hypnotized subject relived being asleep, he or she was told by the hypnotist that it was early in the morning and then was asked whether he or she heard some loud noises. Many hypnotized subjects accepted the suggestion inherent in this leading question, and reported hearing noises (such as a car backfiring), and being awakened by them. Subsequently, subjects were told to remember all that had happened. Interestingly, approximately half of the subjects later reported, in the wake state, that they awoke on the night in question, early in the morning, because of some loud noises. "Even when they were told, during debriefing, that the hypnotist had actually suggested the noises to them during hypnosis, these subjects still maintained that the noises had actually occurred" (Laurence & Perry, in press, p. 5). Thus, the memories created by the leading question in hypnosis were experienced as if they were preexisting recollections that were unrelated to the hypnotic experience.

Though further research is needed, it is likely that additional work in this area will continue to demonstrate that hypnosis increases a subject's responsiveness to subtle bias and influence beyond that found in the waking state. It will be important to delineate the numerous ways in which the hypnotist's beliefs, particularly those not intentionally communicated, impact upon the

hypnotized individual's subsequent memory. Finally, perhaps most disturb-
ing in the increased tendency of hypnotized subjects to be influenced or
biased is not the potential for increased inaccurate remembrances but,
rather, the extent to which memories created during hypnosis are confounded with earlier recollections and the extent to which hypnosis
increases the subject's conviction that his or her memories – regardless of
their accuracy or source – are reliable.

Changes in confidence and credibility due to hypnosis

The degree to which a witness or victim feels confident about remembered
details of an event is crucial for testimony in court but less important for
investigative purposes, especially when corroborating physical evidence can
be found. In court the confidence an accuser or witness places in his or her
recollections bears directly upon the extent to which the individual can withstand cross-examination and upon his or her perceived credibility.

Very few investigations of hypnotic hypermnesia have required confidence
or certitude ratings from subjects concerning details of their recollections.
Fortunately, ratings were obtained in most of the studies using simulated
accidents or mock crimes as memory stimuli, and the results are generally
consistent.

Sheehan and Tilden (1983) and Dywan (1983) found that the confidence
that subjects placed in their memories, as well as the degree to which they
were certain that their answers were correct, was significantly increased for
all subjects by the hypnotic procedure. The effect was particularly marked
among the more highly hypnotizable individuals. This increase in subjective
certainty was not, however, accompanied by a concomitant increase in
accuracy beyond that found for nonhypnotic remembering.

The investigations of Putnam (1979) and Zelig and Beidleman (1981)
yielded results that are not inconsistent with this finding. Though these
studies found that confidence ratings for recognition memory during
hypnosis were not significantly different from ratings from nonhypnotic
recognition memory, there was more inaccuracy in hypnosis (due to leading
questions). Furthermore, Putnam (1979) notes that subjects who underwent
hypnosis believed that they were more accurate than they would have been
without hypnosis. Thus, subjects were as confident, if not more so, of
remembrances from hypnosis, despite the fact that they were more inaccurate. Similarly, Timm (1982) reported that hypnotizable individuals who
recalled in hypnosis were more certain that their inaccurate recollections
were accurate than were unhypnotizable subjects who recalled without hypnosis. Timm (1981, 1982) also noted that in hypnosis, subjects gave substan-

tially fewer "I don't know" responses, without a demonstrable increase in accuracy.

It appears, therefore, that hypnosis can either increase the inaccuracy of recollections (through misleading information) without diminishing confidence in these "memories," or it can actually increase confidence in memory reports without concomitantly increasing accuracy. The amount of confidence and certitude an individual associates with his or her remembrances is more a function of hypnotic responsiveness than accuracy (Sheehan & Tilden, 1983; Zelig & Beidleman, 1981). Hypnosis thus dissociates accuracy of memory from the confidence that a person places in his or her memory reports. With nonhypnotic memory, confidence and accuracy are generally correlated (see Loftus, 1979), though in some situations this relationship can be manipulated.

When a witness is instructed to guess about details of an event, these guesses not only later tend to be reported as part of the original memory, but the witness may later be more confident about their accuracy (Hastie, Landsman, & Loftus, 1978; Wells & Leippe, 1981). Similarly, witnesses who are briefed (before testifying) about former recollections became more confident of these recollections, especially when they were originally inaccurate (Wells, Ferguson, & Lindsay, 1981). The use of hypnosis, however, brings about an increase in certitude without manipulating the individual either by asking him to guess or briefing him about his former recollections. In other words, hypnosis creates a situation where misplaced confidence in memories can easily occur, which is much less likely to be the case if hypnosis had not been used.

Such misplaced confidence in inaccurate recall, or heightened certitude of accuracy in the absence of a bona fide gain in accuracy, with hypnosis necessarily means that the individual becomes a more credible witness by virtue of having been interviewed in hypnosis. This is so because the confidence that an individual places in his or her memory reports has been shown to affect his or her perceived credibility, such that greater confidence yields greater credibility (cf. Lindsay, Wells, & Rumpel, 1981; Wells & Leippe, 1981; Wells, Lindsay, & Ferguson, 1979; Wells, Lindsay, & Tousignant, 1980). Moreover, credibility can be enhanced by other factors, such as the amount of peripheral detail a witness provides even though he or she may be incorrect on substantive matters (cf. Neisser, 1982; Wells & Leippe, 1981).

This last point is particularly troubling in terms of the forensic use of hypnosis. Even if efforts are made to reduce the possibility of biasing the hypnotized subject, and even if there is no appreciable change in confidence as a result of hypnosis – an outcome that is difficult to assess in applied situations – the witness is still likely to become more credible to jurors through the use of hypnosis because more detailed information is typically reported. That is, the shift to a laxer response criterion that appears to occur with hypnosis and the increased confabulation that also often occurs, even with a free narrative recall, result in more detail being reported. Some may be accurate and some may not be, but without independent corroboration of the detail reported, there is no way of ensuring that the hypnotized person is more accurate or more worthy of being believed simply because he or she produces more detailed information that seems plausible. The same problems exist for accepting as credible the recall of a victim or witness in hypnosis who provides an emotionally moving recollection when there was little or no affect before the use of hypnosis.

In summary, the data reviewed clearly suggest that hypnosis creates changes in memory and the confidence placed in it, relative to nonhypnotic recollections. These changes are not desirable, however, because hypnosis frequently increases inaccurate as well as accurate memories, and the changes are not easily undone once the technique has been used.

Such changes are likely to be greatly enhanced in the applied forensic situation, where the witness or victim to be hypnotized is intensely motivated to help the authorities, where the belief is instilled that hypnosis will elicit accurate recall or recognition, and where the hypnotist reinforces the subject for material of interest that is brought forth in hypnosis. Furthermore, after hypnosis has been used to "refresh" the recollections of a witness or victim, there is no way of determining whether the new "memories" or the increased confidence in them shown by the witness are due to accurate reports of previously unremembered events. The new "memories" could as easily be pseudomemories, and the new confidence could as easily be misplaced. Examples of these kinds of problems in forensic cases are discussed in the literature (e.g., Orne, 1979; Spiegel, 1980).

The widespread belief that hypnosis will enhance memory, and the increased detail, emotion, and confidence that typically characterize recall after hypnosis, serve to make the person's testimony more certain, regardless of its accuracy; this, in turn, is likely to make the testifying individual impervious to cross-examination and more credible to the trier of fact! Although hypnosis holds some limited possibility for increasing accurate recall in some circumstances, these other changes, as well as the potential for increased biasing resulting from undue suggestiveness, make it inappropriate to recommend the application of hypnosis prior to testimony in court. Testimony based upon "hypnotically refreshed" recall may seriously jeopardize those procedures within the criminal justice system that are designed to permit a full and fair evaluation of the facts.

The forensic use of hypnosis

The legal concerns over the admissibility of "hypnotically refreshed" recall as the basis of testimony came about through the increasing use of hypnosis by law enforcement officials. Consequently, the manner in which hypnosis has been used in forensic contexts has very much shaped the nature of the controversy. The empirical data that we have reviewed bear directly on three broad issues in the application of the technique by law enforcement officials. These include situations in which hypnosis is to be used, the perspective of the individual who actually administers the procedure, and the nature of the specific technique used to suggest memory enhancement with hypnosis.

Risks in different forensic applications

Hypnosis was first introduced in the forensic context at the beginning of the 20th century in an attempt to ascertain the truth, much in the way that certain drugs were later touted as "truth serum." It was soon discovered, however, that hypnosis (as well as these drugs) was not a reliable method for determining factual information. Its use in this capacity was therefore rejected by the courts (*People* v. *Ebanks*, 1897; *People* v. *McNichol*, 1950). The impetus for its revival in forensic contexts began with the growing acceptance of hypnosis as a useful therapeutic technique and with its official recognition by the American Medical Association (1958) and by the American Psychological Association (1960, as cited by Hilgard, 1965). Encouraged by this therapeutic legitimization, attorneys and law enforcement agencies began exploring the value of hypnosis as a forensic technique, especially for helping victims' and witnesses' recall.[8] Continued optimism over the effectiveness of hypnosis to aid memory ultimately led to its application in a great variety of criminal and civil cases.

The empirical evidence suggests that this almost indiscriminate application of the technique harbors potential problems. Although all forensic uses of hypnosis may appear superficially similar, different situations entail vastly differing risks for the miscarriage of justice. One basic criterion for evaluating the appropriateness of hypnosis is the extent to which information concerning the events in question may be communicated intentionally or inadvertently to a hypnotized subject and thereby appear in confabulated hypnotic recall, which is later confused by the subject with previous non-hypnotic memories.

Hypnosis is most likely to provide useful information with minimum risk in investigative situations where the facts in question are not known or presumed by law enforcement authorities, the public, or the media – the license plate number sought in the Chowchilla kidnapping (Kroger & Doucé, 1979) is a good example of this. Where there are minimal preconceptions, hypnosis may directly or indirectly enhance memory, and the relaxed environment of a sensitively conducted hypnotic session may help to diminish anxiety that may otherwise be interfering with attempts to recall. If the sole purpose of the hypnotic session is to provide clues that ultimately lead to the collection of independent evidence, its application becomes a means to an end that is no different from the use of other unreliable sources by the police.

In contrast to this investigative use of hypnosis are situations where the procedure is utilized to help provide eyewitnesses who can testify in court. As the emphasis shifts away from the search for clues that will lead to reliable independent evidence and focuses more on helping to prepare witnesses to give eyewitness testimony, the difficulties that hypnosis creates for the administration of justice become increasingly greater. The next step along this continuum is the situation in which a witness is hypnotized ostensibly only for investigative purposes but later testifies in court concerning recollections of the event in question.

The extreme case in terms of risk of miscarriage of justice is that in which hypnosis is used to "refresh" a witness's or victim's memory about aspects of a crime that are presumed or known to the authorities, the media, or the hypnotist. In such cases, a "memory" can be created in hypnosis where none existed before, and the witness's memory may be irreversibly contaminated (see Orne, 1981b, for examples). The hypnotic subject may obtain information about the event from the media, from comments made prior to, during, or after an interrogation, or during the hypnotic session itself. Based on what is currently known about hypnosis and its effects on memory, there is a significant likelihood that this information will form the basis of confabulation and will become inextricably intertwined with the witness's or victim's own memories of the event.

This altered memory will tend to persist, and the more frequently the subject reports the events, the more firmly established the altered memory will become. These "hypnotically refreshed" memories are often accompanied by increased confidence and are, therefore, often not subject to fair testing through the usual process of cross-examination or application of standard indicia of reliability.

Another inappropriate use of hypnosis in legal cases is to create an apparently reliable and confident witness. The authorities are frequently presented with witnesses who tell somewhat different stories each time they are asked to recall what occurred. These differences may relate to important details of the crime. The effect of hypnotizing such witnesses is often dramatic. Even if the subject is only modestly responsive to hypnosis, reviewing the events in the hypnotic context and having the memories legitimized by a supportive hypnotist will generally fix one particular version of the testimony in the witness's mind, which is then faithfully and reliably produced on demand. In these cases hypnosis need not produce any new information, but the procedure can bolster a formerly unreliable witness whose credibility might easily have been destroyed by cross-examination.

Finally, scientific evidence to the contrary, there is a widely held belief among the public in general, and within the law enforcement community in particular, that hypnosis is a means of getting at the truth. For example, in *State* v. *White* (1979) a senior member of the Wisconsin State Police was asked why he felt that hypnosis was useful, and he testified that hypnosis lends "credibility and strength to your investigation" (Trial Transcript, p. 13). One of the reasons why hypnosis has had such a strong appeal for law enforcement officials is their hope of using it as a kind of a lie detection procedure, especially with witnesses who are not fully trusted. Unfortunately, as discussed earlier, individuals are capable of lying during hypnosis and are capable of feigning hypnosis successfully if they choose to do so. The observer of the hypnotic session, however, is very likely to accept statements of an apparently hypnotized individual at face value. Hypnosis used in this fashion may seriously mislead both law enforcement officials and prosecutors, causing them prematurely to close off potentially fruitful avenues of investigation, and in some instances resulting in inappropriate or unjustified indictments (e.g., *State* v. *Douglas*, 1978).

Issues of involvement and qualifications of the hypnotist-interviewer

The empirical data on the nature of hypnosis and its effects not only bear upon when hypnosis should be used but also relate to how it should be used. One clear indication from the research is that hypnosis can greatly increase the potential of the individual to be inadvertently led or misled by the hypnotist. Within the legal controversy over the admissibility of "hypnotically refreshed" recall, the question has been raised as to who is qualified to administer the hypnotic procedure in a forensic investigative setting.

Some law enforcement groups feel that police officers trained in "forensic hypnosis" are best qualified to perform it. They point out that police, as professional criminal investigators, are trained and experienced in following legal procedures in their interrogations of victims and witnesses and routinely interview people who have undergone traumatic experiences. They are also more likely to be available for hypnosis and subsequent testimony, and the cost is apt to be less than that involved in using a hypnotist not in law enforcement.

Major professional groups concerned with the use of hypnosis, on the other hand, have taken the position that only trained mental health professionals should be permitted to use hypnosis in a forensic context.[9] This position emphasizes that mental health professionals are committed above all to helping clients avoid interventions that would harm them. Although most law enforcement investigators deal with victims and witnesses compassionately, their professional orientation is fundamentally different from that of the clinician. While they may be working *with* a victim or witness, they are working *on* a case, and it is their progress in solving this case that determines their professional success or failure.

Mental health professionals experienced in hypnosis are not only more aware of what may harm an individual and of the potential for biasing the person in hypnosis, but they are qualified to evaluate psychopathology, including those disorders that may result from traumatic experiences.[10] Most important, however, they are less likely to have information or preconceptions about details of the case, and to the extent that they lack information, they are not in a position to bias, unduly influence, or contaminate the hypnotized individual's recollections. Thus, if hypnosis is to be used in an attempt to "refresh" memory, it should be administered by an expert who has minimal preconceptions about the to-be-remembered event and little investment in the ultimate disposition of the case.[11]

Issues of hypnotic technique

The free narrative recall procedure is the technique whereby hypnotic hypermnesia may occur but the risks of confabulation and response criterion shifts remain. Once this free report has been obtained, specific questions can be asked, with the recognition that these are more likely to create inaccurate recollections that the subject nevertheless accepts as accurate (Hilgard & Loftus, 1979). In addition, these may serve to increase the individual's confidence in his recollections without any substantive change in accuracy.

The specific type of memory metaphor used with hypnosis depends upon the circumstances of the situation. Age regression may be desirable for a traumatized person to permit him or her to deal constructively with the horror of the events to be remembered (though what is recalled is not necessarily accurate). A number of recall metaphors and hypnotic techniques are available, but one in particular has been frequently used in forensic settings and requires consideration. This is the videotape or television metaphor of memory and recall (Reiser, 1976). With this technique the hypnotist

indicates that the subject in imagination, will be watching a special documentary film on television from a safe, secure, and comfortable place. This special documentary can be speeded up, slowed down, stopped, reversed, with close-ups possible on any person, object, or thing in the film. The sound can be turned up high so that anything that is said, even a whisper, can be heard very clearly. This will be a documentary film of the incident in question and will depict accurately and vividly everything of significance and importance the subject perceived and experienced in relationship to that crime scene. And even though what occurred was very traumatic, the subject watching the TV documentary will be able to remain calm and relaxed, feeling detached from what is happening on the television set. The subject will be observing it as a reporter, covering an event to be written up accurately for a news story. (Reiser, 1980, p. 159)

Proponents of the television technique tend to believe that in addition to the usual conscious memory, all sensory inputs are continuously recorded by the "subconscious mind" (which, according to Reiser, includes both the preconscious and the unconscious). "The subconscious mind is alert and on duty 24 hours a day, seven days a week; it never sleeps" (Reiser, 1980, p. 11). Moreover, this material – not normally available to consciousness – is assumed to be retrievable with hypnosis. Whether this view of memory and hypnotic recall is taken literally, or merely employed as a powerful metaphor, the subject is likely to uncritically accept this superficially plausible notion. In fact, as presented, the TV metaphor includes both an implicit suggestion that the details of the event are (as opposed to "may be") in the person's memory and an explicit suggestion that the recollections that are obtained in hypnosis will be vivid and factually accurate.

The striking impact of the television technique becomes clear if one considers the state of mind of a witness about to testify concerning events that occurred 6 months ago. If by chance an actual videotape recording of the events were available and the witness had the opportunity of viewing the videotape shortly before the trial, one could predict with a high degree of assurance that the witness's memory would indeed be refreshed and the testimony would be given with far greater accuracy and certainty than would otherwise be possible. Further, the witness would not see himself or herself as testifying from the videotape, but rather as reporting the events he or she saw 6 months ago.

If such a videotape were available, it would be largely academic whether the memories stemmed from the original event or from the videotape, because the tape would be the most reliable evidence and its effect would be a somewhat stronger version of reviewing notes made at the time of the event. In contrast, watching an imaginary "documentary" during hypnosis may produce the subjective experience of observing the events of 6 months ago but is certainly not an accurate, reliable representation of the facts. Telling people in hypnosis that they are watching a "documentary" is, however, a powerful suggestion that what they see and report is what actually happened.

Given the increase in responsiveness to suggestions that ensues with hypnosis, the suggestion of watching a "documentary" also places considerable pressure on the subject to bring forth additional helpful details and to believe that they actually occurred. When he or she subsequently testifies, he or she will testify from what is believed to be the recollection of the original event. In fact, however, his or her testimony will be based on memories *created* during hypnosis, which may be at gross variance with both prehypnosis recollection and the actual facts.

In an effort to improve the accuracy of hypnotic recall and minimize confabulation, some hypnotists have given explicit suggestions to the effect that the subject should recall accurately and report only the events that really happened, no more and no less. Such an instruction is impressive to lay observers, but it is totally negated by the forensic context of hypnosis, which pressures the subject to provide more details. Unfortunately, in such a context, the net effect of the conflicting demands of these suggestions will not be any increase in accuracy of recall but instead an increase only in the subject's conviction that his or her recall is accurate.

Finally, witnesses who have been hypnotized often assert later that their new recollections preceded rather than followed the hypnotic session. Exceptions occur when the subject had absolutely no recollection prior to hypnosis; he or she may then correctly identify the absence of prior recall. Even in such situations, however, one may find subjects who insist that they actually remembered the event or detail before being hypnotized but did not talk about it. On the other hand, a subject may vividly remember someone wearing a blue shirt prior to hypnosis, and on the imaginary videotape "see" that the individual had "actually worn" a red shirt. Sometimes such a discrepancy is sufficiently striking that it is recalled, but the subject then tends to accept the hypnotic version as true. On the whole, however, the sources of memories become confounded, and no instructions or suggestions can reliably prevent this from occurring in real-life situations.

These are the issues at the core of the controversy over "hypnotically refreshed" recall when it is the basis of testimony in a court of law. Similar controversies over these issues have been raised in Canada (Perry & Laurence, 1983), in Australia (Sheehan, 1982), and in the United Kingdom (Wagstaff, 1982b; Waxman, 1983). The scientific evidence for hypnotic hypermnesia and the forensic techniques employed to produce hypnotic hypermnesia have frequently been at odds, and this discrepancy has led to numerous legal challenges and adjudications over the admissibility of testimony following a hypnotic intervention designed to "refresh" memory.

The legal controversy: Enhanced memory or tampering with evidence?

The basic issue that has had to be adjudicated by the courts during the past 15 years concerns the admissibility of testimony of witnesses and victims following a pretrial hypnotic intervention for the purpose of "refreshing" recall. Those wishing it excluded as a matter of law have argued that the procedure is unreliable, making the testimony based upon it unreliable, and therefore inadmissible as evidence. The counterargument is that hypnosis is one of several procedures to refresh recall; as such, it should be permitted under the rules of evidence and left to the trier of fact to decide the credibility and reliability that should then go to the weight of the evidence. (For a thoughtful review of these issues, see Udolf, 1983.)

The first landmark decision on this issue was that of the Maryland Special Court of Appeals in *Harding* v. *State* (1968), where testimony based upon hypnotic recollection of a prosecuting witness was admitted and allowed to go to the jury. In this case, the memory testified to was clearly brought forth for the first time in hypnosis. Though the court recognized that "hypnotically refreshed" memory might not be fully factual and cautioned the jury not to attach greater weight to the testimony based upon hypnotic recall, the testimony was nevertheless admitted into the trial because "refreshing" memory with hypnosis was conceptualized as not different in kind from refreshing memory in other acceptable ways, such as by looking at notes or memoranda.

Subsequent to this decision, a number of courts faced with similar issues followed the precedent of *Harding* v. *State* (1968) and admitted testimony based upon "hypnotically refreshed" recall (e.g., *Kline* v. *Ford Motor Co., Inc.*, 1975; *State* v. *Jorgensen*, 1971; *State* v. *McQueen*, 1978; *United States* v. *Adams*, 1978). There were, however, serious shortcomings in the *Harding* decision and its progeny, which were not made clear until sometime later (see Dilloff, 1977). Most notable among the shortcomings was the failure of the original legal approach to provide an adequate record of the scientific opinion and consensus on the matter of reliability of "hypnotically refreshed" recall.

Consequently, when the Minnesota Supreme Court was faced with ruling on the admissibility of testimony concerning recollections adduced at a pretrial hypnotic interview in the case of *State* v. *Mack* (1980), the court engaged in a first-impression review of the expert opinion on hypnosis to aid memory. The court recognized that "the fact that a witness' memory results from hypnosis bears on the question of whether her testimony is sufficiently competent, relevant, and more probative than prejudicial, to merit admission at all" (pp. 10–11).

After examining expert opinion based upon clinical and scientific uses of hypnosis, the Minnesota Supreme Court ruled against the admissibility of testimony from a witness whose memory was "refreshed" through the use of hypnosis. In deciding the issue, the court cited the lack of reliability (in terms of accuracy) of hypnotically induced recall, the increased suggestibility of individuals who are attempting to recall in hypnosis, and the increased confidence and credibility that can result from a hypnotic intervention. These concerns were all abundantly supported by facts in the case of *State* v. *Mack* (1980), and they are evident in the empirical literature reviewed earlier.

Since the Minnesota ruling, the Maryland[12], Massachusetts, Pennsylvania, Michigan, California, Arizona, Nebraska, and Indiana supreme courts have taken a similar point of view and have excluded testimony based upon "hypnotically refreshed" recall (*Collins* v. *State,* 1982; *Commonwealth* v. *Kater*, 1983; *Commonwealth* v. *Nazarovitch*, 1981; *People* v. *Gonzales*, 1982; *People* v. *Shirley*, 1982; *State* v. *Mena*, 1981; *State* v. *Palmer*, 1981; *Strong* v. *State*, 1982) with only the Wyoming Supreme Court admitting it (*Chapman* v. *State*, 1982). In most of these cases the question of the admissibility of testimony from a person who has undergone pretrial hypnosis was subjected to the *Frye* criterion (*Frye* v. *United States*, 1923). This widely applied "general acceptability test" concerns whether a special procedure has gained acceptance among the scientific community of the particular field to which it belongs.

In applying the *Frye* criterion, recent state supreme court rulings have tended to recognize that use of hypnosis to "refresh" recall is not accepted as a reliable technique among the relevant scientific community,[13] making admissibility of testimony based upon the technique unacceptable. The decision by the California Supreme Court in *People* v. *Shirley* (1982) is an excellent example of the exclusion by this criterion of hypnotically induced testimony. A carefully written legal review by Diamond (1980) was influential in the *Shirley* case. This review concludes that the danger of mischief with the pretrial use of hypnosis is sufficiently serious that no witness should ever be permitted to testify in a case where the authorities have previously used hypnosis to "refresh" recall.

Perhaps the best illustration of the extent to which expert opinion has affected the adjudication of the issue is the changes that have taken place in the state of Maryland concerning the admissibility of testimony from a previously hypnotized witness. The *Harding* case in this state set the initial precedent in favor of admissibility. After the careful review and adjudication of the issue by the Minnesota Supreme Court in the *Mack* case, however, the Maryland Court of Special Appeals ruled again on the issue in *Polk* v. *State* (1981). This time the court modified its original position and required that the trial court make specific rulings and evaluations if hypnosis is involved in the retrieval of memories that are to be presented in court; these evaluations were to be based upon the *Frye* criterion, which had been adopted in Maryland in *Reed* v. *State* (1978), a decade after the *Harding* decision.

Not long after this the Maryland Court of Special Appeals applied the *Frye* criterion to "hypnotically refreshed" recall and resolved the matter in *Collins* v. *State* (1982). In this ruling the court completely reversed its original position in *Harding* and concluded:

After a complete and careful review of the record in this case, as well as the decisions of other jurisdictions and the scientific literature which has been called to our attention, we are convinced that applying the standards explicated in *Frye* for the use of hypnosis to restore or refresh the memory of a witness is not accepted as reliable by the relevant scientific community and that such testimony is therefore inadmissible. To the extent that previous cases in this jurisdiction have permitted the admissibility of hypnotically induced testimony, we hereby overrule those cases. (pp. 20–21)

Thus, the state that originally permitted such testimony to go to the trier of fact now totally precluded its admissibility as a matter of law.

Though state supreme courts that have ruled on the matter thus far have tended to exclude testimony resulting from a pretrial hypnosis intervention, there are differences of opinion among them about whether testimony from any witness who has been hypnotized to "refresh" memory should be inadmissible altogether, or whether recollections made by the witness prior to hypnosis are admissible. Recently the Arizona Supreme Court modified its earlier decision of total exclusion, reached in the *Mena* case, to permit testimony to "matters that the witness was able to recall and relate prior to hypnosis" (*Collins* v. *Superior Court of State of Arizona*, 1982, p. 2157).

It is unclear, however, whether a witness can distinguish between recollections made prior to hypnosis and those reported during and after hypnosis (cf. Orne, 1979). Similarly, the individual may, as a result of hypnosis, become more confident or certain of the factual accuracy of recollections made prior to hypnosis. The extent to which such problems occur can best be judged if an adequate record exists and other procedural guidelines (see Orne, 1979) are carried out before, during, and immediately after the hypnosis interviews. Thus, the state of Maryland (*Collins* v. *State*, 1982) not only ruled hypnotically influenced testimony inadmissible but also required that even when hypnosis is used for strictly investigative purposes – to obtain leads – such guidelines must be followed.

One court has based the admissibility criterion on such safeguards. In *State* v. *Hurd* (1981), the New Jersey Supreme Court ruled that the guidelines first proposed by Orne in *Quaglino* v. *California* (1978) be required for consideration of testimony following pretrial hypnosis. In its decision, the New Jersey court opted for a different approach from that taken by its predecessors to the issue of admitting "hypnotically refreshed" testimony. Such testimony was neither excluded per se (as in the Minnesota decision of *Mack*), nor was it automatically admitted into court (as in the early Maryland decision of *Harding*). Rather, the New Jersey Supreme Court ruled, "Therefore, we hold that testimony enhanced through hypnosis is admissible in a criminal trial if the trial court finds that the use of hypnosis in the particular case was reasonably likely to result in recall comparable in accuracy to normal human memory" (*State* v. *Hurd*, 1981, p. 25). Further, the court held that this question could not be resolved unless the guidelines were adhered to: therefore, in New Jersey, compliance with the guidelines is a prerequisite to adjudication of the admissibility of "hypnotically refreshed" testimony.[14]

Though most recent state supreme court rulings have held that, as a matter of law, testimony must be excluded concerning matters dealt with in a pretrial hypnosis session, nearly all have recognized the legitimate use of hypnosis solely for investigative purposes. Used in this way, hypnosis may provide leads that can be followed up in order to obtain corroborating physical evidence, and the remembered material itself is not subsequently used in court. Even in these investigative situations, however, guidelines concerning the appropriate use of hypnosis are warranted (see *Collins* v. *State*, 1982; *State* v. *Mack,* 1980).

Guidelines for the investigative use of hypnosis

The present state of scientific knowledge is consistent with the rulings of a number of state supreme courts that memories retrieved through hypnosis are sufficiently unreliable that their use is precluded as eyewitness testimony in criminal trials. The nature of hypnosis and of its effects on memory leads to the possibility that beliefs of the hypnotist or subject may be transformed into inaccurate memories that the subject reports, believes, and subsequently is willing to testify to under oath. There is currently no available method for eliminating this possibility or for accurately determining in real-life situations the balance of increased recall versus increased distortion that may occur following hypnosis, because ground truth cannot be known with certainty. It is therefore appropriate at the present time to restrict the forensic use of hypnosis to investigative situations where the potential gains are likely to be greater than the risks, provided that suitable guidelines are followed.

The use of hypnosis for investigative purposes only, together with an adequate record of its application in a given case, appears to offer potential benefits – for new leads – that outweigh the risks of false information or misplaced confidence. This use can be justified, however, only in cases where a defendant has not been identified to the subject, where there has not been widespread publicity involving speculations about the perpetrator, and where law enforcement officials do not have compelling beliefs about details of what actually transpired. It becomes crucial to follow procedures that provide a detailed record of precisely what has or has not been discussed in the hypnotic interview, and to show that every effort has been made to minimize the potential effect of hypnosis in distorting memory.

As has been pointed out, hypnosis should not be used to prepare a witness to testify in court, such as in an attempt to improve the recall of a previously unreliable or uncertain witness.[15] If a witness becomes confused or distressed during questioning, a nonhypnotic interview conducted in a calm, quiet environment and in a nonconfrontational, supportive manner is likely to help the witness or victim clarify recall without the risk of the distortion that is inherent in the use of hypnosis. Finally, hypnosis should never be used to encourage a witness to report details when it was physically impossible for such details to have been observed – as when a witness is asked to zoom in on the face of someone who was never viewed except at a distance of 90 yards in semi-darkness or to remove the mask from a perpetrator whom the subject had never seen without a mask! In other words, hypnosis does not retrospectively allow the individual to transcend normal perceptual abilities.

To protect the law enforcement agency, the rights of the defendant-to-be, and the health and welfare of the witness or victim to be hypnotized, as well as to allow for the possibility that he or she can subsequently testify to matters not dealt with in hypnosis, the following guidelines for using hypnosis for investigative purposes are proposed. Earlier variants of these guidelines have been adopted by the Federal Bureau of Investigation (Ault, 1979) and by the criminal investigative branches of the armed services, as well as by New Jersey (*State* v. *Hurd*, 1981) and Maryland (*Collins* v. *State*, 1982).

Qualifications and knowledge of the hypnotist. The forensic use of hypnosis should be performed by a psychiatrist, psychologist, or an equivalently qualified mental health professional who has had training both in the clinical use of hypnosis and in its forensic applications. This individual should be an impartial expert whose professional status is independent of the law enforcement investigators, prosecution, and defense (though it is likely that a given expert will have had prior professional contact with these persons).

The expert should ideally know little or nothing about the case. In most situations, however, it is virtually impossible to prevent communications from law enforcement personnel or legal counsel concerning those aspects that they view as important to the disposition of the case. The most viable solution, therefore, is to permit no information to be given orally to the hypnotist from individuals involved directly in the case but, rather, to require written communications that specify those details that are considered essential for the expert to know in order to carry out the hypnosis interview. This procedure will ensure the possibility of subsequently evaluating the extent of the information available to the hypnotist – information that might be unwittingly communicated to the subject. If the hypnotist has learned about the case from outside sources, such as press accounts, he or she should record such information in writing prior to the hypnosis session (withdrawing from the case if this prior information is unduly prejudicial).

Complete videotape recordings. All contact of the hypnotist with the individual to be hypnotized should be recorded on videotape from the moment they meet until their entire interaction is concluded, including the prehypnosis interview, the hypnosis interview, and the posthypnosis discussion. The casual comments passed before or after hypnosis may act as prehypnotic or posthypnotic suggestions and are as important to record as the hypnotic session itself. The camera should be aimed to get *both* the hypnotist and the subject in the picture. A time recording should be incorporated into the record of the session to ensure its continuity. Audio recordings are *significantly* less useful for the subsequent evaluation of the hypnosis session, and stenographic transcripts provide no opportunity to record the nonverbal and paraverbal (tone of voice, pauses, etc.) cues by which information and expectations are often communicated to subjects undergoing hypnosis.

Limitations on those present during the interview. Only the hypnotist and the subject should be present during any phase of the preinduction, hypnosis, or posthypnosis session. This is important because it is all too easy for observers inadvertently to communicate to the subject what they expect, what they are startled by, or what they are disappointed by (even if the subject's eyes are closed and he or she has been told to hear only the hypnotist's voice). If investigators or representatives of the prosecution or the defense wish to observe the hypnosis session, they may do so only if they use a one-way screen or a remote television monitor to watch the interview – to prevent jeopardizing the integrity of the session.

Deviations from this guideline must be evaluated carefully. In some situations adequate videotape recording may require the presence of a technician in the room to operate equipment.[16] This individual should not have any prior knowledge of the case and should document this in writing. Other special situations, such as a child who requests, or who an involved clinician believes requires, the presence of a parent during the session, must be evaluated on a case-by-case basis. The primary consideration here, as in other aspects of conducting the hypnotic session, must be the protection of the witness or victim who has consented to serve as a hypnotic subject.

A more difficult problem arises in situations where all the requisite expertise needed to conduct the hypnotic interview is not available in one person. A psychiatrist or psychologist skilled in clinical uses of hypnosis may lack any experience with forensic interviewing techniques. In this situation, a law enforcement professional who is skilled in avoiding leading questions and who has no knowledge of the specific case[17] might conduct the actual interview following hypnotic induction by the clinician and transfer of rapport. The clinician, however, remains responsible throughout the procedure and terminates hypnosis. The law enforcement professional who conducts the interview should, like the clinician, be given a written summary of the facts he or she is to know about the case and should submit, in advance of the hypnotic session, a written statement detailing any other prior knowledge that he or she may have concerning the case.

Prehypnosis evaluation. At the beginning of the session a brief psychological evaluation of the subject should be carried out by the mental health professional, and the existence of a full, written, informed consent for the procedure confirmed. *Before* the induction of hypnosis, the mental health professional should elicit from the victim or witness a detailed narrative description of the facts as the subject remembers them, being careful to avoid adding any new elements through direct or indirect suggestions. This preliminary procedure is important because it provides a recorded baseline for evaluating the subject's memories of the incident before anything has been added or changed through hypnosis. Moreover, witnesses are sometimes able to recall more or different memories while talking to a psychologist or psychiatrist than during interrogation by an investigator.

If significant new information emerges during this prehypnosis interview, consideration should be given to stopping the procedure at this point and thus avoiding some of the problems inherent in the use of hypnosis. If the decision is made not to induce hypnosis, the subject should then be interviewed nondirectively as to what he or she believes happened during this interview, because, having come for the purpose of being hypnotized, the subject may believe that he or she was hypnotized. In any case, the videotaped record of the entire interaction should be preserved. If the decision is made to proceed with the induction of hypnosis, the subject should be questioned first as to his or her expectations so that their effect may be evaluated subsequently and any remaining serious misconceptions about hypnosis or its effects may be corrected.

Appropriate hypnotic induction and memory retrieval techniques. Hypnosis should be induced by one of the standard methods and incorporate sufficient test suggestions to allow assessment of the subject's hypnotic responsivity. Following the induction of hypnosis, the psychiatrist or psychologist should suggest an appropriate cognitive strategy to aid focusing on the events in question and first obtain a free narrative report. During this report, the hypnotist should encourage the narrative flow but avoid interrupting, asking questions, or otherwise adding any new elements to the witness's description of his or her experiences, including those discussed in the preinduction interview, lest the nature of the witness's memories inadvertently be altered or constrained by a reminder of his or her prior, nonhypnotic memories. Once the subject begins to describe the events in question, minimal verbalization by the hypnotist is desirable. When the subject pauses, comments such as, "Go on," "Continue," "Yes?" "Mm hm?" – indicating the clinician's interest in what the subject says but avoiding communicating concern about specific content – are particularly useful.

If the free narrative fails to elicit needed details, a more directive technique may be employed subsequently, but it should be kept in mind that questioning or otherwise pressuring about specific details will inevitably increase the number of items reported and also increase the probability of inaccurate details being supplied.

Communication with the hypnotist. There may well be questions that need to be resolved by the observers who are not in the room but who are familiar with the case. For this reason, it is desirable for the hypnotist to arrange very brief breaks – leaving the videotape continuously recording the subject – at the end of the prehypnosis interview, and again at the end of the free narrative recall obtained during hypnosis. Observers should put in writing any requests or suggestions for the hypnotist concerning material to be elicited, which can be given to the hypnotist during these breaks. In this fashion a permanent record is obtained concerning when and by whom specific issues are raised during the session; this record should be archived with the videotapes.

Posthypnosis discussion. During the termination of hypnosis or immediately thereafter while the subject is still in a hypersuggestible state, explicit or implicit posthypnotic suggestions should be avoided concerning the nature, extent, or reliability of the subject's subsequent nonhypnotic memory of the event (e.g., "It will be easy for you to remember things now that you did not remember before"). After hypnosis is terminated, it is important to explore the subject's experiences during hypnosis, which provide needed information about the individual's hypnotic responsivity and whether he or she felt that hypnosis changed anything concerning his or her memories. Before ending their contact the hypnotist should invite the subject to reflect on what the subject believes took place during the session, its causes, and implications. Videotape recording of the session should be terminated only after the hypnotist and the subject have parted company and all immediate posthypnotic interviews of the subject by involved personnel have been concluded.

Provision for clinical follow-up. The planning of the hypnosis session should include provisions for making clinical follow-up available to the victim or witness who has served as a subject if it appears to be clinically indicated or if the subject requests it. This follow-up may be provided by the hypnotist, by a clinician who has been working with the subject, or by referral to a suitable clinician in the area where the subject lives. The subject should be informed of these arrangements before leaving the hypnotic session. If repressed traumatic memories have been recalled under hypnosis, these provisions are especially important and should be of an active rather than a passive ("Call if you have any problems") nature.

Technical considerations. The individual responsible for carrying out the hypnosis session should check well in advance the suitability of the setting and whether the videotape recording equipment is working properly. Aside from ensuring that the quality of the picture is adequate and that both hypnotist and subject are going to be clearly displayed in the picture, the hypnotist should ascertain that the audio recording system is carefully tested to ensure that it is capable of picking up very quiet conversation – hypnotized subjects often speak in soft or low voices. As a test of the adequacy of the videotape recording equipment, a brief sample tape should be recorded and evaluated prior to the session. (Obvious errors like placing a microphone on or too near a videotape machine will result in inaudible tapes, thereby completely compromising the intended monitoring of the session.) Finally, provisions should be made to videotape all materials to be shown to the subject, such as pictures or photo lineups.

Cautionary note on hypnotizing suspects. There is no justification for the authorities to hypnotize suspects in a case. Because individuals may successfully simulate hypnosis and because even hypnotized individuals are capable of willfully lying, a suspect's report in hypnosis is not useful for the purpose of exoneration. Similarly, confessions obtained during hypnosis are not admissible because the use of such a technique to elicit a confession involves undue coercion (*Leyra* v. *Denno*, 1954).

With the increased investigative use of hypnosis, an individual who had been hypnotized as a witness may at some later time become a suspect. In such an event, special procedures must be observed with regard to the subsequent waking interrogation because the memory of the witness/suspect may have been altered by the hypnosis session. During interrogation the authorities may wittingly or unwittingly use the hypnotically elicited "information" – especially information that placed the subject at the scene of the crime – in order to elicit a confession.

Because the hypnotically elicited "information" may have been confabulated, the witness subjected to hypnosis procedures may be more vulnerable to later interrogation. Therefore, it is essential that the waking interrogation of a previously hypnotized witness be recorded – ideally videotaped, but at least audiotaped. The taped record is crucial to determining whether admissions or confessions were elicited voluntarily or whether the interrogator capitalized upon "memories" created during hypnosis (such as those produced by the "zooming-in" technique in order to convince the suspect that he or she must have been at the scene of the crime because he or she could not otherwise have seen the details reported).

Conclusions concerning uses of hypnosis to "refresh" memory

The use of guidelines is designed to permit the subsequent evaluation of a hypnosis session by independent experts, in order to determine whether undue suggestiveness was present. Nonetheless, even when hypnosis has been used appropriately in a forensic situation and when the session has been monitored and conducted in a manner that is likely to minimize undetected biasing, inadvertent distortions of memory may still occur. Although the recommended guidelines for conducting the hypnosis session help determine what was done during the session, they do not prevent (nor is there any reliable way to prevent) subjects from confounding distorted hypnotic memories with prior and subsequent nonhypnotic recall or from placing undue confidence in these distorted recollections. Thus, the use of the results of hypnosis applied in forensic situations, as well as the use of the procedure itself, demands extreme caution.

"Hypnotically refreshed" memories cannot be used to "verify" facts for which no adequate evidence exists, especially when subsequent investigation has failed to produce any substantial independent corroboration and the individual did not recall the fact or was not confident of it prior to hypnosis. As long as the detail recalled is verified by independent physical evidence, the utility of hypnosis can be considerable and the risk attached to the procedure – if properly conducted – minimal. There is no way, however, by which anyone (including an expert with extensive experience in hypnosis) can for any particular piece of information obtained in hypnosis determine whether it is an actual memory or a confabulation. For these reasons, hypnotically induced testimony is not reliable and ought not be permitted to form the basis of testimony in court.

Notes

1 In a forensic context to assume otherwise would encourage extensive litigation concerning whether an individual actually had been hypnotized. It is, in fact, a very difficult task, requiring the use of special empirical paradigms, to establish the degree of hypnosis that has taken place (see Sheehan & Perry, 1976). Nevertheless, the assumption that hypnosis has taken place after a hypnotic induction has been administered is consistent with the view held by many subjects. For example, in studying hypnotic hypermnesia, Shaul (1978) found that 67% of those receiving an induction felt that they were moderately to deeply hypnotized compared with only 5% of subjects who had equivalent hypnotizability and the same recall instructions but no hypnotic induction procedure.

2 The extent to which the process of confabulation may be stimulated by hypnosis becomes obvious when, instead of being asked to relive a prior event, the subject is given suggestions to experience a future event – about which no memories could possibly exist. For instance, in age progression (Kline & Guze, 1951), a subject is given the suggestion that it is the year 2000 and is asked to describe the world around him. Often this will lead to a vivid and compelling description of all kinds of scientific marvels. Obviously, the plausibility and the precise nature of a subject's description will depend upon the scientific knowledge and imagination of that subject.

3 What these generally negative results for nonsense syllables and word lists indicate is that the memory system does not store sensory inputs like a tape recorder. Thus, hypnosis is not simply a matter of replaying a "videotape" stored in the mind – a metaphor used in the television technique (Reiser, 1980), and one that is sometimes taken literally by its proponents – because recall of this kind would not distinguish between meaningful and meaningless material.

4 Unfortunately, most of these recent studies on hypnotic hypermnesia have failed to distinguish between free recall, where the subject reports his or her recollections in narrative form, and recognition memory, where the subject is given a choice between several alternatives, as in multiple choice, true or false, or photo lineup. Research with normal human memory has clearly demonstrated waking hypermnesia effects with free recall (Erdelyi & Kleinbard, 1978), but not with recognition memory, except under very special circumstances (Erdelyi & Stein, 1981). One would, therefore, anticipate that hypnotic hypermnesia would be more likely to occur with free recall memory than with recognition memory. Recognition memory is, nevertheless, important for studying the effects of hypnosis on susceptibility to distortions from biasing or leading questions.

5 This discrepancy between results from hypnotic hypermnesia studies using structured or pressured recall and results from studies using an unstructured free recall parallels that observed between nonhypnotic recall from a narrative interview and nonhypnotic recall

from an interrogatory interview (Hilgard & Loftus, 1979; Loftus, 1979). In the narrative interview the subject is asked to report the event as he or she remembers it with no guidance from the interviewer. In this case, less detail but fewer errors are obtained than in an interrogatory interview, where the subject's attention is focused on possibilities and details of interest to the interviewer (Cady, 1924; Lipton, 1977; Marquis, Marshall, & Oskamp, 1972). Thus, the interrogatory interview is structured in certain ways and yields more detailed information that is both correct and incorrect.

6 Dywan and Bowers (1983) not only used the forced recall procedure but also attempted to maximize waking (nonhypnotic) hypermnesia prior to testing in hypnosis. More work is needed in this area to determine if the effects of hypnosis on recall are different (e.g., more rapid) than the effects of repeated forced attempts at remembering without hypnosis. Erdelyi's original observation of improved recall due to repeated attempts at recall (cf. Erdelyi & Kleinbard, 1978) has now been replicated. This waking hypermnesia paradigm provides a rigorous empirical baseline against which hypnotic hypermnesia must be tested.

7 It is important to note that the difference between a leading and a nonleading question is remarkably small in terms of the manner in which the question is phrased (Loftus & Zanni, 1975). For example, a nonleading question such as, "Did you see a stop sign?" can be made into a leading question by merely substituting the word *the* for the word *a* ("Did you see the stop sign?"), as was done by Putnam (1979).

8 In 1972 the Los Angeles Police Department (LAPD) initiated training of police officers in "investigative hypnosis." A Law Enforcement Assistance Administration sponsored research project was carried out by the LAPD in 1975–1976, and in 70 cases hypnosis was employed (to aid memory) by 13 carefully selected senior police officers trained in hypnosis for purposes of interrogation (Reiser, 1980). Since that time, approximately 1,000 police officers have been trained by individuals associated with the LAPD, and it is estimated that substantially more than 5,000 law enforcement officers have been trained nationwide. Officers are typically trained by proprietary corporations such as Reiser's "Law Enforcement Hypnosis Institute." This institute, which is probably the most widely known in law enforcement circles, offers a "comprehensive program" that lasts "four days, consisting of 32 class hours of theory, demonstration, and practice" (Reiser, 1980, p. xvi). Even shorter training programs are run by various other proprietary groups throughout the country.

9 The International Society of Hypnosis (ISH) and its Constituent Societies in the United States (the American Society of Clinical Hypnosis and the Society for Clinical and Experimental Hypnosis) have a membership restricted to physicians, psychologists, dentists, and clinical social workers. In 1979 the International Society and its United States constituents adopted a Resolution (ISH, 1979) stating that the Society "is strongly opposed to the training of police officers as hypnotechnicians and the use of hypnosis by the police officer." As major reasons for limiting its use, the Resolution points to the potential abuse of hypnosis in the creation of pseudomemories and biasing of the recollections of the hypnotized individual without the hypnotist's awareness. In 1980 a ballot regarding this Resolution was sent to all 2,692 members of the International Society of Hypnosis. Over half (54.4%) of the membership voted; of the 1,465 signed, verified ballots returned, 1,359 (92.8%) voted in favor of adopting the Resolution. This indicates a remarkably high degree of consensus within the relevant scientific community against the use of hypnosis by police officers to "refresh" recall and concern for the reliability of the recollections obtained. At the 1982 International Congress, the governing body of the Society reviewed and reaffirmed this position.

10 Often a person who has undergone a traumatic event has the need to relive the experience and share it with a sympathetic therapist. In forensic contexts, however, the subject may be told by the lay police hypnotist that he or she need not relive the experience when recalling it (as when the television metaphor is combined with suggestions to view the event "objectively"), but there nevertheless will be a strong tendency to do so. Individuals without men-

tal health training and experience who carry out hypnosis are likely to try to prevent the subject from reliving the traumatic events, partly in the mistaken notion that this is being kind, and partly because of their own difficulty in dealing with the person's pain. The result can be quite destructive because it can communicate to the subject in this highly suggestible condition that the feelings are so terrible that the hypnotist does not want to know about them. This may lead to considerably greater emotional distress and make subsequent psychological treatment more difficult. Trained mental health professionals are also in a better position to foresee and manage some of the possible negative consequences of the retrieval of repressed traumatic memories, such as the development of neurotic symptoms based upon fear of retribution for providing incriminating evidence, or the pathological guilt for not fighting back that is developed by some victims of assault (e.g., Kleinhauz, 1982).

11 The Federal Bureau of Investigation (FBI), the Department of the Treasury, and the criminal investigation branches of the U.S. Army, Navy, and Air Force have adopted policies that investigative hypnosis be administered exclusively by individuals trained in medicine or psychology with special expertise in the use of hypnosis, and that investigators intimately familiar with the problems of hypnosis but unfamiliar with the details of the specific case coordinate its use in interrogation (see Ault, 1979, for FBI guidelines).

12 In criminal matters the Maryland Special Court of Appeals is considered the highest court of appeal in this state. Both the original *Harding* v. *State* (1968) decision and its reversal in the *Collins* v. *State* (1982) decision were rulings by this court.

13 See note 9.

14 The Wisconsin Supreme Court in *State* v. *Armstrong* (1983) also explicitly ruled that "hypnotically refreshed" testimony was neither automatically admissible nor excluded per se. Instead, the court mandated a case-by-case evaluation with the burden of proof to demonstrate admissibility and the absence of undue suggestiveness resting upon the side that wishes to introduce the "hypnotically refreshed" testimony. Although the court took judicial notice of the proposed guidelines for the use of hypnosis, it did not specifically require them, emphasizing that it is the trial court's responsibility to evaluate the manner in which hypnosis was used.

15 It may be desirable, however, to use hypnosis in the context of investigation to explore issues that the subject would *not* subsequently be testifying about, leaving open the possibility that the individual might be able to testify about matters that are not dealt with in the hypnosis interview. A variant of this issue involves the use of hypnotically elicited "recollections" brought forth during the therapeutic use of hypnosis (such as in the treatment of traumatic neuroses) – recollections later forming the basis of testimony. Some clinicians have argued that the exclusion of testimony following therapeutic hypnosis denies the patient (e.g., rape victim) the right to the treatment of choice (i.e., hypnosis). Hypnosis has not, however, been considered the treatment of choice by any of the leading crisis intervention or rape treatment centers. Thus, the argument is misleading in that alternative therapeutic approaches exist and are more widely employed.

16 When police artists are used to help the witness or victim construct a facsimile of their mental image of the perpetrator, it is most desirable to conduct this outside of hypnosis. The interaction between the police artist and the hypnotized individual is such that the subject's mental image may easily be altered. Nonetheless, some police artists prefer to work with the individual during hypnosis. If this is to be done it becomes absolutely vital to determine any possible preconceptions of the artist concerning the appearance of the perpetrator. Because talented police artists are rare, he or she may have worked with another witness in constructing a facsimile, making the attempt with the hypnotized subject prone to the effects of his or her acquired biases. In any case, the careful videotaping of such an interaction in hypnosis would be mandatory.

17 The Federal Bureau of Investigation tries to ensure the interviewer's lack of familiarity with the specific case by using an agent from a different jurisdiction.

10 Detecting deception in eyewitness cases: problems and prospects in the use of the polygraph

Frank Horvath

Eyewitness accounts of a criminal event may be erroneous for many reasons. When a witness goes beyond what may be attributed to human error, however, and deliberately distorts what was seen or fabricates a story about what was not seen at all, justice must certainly be a doubtful outcome. Because those involved in the administration of our system of justice – police, prosecutors, defense attorneys, and judges – know that a lying witness can have a devastating effect, they develop a certain eye for dissimulation. They also recognize that even when they have no suspicion that an eyewitness is lying, there may be good reason to doubt the accuracy of the eyewitness's account. In instances like these, the polygraph is commonly used to help determine the accuracy of the eyewitness account.

Whether used to detect that an eyewitness is lying, to verify doubtful eyewitness accounts, or for other purposes, the polygraphic examination plays a very important role in justice today. In fact, the versatility and utility of the polygraphic examination make it one of the most important applied psychological techniques ever developed for use in our system of justice. It is perhaps for that reason that the use of the polygraph – indeed, the mere mention of the device – seems to provoke controversy. Unfortunately, that controversy is in large measure attributable to the lack of thorough scien-

The author gratefully acknowledges the support of Robert Trojanowicz, director, School of Criminal Justice, Michigan State University, and the assistance of the Social Science Research Bureau, AUR grants, in the preparation of this chapter. Dr. J. Siegel, L. Marcy, S. Slowik, J. Buckley, and K. McCracken made helpful comments on an earlier draft of the manuscript. I am also indebted to Kathy Riel who, in difficult circumstances, managed to do the typing and to the many polygraphic examiners who offered their help in describing some of their cases, most of which, for lack of space, I was unable to present. Portions of this chapter, reprinted and adapted here with permission, appeared previously in *Polygraph* (1976, *5*, 127–145) and the *Journal of Forensic Sciences* (1982, *27*, 340–351, copyright ASTM, 1916 Race St., Philadelphia, Pennsylvania 19103).

tific knowledge, both empirical and theoretical, about polygraphic testing. We know surprisingly little about the use of the polygraph in field settings, but the past decade has been one of considerable scientific and popular interest in polygraphic procedures. It is the purpose of this chapter, therefore, to discuss the theory and evidence pertaining to polygraphic testing. First, I shall describe two eyewitness cases in which the polygraph was used.

On January 2, 1981, Sandra Dennis complained to the police that on that day she had been the victim of a purse snatching. As she was walking on Desmond Avenue someone came from behind and tapped her on the shoulder; she turned around and was confronted by a young man who grabbed her purse and from it took a wallet containing $170 in cash along with her driver's license, charge cards, and personal papers. The youth then turned and ran. Ms. Dennis described her assailant as about 18–20 years old, white, male, wearing blue jeans and a gold and maroon high school athletic jacket; he had dark shaggy hair, parted in the middle, and brown eyes and a drooping mustache; he weighed, she guessed, about 140 pounds. The police officers who responded to Ms. Dennis's call checked the immediate area but could not locate anyone fitting the description. Eleven days later, however, two police officers who were working a special detail in a local shopping mall responded to another call from Ms. Dennis, who was shopping in the mall. When they arrived, she told them that the youth who had stolen her purse was now a customer in the mall's hobby shop.

The youth, Chris Boutz, was arrested; Ms. Dennis confronted him and stated positively that he had been her assailant. Upon returning to the police station, Ms. Dennis again said she was certain he was the thief. Boutz denied it and claimed that on January 2, 1981, he had stayed home all day; furthermore, he denied owning a jacket or clothes similar to those described by the victim. These statements were all verified by Boutz's parents; a search of the Boutz home failed to reveal clothing like that described. The investigators decided to ask Boutz to take a polygraphic examination about the purse snatching; he agreed. The examiner concluded that Boutz was definitely telling the truth in his denial of the purse snatching. Boutz was temporarily released. Shortly thereafter another youth – who looked rather like Boutz – was arrested for purse snatching; he subsequently was charged with and pleaded guilty to the attack on Ms. Dennis. Consequently, Boutz was, of course, never prosecuted.[1]

In cases like the one just described, the polygraphic results not only helped in the investigation but, more important, protected an innocent defendant from unwarranted involvement in the justice system and from a criminal conviction that might have ensued. Although there are no uniform statistics on how frequent such cases are, there is little doubt that there are numerous cases in which polygraphic results either directly or indirectly lead to the exoneration of or dismissal of charges against a defendant erroneously identified by an eyewitness. In fact, even though polygraphic results are not regularly admitted as evidence in court proceedings, they are regularly used by police and prosecutorial officials to decide whether criminal charges should or should not be brought. In cases of doubtful or suspicious circumstances, particularly those involving eyewitnesses whose truthfulness is questionable, prosecutors routinely make use of polygraphic results; those results often tip the balance in favor of either dismissal of charges or formal criminal proceedings.

Perhaps the most widely publicized case involving the use of the polygraph in recent years is that of Floyd Fay. Because this case involved eyewitness identification and because the polygraph played an important but controversial role in the case, it will be discussed in some detail.

On March 28, 1978, the Perrysberg, Ohio, Police Department received a call that there had been a shooting at a local grocery store. At the scene the police found that Fred Ery, the owner of the store, had been critically wounded in an apparent robbery attempt. A witness to the shooting who had been making a purchase in the store, told the police that Ery's assailant had entered the store wearing a ski mask, pointed a gun at Ery and then shot him, without saying anything and without paying any attention to the witness. Although the witness could not identify Ery's assailant, Ery made several dying declarations that Floyd Fay had been his assailant. The police investigated Fay and reportedly found that Fay had been near the crime scene at the time and that at sometime in the previous year Fay had threatened to "blow Ery's head off" because Ery had made advances to a girl friend of Fay's.

Eventually, Fay was arrested for and charged with the murder of Ery. Before the trial the prosecutor requested that Fay take a polygraphic examination to be carried out by an examiner who at that time was employed by the Bureau of Criminal Identification of Ohio. Fay stipulated that if he failed, the results of the examination were to be admissible as evidence against him at trial, and if he passed, the charges against him were to be dismissed. Moreover, Fay also stipulated that if he failed, he be allowed to take a second examination from an expert of his choice. If the results of the two examinations were in conflict or if either was inconclusive, neither could be admitted as evidence. Fay failed both examinations. At trial the polygraphic findings and the circumstantial evidence led to Fay's conviction by a jury, after only 5 hours of deliberation. Reportedly, the jurors and other legal observers questioned after the trial said that Fay's conviction turned not on the polygraphic results but rather on Ery's dying declarations and Fay's failure to testify in his defense at trial. (Fay's attorney told the jury in his opening statement that Fay would testify.)

While in prison, Fay wrote to several polygraph experts and a critic of the polygraphic field seeking their review and assistance with respect to his first polygraphic examination. Gordon Barland, a private polygraphist, reviewed the polygraphic data of the first examination and concluded that the results were inconclusive. David Lykken, a critic of the polygraphic field, reported that the data did not show anything at all. I also reviewed the polygraphic results and reported to Fay that they were inconclusive and that another, more thorough examination was necessary to determine Fay's truthfulness. David Raskin, a psychologist researching polygraph testing, reported to Fay that although the examination had not been carefully structured his analysis showed that Fay's first polygraphic results indicated truthfulness.

Subsequent to, but not as a result of, the additional analyses of Fay's first polygraphic examination, three other people were charged with the murder of Ery. Fay was released from prison.

The Fay case illustrates how prosecutors may rely on polygraphic examinations to determine whether to go to trial. Even without a stipulation, of course, prosecutors may and do use polygraphic results to decide whether charges should be dismissed, especially in those instances in which eyewitness identification is of doubtful validity. The Fay case is atypical, however, in that the polygraphic results were entered into evidence (such stipulations are legally permissible in many states; see Ansley, 1980); the results were reviewed by several experts, all of whom have both scientific and practical training in the polygraphic field; and Fay was later exonerated by the conviction of those who were apparently guilty – a very infrequent happening in our criminal justice system (Ferguson, 1971). The issues raised by the Fay case with respect to polygraphic testing will be discussed further later in this chapter.

The polygraphic industry

There are today more than 3,000 active polygraphic examiners in the United States. Almost every major law enforcement agency in the country employs at least one examiner, and many large agencies employ several full-time examiners. Apart from those who conduct polygraphic examinations for law enforcement agencies, there are also those who work for other agencies of the justice system, such as courts and prosecutors and within the governmental intelligence community (e.g., for the Central Intelligence Agency). Still, it is probably the private, commercial polygraphic examiner, who conducts polygraphic examinations for a fee, who does the bulk of polygraphic testing in the United States. A commercial examiner may carry out testing for businesses in order to resolve privately a crime committed on their premises or to assist the company in the selection of applicants for employment. The use of the polygraph for the latter purpose is highly controversial, and because the issues involved in that controversy are not pertinent to the present work, they will not be discussed further here. Private, commercial polygraphic examiners, however, also conduct examinations for officials involved with the justice system. For instance, it is not uncommon for a prosecutor or judge to request a privately conducted polygraphic examination of a criminal defendant in situations in which an examination carried out by a law enforcement agency would be either inappropriate or unavailable. Even more common, however, is the use of commercial polygraphic services by defense counsel. Many lawyers routinely require their clients to undergo private polygraphic examinations to determine whether they have told the truth about the incident in question. Because these private examination results are confidential, defense attorneys use them in preparation of a trial defense or to help decide whether or not to seek a plea bargain with the prosecutor.

Historical development of polygraphic procedures

There are already available excellent accounts of the early history of field polygraphic procedures and the development of the instrument (Larson, 1932; Trovillo, 1939). The following review of this area will, therefore, be brief.

It was not until about 1895, when Cesare Lombroso, an Italian physiologist, and his student Mosso used the hydrosphygmograph and the "scientific cradle," that objective measurement of physiological changes became associated with the detection of deception (Trovillo, 1939). Following Lombroso and Mosso, Hugo Munsterberg (1908), made reference to the effect of lying on breathing, cardiovascular activity, involuntary movements, and the galvanic skin response (GSR). Vittorio Benussi (1914) reported a relationship between the inspiration–expiration ratio in breathing and deception. His findings were later confirmed by Harold Burtt (1921a, 1921b), who added that systolic blood pressure was yet more indicative of deception than was respiration. William Marston's (1917) findings agreed with Burtt's that discontinuous measures of systolic blood pressure were superior to either respiration or GSR for detecting deception. John Larson (1921) modified Marston's blood pressure test and developed an instrument and procedure for making a continuous recording of both blood pressure–pulse rate and respiration. Leonarde Keeler, generally credited with developing the prototype of the polygraphic instrument now used in most field settings, further refined Larson's apparatus by adding a device for measuring and recording electrodermal activity (Keeler, 1930).

The discussion up to this point should not be taken as an indication that respiration, cardiovascular activity, and GSR are the only physiological processes that have been found to be associated with deception. There has also been limited success at detecting deception by measuring other physiological activity – for example, electroencephalic activity (Oberman, 1939), pupil dilation (Berrien & Huntington, 1943), oculomotor activity (Berrien, 1942), voice modulation (Alpert, Kurtzberg, & Friedhoff, 1963; Fay & Middleton, 1941), oxygenation of the vascular system (Dana, 1958), and covert muscular movements (Reid, 1945). More recently, it has been claimed that a voice microtremor, detectable with specialized instrumentation, is related to deception – a claim that has not been supported in the scientific literature (Horvath, 1978, 1979, 1982; Kubis, 1974). What is now fairly well agreed upon by field examiners is that any attempt at detecting deception must be made with an instrument that records at least cardiovascular, respiratory, and electrodermal activity.

Field polygraphic procedures

There are two major field lie detection procedures in use today: the relevant/irrelevant (R/I) and the control-question (C-Q) techniques. I will now discuss these techniques in some detail, to aid in the understanding of the literature about the research bearing on field uses of the polygraph.

The relevant/irrelevant technique

Many of the early practitioners considered the primary benefit of polygraphic testing to be that it enhanced their ability to obtain confessions of guilt or admissions of lying from criminal suspects (Inbau, 1942). It is not surprising then that polygraphic testing and interrogation (intensive or accusatory questioning designed to secure a confession) were often considered identical, and perhaps inseparable, processes; that is, the two processes were blended or combined in such a way that the psychological effect of the polygraphic instrument and the consequent physiological recordings could be maximized to secure confessions of guilt.

The pretest interview. Simply stated, the R/I technique is relatively unstructured, consisting of an interview, or perhaps intensive questioning, followed by or combined with polygraphic testing (Harrelson, 1964). During the interview the examiner discusses with the subject background information relative to the investigation at hand and exploits any hesitancy or uncertainty in the subject's answers to questions; he also observes the subject's behavior in order to locate sensitive areas that may be useful in the testing. The examiner also explains the purpose of the testing and nature of the polygraphic instrument, implying that it is futile for the subject to harbor any thoughts of "beating" the test. It is also the examiner's purpose during the interview to establish rapport with the subject and to become familiar with the subject's language and personal history in order to ensure that the test questions, which may or may not be reviewed before the testing, will be effectively worded.

The length of the interview is determined by the examiner, according to his impression of the subject's emotional accessibility. A high-strung subject generally requires a lengthier interview; a relatively passive subject must be aroused, and so forth.

Polygraphic testing. Polygraphic testing in the R/I technique usually consists of asking a series of questions relevant to the crime interspersed with irrelevant or noncritical questions; other types of questions such as those that might expose a guilt complex may be asked at the discretion of the examiner. The precise nature, wording, and ordering of the test questions is determined by the examiner as testing progresses, as is the length of any one test. Most often, however, general questions precede specific questions, an order believed helpful because it recapitulates the steps in the commission of an offense.

The length of any given test, the asking of the relevant and irrelevant questions at least once in a series, is determined by the examiner and is dependent primarily upon the subject's ability to withstand the effects of the apparatus used for recording cardiovascular activity. (A standard blood pressure cuff, inflated for the duration of a question sequence, causes moderate discomfort in some persons.) Within any given polygraphic examination two R/I tests may be conducted before a determination of deception (or truthfulness) is made, although proponents of the method feel that in most cases such a determination can be made after one test.

Proponents of the R/I technique assume that truthful people will not react differently, to any great degree, to relevant and irrelevant questions, whereas people who are lying will. In other words, determinations of truth-telling and lying depend upon perceptible differences in physiological responses to the stimulus of noncritical and critical items. Moreover, during any given test or between any two tests, such differential reactions constitute cause for intensive questioning of the subject by the examiner. Proponents of this technique believe that interrogation for the purpose of securing a confession or admission of lying at any time during the pretest interview or the testing is justified if, in the examiner's judgment, it seems warranted. The lack of an adequate control response is believed by many to make the R/I technique an interrogation capitalizing on the psychological effect of the polygraphic instrument and recordings; R/I tests, then, for reasons to be explained further, are usually considered by proponents of the C-Q technique inadequate for making decisions about a person's truthfulness or deception on the basis of the polygraphic recordings exclusively (Backster, 1962).

The control-question technique

Many leading polygraphic examiners today distinguish between interrogation and polygraphic testing. The major impetus of this change in approach was the "control question" as developed by John E. Reid (1947). Since Reid's first publication on this topic, he and other practitioners have so refined the use of control questions and the procedure used for giving polygraphic tests that it is now believed that polygraphic testing and interrogation must be considered separately. That is, most proponents of the C-Q technique believe that polygraphic testing provides a substantially accurate means of determining a person's truthfulness or deception independent of interrogation; in fact, interrogation before or during the testing proper is believed detrimental to testing (Reid & Inbau, 1977).

The C-Q technique consists of two distinct components: the pretest interview and polygraphic testing. Although some examiners maintain that posttest interrogation is a third component (Barland & Raskin, 1973), such a contention is not in keeping with the notion that interrogation and polygraphic testing are separate phenomena.

The pretest interview. The pretest interview as used by proponents of the C-Q technique is done before testing, when the examiner discusses with the subject the purpose of the examination, the nature of the polygraphic instrument, and, in general, seeks to prepare the subject for the testing. Unlike the interview used in the R/I technique, however, there usually is no intensive questioning on the issue at hand. Moreover, during the interview the examiner makes it a point to review with the subject the exact test questions that will be asked, and the subject himself participates in the formulation of these questions. Such participation is considered essential to the functioning of the testing procedure, particularly with respect to the control questions.

There are, of course, variations among examiners in the way a pretest interview is conducted. Some examiners conduct a lengthy interview and acquire detailed background information (e.g., medical history), whereas others do not. Some use specialized interview techniques to become familiar with behavioral characteristics that may be helpful in judging truthfulness or deception. Some examiners spend considerable time explaining the nature of the polygraphic instrument, the way in which autonomic responses are used to detect deception, and the futility of trying to beat the test. More detailed information about variations in the pretest interview can be found in Reid and Inbau (1977), Horvath (1973), or Barland and Raskin (1973).

Polygraphic testing. Although there are differences between pretest interviews in the R/I and C-Q procedures, the essential difference between the two methods lies in the nature of the questions asked during polygraphic testing and the manner in which response data are evaluated. In C-Q testing, three basic types of questions are asked: irrelevant, relevant, and control questions, although, as in the R/I technique, other types may also be used (Arther, 1969; Reid & Inbau, 1977). Irrelevant questions are those used for establishing "normal" or truthtelling patterns: "Do they call you Joe?" "Are you over 21 years of age?" Relevant questions are those that pertain to the matter under investigation: "Did you shoot John Doe?" "Did you fire the shots that killed John Doe?" Control questions are those growing out of interaction between the examiner and the subject; in general, they deal with matters similar to, but of presumed lesser significance than, the offense being investigated. Although the interaction between the subject and the examiner determines the exact nature of these questions, examples in a burglary investigation might be: "Did you ever steal anything?" "Except for what you have already told me about, did you ever steal anything else?" The examiner seeks to frame these questions in such a way that the subject will answer no but will in all probability be lying or at least have some doubt or concern about the truthfulness or accuracy of his answer. After the formulation of all test questions and at the completion of the pretest interview, polygraphic testing is conducted.

In the polygraphic testing, the examiner asks the subject the previously reviewed irrelevant, relevant, and control questions in a series of polygraphic tests. Each test, usually lasting about 3 minutes, generally consists of 10 or 11 questions, 4 of which are irrelevant, 2 or 3 control, and 4 or 5 relevant. All questions are asked once during one test, and at about 20-second intervals. A complete examination consists of the repetition of several of these tests. It is generally agreed that for an examiner to ascertain with any degree of accuracy the deception or truthfulness of the subject's answer to a relevant test question, that question should be asked at least once on each of two separate tests; sometimes, four or five separate tests may be conducted before a determination of deception is made (Reid & Inbau, 1977).

Upon completion of several tests, the examiner briefly reviews the accrued polygraphic recordings (charts) and decides whether further testing is necessary. In some cases response data from the first two control-question tests are sufficient to indicate the subject's truthfulness or deception (Reid & Inbau, 1977). More often, however, further testing is indicated and one or more specialized tests are given, such as a mixed-question test, or yes test (Reid & Inbau, 1977), or a silent-answer test (Horvath & Reid, 1972).

Stimulation procedures. Proponents of the C-Q technique have developed various tactics to clarify response data; that is, these tactics are used not only to augment responsiveness to testing but, more important, to direct the subject's attention (psychological set) to those test questions that constitute the greatest threat to his well-being. Presumably, for persons telling the truth these tactics augment responses to control questions; for those lying they stimulate response to relevant questions. Such tactics may take the form of specialized tests – the card test, the silent-answer test, and so on – or may consist of various forms of examiner–subject interaction.

The various tactics used by examiners to stimulate subjects are too numerous to detail here. It should be noted, however, that the tactics are rather indirect in nature; they are not accusatory and do not usually make reference to particular test questions; and, most important, they pre-sumably make a significant contribution to the functioning of the C-Q procedure (Horvath, 1976; Reid & Inbau, 1977).

While the testing procedure just outlined is representative of that used by many field examiners employing the C-Q technique, there are other spe-cialized tests and other variations of the procedures. Some of these variations are in the number of individual tests that will be conducted during an examination, the organization of the tests, the order of questions within tests, and the procedure followed by the examiner during the break between tests. For a more thorough discussion of these variations see Reid and Inbau (1977), Barland and Raskin (1973), or Backster (1969a, 1969b).

Regardless of the various administrations of the C-Q technique, its pro-ponents argue that control questions embedded within the series provide a better tool for assessment of a person's truthfulness or deception to rel-evant issues than does the R/I procedure. The variations do not imply unstructured procedure, however, because each variation is controlled by its particular rules. Presumably, once informed of each other's rules, examiners using the different procedures of examination can evaluate each other's results.

Peak-of-tension testing

A type of testing occasionally encountered in field settings is the peak-of-tension (POT) test. Although the principle behind this test is often relied on by proponents of both the R/I and C-Q procedures, especially in the ordering of questions in the test series, the POT test is not a standard part of either of these procedures.

Arther (1967) has termed the two general forms of the POT tests the searching test and the known-solution test. The searching POT consists of the asking of a series of similar questions, usually with specific focus, such as the location of a murder weapon. For example, a subject tested by control-question testing may give the examiner reason to think the subject is in fact implicated in a certain murder and, further, has hidden or discarded the weapon. Under these circumstances, the searching POT test would include a series of questions – "Do you know if the gun used to kill John Jones is *under water*?" "Do you know if the gun used to kill John Jones is *buried in the ground*?" – such questions being asked throughout a number of individual tests until the examiner believes the location of the murder weapon has been determined (Arther, 1970; Reid & Inbau, 1977).

On the other hand, the known-solution POT test, although similar to the searching test in that it consists of a series of about seven questions, presupposes that the examiner is aware of particular details of a crime of which the subject denies any knowledge. For example, the examiner may know that in a certain burglary $200 in quarters has been stolen. The subject is then asked a series of questions: "Do you know if dimes were stolen in the such-and-such burglary?" "Do you know if nickels were stolen in the such-and-such burglary?" The critical question is usually put in the fourth position in the series: "Do you know if quarters were stolen in the such-and-such burglary?"

Regardless of the type of POT test employed, interpretation of the polygraphic charts thus obtained is standard. It is assumed that if a subject is in fact familiar with the critical item in the series, the polygraphic recordings (especially the cardiovascular and GSR tracings) will appear to "peak" at the critical item or will show a reaction of the greatest magnitude there. Further ramifications of the POT test and its interpretation, as well as necessary precautions in its use, are recorded in the literature (Arther, 1968; Reid & Inbau, 1977).

Contrary to what some writings say (Orne, Thackray, & Paskewitz, 1972), the POT test is not a field technique in the sense that the control-question and relevant/irrelevant procedures are "techniques." Rather, the POT is merely a specialized type of polygraphic test normally used only after testing by either the C-Q or R/I procedure; the POT test is used to determine whether a given person has guilty knowledge of specific details of a particular offense. Hence, its use is limited to those types of offenses where such details are evident. On the other hand, the C-Q and R/I procedures are diagnostic techniques not predicated on awareness of particular details of an offense. These techniques can be administered in a variety of ways, the examiner having at his disposal the specialized card test, mixed-question test, yes test, silent-answer test, and others, all of which can be used within the framework of either the C-Q or R/I technique.

Evaluation of polygraphic response data

The visual inspection technique. Field examiners rarely, if ever, employ strictly objective measurements in interpreting the significance of response data – changes in cardiovascular, respiratory, or GSR tracings recorded polygraphically. Rather, visual inspection techniques, progressing from a general appraisal of all charts (tests) down to particular analysis of reactions to particular test questions, are usually performed. Most often, changes – extent and duration of cardiovascular, respiratory, or GSR response – in any of the recorded measures are evaluated according to specifiable criteria for each as set forth in texts (Reid & Inbau, 1977) or in training manuals (Backster, 1969a).

Some writers have overgeneralized the evaluation of field-derived polygraphic charts to the point where any change from prestimulus levels is said to be indicative of deception. Although it is true that polygraphic charts indicate any changes from prestimulus levels, such changes must be considered both quantitatively and qualitatively: they cannot be summarily assumed to be indications of deception. Consider evaluation in the control-question technique, for example. Simply stated, responses in the polygraphic measures that occur more consistently over a series of tests and that are of a greater intensity to control questions than to relevant questions indicate truthfulness to the relevant questions. Conversely, responses of a consistently greater intensity to the relevant questions than to the control questions suggest deceptiveness regarding the relevant questions. The key points in this oversimplified description are that any changes have little significance unless they occur consistently, and even then they cannot be seen as significant until they are compared with other changes.

Numerical evaluation technique. One of the noteworthy variations in evaluation of polygraphic recordings is a numerical scoring system developed by Backster (1969a), a well-known field examiner. In this system, examiners assign a number ranging from -3 to $+3$ to reflect the perceived difference between responses to control and relevant question pairings for each of the physiological measures recorded; the magnitude and direction of the numbers assigned to such comparisons form the basis for decision making. For example, the examiner pairs relevant and control questions and then observes whether or not a particular question in each pair provokes an outstanding response. If the response to the relevant question is greater, a number from -1 to -3, depending upon the extent of the difference, is assigned. On the other hand, if the control-question response is greater, a number from $+1$ to $+3$ is assigned; if there is no difference between the paired responses, a zero is assigned. Such a procedure is carried out separately for each question pair for each physiological measure of all the tests administered. The numbers assigned are then added; a positive total greater than 5 and a negative total less than 5 usually are established as cut-off points to indicate truthfulness and deception, respectively. Total scores ranging between $+5$ and -5 are usually considered inconclusive.

There are some disadvantages apparent in the numerical scoring system: (a) it is possible that scoring data in such a way filters out recorded trends that might be useful in evaluation; (b) it assumes that response data are the only indices of deception (in actuality, deception is sometimes indicated not so much by specific response as by generally abnormal or erratic recordings), and (c) it makes no provision for artifacts deliberately produced by some subjects (Reid & Inbau, 1977). Within its limits, however, the numerical scoring system appears to be highly reliable and an especially useful research tool (Barland, 1972).

Summary

From this discussion of the major procedures used in the field, it should be evident that it is extremely difficult to separate the polygraphic testing or the polygraphic charts themselves from the procedure used in obtaining them. That is, the examiner–subject interaction before and during polygraphic testing is an integral part of the procedure whether or not R/I or C-Q procedures are considered. The most prominent distinction between these procedures seems to be that proponents of the C-Q technique believe that control questions are a necessary basis for objectivity in evaluation of polygraphic charts; that is, that the use of control questions results in polygraphic recordings that are valid indicators of a person's truthfulness or deception.

Laboratory lie detection procedures

Laboratory studies of lie detection have usually involved two testing paradigms characterized here as concealed-information tests and information recognition tests, the two not necessarily mutually exclusive. Neither of these approaches is similar to the control-question technique most commonly used by field examiners today. Therefore, only a brief discussion of these typical laboratory procedures will be offered.

Concealed-information tests

In concealed-information testing, both the examiner and the subject know that information is being concealed by the subject. Here, the examiner's task and the purpose of the testing is to determine merely which item among a group of items is the one being concealed. For instance, a subject is instructed to choose a number between one and seven and to write that number on a slip of paper, all the while concealing the chosen number from the examiner. Physiological responses, usually electrodermal, to all items are then inspected to determine whether the concealed item can be detected; accuracy rates for detection of concealed items are usually in the 60% to 70% range, against a typical chance expectancy of .20. Not surprisingly, however, concealed-information tests are very susceptible to countermeasure attempts, the most straightforward being merely a subject's enhancement of a response to a noncritical item. To overcome such countermeasures, the testing strategy might include the repetition of items (thereby allowing for the averaging of response magnitudes across repetitions), the reordering of items, or perhaps merely a simple warning to the subject. Except in stimulation tests it is extremely rare for a field examiner to know that a person is concealing information; thus, the concealed-information paradigm may not bear particular relevance to basic field procedures.

Although there has been a considerable amount of laboratory research using a concealed-information paradigm (Ellson et al., 1952; Geldreich, 1941; Orne et al., 1972; Ruckmick, 1938), field examiners make only limited use of such testing. It is not uncommon, for instance, for field examiners to use various forms of concealed-information tests as stimulation devices. As a part of field examination, a subject might be asked to choose a card from a small deck of cards (Reid & Inbau, 1977). The subject is instructed to lie about the chosen card as the examiner attempts to detect the lie with polygraphic equipment. Subjects' physiological responses are thereby enhanced in subsequent control-question testing (Bradley & Janisse, 1981; Senese, 1976). Thus, field examiners' use of concealed-information tests is a specialized one not directly related to their determination of a subject's truthfulness about a criminal or other incident.

Information recognition tests

In information recognition tests, the examiner's intent is to determine whether a subject recognizes which item in a group of items is the critical one; physiological response patterns that show recognition of the correct item in a series of tests, each referring to different aspects of an offense, lead to an inference that a subject committed the offense. In such situations the examiner knows in advance which item is critical and which is not. Thus, his testing strategy, as well as the manner in which physiological data are interpreted, may be different from what is done in concealed-information tests. One variation of the information recognition paradigm, for instance, is what Lykken (1959) has termed the guilty-knowledge technique. In this technique, subjects are questioned about their awareness of particular details pertaining to a certain event, a mock crime, for example. In the mock crime the "guilty" person may have had to "steal" a blue scarf from the top drawer of a brown desk in Room 12 of a certain building. Some subjects, of course, are assigned to carry out the mock crime and some are assigned to act as innocent subjects. Testing is then administered to determine who are the guilty subjects and who the innocent ones – or, more precisely, who recognizes information only the perpetrator should recognize. The testing consists of a series of multiple-choice questions in which a critical item is put among noncritical ones. For instance, one question might be: "Was the item that was taken a (a) belt, (b) shirt, (c) sweater, (d) scarf, (e) hat, (f) handkerchief?" Another might be: "Was the item taken (a) green, (b) red, (c) blue, (d) purple, (e) white, (f) orange?" Typically, a series of five or six such questions are asked, each only once. In the series of tests, it is assumed that only the person who actually committed the crime would recognize the critical items in each test – thus, that subject would be expected to respond physiologically (the measures are usually electrodermal) to a greater degree and more often to the critical than to the noncritical items. The responses of innocent subjects, on the other hand, would be expected to be randomly distributed across the items and across the tests.

Laboratory studies in which the information recognition paradigm have been used usually show quite high discrimination between guilty and innocent subjects, 90% to over 95%. This is true, by the way, even when relatively simple scoring schemes are used to evaluate response data.

By using the guilty-knowledge technique and establishing an arbitrary cutoff point for objective analysis of GSR reactions, Lykken (1959) was able to classify correctly subjects by group 89.9% of the time and to identify the guilty and the innocent 93.9% of the time. In a follow-up study to assess the effects of faking on the guilty-knowledge technique, Lykken (1960) achieved 100% correct classification of subjects who concealed items of personal information. Studies by other investigators have also reported success of varying degrees using GSR in the guilty-knowledge technique (Balloun & Holmes, 1979; Ben Shakhar, Lieblich, & Kugelmass, 1970; Davidson, 1968; Podlesny & Raskin, 1978).

It is of some interest to note that the so-called known-solution peak-of-tension test as used by field examiners is a variation of the information recognition paradigm. In the laboratory, the critical item is usually randomly inserted among the noncritical items. Field examiners, however, most often sequence items (for each multiple-choice question) in such a way that the critical item comes near the middle of the sequence. This, it is believed, capitalizes on the anticipation that would be expected in a subject who knows what the critical item is. Because field examiners may repeat a question and all the items asked in one test, in the repetition the subject knows the order of the items. Thus, it becomes possible to determine not only whether the subject shows a more pronounced physiological response to the critical item(s) but also to determine whether the subject anticipates the critical item, gradually becoming more tense until the critical item appears and relaxing afterward – thus the name "peak-of-tension" test.

Although the information recognition paradigm has been used quite often in the laboratory, its use in field settings is quite limited. It may be true that that paradigm has greater use in the field than field examiners believe; it is also the case, however, that criminal cases in which the examiner has particular information about the case and about which only the guilty person would be aware are not frequent. Such cases are rare because police investigators reveal details of the investigation to the media and to suspects and because the majority of criminal offenses get very little investigative effort that would lead to the discovery of the kind of information necessary for the proper construction of information recognition testing.

Because laboratory research in lie detection has typically involved the concealed-information or the information recognition paradigms, the degree to which the results in such research generalize to what occurs in the field is not certain. Moreover, there are other differences between typical laboratory and field procedures that may account for the dissimilarity between most laboratory findings and the claims of field examiners. For example, (a) most laboratory researchers use a measure of electrodermal activity as the only dependent variable (Chappell & Matthew, 1929; Marston, 1921;

Podlesny & Raskin, 1977); (b) the level of subject effect and the motivational characteristics differ in the laboratory and in the field (Davidson, 1968; Gustafson & Orne, 1963; Kugelmass & Lieblich, 1966; Kugelmass et al., 1968; Lykken, 1959; Thackray & Orne, 1968); (c) laboratory and field testing apparatus are dissimilar (Orne, 1975); (d) objective scoring of response data as typically done in the laboratory may "mask out" important information (Kubis, 1962; Kugelmass, 1963); and (e) most laboratory research has not involved the use of "control questions" as proposed by either early investigators (Kubis, 1945, 1950; Summers, 1939) or leading field examiners (Reid & Inbau, 1977). To put it simply, control questions in the field are designed to channel the psychological set of truthful subjects away from relevant questions and toward the control questions. Lying subjects, on the other hand, are presumed to be "psychologically set" to the relevant questions. Hence, consistently greater physiological responses to control questions are considered indicative of truthfulness regarding the relevant questions, whereas consistently greater responses to relevant questions are suggestive of lying. The use of control questions reportedly has significantly increased the ability of field examiners to discriminate between truthful and lying persons and at the same time has lowered the number of inconclusive tests (Reid & Inbau, 1977). Because control questions as used in field settings are individually developed with the subject to ensure that they involve personally relevant material and that the subject will either lie or have doubts about the accuracy of his answer, it is likely that the proper use of those questions heightens a person's concern for the test. Thus, it might be expected that the use of field-type control questions in laboratory studies would increase physiological responsiveness much as the use of other personally relevant material does (Berkhout, Walter, & Abey, 1970; Thackray & Orne, 1968).

Control-question tests

In recent years significant attempts have been made to overcome the many differences between typical laboratory research and field lie detection. These attempts involve the use of field control-question procedures in laboratory-contrived but realistic situations; these studies, as a group, therefore, are more directly pertinent to polygraphic testing as it is practiced in the field.

Barland and Raskin (1975) reported the first laboratory study in which field control-question procedures were used. In that study 72 students were randomly assigned to a "guilty" or "innocent" condition. Those 36 subjects assigned to the former condition were instructed to commit a theft of $10 from a certain desk drawer; they were also told that if they convinced the polygraphic examiner that they had not taken the money, they could keep it. The innocent subjects were told the details of the "crime" the guilty subjects committed and were warned that if they failed to appear innocent, they could lose credit for participation. Thus, both innocent and guilty subjects were motivated, though not in an equivalent manner, to appear innocent.

All subjects were given field polygraphic examinations similar to that described previously in this chapter, except in this instance none of the subjects was asked control questions that were individually developed, as they are in the field. Rather, the control questions used in this study were standardized for all subjects, a practice that field examiners would believe to result in less than desirable differentiation between control and relevant questions (Harman & Reid, 1955; Reid & Inbau, 1977). These examinations were carried out in a "blind" manner by Barland, who had previously completed a standard field polygraphic training course. Upon completion of all polygraphic examinations, the polygraphic charts produced were subjected to evaluation in three ways. First, Barland numerically scored all polygraphic charts. Using field criteria for scoring, and applying a decision rule to those scores in which all total scores over $+4$ indicated truthfulness (greater and more consistent responses to control questions than to relevant questions) and all those less than -4 indicated deception (greater and more consistent responses to relevant than to control questions), Barland correctly categorized 53% (23 guilty and 15 innocent) of all subjects; 12% were incorrectly categorized and the scores of 35% of the subjects were reported to be "inconclusive" (their total numerical score was between ±4 inclusive). Excluding the inconclusive category, 81% ($p < .05$) of the subjects were correctly categorized.

Second, Barland and Raskin also had five trained field examiners evaluate the charts of the 72 subjects. In the evaluation, the examiners had no information about the examinations other than the polygraphic data; yet, the mean percentage of correct decisions was 82% and the range was from 79% to 86%. On the average, therefore, these examiners had an accuracy rate almost identical to that obtained by the actual examiner.

The third evaluation of the polygraphic data in the Barland and Raskin study was an objective, quantitative analysis of all chart-based data. Polygraphic responses to all control and relevant questions were measured to determine whether, as would be predicted from the theory of the C-Q technique, guilty subjects showed larger responses to relevant questions, and innocent subjects showed greater responses to control questions. The predicted effects were observed for four dependent variables: decreases in respiration amplitude, increases in respiration cycle time, decreases in skin resistance, and increases in blood volume. Thus, both the objective and the field scoring of the polygraphic data in the Barland and Raskin study were supportive of predictions derived from the theory on which the field control-question technique is based. In addition, the results of this study supported some of the empirical evidence already reported in field-based studies (this evidence will be further discussed at a later point in this chapter): specifically, that polygraphic charts derived from properly conducted control-question polygraphic examinations can be interpreted with a high degree of interrater agreement by trained persons who have access to only the polygraphic data.

Raskin and Hare (1978) reported a study designed to deal with some of the shortcomings apparent in the Barland and Raskin (1975) report. In this study a sample of 48 prisoners, half of whom were diagnosed as psychopaths according to Cleckley's (1964) outline, were used as subjects; thus, the subjects here were apparently more representative of the subject population encountered in some field settings, particularly those involved in criminal violations under investigation by law enforcement agencies, than in the Barland and Raskin study. One-half of the psychopaths and half of the nonpsychopaths were randomly assigned to carry out a mock theft of $20; the other half of each group was assigned to an innocent condition. The innocent subjects were aware of the crime committed by the guilty subjects and they were instructed to deny having taken the $20. Each group of subjects was motivated to appear innocent by the promise of a $20 bonus for doing so successfully.

All subjects were given polygraphic examinations consistent with the control-question procedure used by Barland and Raskin (1975), except that in this instance the control questions were adjusted to fit each individual. Therefore, the study more closely approximated typical field procedure than did the Barland and Raskin study, in which the control questions were not modified to accommodate individual perceptions of the content and scope of the control questions.

Raskin, who had carried out the polygraphic testing of all subjects, analyzed all polygraphic data by numerically scoring each subject's charts. A score of +6 or greater resulted in a decision of truthfulness (innocent), whereas a −6 or lower was judged deceptive (guilty). All scores between ±5 were reported as inconclusive decisions. In addition to the numerical scoring, all polygraphic charts were also subjected to objective quantification by a person who had no knowledge of either the numerical scores assigned by Raskin or the treatments administered to the subjects.

The numerical evaluation of the polygraphic charts produced 88%

correct decisions, 4% wrong, and 8% inconclusive. Excluding inconclusives a 96% accuracy rate obtained. Two errors were made; both of them were false positives, that is, truthful subjects who were erroneously reported to be deceptive. One of the errors was made on a psychopathic subject and one on a nonpsychopath. There were no statistically significant differences in the accuracy rates for psychopaths and nonpsychopaths.

The objective quantification of the polygraphic data in this study showed, as in the Barland and Raskin (1975) study, that predictions derived from control-question theory obtained for a number of physiological measures. For example, in respiratory, electrodermal, and cardiovascular measures, truthful subjects showed certain response patterns to a greater degree to control questions than to relevant questions; on the other hand, responses of deceptive subjects in those measures were more pronounced to relevant questions than to control questions. Thus, this study again demonstrated in both the field numerical-scoring results and the objective quantification of response data that the control-question technique functions essentially as expected. Although the results of this study with respect to the detectability of psychopaths is a matter of controversy (Lykken, 1978; Raskin, 1978), the findings nevertheless support the effectiveness of the C-Q technique in a population more closely approximating that encountered in some field settings.

Three additional laboratory studies provide further support for the effectiveness of the C-Q technique. In two of these studies, reported by Podlesny and Raskin (1977) and Rovner, Raskin, and Kircher (1979), the subjects were recruited from the general community by advertisements in newspapers. In both studies the accuracy of decisions based on blind numerical scoring of the polygraphic charts was very similar to that reported in the Raskin and Hare (1978) study; moreover, objective quantification of the polygraphic data generally replicated the finding of Barland and Raskin (1975) and Raskin and Hare (1978) that field-type control questions function as predicted with a number of physiological measures. The third study, reported by Dawson (1980), was carried out in a manner almost identical to the studies previously discussed in this section except his subjects were trained actors who were instructed to try to beat the control-question testing by using methods learned in acting school; none of the guilty subjects was able to beat the test. The accuracy of decisions made in blind evaluation of the polygraphic data and the results of objective quantifications of those data were supportive of the findings reported by Raskin and his colleagues.

Table 10.1 shows the distribution of the decisions made in the various laboratory studies of the C-Q technique that are discussed in this section.

Table 10.1. *Accuracy of control-question testing in laboratory studies*

Type of control questions	n	Decisions			% false positive	% false negative	% correct excluding inconclusives
		% correct	% wrong	% inconclusive			
Nonadjusted							
Barland & Raskin (1975)	72	53	12	35	17	8	81
Adjusted							
Raskin & Hare (1978)	48	88	4	8	8	0	96
Podlesny & Raskin (1978)	20	85	5	10	0	5	94
Rovner, Raskin, & Kircher (1979)	48	88	4	8	8	0	95
Dawson (1980)	24	88	8	4	17	0	91
M for adjusted control studies		87	5	7	8	1	94

One of the important points to be made with respect to those studies concerns the degree to which field procedures, particularly the development of control questions, were adhered to. Field examiners, for instance, report that in order for control questions to function optimally they must be individually adjusted (Reid & Inbau, 1977). Without such adjustment it would be expected that control questions would be relatively ineffective; that is, improper or nonadjusted control questions would have less arousal value for innocent subjects and would, therefore, be less apt to direct their "psychological set" away from relevant questions. Thus, it would be predicted that in situations in which control questions are not properly developed, there would be a higher rate of false positive (truthful subjects incorrectly reported as deceptive; or, in other words, truthful subjects showing greater physiological responses to relevant than to control questions) and inconclusive (i.e., equal magnitude of responses to both relevant and control questions) decisions. The data shown in Table 10.1 are suggestive of support for that prediction. In the Barland and Raskin (1975) report, the only laboratory study in which the control questions were not individually adjusted, only 53% of the decisions were correct, 12% were wrong, and 35% were inconclusive; 17% of the decisions were of the false positive type. On the other hand, in each of the other studies shown in Table 10.1 the control questions were individually adjusted; the mean percentage of correct decisions in those studies was 87, whereas the mean percentage of wrong, inconclusive, and false positive decisions was 5, 7, and 8, respectively.

Thus, taken together, all of the laboratory studies discussed in this section yielded findings strongly supportive of the basic theoretical premise of the field developed control-question technique. A study reported by Bradley and Janisse (1981) offers further support for that premise. In their study it was found that innocent subjects tested with the C-Q technique reported that they perceived themselves as responding more to control questions than to relevant questions, whereas guilty subjects reported the opposite perception. These subjective impressions were supported by electrodermal response data that showed that 86% of the innocent subjects responded more to control questions and about the same percentage of guilty subjects responded more to relevant questions.

In spite of the empirical support for the effectiveness of the C-Q technique in a variety of subject populations as shown in the laboratory studies, there is, nevertheless, considerable controversy about the generalizability (external validity) of those findings. Lykken (1980), for instance, apparently believes that it is not possible to extend laboratory findings to field situations in which an innocent person, fearing prosecution and perhaps conviction for a serious crime, is motivated by entirely different forces from those obtaining in the laboratory. Podlesny and Raskin (1977), on the other hand, have expressed the belief that carefully constructed laboratory studies can and do approximate the field situation.

Findings from the field

As already pointed out in this chapter, field situations in which the control-question technique is used differ in many important respects from laboratory situations, even those in which there is an attempt to simulate field conditions by using a realistic mock crime, subjects who are more representative of those encountered in field settings, and control-question testing procedures as used in the field. Those and other procedural and contextual differences notwithstanding, however, field situations also differ from laboratory situations in the availability and certainty of a criterion for establishing ground truth. In a laboratory it is relatively easy to structure an experiment in which innocence and guilt are known; in the field, guilt and innocence are seldom known with a high degree of certainty. Some cases, of course, are verified by the confession of a guilty person, some by a court decision; but, even these criteria are limited in their usefulness. Confessions, for instance, may be false; similarly, courts' judgments may be in error because they may, and commonly do, turn on legal as opposed to factual issues. Moreover, a large proportion of field polygraphic decisions is never resolved satisfactorily by either a confession or a court judgment. Thus, the ground truth problem in field settings is a very hard one to deal with.

There have been two major approaches to estimating the accuracy and effectiveness of the C-Q technique in the field. The first of these is what I will term the independent-criterion method. In this, a criterion measure that is free of influence by polygraphic results is used to establish ground truth. In the second approach, the dependent-criterion method, confessions made to polygraphic examiners following their examination of guilty subjects in various investigations are used to establish ground truth. Usually these confessions are corroborated by other evidence and there is little doubt that the confessors are factually guilty. Sometimes, of course, the confession of a guilty subject in an investigation completely exonerates other subjects who may also have been given polygraphic examinations in the same investigation; these subjects are therefore known to have been innocent of involvement in the matter under investigation. Because any confessions made in field situations almost always occur after a polygraphic examination and because they are usually made directly to the polygraphic examiner, they are clearly dependent on a judgment by the examiner that the subject was deceptive (guilty). In other words, in the field polygraphic setting, confessions are seldom made to a person who had no knowledge of or was uninfluenced by the confessors' polygraphic results.

Early claims of accuracy

Many of the early lie detection practitioners used procedures and instrumentation that by today's standards appear unsophisticated. In spite of this deficiency, however, there are numerous reports of impressive validity (Arther & Caputo, 1959; Benussi, 1914; Inbau & Reid, 1953; Larson, 1932; Lyon, 1936; MacNitt, 1942; Marston, 1917; Summers, 1939). It is unfortunate, however, that the majority of these reports are quite old and did not employ polygraphic instrumentation (MacNitt, 1942; Summers, 1939), did not use procedures commonly used today (Lyon, 1936), or, in some cases, did not properly analyze data (Orlansky, 1964). Moreover, many field reports of the accuracy of the polygraph rely on anecdotal evidence, which, although interesting, is not an acceptable method of determining validity (Larson, 1932).

Independent-criterion studies

To date, only two scientifically acceptable independent-criterion studies of the validity of lie detection in the field have been reported. Although these studies (Barland, 1975; Bersh, 1969) represent relatively solid examples of the independent-criterion approach, they are not without problems. Both studies found relatively good agreement (about 90%) between independent judgments by a panel of lawyers and the results of polygraphic examinations. In both studies, however, it is possible that the examiners' judgments were influenced by factual information, subjects' behaviors, and other extrapolygraphic data as well as the polygraphic recordings themselves. In general, independent criterion studies suffer from the fact that there is no completely adequate ground truth criterion with which examiners' judgments can be compared. The criteria that have been or can be used, such as independent evaluations of extrapolygraphic information, and the outcome of judicial proceedings, do not establish with certainty a person's actual truthfulness or deception. In particular it may be assumed that panel decisions and trial outcomes would tend to favor a judgment of innocence, particularly in situations in which the factual information is inadequate or weak. In those instances, of course, a decision of guilt based on polygraphic data would be recorded as a false positive error even though it was the panel decision that was actually incorrect. Finally, because procedures used in giving polygraphic examinations are, in essence, diagnostic procedures, it is difficult to separate the influence of the examiner's interaction with the subject from the polygraphic recordings themselves; that is, the recordings are not necessarily independent of the examiner's attitudes, behavior, and information about the subject's involvement in the offense being investigated.

Dependent-criterion studies

The second approach to estimating the accuracy of present-day field control-question tests, the dependent-criterion method, has involved blind analysis of confession-verified polygraphic charts. In such analysis it is possible to ensure that extrapolygraphic information does not influence decision making. To illustrate the manner in which such studies are carried out, I will describe the first reported study of this type in some detail; then, after reviewing similar studies, I will focus on the issues raised by all of them.

Horvath and Reid (1971) reported a study in which they selected from a total of 75 subjects' polygraphic charts a purposive sample of 40 subjects' charts. These 40 charts were selected because they seemed to be the hardest to interpret. Of the 40 charts, 20 were those of subjects who, subsequent to their polygraphic examination, confessed their guilt (deception), and 20 were those of subjects whose innocence (truthfulness) had been established by the fully corroborated confession of the guilty person involved in the crime. All of the polygraphic examinations had been carried out by Horvath, at that time an examiner for J. Reid and Associates, a large, well-known commercial polygraphic testing firm. All examinations involved criminal matters, although they were carried out for private, not public law enforcement, purposes.

The 40 subjects' polygraphic charts were reviewed in a blind manner by 10 examiners (evaluators) on the staff of Reid and Associates; 7 of the evaluators were experienced, and 3 had not yet completed their 6-month training program. All evaluators were asked to review the charts and to decide whether each subject was telling the truth or lying about the issue under investigation.

The 10 evaluators averaged an 88% accuracy in correctly identifying the innocent and the guilty subjects. The experienced evaluators, however, averaged 91% correct decisions, whereas the inexperienced group produced a 79% accuracy rate. In addition, of the 200 judgments on innocent subjects made overall by the evaluators, only 9% were in error (false positives); of the 200 judgments on guilty subjects, 15% were incorrect (false negative).

Since the Horvath and Reid report, four other studies have been reported by the Reid organization. Hunter and Ash (1973) drew a sample of 20 subjects' polygraphic charts from examinations carried out by the first author; there were 10 charts of the verified guilty and 10 of the verified innocent type. All charts were evaluated blind by 7 evaluators on the Reid staff, who correctly identified 86% of the innocent subjects and 90% of the guilty subjects. Wicklander and Hunter (1975) selected the polygraphic charts of 20 confession-verified polygraphic subjects, 10 innocent and 10 guilty, from examinations previously carried out by both authors. Six evaluators on the Reid staff, who analyzed the polygraphic data only, averaged 94% correct decisions on the innocent subjects and 91% correct decisions on the guilty subjects.

Slowik and Buckley (1975) drew a random sample of 30 confession-verified polygraphic charts, 15 innocent and 15 guilty, from the case files of Reid and Associates. Seven Reid-trained evaluators, who analyzed these charts in a blind manner, averaged 89% correct judgments; 93% of the decisions on innocent subjects and 85% of the decisions on guilty subjects were correct. A similar, unpublished, study by Senese and Buckley (1979), involving blind analysis by 9 Reid-trained evaluators on a random sample of 20 verified guilty and 20 verified innocent subjects' polygraphic charts, produced results similar to the other Reid-based findings: Overall, 90% of the decisions were correct, and 88% of the decisions on innocent subjects and 92% of the decisions on guilty subjects were correct.

Another study of the type illustrated by those just described was reported by Raskin, Barland, and Podlesny, (1977). In their study, Raskin and colleagues selected confession-verified polygraphic charts of 16 criminal suspects who were tested for private, commercial purposes by the authors; 12 of the subjects were verified guilty and 4 were verified innocent. These 16 subjects' charts were then analyzed blind by 25 polygraphic examiner-evaluators from a variety of training backgrounds. Overall, the 25 evaluators averaged 90% correct decisions, and 9 of them achieved 100% accuracy. (The data were not reported separately for decisions on guilty and innocent subjects.)

All of the dependent-criterion studies discussed so far have involved charts drawn from the files of commercial polygraphic firms. Two other studies that are similar, but for which charts were drawn from the verified case files of law enforcement agencies, have also been reported. In the first of these, Holmes (1958) selected a systematic sample of the charts of 20 verified guilty and 12 verified innocent subjects. He then had these charts reviewed blind by 6 examiners employed by law enforcement agencies. They averaged 74% correct decisions overall; data were not reported separately for guilty and innocent subjects. Unfortunately, it is not clear whether Holmes's charts had been obtained in a way consistent with the control-question technique as described in this chapter and elsewhere (Barland & Raskin, 1973). It is not possible, therefore, to determine the degree to which the Holmes report bears on the C-Q technique as used today.

The second study involving polygraphic charts drawn from law enforcement files was reported by Horvath (1977). In this study, a multistage random sample of 56 subjects' polygraphic charts was drawn from the verified case files of a law enforcement agency; half of the charts were of the verified innocent type and half were of the verified guilty.

Ten evaluators, all of whom were trained, experienced polygraphic examiners employed by a law enforcement agency, then reviewed these charts blind. On average, the 10 evaluators correctly identified the innocent and guilty subjects 64% of the time. On the charts of the verified innocent subjects the evaluators averaged 51% correct decisions; on those of the verified guilty the decisions were correct 77% of the time.

Table 10.2 displays the average percentage of correct decisions in all of the reported dependent-criterion studies. In the six studies involving verified polygraphic charts drawn from the files of commercial firms, the average percentage of correct decisions was 88. Including the Holmes data, the average percentage of correct decisions on charts drawn from law enforcement files was 68. I will discuss the difference between the commercial and law enforcement–based studies, but first a number of other issues require attention.

In the Horvath and Reid (1971) study, remember that the sample of charts selected was an arbitrary one; it included only those charts the authors felt were difficult to interpret. Because such a sample is essentially nonreplicable, Lykken (1980) has been highly skeptical of the results in that study. Because the sample was a selected, presumably unrepresentative one, he claims, it is not likely that those results are generalizable to the typical field situation. Although Lykken's point has merit, the Horvath and Reid (1971) results have been closely replicated in five similar studies in which the sample of charts was not an arbitrary one, which strongly suggests that the findings reported by Horvath and Reid were not unduly biased by the sampling process. In fact, in the Slowik and Buckley (1975) study the sample clearly was a random one, yet the results were very close to those reported by Horvath and Reid. Moreover, because the other five studies involved a total of 54 different examiner-evaluators and a total of 126 different polygraphic charts, it seems exceedingly unlikely that such a close correspondence between the findings in those studies and those reported by Horvath and Reid (1971) would obtain if the results in that study were

Table 10.2. *Percentage of correct decisions in blind analysis of confession-verified field polygraphic charts*

	Innocent		Guilty		Overall % correct
	n	% correct	*n*	% correct	
Commercial cases					
Horvath & Reid (1971)	20		20		
Inexperienced evaluators (*n* = 3)		83		75	79
Experienced evaluators (*n* = 7)		94		89	91
Hunter & Ash (1973)	10		10		
Evaluators (*n* = 7)		86		90	88
Slowik & Buckley (1975)	15		15		
Evaluators (*n* = 7)		93		85	89
Wicklander & Hunter (1975)	10		10		
Evaluators (*n* = 6)		94		91	93
Raskin, Barland, & Podlesny (1977)	4		12		
Evaluators (*n* = 25)		—		—	90
Senese & Buckley (1979	20		20		
Evaluators (*n* = 9)		88		92	90
M		90		87	88
Law enforcement cases					
Holmes (1958)	12		20		
Evaluators (*n* = 6)		—		—	74
Horvath (1977)	28		28		
Evaluators (*n* = 10)		51		77	64
M		51		77	68

Note: Dashes mean data not reported.

unrepresentative.

From inspection of the data shown in Table 10.2 it can be seen that the results reported by Horvath (1977) were considerably different from those reported in the commercial-based, dependent-criterion studies. Interestingly, Lykken (1980) argues that the Horvath results are the only dependable findings; he maintains, incorrectly, that the chart sample in that study was the only unselected (random) sample employed in any of the studies. On the other hand, Raskin (1978), generally a proponent of the polygraph, dismisses Horvath's findings because they were not consistent with other reported findings and because he apparently believes that the examiner-evaluators in that study were not trained properly in the interpretation of polygraphic data.

Although the reasons for the difference between the Horvath (1977) findings and those reported in the other dependent-criterion studies are not clear, there are two likely possibilities. First, however, I want to discuss briefly Raskin's claim that the evaluators in that study were not trained properly in chart evaluation. In that study there were eight evaluators who were trained in a facility that is known to emphasize the value of extrapolygraphic information to decision making. If those eight evaluators had produced results considerably different from those of the two evaluators who did have "proper" training, Raskin's claim would be more plausible, but they did not. The two "properly trained" evaluators interpreted the charts with essentially the same degree of accuracy as did the eight "improperly trained" evaluators. Moreover, calculation of Hoyt's intraclass correlation coefficient on evaluator's judgments, irrespective of the accuracy of the judgments, showed substantial (.89) agreement among evaluators.

One of the major differences between the Horvath (1977) study and the other dependent-criterion studies was that in the former all charts were selected from examinations originally carried out by a variety of examiners, some of whom were, at the time they conducted the examination, still undergoing internship training. In the other studies, charts were drawn from cases in which the examiners had been fully trained and had had considerable experience; in fact, in most of these studies the charts were selected from examinations carried out by only one examiner. Thus it seems quite possible that the difference between Horvath's (1977) findings and those reported in similar studies can be accounted for not by the lack of proper training of the evaluators but rather by the lack of adequate training and experience of the examiners in the Horvath study who actually carried out the polygraph testing. In other words, the charts, not the evaluators, used in the Horvath study were possibly qualitatively different from those used in the other dependent-criterion studies. That such a qualitative difference in the manner in which control-question tests are administered can account for a large proportion of the variation in which charts can be accurately blind-reviewed is suggested by the available laboratory evidence previously described. Barland and Raskin's (1975) results, for instance, show in comparison with other laboratory findings (see Table 10.1) that when control questions are not properly developed, control-question tests are less accurate and more often inconclusive than when those questions are developed properly.

The data displayed in Table 10.2 show that in the commercially based, dependent-criterion studies the average accuracy of blind reviewers of charts was 88%, whereas in the law enforcement–based studies, including the Holmes study, the average accuracy was 68%. It is possible to suggest, therefore, that there may be yet other differences between the two situations that account for the disparity in the findings. These might include factors such as the personality characteristics of the subject populations encountered, the motivational characteristics present in the two situations, or some combination of these and other factors.

These factors notwithstanding, an important difference between the two situations is that law enforcement examiners are traditionally experienced investigators who strongly appreciate the value of confessions in police work (Wilson, 1978); commercial examiners, certainly those who were involved in the commercially based, dependent-criterion studies, emphasize polygraphic findings, because in much of their work (e.g., testing for defense attorneys) attempts to obtain confessions are sometimes prohibited, or at least played down. This difference suggests that some police examiners, given their orientation and that they typically have a great deal of investigative information at their disposal before a polygraphic examination, may tend to be less attentive to, or may find it harder to attend to, how they carry out control-question tests (e.g., how they develop control questions) than some commercial examiners. Blind reviews of law enforcement–based charts might be expected, therefore, to manifest that distinction, to show less accurate discrimination of liars and truthtellers.

It is possible, of course, that none of the hypotheses advanced here adequately explains the discrepancy between the two types of the dependent-criterion studies. We have research currently under way at Michigan State University to shed some light on that problem.

Much of the controversy about the dependent-criterion studies concerns the degree to which they provide an estimate of the validity of the C-Q technique in the field. It is my view, as I have indicated elsewhere (Horvath, 1977), that such studies estimate merely how much field examiners could have relied on polygraphic data exclusively to make decisions of innocence and guilt. That is, although such studies offer some insight into the possible contribution made to field examiners' judgments by the polygraphic data alone, they do not bear directly on the validity of the field examination process. To state the issue in another way, when charts are sampled ex post facto from confession-verified cases, one knows only that the testing examiners made correct judgments on all subjects in those cases. Whether they made judgments on the basis of the charts alone or on some combination of the charts and extrapolygraphic information is not known. Because the examiners' chart-based decisions are not known, the results of the dependent-criterion studies estimate merely the extent of agreement between examiners' judgments based on all information available and evaluators' judgments based solely on polygraphic data. Moreover, because verified cases are, ipso facto, those in which it is known that examiners' made correct judgments, selecting charts from such cases allows for the possibility that those charts were contaminated by unusually effective pretest interviews (Horvath, 1973), which, in turn, led to readily recognizable physiological responses. Thus, as Orne (1975) has pointed out, that evaluators can identify physiological responses in such instances suggests merely that those responses can be reliably interpreted.

Summary

Undoubtedly, the problems inherent in establishing the validity of field polygraphic procedures will continue to plague researchers for some time to come. The inadequacies in ground truth measures that are independent of polygraphic outcomes are a particularly troublesome problem. Similarly, that confessions made to polygraphic examiners most often depend on a finding of guilt in a polygraphic examination contaminates the selection of charts from such confession-verified cases. Because only a small proportion of all polygraph cases is ever verified by a confession, there is a question of whether the accuracy of blind interpretation of those charts generalizes to findings that would obtain on charts not so verified. The limited evidence now available (Horvath, 1977) suggests that there may be only small qualitative differences between verified and nonverified charts, but the issue needs much more research.

Both the laboratory and the field research now available show that the theoretical foundation for the control-question technique has considerable merit and that control-questions tests can, in the proper circumstances, yield a surprisingly high degree of discrimination between liars and truthtellers. Nevertheless, it is clear that some of the controversial issues evolving from the studies already reported will not be resolved without a considerable amount of continued research and ingenuity.

One of the critical issues about field polygraphic examinations that has not been adequately addressed is whether and to what degree extrapolygraphic sources of information – for example, factual information, investigators' reports and impressions, and a person's behavioral characteristics while undergoing a polygraphic examination (Horvath, 1973) – should, and do, contribute to accuracy in the field. Some persons assume, for example, that the use of such outside information is both unscientific and unsound. Others, particularly certain schools of field examiners, maintain that such information is essential in both the proper application of the control-question technique (e.g., in working up proper control questions) and in preventing diagnostic errors (Reid & Inbau, 1977). Thus, it would be extremely useful to investigate the validity of each of these items separately and collectively to determine whether there is merit in the position of field examiners. Such an approach has not as yet been undertaken.

Interevaluator agreement on polygraphic data

Aside from dealing with the accuracy of the C-Q technique the research literature also shows concern about the degree to which polygraphic charts can be reliably interpreted – that is, whether interevaluator agreement on polygraphic charts, irrespective of the correctness of the judgments, can be accomplished within acceptable limits. In discussing this issue I will ignore the major results of the dependent-criterion studies and, instead, focus on other findings, starting with a brief review of the results from laboratory studies. It is important to note that because validity cannot exceed reliability the results presented here are no less valuable than those previously presented.

Laboratory studies

There are numerous laboratory reports that show high rates of inter-evaluator agreement on polygraphic response data (Bitterman & Marcuse, 1947; Heckel et al. 1962; Kubis, 1962; Van Buskirk & Marcuse, 1954). More recent and perhaps more pertinent results with respect to interevaluator agreement have been reported in a number of other laboratory studies that involved both hypothetical crimes and the use of the control-question technique. Dawson (1980), for example, in the study already described, reported that the correlation (r) between his numerical scores on the charts in his study and those obtained by an independent evaluator was .94. Similarly, Podlesny and Raskin (1978) reported a correlation of .97 between numerical scores assigned by the examiner in their study and those assigned by a "blind" evaluator. Finally, Barland (1972) submitted the polygraphic charts of 72 subjects involved in a hypothetical crime to a group of five field polygraphic examiners. The examiners were asked to score each subject's charts numerically. By considering evaluators in pairs, and including his own numerical scores, Barland found that the correlations (Pearson's r) between all possible pairs of evaluators ranged from .78 to .95, with a mean of .86; out of 559 instances of two evaluators' making a definite judgment, agreement occurred 534 times, or 95.5% of the time.

Field studies

Before discussing results from the field pertinent to interevaluator agreement I wish to return to the Floyd Fay case described at the beginning of this chapter. It will be recalled that in that case Fay's control-question polygraphic charts were evaluated independently by four trained field examiners – the original examiner, Barland, Horvath, and Raskin. The original examiner judged Fay to be deceptive, whereas Raskin judged him to be truthful. Both Horvath and Barland reported that their evaluations indicated an inconclusive outcome; they called for another, more carefully structured control-question test of Fay. Obviously, Fay's charts were not scored with a high degree of interrater agreement (a point I will return to at the end of this chapter), an unusual outcome, given findings reported in both laboratory and field research.

In the study reported by Horvath (1977), described earlier, it was found that of the 10 examiner-evaluators who analyzed a total sample of 112 polygraphic charts (56 were confession-verified and 56 were not so verified), 6 or more of them agreed in their judgments of truthfulness (innocence) and deception (guilt) on 104 of the charts in the sample. The percentage of agreements in judgments between all possible pairs of the 10 evaluators ranged from 53% to 90%, with a mean of 69%. Calculation of Hoyt's intra-class correlation coefficient on the trichotomous judgments (truthful, deceptive, inconclusive) of the evaluators showed a substantial degree of interevaluator agreement in evaluation of both the 56 confession-verified charts and the 56 unverified charts, .89 and .85, respectively.

In the Barland (1975) study, also described previously, Barland numerically scored his charts of 77 criminal suspects on two occasions, first at the time of testing and then 6 months later, without knowledge of the original scoring. Sixty-five of his 77 rescores (84.4%) resulted in the same decision of guilt and innocence (and in no case was a decision reversed), differences between score-rescore results being due to a greater number of inconclusive determinations in the rescoring. Pearson's *r,* calculated on the total numerical scores in the first scoring and those assigned in the rescoring, was .92.

In a paper reported by Raskin et al. (1977), the numerical scores assigned to 102 criminal suspects' control-question charts by Barland at the time of testing were correlated with scores assigned by Raskin, who blind evaluated the same charts. The correlation (*r*) between the two scorings was .91. When both evaluators made a decision of either truthfulness or deception on the basis of their numerical scores, they were in agreement 100% of the time. In that same study Barland and Raskin also blind evaluated a total of 419 criminal suspects' polygraphic charts drawn from a variety of field agencies. Their rate of agreement with the actual decisions made in the agencies was 85% when inconclusive outcomes were excluded.

Finally, Hunter and Ash (1973) had seven field examiners blind evaluate the same set of 20 criminal suspects' polygraphic charts on two occasions about 3 months apart. The rate of agreement between the evaluators' decisions at the two times averaged 85%, ranging from 75% to 90% for individual evaluators.

Important unresolved research issues

Aside from the validity and reliability of control-question testing there are other important controversial issues about such testing. Most of these have received little attention in the research literature; thus, my discussion of each issue will be somewhat limited and will focus on the major findings and the points of view that have been expressed in each topical area. I make no claim that the issues presented are exhaustive, only that they are among the most pressing matters in need of research. For further information about these and other issues the reader is referred to Barland and Raskin (1973), Horvath (1980), Podlesny and Raskin (1977), and Lykken (1980).

Nature of errors

One of the critics of control-question testing in the field has in various recent publications (Lykken, 1978, 1979, 1980, 1981) expressed the point of view that the theoretical premise of control-question testing is psychologically implausible. Because, he argues, both innocent and guilty persons can readily identify the accusatory, relevant questions in such tests, it is naive to believe that innocent subjects will show less physiological response to those questions than to field-type control questions. Thus, he asserts that control-question testing leads to a very high rate of false positive errors, that a great proportion of actually truthful people will not "pass" such tests.

Table 10.1 shows the results of laboratory studies of the control-question technique with respect to the proportion of false positive and false negative errors made in those studies. It is clear from those data that in all but the Podlesny and Raskin (1978) study, errors were predominately false positives, not false negatives, the mean for each across all five studies being 10% and 3%, respectively. If the Barland and Raskin (1975) study, in which the control questions were not individually adjusted, is excluded, false positives averaged 8%, false negatives 1%.

In one of the independent-criterion field studies, Bersh (1969) reported that when the "panel" criterion was unanimous agreement among panelists, polygraphic (control-question testing) outcomes agreed with the panel's decisions on 82 of 89 cases; of the seven errors, three of them were false positives and four were false negatives; thus, in that study the types of errors made by the examiners slightly favored false negatives. Barland's (1975) similar independent-criterion study showed conflicting results. He reported that when unanimous panel judgments were compared with polygraphic outcomes, the two polygraphic errors were false positives.

Evidence of polygraphic errors in the dependent-criterion studies is, as in the other field research, somewhat ambiguous. In Table 10.2 it can be seen that in the commercially based studies the mean accuracy on truthful subjects was slightly higher than that obtained on deceptive subjects, 90% to 87%; thus, false negative errors exceeded false positives. In the Horvath (1977) study, dealing with law enforcement–derived charts, 49% of the truthful subjects' charts were scored deceptive, whereas only 23% of the judgments on deceptive subjects' charts were in error.

If the laboratory findings are excluded it is clear that at this time the relative distribution of false positive and false negative errors in the field is not well defined. Many field examiners (Reid and Inbau, 1977) claim that in their situation, because of their inclination to be conservative in making judgments of deception (guilt) and because of their use of extrapolygraphic information, false negatives occur much more often than false positives. But evidence in support of such a claim is unclear.

Given that laboratory research generally shows control-question test errors to be of the false positive type, Raskin (1978; 1981) has advanced the interesting contention that that fact enhances the value of polygraphic results in some situations. For instance, our justice system is structured in such a way that it tends to favor errors of the false negative type. Therefore, because polygraphic outcomes of guilt (deception) tend to be in error more often than innocent outcomes, an innocent outcome is one in which officials in the justice system can have greater confidence. Thus, a criminal suspect who passes a polygraphic examination is able to show that there is "reasonable doubt" of his guilt, perhaps a sufficient basis for a prosecutor to dismiss the charges.

Because the degree to which laboratory findings apply to field situations is not yet known, whether Raskin's contention is meritorious is a matter of some controversy (Lykken, 1980; 1981). What is clear, judging from the available evidence, is that control-question testing, whatever its accuracy, does result in both false negative and false positive errors. The relative proportion of these errors in the field can be determined only by further empirical developments.

Extrapolygraphic information

Leading field examiners (Reid and Inbau, 1977) have long maintained that field procedures are essentially diagnostic in nature, that decisions of truthfulness and deception depend (or ought to depend) on the integration of a variety of information sources besides polygraphic data. Factual information available to the examiner, for instance, must be viewed as important to the testing process and the outcome, because it is that information that determines not only the scope and content of the test questions but also to some degree the "quality" of the resultant polygraphic charts. In short, improper or poorly worded test questions can yield misleading polygraphic data. Field examiners contend, therefore, that only by balancing the charts against the factual and other such extrapolygraphic information available at the time of testing can the optimum in accuracy be obtained.

Of the variety of extrapolygraphic data available to field examiners, the least understood and the most controversial are assessments of subjects' behavioral characteristics during polygraphic examinations.

Some critics (Lykken, 1980) and some proponents of the polygraph (Raskin, 1978) assert that such assessments are unscientific and that polygraphic decisions should be based exclusively on blind interpretation of polygraphic charts. Whether such assessments should play a role in field examiners' decisions is, of course, a value judgment that ultimately depends on the assumptions made about the nature of field polygraphic testing. If, however, it were empirically demonstrated that behavioral assessments enhanced the accuracy of field decisions, as some field examiners contend, it would be possible to determine what role such assessments should play in decision making. Unfortunately, the available empirical evidence on this issue is full of problems.

There are two reports of field examiners that suggest that the behavioral characteristics of guilty subjects undergoing polygraphic examinations differ from those of innocent subjects. Reid and Arther (1953), for example, found that liars (guilty subjects) tended to exhibit certain mannerisms not generally displayed by truthtellers (innocent subjects); liars, moreover, tended to express reservations about their testing more often than truthtellers. These data were supported in a study reported by Horvath (1973); in that study, a tabulation of both the verbal and nonverbal behavioral characteristics made by examiners showed statistically significant ($p < .05$) differences between liars and truthtellers. Both studies, however, were largely based on impressionistic data and in neither was there any attempt to determine what contribution, if any, the behavioral assessments made to the decisions that were based on the polygraphic data.

In his field study of the validity of control-question tests, Barland (1975) reported that 87% of his behavior-based assessments correctly predicted test outcomes on guilty (deceptive) subjects, whereas only 50% of the assessments of innocent (truthful) subjects were predictive of their polygraphic findings. Barland also reported, as many field examiners contend, that his assessment of a subject's behavior provided an important reality check on his polygraph results; when he found much inconsistency between behavioral assessments and polygraph charts, he was careful to make certain that his polygraphic data were complete. Unfortunately, Barland's data were also impressionistic; that and the small number of innocent subjects in his sample make it difficult to draw generalizations from his report.

Some laboratory studies have attempted to validate the usefulness of behavioral assessments in relation to polygraphic outcomes. Podlesny and Raskin (1978), using a very weak approximation to field pretest interview procedures as reported by Horvath (1973), found that on the basis of behavioral assessments of subjects involved in a mock crime, 86% of their decisions on 30 guilty subjects were correct and 48% of the decisions on 30 innocent subjects were correct. Overall, 69% ($p < .05$) of the behavior-based decisions were correct. Kubis (1974) has also demonstrated that on the basis of observations of the behavior of subjects involved in a hypothetical crime, discrimination between guilty and innocent subjects can occur at levels greater than chance. Neither of these reports, however, shows that behavioral assessments make a contribution to detecting deception separate from or in addition to that made by the polygraphic data themselves.

An excellent review of the available research literature on detection of deception from verbal and nonverbal cues has recently been published by Zuckerman, DePaulo, and Rosenthal (1981). As those authors point out, the great majority of the research in that area has been done in the laboratory; the ecological validity of those findings, therefore, is suspect. What is sorely needed in the lie detection field is a careful, systematic assessment of subjects' behavior during polygraphic testing. Not only must it be determined to what extent careful behavioral assessments can predict deception, but it is equally important to discover how examiners' assessments contribute to, or detract from, the physiological data. It would be naive in the extreme to believe that the interaction between the examiner and the subject has no effect on the polygraphic data. If, as many field examiners (Reid & Inbau, 1977) claim, behavioral assessments are needed to determine the value of control questions, to assess the possibility of error (particularly false positives) in polygraphic data, and to structure properly the interaction between examiner and subject during the testing protocol, then clearly we now have very little knowledge about very important issues.

Evaluation of polygraphic data

Traditionally, field examiners have evaluated polygraphic charts relatively unsystematically. In recent years, however, it has become quite common for those examiners to apply a numerical scoring system, as described previously, to polygraphic response data. The report of Raskin et al. (1977) has had considerable influence on this change; in that report, for instance, it is recommended that the results of all control-question examinations always be determined by numerical scoring of the response data.

Part of the support for the recommendation by Raskin et al. (1977) is found in the fact that various laboratory studies of the C-Q technique have shown that numerical scoring yields high accuracy in decisions and that such scoring also yields a high degree of interrater agreement. Field research also appears to support that recommendation.

Raskin et al. (1977) had 25 field examiners blind evaluate a sample of 16 confession-verified polygraphic charts of criminal suspects. Seven of the 25 evaluators used the numerical scoring system to render decisions; their accuracy (99%) was reported to be significantly higher than that of the 18 evaluators who did not use numerical scoring (88%). In addition, among the 13 evaluators who had been specifically trained in numerical scoring, the accuracy of the decisions made by the 7 who used that scoring (99%) was significantly greater than that attained by the 6 evaluators who were familiar with the technique but did not use it (88%).

Unfortunately, the report of Raskin and colleagues is not clear about the comparisons that were made. It was not reported, for instance, what method of evaluation was used by the evaluators who did not use numerical scoring. Nor was it known whether those who used numerical scoring did so simply because they were more conscientious than the others or were simply more familiar with the structure of the control-question variation that had been used to obtain the polygraphic data. Thus, whether the difference in results between those who used and those who did not use numerical scoring was attributable solely to the use of that technique is questionable.

It seems highly likely that any blind-scoring approach to chart evaluation in which evaluators are forced to attend to all response data in the charts is preferable to less systematic schemes. Reid-trained examiners, for instance, do not generally employ numerical scoring. Rather, they use a system in which responses to relevant questions are rank ordered against responses to control questions; ranks are indicated by a "checking" scheme rather than by numbers. Although that approach is clearly less sophisticated than numerical scoring, the results of the Reid-based studies in which there was blind scoring of charts have not shown any appreciable difference in accuracy compared with results in studies in which numerical scoring was used (see Table 10.2). That fact, by the way, casts further doubt on Raskin's position with respect to the difference in results between the Horvath (1977) study and the other dependent-criterion studies. Raskin maintains that the Horvath findings are unrepresentative because most evaluators in that study had been trained in a facility known to emphasize the use of extrapoly-graphic information – specifically, behavioral observations – in decision making (Raskin, 1978). Yet, it is also known that Reid-trained examiners are explicitly schooled in making appropriate behavioral observations and in integrating them into the decision-making process. Even when they were denied the use of those observations, however, as in the dependent-criterion studies, their accuracy in blind evaluation of response data was well within the range of the "accuracy" reported by Raskin et al. (1977), who do not explicitly use behavioral assessments.

As indicated earlier, there are limitations apparent in the field numerical scoring system. Furthermore, as I have suggested elsewhere (Horvath, 1980), it is a mistake to assume that numerical scoring alone is a panacea for the complex and difficult problems inherent in properly structuring control-question tests. That is, numerical scoring of charts, no matter how carefully done, does not overcome improper procedures used in obtaining poly-graphic information; assiduous attention to the administration of control-question tests is a prerequisite to meaningful response data.

Competence of examiners

Because it is likely that the structure of control-question tests and the inter-action between the examiner and the subject affect polygraphic outcomes, it is exceedingly important to determine how much the competence of examiners influences field procedures and results. At the present we know very little about this problem. Although Horvath and Reid (1971) demon-strated that experienced examiner-evaluators were apparently more adept at evaluating polygraphic response data than those who were less experienced, those results were not informative of the possible effect of differences among examiners in the administration of control-question tests.

There are now about thirty polygraphic training facilities in the United States and several others in foreign countries. The training offered in these facilities is highly diverse with respect to the testing procedures emphasized, the qualifications and backgrounds of students, and the experience and qualifications of the instructors. Efforts by the American Polygraph Asso-ciation and by various state legislatures have had some favorable influence on this problem (Horvath, 1980); still, it is far from certain that those efforts are sufficient to ensure that all examiners are properly qualified and trained.

What is needed, therefore, is reliable empirical research on the qualitative differences between competent and less competent examiners with respect to their personal and professional qualifications and with respect to the impact of those differences on testing outcomes. Because almost all of the field-based research now available has involved only two variations of control-question testing (Barland & Raskin 1973; Reid & Inbau, 1977), it is not known whether those results generalize to other variations. If the explanation advanced earlier in this chapter to account for the difference between the Barland and Raskin (1975) study and other laboratory studies of the C-Q technique has merit, it would be of considerable interest to determine how much the training and qualifications of the examiner affect proper development of control and relevant questions. These and, of course, other issues pertaining to examiner qualifications need to be addressed in the research literature.

Offense characteristics

Field examiners have never adequately addressed the issue of whether polygraphic outcomes may differ depending on the characteristics of the offense for which control-question testing is carried out. Rather, it is commonly assumed that polygraphic results are equally valid and useful in a variety of case types. Yet, the report by Horvath (1977) suggests that the accuracy of blind evaluation of polygraphic charts of subjects involved as suspects in criminal investigations may vary as a function of the type of offense (property crimes or crimes against a person). Contradictory evidence was reported by Raskin et al. (1977).

Since it may be assumed that the emotional impact of polygraphic test questions depends somewhat on how much they force recall of traumatic events, it is possible that physiological polygraphic data of some subjects, such as rape victims who are suspected of falsifying or concealing details of the offense, may generally be qualitatively different from those of subjects suspected of involvement in less emotional offenses. All of the laboratory studies of control-question testing, unfortunately, have involved mock thefts; those findings, therefore, are silent about this issue. Neither of the two laboratory studies in which more emotionally laden hypothetical crimes were carried out employed control-question testing (Davidson, 1968; Timm, 1979). Thus, the effect of offense characteristics on control-question tests is almost entirely unexplored. Although laboratory experiments to get at this issue would be relatively easy to design, no one has yet done so.

Summary

In the scientific literature on polygraphic procedures the major controversial issue is whether those procedures yield accurate discrimination of liars from truthtellers in field settings. Although that issue is far from being settled the available evidence strongly suggests that when field procedures are carefully carried out, polygraphic results can be highly accurate. Thus, such results can and do make an important contribution to our justice system. This is especially true in those instances in which eyewitness testimony plays an important role in a prosecutor's decision to charge and to try a defendant. In many, perhaps the majority, of such cases, eyewitness identification and testimony is the foundation of a prosecutor's case. Yet, as demonstrated in this volume, eyewitness accounts of a criminal event are subject to a variety of possibilities for error. Moreover, as the case presented at the beginning of this chapter illustrates, polygraphic results frequently provide the only reliable defense available to a wrongly accused defendant; were it not for the polygraph there would undoubtedly be a far greater number of persons subjected to the often debilitating and sometimes demeaning justice system than at present.

Ultimately the value of polygraphic results to our justice system boils down to a practical, not a scientific, question: Do such results merit probative evidentiary weight comparable to what can be obtained by other more traditional and accepted forms of evidence on which our justice system now relies? That is, against other scientific and nonscientific forms of evidence, how do polygraphic results stack up? The research literature on this issue shows results quite favorable to the polygraph. Studies of eyewitness accounts, for example, frequently demonstrate lower levels of accuracy than are obtained in properly conducted polygraphic examinations. Moreover, scientific analyses of physical evidence, in spite of the common belief to the contrary, have been shown to yield misleading and inaccurate findings, particularly when, as with the polygraph, techniques used in those analyses are not carefully and properly applied (Horvath 1977, Summary). More direct evidence pertinent to this issue was reported by Widacki and Horvath (1978). In their experimental laboratory study, they showed that the accuracy of polygraphic results in resolving mock crimes compared very favorably with results obtained in fingerprint identification and handwriting analysis: 95%, 100%, and 94%, respectively. In that study, eyewitness identification produced only a 64% accuracy rate. Furthermore, the polygraphic results were less-often inconclusive – that is, had greater utility – than were these other forms of evidence. Although the approach taken by Widacki and Horvath has not yet been seen in other studies of the polygraph's accuracy, such research would be extremely useful in determining the contribution that polygraphic results could make to our justice system.

I wish now to return once again to the Floyd Fay case to illustrate two important points about polygraphic testing. First, it will be recalled that in that case three experts independently reviewed Fay's polygraphic charts from his first examination. (To my knowledge Fay has never asked for similar independent review of his second polygraphic examination.) All of them agreed that Fay's first examination had been improperly structured, specifically that the control questions were inadequate. Consequently, it can be concluded that the polygraphic testing of Fay was not consistent with ordinary and accepted practice in control-question testing. That two of the independent reviewers of Fay's charts, Barland and Raskin, have been shown to have high interrater agreement on polygraphic data when those data were carefully collected (Raskin et al., 1977) and that their evaluations of Fay's charts were not in agreement reinforces the argument advanced previously in this chapter: Proper collection of control-question polygraphic charts is just as important a determinant of chart-based outcomes as is the degree to which chart-scoring techniques are applied. In short, no chart-scoring scheme now available, no matter how carefully applied, can overcome basic deficiencies in the manner in which control-question tests are carried out. Second, it will be recalled that neither the jurors nor the independent observers in the Fay trial were unduly swayed by the polygraphic results. Thus, neither the Fay case nor the available empirical evidence (Barnett, 1973; Carlson, Pasano, & Jannuzzo, 1977; Cavoukian & Heslegrave, 1980) support the contention made by some legal observers (Abbell, 1978) that polygraphic results have, or will have if more generally used, an overbearing effect on our justice system. The justice system, after all, seeks to determine legal, not necessarily factual, guilt; to the extent that the latter is important, the available evidence demonstrates that the polygraph, as well as a variety of other scientific evidence, can make a substantial contribution.

As shown in this chapter, a great number of questions related to polygraphic testing remain unanswered. The controversy about many of these questions cannot be resolved when evidence, both theoretical and empirical, is lacking. Given the potential that the polygraph has for use in our justice system, particularly for protecting the wrongly accused, the usual clarion call for continued, intensive, and reliable research is perhaps nowhere more appropriate than here.

Notes

1 The case presented here describes actual events, with some alteration of identifying information. Almost all professional polygraph examiners regularly have cases like this, in which eyewitness accounts are disproved by polygraph results. Other more complex and more singular cases can be found in the *American Polygraph Association Newsletter;* see, for example, *APA Newsletter,* 1981, *14,* 8–13.

11　How adequate is human intuition for judging eyewitness testimony?

Gary L. Wells

Justice would less often miscarry if all who are to weigh evidence were more conscious of the treachery of human memory. Yes, it can be said that, while the court
makes the fullest use of all the modern scientific methods when, for instance, a drop
of dried blood is to be examined in a murder case, the same court is completely satis-
fied with the most unscientific and haphazard methods of common prejudice and
ignorance when a mental product, especially the memory report of a witness, is to be
examined. (Munsterberg, 1908, p. 45)

One of the most interesting and fundamental questions in eyewitness
research revolves around Munsterberg's insistence that experimental psychology has answers that neither judge nor juror could intuit. The courts
still are reluctant to allow expert psychological testimony on eyewitness
matters. It is generally believed that this reluctance stems from three questions asked by the courts: Does psychology have an "accepted" body of scientific evidence on eyewitness testimony? Does this testimony invade the
province of the jury? and Is the scientific evidence redundant with the common knowledge of the juror?

I will not attempt to address the first question because the term *accepted*
is vague. Presumably, "accepted" refers to consensus among experts. But
how is this to be defined? Clearly, much eyewitness research has withstood
the scientific rigors and editorial process of many of psychology's best jour-
nals, such as the *Journal of Applied Psychology, Journal of Experimental
Psychology, Journal of Personality and Social Psychology, Psychological
Bulletin,* and many more. It is not clear what criteria apply to the question
of whether or not or when something is an accepted body of literature.
(Also see Yarmey & Jones, 1983, for some evidence on consensus among
eyewitness experts.) The question regarding the expert's possible invasion of
the jury's province is a different matter. Still, (a) there are numerous

The research and writing for portions of this chapter were assisted in part by Social
Sciences and Humanities Research Council Grant #410-81-0400-R1 to the author.

examples of how expert testimony on eyewitness matters can be delivered without invading the jury's freedom to decide (e.g., see Loftus, 1979, appendix section), and (b) the 1975 *Federal Rules of Evidence* (United States) abolished this form of reasoning for excluding expert testimony. The third issue (i.e., is scientific evidence redundant with common knowledge) is, however, of considerable importance and is the focus of this chapter.

The courts' concern (i.e., that scientific evidence on eyewitness testimony is redundant with common sense) stems from a belief that people have adequate intuitive theories of memory. It could be argued that triers of fact have developed these theories through repeated experiences with their own and other individuals' memories. Although intuitive theories of memory do not necessarily contain notions inherent in formal, scientific theorizing (e.g., propositions, corollaries), the intuitions are considered to be reasonably accurate.

The notion that intuitive theorizers have valid theories is an appealing one, but there are reasons to doubt such a notion. Extensive research on people's intuitive theories of events in other psychological domains shows that people are likely to perceive correlations where none exist (e.g., Chapman & Chapman, 1967), to perceive similarities or commonalities more easily than differences (Kreuger, 1978; Tversky, 1977), to test intuitions selectively by searching only for confirmations (e.g., Wason & Johnson-Laird, 1972; Snyder, 1981), and to base intuitions on a small number of observations (Tversky & Kahneman, 1971).

These problems with the intuitive scientist are, of course, only indirect bits of evidence on which to question the adequacy of triers of fact in judging eyewitness testimony. Direct evidence can be obtained only by comparing the lay person's intuitions with current scientific evidence on the specifics of eyewitness testimony. Until about 1979, this topic was not subjected to empirical tests. Since that time, however, several studies have examined people's intuitions about eyewitness testimony.

Because these studies are recent and their number still relatively small, a major purpose of this chapter is to develop an elementary framework for conceptualizing, designing, and interpreting research devoted to the lay person's understanding of eyewitness testimony. This chapter will not address directly the issue of whether or not expert testimony is desirable or useful. Instead, it is designed to describe current knowledge regarding how the trier of fact normally goes about the process of judging eyewitness matters. The two chapters that follow in this volume directly address the issue of expert testimony.

In this chapter I have distinguished between four methods used to examine the lay person's understanding of eyewitness testimony: (a) the questionnaire approach; (b) the prediction study; (c) the written or videotaped trial; and (d) the cross-examination of eyewitnesses to staged crimes. Each method has strengths and weaknesses, some shared and some not. At the outset I should note that I consider all four approaches to be important. To the extent that one method produces results that are similar to other methods, our uncertainty about that result is reduced. A multimethod approach will be valuable in the long run.

Questionnaire studies

One of the approaches to estimating the knowledge that people have of eyewitness matters has been to use multiple-choice questionnaires. The following example is extracted from a study by Yarmey and Jones (1983):

There are two eyewitnesses to a criminal assault that was committed under poor lighting conditions. When giving evidence some time later, one witness is very positive about his ability to identify the criminal. The other witness is not absolutely positive about his ability to identify the criminal. Which statement best reflects your belief in their testimony?
(a) The positive person is more likely to be accurate than the less positive person.
(b) The less positive person is more likely to be accurate than the more positive person.
(c) The persons are equally likely to be accurate.
(d) If the less positive person's testimony does not agree essentially with the more positive person's, then the less positive person's testimony will be accurate.

This question is addressed in more detail later.

The questionnaire approach has yielded some interesting results. Loftus (1979, chap. 9) for example, asked registered voters in the state of Washington several questions about their knowledge of factors affecting eyewitness accuracy. Her results revealed that some people might not appreciate the effects of stress on perception and recall. Approximately one-third of the respondents indicated a belief that extreme stress would produce an increased ability on the part of the witness to recall details of the witnessed event. Also, approximately two-thirds of the respondents indicated a belief that eyewitnesses would remember details of a violent crime better than they would remember details of a nonviolent crime.

Yarmey and Jones (1983) extended Loftus's (1979) questionnaire to include additional items on such factors as time perception, police versus civilians as eyewitnesses, decay of memory for faces over time, the influence of mug-shot identifications on later identifications from a lineup, the relationship between eyewitness confidence and eyewitness accuracy, and the effects of age of a witness on eyewitness testimony. In addition, Yarmey and Jones tested various populations, such as legal professionals, law students, other students, and citizen jurors. There was no consistent superiority of any one of these populations over any other population. This is important because studies using university students could be criticized for using respondents who are unrepresentative of actual jurors. The following results represent the findings for citizen jurors: Approximately two-thirds failed to indicate awareness that eyewitnesses are prone to overestimate the length of time involved in a witnessed crime (however, see, e.g., Shiffman & Bobko, 1974); approximately two-thirds believed that police would be superior to civilians as eyewitnesses (however, see, e.g., Tickner & Poulton, 1975); 15% indicated that they believed eyewitnesses' memory for faces would be 90%–95% accurate several months after first seeing the face (however, see, e.g., Egan, Pittner, & Goldstein, 1977); over one-half failed to show awareness that an eyewitness's identification of someone from a set of photographs is likely later to produce an identification of the same person from a lineup regardless of whether the identified person is guilty or not (however, see, e.g., Gorenstein & Ellsworth, 1980); two-thirds indicated that they thought there to be some kind of relationship between eyewitness accuracy and eyewitness confidence (however, see Chapter 8 in this book); and over half failed to indicate awareness that a physically healthy 70-year-old woman would be as likely accurately to identify a thief as would a 20-year-old woman (however, see Chapter 7 in this book).

Thus, there seem to be many areas where the lay person's intuitions disagree with the results of experimental studies on eyewitnessing. Recent questionnaire studies by Deffenbacher and Loftus (1982) and by Rahaim and Brodsky (1981) seem to corroborate this general conclusion.

Evaluation of the questionnaire method

Although the results of these questionnaire studies are important, some caution is required. There are several possible limitations to the questionnaire method that must be fully explored. First, a questionnaire respondent is an active theorizer who might try to second-guess the questionnaire administrator. Consider the Yarmey and Jones (1983) question on the confidence–accuracy issue. Their results showed that only 38% of the student jurors and 33% of the citizen jurors answered correctly (i.e., no confidence–accuracy relationship). Interestingly, however, 35% of the student jurors and 38% of the citizen jurors answered by saying that the *least* confident of two eyewitnesses is most likely to be accurate. Do these people really believe that accuracy and confidence are negatively correlated? Or, are they trying to reverse their intuitions on the assumption that the correct answer must be counterintuitive (otherwise, why ask such a question?). The tendency for a questionnaire respondent to second-guess the questionnaire administrator can make the respondent more or less accurate, depending on various factors. We do not know the extent to which the eyewitness-knowledge questionnaire results are influenced by this kind of process. However, the foregoing example, wherein over 30% of the respondents indicated that the confidence–accuracy correlation is negative, suggests that some questionnaire items could be reactive.

A second possible problem with the questionnaire approach is that it fails to preserve the ecology of the real-world situation in which these issues are encountered. Actual jurors, for example, have the benefit of discussion and "group knowledge" of these eyewitness factors. There is evidence indicating that people will sometimes shift toward the correct answer held by a member of a group as a function of group discussion (e.g., see Vinokur & Burnstein, 1974).

Do groups make better decisions on eyewitness matters than do individuals? I used a subset of items from Yarmey and Jones's (1983) questionnaire to test this idea. Groups, each composed of five students, were given a six-item questionnaire and told either to answer the questionnaire individually or to discuss each item as a group and subsequently indicate their private beliefs. The students that were asked to deal with the items individually were required to spend 30 minutes with the questionnaire weighing the merits of each answer. This was the same amount of time given to the interacting groups for discussion. The six items dealt with the effects of stress on eyewitnesses, time estimation by eyewitnesses, cross-race identification evidence, the effects of mug-shot identifications on later lineup identifications, the relationship between confidence and accuracy, and the effects of age of witnesses on their reports. The results are presented in Table 11.1. Although one of the items (stress) showed no effect for group discussion, the overall effect of group discussion appears beneficial and is statistically reliable. This suggests that the standard questionnaire approach might underestimate the joint knowledge of people who have the benefit of deliberation. On the other hand, the benefit of discussion was not profound; the majority of respondents continued to express beliefs about eyewitness matters that conflicted with scientific evidence.

Thus, instead of negating the questionnaire studies, this group discussion study could be considered corroborative of the general conclusion that most people have mistaken views on these matters. Still, we must be cautious in our conclusions.

Questionnaire results are no better than the items on which they are based. I will not quibble with the wording of each specific item contained in the questionnaires of Deffenbacher and Loftus (1982), Loftus (1979), Rahaim and Brodsky (1981), and Yarmey and Jones (1983). I will, however,

Table 11.1. *Correct answers from student-jurors about the role of eyewitness variables as a function of group discussion (in %)*

Variable	Individuals ($n = 60$)	Groups ($n = 60$)
Stress	57	56
Time estimation	21	27
Cross-racial identification	41	57
Previous use of mug shots	24	46
Confidence–accuracy relationship	21	34
Age	30	41
M	32	43

use one item from one of these questionnaires to illustrate some points. Consider the following item:

Appropriate to the situation where people of one racial group view those of another, you may have heard the expression "They all look alike." Which of the following statements best reflects your personal view of this expression.
(a) It is true
(b) It is a myth
(c) It is more applicable to whites viewing nonwhites than the reverse
(d) It is more applicable to nonwhites viewing whites than the reverse

Deffenbacher and Loftus (1982) reported that only 19% of their respondents chose Alternative a, and 40% chose Alternative b. What does this mean? Would the people who chose Alternative b, if serving as jurors, not consider a cross-racial identification to be less reliable than a within-race identification? Not necessarily. The respondent may believe that cross-racial identifications are somewhat unreliable and still believe that it is a myth that "they all look alike." Note also that the wording of the question is ambiguous as to whether the respondent believes that other people think they all look alike or whether the respondent personally thinks they all look alike.

In fairness to Deffenbacher and Loftus, it should be noted that the majority of their questionnaire items are better constructed than is this unfortunate example. Still, the general point remains that a questionnaire item does not necessarily tell us how the respondent would act in a specific, concrete situation (see Fishbein & Ajzen, 1975). Thus, although these questionnaire studies are important, they need corroboration from other methods.

One of the major limitations of the questionnaire approach is that people often cannot report accurately on the factors that would influence their decisions in concrete cases (e.g., see Nisbett & Wilson, 1977). Thus, people may report that they would be less likely to believe an eyewitness who made

Table 11.2. *Correct eyewitness identifications and students' predictions as functions of theft seriousness and the time of eyewitnesses' knowledge of theft seriousness (in %)*

Time of knowledge of seriousness	Low seriousness theft	High seriousness theft
Before theft	19 (66)	56 (65)
After theft	35 (53)	13 (60)

Note: Students' predictions are in parentheses.

a cross-racial identification yet not behave in a manner consistent with that belief when actually serving as a juror. Care must be taken, therefore, to corroborate self-report questionnaire results with the use of other methods.

Prediction studies

An alternative to the questionnaire approach is one that could be described as a prediction approach. The prediction approach to assessing intuitive knowledge of eyewitness testimony involves the describing of an actual eyewitness experiment to people and asking them to predict the results. These predictions can then be compared with the actual results of the experiment.

Saul Kassin conducted a study exemplifying this approach. Kassin (1979) presented students with a summary description of an eyewitness identification study conducted by Leippe, Wells, and Ostrom (1978). The study involved a staged theft in which the stolen object made it a serious theft (a calculator) or a trivial theft (a pack of cigarettes), and the witnesses either knew the identity of the object before the theft occurred or found out about the relative seriousness of the theft only after the thief had vanished. Table 11.2 presents the percentages of witnesses who were able to identify accurately the thief from a six-person photo array. In parentheses are the prediction estimates made by students who were asked to guess the outcome of the study.

Note that the students' predictions in Table 11.2 show no appreciation for the effects of the seriousness variable or the timing variable. Note also that the students tended to overestimate the percentage of witnesses who would be accurate under these conditions. These results have been replicated in a prediction study by Brigham & Bothwell (1982).

I used the same experiment used by Kassin (i.e., Leippe, Wells, & Ostrom, 1978) to do a prediction study involving the confidence of eyewitnesses. In this study students read the procedure section of the experiment

Table 11.3. *Correct items from hypnotized and unhypnotized eyewitnesses,*
by type of question, and students' predictions of the outcomes (in %)

	Leading questions	Nonleading questions
Hypnosis	78 (92)	63 (91)
No hypnosis	86 (55)	67 (63)

Note: Students' predictions are in parentheses.

by Leippe and colleagues and were given a target case to predict. The target case was an eyewitness who made an identification and was "completely certain" that he had identified the true thief. Other students were given a target case who was described as "somewhat uncertain" that he had identified the thief. The students were then asked to estimate the probability that the eyewitness had identified the thief. The actual experiment conducted by Leippe and colleagues showed no relationship between certainty and accuracy. Thus, the students' predictions should have been equal in these two conditions. The students, however, predicted a .83 probability that the "completely certain" witness had made an accurate identification and predicted a .28 probability of accuracy for the "somewhat uncertain" witness.

I also used the prediction method to investigate the agreement between scientific evidence and people's intuitions regarding the validity of eyewitness reports when the eyewitness reports were obtained from hypnotized witnesses. Recent evidence indicates that hypnosis has no beneficial effect on eyewitness memory (e.g., Orne, 1979) and that the hypnotized subject is actually more susceptible to the distorting properties of leading questions (e.g., see Chapter 6, by Hall, Loftus, & Tousignant, in this volume) than is a no-hypnosis control subject. To see if this is congruent with the intuitions of the lay person, I extracted relevant information from the procedure section of a study on this topic conducted by Putnam (1979). Students ($n = 120$) read this procedure and were asked to predict the average percentage of items that hypnotized and nonhypnotized eyewitnesses got correct under conditions of leading versus nonleading questions.

Table 11.3 shows the actual data obtained by Putnam (1979) along with the students' predictions. The students predicted a result that is the precise opposite of the outcome of the data. These students show a general, indiscriminating tendency to predict superior memory performance under conditions of hypnosis.

I conducted another prediction study based on an experiment by Malpass and Devine (1981a). Malpass and Devine staged an act of vandalism as an eyewitness event and used a lineup that either included the vandal or not. In

Table 11.4. *Eyewitnesses' choices from lineup as functions of the vandal's presence or absence and biasing instructions, and students' predictions (in %)*

	Choice of vandal	Choice of innocent person	No choice
Vandal present			
Biased instructions	75 (79)	25 (12)	0 (10)
Unbiased instructions	83 (74)	0 (15)	17 (12)
Vandal absent			
Biased instructions	–	78 (16)	22 (84)
Unbiased instructions	–	33 (18)	67 (81)

Note: Students' predictions are in parentheses. Dashes indicates that the situation cannot occur.

addition the lineup conductor either told the eyewitnesses that the vandal was probably present (biased instructions) or told witnesses that he did not know whether or not the vandal was present in the lineup (unbiased instruction). I gave the description of Malpass and Devine's procedure section to 80 students (20 in each of the four conditions) and asked them to predict the outcome of the study. (Malpass and Devine's procedure section was followed closely except that use of the terms *biased* and *unbiased* were deleted as these terms suggest the nature of the experimenter's hypothesis.) Table 11.4 presents the distribution of witnesses' responses reported by Malpass and Devine and the distributions predicted by students. Once again we see a considerable discrepancy between students' estimates and the experimental data. Those who read a version in which the witnesses received biased instructions were seemingly oblivious to the fact that such instructions greatly increase the likelihood of the witness's choosing an innocent person (especially in the vandal-absent conditions).

Evaluation of the prediction method

The prediction method seems to capture much of what we mean when we question the extent to which eyewitness research findings are intuitive. A particular advantage of the prediction method over the questionnaire method is the fact that the prediction method preserves the original setting. That is, the prediction method describes for the predictor, as well as possible, the same eyewitness setting that yielded the results with which the predictors' estimates will be compared. This contrasts somewhat with typical questionnaire items, which are often cast in a manner that fails to represent the original setting. For example, a questionnaire item dealing with hypnosis might begin, "Suppose an armed robbery took place in a grocery store," when in fact the relevant research has not involved that type of setting. Thus, the questionnaire method generally involves a greater leap in one's faith regarding the "correct" answer than does the prediction method.

On the other hand, the existing prediction studies can be criticized for having some of the same possible limitations as the questionnaire studies. For example, the effects of group discussion may be similar to those observed in the questionnaire study reported in the previous section. Recall also that it was argued that a questionnaire result cannot be better than the item(s) on which it is based. Prediction studies can suffer a similar fate. Specifically, a prediction study strongly relies on the predictors' interpretation of the witnessing conditions. Thus, predictors' may predict outcomes from an eyewitness study that differ from the actual outcome of the study because the predictor received a poor description of the experiment.

Perhaps the major limitation on prediction studies is that such studies do not necessarily tell us how the person would judge a given eyewitness. There is considerable evidence that people's individual judgments can be quite different from their perceptions of prior probability (e.g., Kahneman & Tversky, 1973). It would not be surprising, therefore, to find a person who believes that 85% of all eyewitnesses would have accurate memories under certain witnessing conditions yet refuses to believe the testimony of individual eyewitnesses under these conditions. Similarly, it would not be surprising to find that a person who believes that only 10% of all eyewitnesses would be accurate under certain conditions is prone to believe most of these eyewitnesses when they are evaluated on the basis of their actual testimony.

Finally, the prediction method fails to account for any beneficial effects that might accrue from cross-examination. For example, would people overlook the damaging effects of biased lineup instructions (see Table 11.4) if the opposing attorney argued that such instructions were unfairly suggestive?

Studies using written or videotaped trials

Another approach to investigating the intuitions of the trier of fact regarding eyewitness matters is to present a written or videotaped trial. Within the fictitious trial one can manipulate eyewitness variables (e.g., high- versus low-confidence eyewitnesses) to see what impact those variables have on the perceived credibility of the eyewitness(es), on the verdicts rendered by mock jurors, or on both. This is a method of assessing people's intuitions regarding eyewitness matters that can preserve most of the crucial elements of an actual trial. In addition, this method requires the trier of fact to distinguish the relevant information from the irrelevant information.

Most eyewitness research using written or videotaped trial information has been devoted to examining the impact of expert testimony. Loftus (1980b), for example, presented subject-jurors with a brief written summary of an actual assault case, including the testimony of an eyewitness. The principal focus of the study was to see if expert psychological testimony on eyewitness identification matters would affect the way in which the subject-jurors processed the trial information. The results showed that the subject-jurors who received expert testimony spent significantly more time in deliberation and were significantly less likely to render a guilty verdict than were their no-expert-testimony counterparts.

Studies such as Loftus's (1980) that examine the effects of expert testimony do not provide direct information regarding the intuitions of triers of fact. Such studies do provide, however, some indirect evidence on the question. Specifically, if the expert testimony serves to alter the process or outcome of deliberation, or both, then the content of that testimony was probably not redundant with the prior intuitions of the triers of fact. A number of studies indicate that expert testimony on eyewitness matters has a strong impact on the processing strategies and verdicts of subject-jurors (e.g., Hosch, Beck, & McIntyre, 1980; Weinberg & Baron, 1982; Wells, Lindsay, & Tousignant, 1980). Thus, it may be fair to conclude that the way in which expert testimony has been operationalized in the aforementioned studies is not redundant with the intuitive theories of the triers of fact. Alternatively, one could argue that the expert testimony served to give the factors mentioned by the expert more weight than would be given normally.

The expert testimony studies, however, still do not tell us much about how the trier of fact arrives at some decision regarding the credibility of an eyewitness. One approach to this could be to present a case to subject-jurors involving eyewitness testimony, record the deliberations, and analyze the verbal information for themes or hypotheses regarding the eyewitness testimony. Hastie (1980) has conducted such a study. In this study six-person mock juries were convened and watched a half-hour reenactment of an armed robbery trial. At the conclusion of the trial each jury was set to the task of deliberating to reach a verdict. The deliberations were videotaped and subsequently subjected to an analysis in which all remarks relevant to eyewitness reliability were identified, summarized, and coded into categories. The results of this analysis showed that the jurors were not blindly accepting of the eyewitness testimony. For example, most juries made reference to the characteristics of the crime event (e.g., duration), characteristics of the perpetrator (e.g., race), characteristics of the witness (e.g., witness stress), retrieval conditions (e.g., format of interrogation), the retention interval (e.g., passage of time or interference), and the certainty or confidence of the witness. In general, then, it seems that juries may be capable of identifying pertinent factors. Hastie notes that the typical deliberation included reference to at least 71% of the issues that might be cited by an expert on eyewitness matters.

The Hastie (1980) study, however, also found that many of the issues identified during deliberation seem to conflict with eyewitness findings. Stress, for example, was mentioned in 10 of the 11 juries in connection with the idea that it would benefit the eyewitness (i.e., high stress produces better accuracy), an idea that would seem to conflict with expert opinion (see Loftus, 1979). In addition, the confidence or certainty of the eyewitness was thought to be positively related to eyewitness accuracy, which is also in conflict with empirical evidence (see Chapter 8, by Wells and Murray, in this volume). Also, there was occasional reference to the idea that interpolated descriptions and photographs can increase accuracy in a subsequent face-to-face identification and that memory accuracy might actually increase with the passage of time.

Evaluation of the method of using written or videotaped trials

The principal advantage of the written or videotaped trial method is that the relevant information regarding witnessing conditions can be presented in a more forensically valid manner than is true in either questionnaire or prediction study methods. Specifically, the trier of fact receives the relevant information by reading or listening to the testimony of a witness under direct examination and cross-examination in conjunction with other trial information. Because this is the manner in which triers of fact in an actual trial receive their information about eyewitnessing conditions, results from this method would seem to have greater face validity than would questionnaire or prediction studies.

Existing studies have focused almost entirely on the effects of expert testimony. A more direct approach to studying the intuitions people use in judging eyewitness testimony would be to manipulate eyewitness variables in the trial script. For example, one could manipulate (for the triers of fact) whether the eyewitness's identification of the accused was obtained from a low-similarity lineup or a high-similarity lineup or whether or not the eyewitness had viewed the accused in a set of mug shots prior to viewing the lineup. Both of these factors should make a difference for the trier of fact's assignments of credibility to an eyewitness's lineup identification (see Lindsay & Wells, 1980).

One of the decisions that must be made in the use of written or video-taped trials is how to characterize the eyewitnesses' testimony. Consider, for example, a study by Hatvany and Strack (1980). Hatvany and Strack presented videotaped cases to subjects that varied in whether or not a key eyewitness was discredited. Among other things, discrediting information included the eyewitness's admission that his or her testimony should be disregarded and even the witness apologizing for testifying. Whether the eyewitness was discredited or not made a considerable difference in the jurors' deliberations. What is unknown, however, is whether or not an eyewitness is likely to withdraw his or her testimony in this manner when exposed to strong cross-examination. In this regard it is important to note that there is evidence that eyewitnesses who are inaccurate in their testimony are not more likely to "give in" under cross-examination than are eyewitnesses who are accurate (e.g., see Wells, Lindsay, & Ferguson, 1979; Wells & Leippe, 1981). Thus, jurors may well believe that they should ignore an eyewitness's testimony if the eyewitness retracts that testimony, but is this a realistic portrayal of the testimony behavior of eyewitnesses? The general question here is how to present triers of fact with eyewitness testimony that is representative of actual eyewitness testimony behaviors.

Studies using testimony of eyewitnesses to staged events

The issue of presenting triers of fact with eyewitness testimony behaviors that are representative of actual eyewitnesses can be partly resolved by using actual eyewitnesses. This was the logic behind several recent studies that used cross-examinations of eyewitnesses to staged events and presented these cross-examinations to subject jurors (e.g., Wells, Lindsay, & Ferguson, 1979).

There are two general advantages to presenting triers of fact with eyewitness testimony given by eyewitnesses who observed staged events. First, the testimony behaviors across witnesses can reflect the variances, means, and relationships that would be expected of witnesses to actual events. The study by Hatvany and Strack (1980), although excellent in many respects, is illustrative of the problem that exists when the eyewitness testimony is actually a script written by an experimenter. As I noted previously, the Hatvany and Strack study portrayed the testimony of an eyewitness who gave identification testimony and then, in some conditions, retracted that testimony under cross-examination. These retraction conditions were referred to as "discrediting information," which Hatvany and Strack argued was generally treated logically by subject-jurors. That is, subject-jurors discounted the eyewitness testimony in those conditions. Although I agree that subject-jurors treated this discrediting information in a logical manner, I believe that the eyewitnesses' behavior was unrealistic. That is, I believe that the testimony retraction behavior of the eyewitness is simply an experimenter's scenario and is not representative of actual eyewitness testimony.

A second general advantage of using the testimony of eyewitnesses to staged crimes is that it is possible to compare directly subject-jurors' judgments (e.g., belief or disbelief of the eyewitness) to a documented reality (i.e., the eyewitness's testimony was accurate or inaccurate). This is, of course, not generally possible when using eyewitness testimony from actual trials and it certainly is not possible when using experimenter-written scripts of testimony. Therefore, using testimony from eyewitnesses to staged crimes allows for a measure of subject-jurors' judgments that is somewhat closer to what we mean when we ask how adequate human intuition is for judging eyewitness testimony.

At the time of this writing, five studies using this method have been published. The prototype study, conducted by Wells, Lindsay, & Ferguson (1979), involved the staging of a theft 127 times for as many eyewitnesses, who attempted an identification of the thief from a set of six photographs. A random sample of 24 eyewitnesses who made an accurate identification and 18 eyewitnesses who made a false identification were then cross-examined individually in the presence of subject-jurors. The subject-jurors' task was to determine whether the eyewitness had accurately identified the thief (belief of witness) or had identified an innocent person (disbelief of witness). The results of this study indicated two important findings. First, there was no evidence overall to indicate that the subject-jurors could detect an accurate witness from one who had made a false identification. Also, the subject-jurors were extremely responsive to the perceived confidence of the witness. Specifically, although the witnesses' confidence accounted for less than 9% of the variance in witness accuracy overall (and zero percent in the random sample of 42), jurors perceptions of the eyewitnesses' confidence accounted for 50% of the variance in jurors' belief decisions. This result, wherein variation in eyewitness confidence affects subject-jurors' judgments more strongly than it should, has been replicated several times (e.g., Lindsay, Wells, & Rumpel, 1981; Wells, Ferguson, & Lindsay, 1981; Wells & Leippe, 1981; Wells et al., 1980). In addition, juror decisions regarding who is and is not an accurate witness do not correlate with the actual accuracy of the witnesses.

These studies suggest that people cannot distinguish, on the basis of viewing cross-examinations of the eyewitnesses, between an eyewitness who has made an accurate identification and an eyewitness who has made a false identification. A study by Lindsay et al. (1981), however, suggests that under some circumstances people can discriminate *between* witnessing conditions even though they cannot discriminate between accurate and inaccurate eyewitnesses *within* conditions. In other words, jurors show no signs of an ability to discriminate between accurate and inaccurate witnesses, but jurors can discriminate between situations that are likely to produce accurate witnesses and situations that are likely to produce less accurate witnesses. In the study by Lindsay and colleagues, three different thefts were staged and 48 eyewitnesses who identified someone from a photo lineup were cross-examined. One of these thefts produced a high rate of false identifications (67%), one produced a moderate rate of false identifications (50%), and one produced a low rate of false identifications (26%). The subject-jurors who viewed cross-examinations of these witnesses were as likely to believe a witness who had falsely identified someone as they were to believe a witness who had accurately identified the thief. Across theft conditions, however, subject-jurors were less likely to believe a given witness in the high-rate-of-false-identification conditions than in the low-rate-of-false-identification conditions.

It is especially interesting to note that the subject-jurors' performance varied as a function of the certainty or confidence of the eyewitness. Specifically, it was found that subject-jurors did *not* take account of witnessing conditions when the eyewitness was confident of his or her testimony (i.e., above the median in confidence). Instead, the subject-jurors seem to have scrutinized the witnessing conditions only when the eyewitness was relatively uncertain of his or her testimony (Lindsay et al., 1981).

Evaluation of the method using eyewitnesses to staged events

As indicated earlier, the cross-examination of eyewitnesses to staged events has two principal advantages over the other methods described in this chapter. First, it provides the triers of fact with eyewitness testimony behaviors that have frequencies, means, variances, and relationships that presumably mimic what one would encounter in actual court cases. Second, and perhaps more important, this method allows for quantitative comparisons between a subject-juror's judgments (e.g., belief or disbelief of a given eyewitness's testimony) and a documented reality (i.e., the accuracy or inaccuracy of an eyewitness's testimony).

Unfortunately, research using cross-examinations of eyewitnesses to staged events has not been entirely satisfactory on several counts. First, this research has been entirely contained in one set of laboratories (University of Alberta). Independent corroboration from other laboratories regarding the general conclusions of these studies is needed. Also, the research has dealt almost exclusively with students, as both witnesses and jurors. Although there is evidence that university students do not differ from jurors in how they evaluate eyewitness matters (e.g., Hosch, Beck, & McIntyre, 1980; Yarmey & Jones, 1982), such differences have not been explored with the staged-event–cross-examination method. Also, the staged-event–cross-examination method typically has not provided subject-jurors with full trial information (such as other forms of physical or testimonial evidence), and the subject-jurors' judgments have typically been without deliberation (i.e., juror decisions rather than jury verdicts). (See Wells et al., 1981, however, for an exception to these last two shortcomings.)

It should also be noted that the staged-event–cross-examination method is an effortful and costly procedure to implement. It requires repeated stagings of events followed by photograph or lineup identifications and then cross-examinations of the eyewitnesses that are either videotaped or presented live to subject-jurors. In some ways it could be argued that the difficulty of implementing a method should not be considered a shortcoming of that method. In terms of pragmatic considerations, however, the difficulty of implementation is undoubtedly a shortcoming because it reduces the number of researchers who can or will use the method and it slows down the rate of data collection.

Conclusions

As indicated in the previous sections, studies assessing human intuition regarding eyewitness matters have used a variety of approaches. Such variety is beneficial in the long run as it will provide us with evidence of conceptual replication. That is, if two different methods produce similar results we can make better judgments about the generality of the findings. For the same reason, if two methods produce different results, then we must take extra caution in interpreting the results. What, however, do we have in the short run? Do we yet have definitive evidence regarding the adequacy of human intuition for judging eyewitness testimony?

At this point in time I am willing to argue that there is at least one important aspect of eyewitness testimony that is misunderstood by the trier of fact, namely eyewitness confidence. All four methods of assessing people's intuitions converge on the conclusion that confidence and accuracy are perceived to be strongly related. The questionnaire studies by Deffenbacher and Loftus (1982), Rahaim and Brodsky (1981), Yarmey and Jones (1983), and myself (reported in this chapter) show that the majority of respondents believe that there is a meaningful relationship between certainty and accuracy. The prediction study showed that subjects expected accuracy from highly confident witnesses and inaccuracy from witnesses whose confidence was low. The taped deliberations in the study by Hastie (1980) showed that subject-jurors spontaneously mentioned eyewitness confidence as a cue to the witness's accuracy. Finally, the series of studies using cross-examinations of eyewitnesses to staged events shows that subject-jurors rely heavily on an eyewitness's confidence to infer the eyewitness's accuracy. Thus, when we compare human intuition (via the methods used in this chapter) with scientific data on the confidence–accuracy issue (see Chapter 8), we must conclude that intuition is inadequate on this matter.

Intuitions of the trier of fact regarding eyewitness matters might also be inadequate in other ways. Questionnaire studies suggest that most people do not appreciate the way eyewitnesses overestimate short temporal durations, the interfering effects of interpolated mug shots, and the nonsuperiority of police as eyewitnesses, all of which have been reasonably well documented through experimentation. Prediction studies suggest that people do not appreciate the effects of crime seriousness, the ineffectiveness and distortion properties of hypnosis, and the effects of biased lineup instructions. Studies using videotaped and written trials suggest that people are reasonably good at identifying pertinent factors such as stress but misinterpret their effects on eyewitness memory. Until these results are corroborated by each of the four methods outlined in this chapter we should be cautious in identifying them as shortcomings of the intuitive theorizer. Nevertheless, the evidence might be sufficient already to suggest that the lay person, as trier of fact, be counseled on these matters.

12   Expert testimony on the eyewitness

Elizabeth F. Loftus

The eyewitness controversy

While psychologists continue their laboratory investigations of eyewitness testimony, legal courts are once again struggling with some of the problems associated with that testimony. An extreme statement of the problem can be found in the writings of a well-known attorney, F. Lee Bailey (1971): "And jurors usually tend to believe eyewitness identifications – another weakness in our system. Mistaken identifications are the greatest single cause of wrongful convictions. Every time someone is convicted on an uncorroborated witness identification, the odds are fifty-fifty that justice has miscarried" (p. 36).

Whether or not one attaches odds of error that match the intuitions of Bailey, it seems clear that there is a chance of a wrong verdict due to mistaken eyewitness testimony. It cannot be denied that errors do occur. Recently there seems to be renewed disagreement over how serious a problem this is and how best to handle it. The U.S. Supreme Court took up the issue again in the recent case of *Watkins* v. *Sowders* (1981). Briefly, John Watkins was convicted in a Kentucky court of attempting to rob a Louisville liquor store. In a separate case, James Summitt was convicted of rape. In both cases the major evidence against the defendants was eyewitness testimony, and in both cases the defendants offered evidence that pretrial police procedures to obtain the identification were impermissibly suggestive. The cases were joined on appeal to the U.S. Supreme Court. Defense counsel argued that the trial courts should have been constitutionally obligated to conduct a hearing outside the presence of the jury to determine whether the identification was admissible. The U.S. Supreme Court decided that although it is prudent for a trial court to determine the admissibility of identification evidence out of the presence of the jury, there is no per se requirement under the due process clause of the Fourteenth Amendment.

The majority in *Watkins* refused to analogize to a previous decision, *Jackson* v. *Denno* (1964), where it was held that there must be a pretrial

273

hearing outside the presence of the jury whenever a confession was sought to be admitted and a question of the voluntariness of the confession was raised. Here the Court required pretrial hearings for confessions by reasoning that confessions are so compelling as evidence that a jury may be unable to follow judicial instructions to ignore involuntary confessions. In contrast, the majority in the more recent case, *Watkins* v. *Sowders,* presumed that juries can follow instructions to assess the reliability of eyewitness identification evidence and will be able to ignore identifications that are impermissibly suggestive. The dissenting opinion in *Watkins* was strong: "Surely jury instructions can ordinarily no more cure the erroneous admission of powerful identification evidence than they can cure the erroneous admission of a confession." The dissent further pointed out that cross-examination in front of the jury is inadequate to test the reliability of eyewitness testimony because cross-examination may often be inhibited by a fear that rigorous questioning of hostile witnesses will strengthen the eyewitness testimony and impress it upon the jury.

Although not directly concerned with the issue of expert testimony, the Watkins case illustrates the differences in opinions that are held on the subject of eyewitness testimony itself. These justices disagree in terms of their views on the impact of eyewitness testimony and they disagree in their views of the ability of jury instructions to cure problems in this area. One group seems to worry about jurors' being overly impressed with the testimony of eyewitnesses, while the other group is not. The strength of these opposing views suggests that legal decision makers will vary tremendously in terms of their receptivity to innovative solutions to problems posed by that testimony.

Expert testimony in practice

One of the proposed safeguards to the problem of jurors' overreliance on eyewitness testimony is to allow judge and jury to hear an expert witness present psychological testimony about factors affecting the reliability of eyewitness accounts. The psychologist typically describes research studies illustrating people's ability to perceive and recall complex events. Factors that may have affected the accuracy of the particular identification in the case at bar are explained to the jury. The goal is to provide jurors with additional information to better equip them to evaluate the identification evidence fully and properly.

An actual case, abbreviated *People of California* v. *DC,* will serve to illustrate the type of testimony that might be offered. On Wednesday, April 1, 1981, at approximately 5:30 in the evening, John Russell and Donny

Serafin, both male prostitutes, were standing together on the sidewalk along Polk Street in San Francisco. Serafin was hustling for "tricks," but his friend Russell was not. Minutes later, a man drove up in a long brown car and stopped directly in front of the two young men; the driver motioned for Serafin to come over. Serafin went over to the car, told Russell that he would be back in an hour, and jumped into the car. A few days later, on April 4, Serafin's dead body was found in a wooded area nearly a hundred miles away. According to preliminary hearing testimony, "a band or cord of some type was tightened about the neck causing asphyxiation and death of the individual."

On April 14, Russell viewed a photographic lineup containing a police suspect, DC. Although Russell was unable to make a positive selection, he did choose two photographs, one of which was of DC. In Russell's words: "I don't know, if I saw a side view I think I could tell. . . . Right now I'm not able to positively say."

On May 7, a lineup was prepared so that the suspect could be viewed by Russell. As the police tell it, after viewing the lineup Russell quickly walked away and lit a cigarette. He looked ill; he was bent over in his seat and his face was white. When asked if he was all right, he volunteered that he had identified the man who drove off with his friend and he was absolutely sure about it. Interestingly, he denied ever having seen a photograph of this man before. On the basis of this identification, DC was tried for murder in October 1981.

Numerous factors that could have influenced Russell's initial perception and memory were brought out via expert testimony. The factors were divided into three major categories – those that affect the initial acquisition of information, those that affect the retention of information, and those that affect the final retrieval of information. At the acquisition stage, an important factor was that Russell had been smoking marijuana prior to going out on the street with the victim. Marijuana is known to affect the formation of new memories, or the ability to store information into long-term memory (Loftus, 1980a; Miller & Branconnier, 1983). Several factors came into play during the retention stage. First, 5 weeks intervened between the initial encounter in San Francisco, and the lineup identification on May 7. Although 5 weeks in and of itself is a reasonably long period of time, what is especially important is that the witness viewed photographs of the suspect during that time. When a photograph of an innocent person is seen between an initial event and a subsequent in-person identification, the likelihood of a mistaken identification is enhanced (Brown, Deffenbacher, & Sturgill, 1977; Gorenstein & Ellsworth, 1980). Finally, there are factors at the retrieval stage that are important. For example, the witness was extremely confident, a fact especially likely to impress a jury. In fact, recent research has shown that there may be little or no relationship between the confidence with which testimony is given and the accuracy of that testimony (Deffenbacher, 1980; Leippe, 1980).

These, then, were some of the specific issues about which expert testimony was offered in the case of *People* v. *DC*. In other cases, the relevant factors are different, and the expert may discuss the effects of extreme stress or the cross-racial identification problem, factors that were not relevant in *People* v. *DC*. In some instances, the expert testimony has remained at a very general level, never mentioning the particular witnesses or victims in the case at bar. Other times, the expert speaks quite specifically about the particular witnesses. Which form the testimony takes depends upon the inclinations of the particular judge who decides on admissibility.

It is natural to ask whether the testimony in this case, or in any case, is appropriate testimony. Will it aid the jury? Will it prejudice the jury? Should the jury be allowed to hear this testimony at all?

Legal considerations

Although expert testimony has been allowed in numerous states around the country, it is highly controversial. Some lawyers and judges worry that it invades the province of the jury, that it will have undue influence on the jury, that it is well within the common knowledge of the jury, or that it will lead to a battle of experts that will detract from the real issues in the case.

The leading appellate decision on the subject is *United States* v. *Amaral* (1973). The defendant, Manuel P. Amaral, was charged in 1973 with the robbery of two national banks. Later that year he was tried. At his trial, defense counsel moved to introduce the testimony of a psychologist with regard to the effect of stress on perception, and more generally, with regard to the unreliability of eyewitness identification. The trial court refused to admit the testimony on the ground that "it would not be appropriate to take from the jury their own determination as to what weight or effect to give to the evidence of the eyewitness and identifying witnesses and to have that determination put before them on the basis of the expert witness testimony as proffered" (p. 1153). Amaral was found guilty. He appealed his conviction on several grounds, one of which was the refusal of the trial court to admit the expert testimony. The Ninth Circuit Court of Appeals affirmed the conviction and noted that the defense had uncovered no uncertainty as to the identity of the robber in any of several witnesses. Although it acknowledged that stress might affect perception, it noted that not all the witnesses were under similar conditions of stress. One witness saw the robber as he sat in his car blocking the exit from the bank parking lot, another saw him from the safety of her house as he fled after robbing the bank, and still another saw him as he entered the bank and approached the teller. Moreover, the court suggested that defense counsel could have questioned the witnesses at cross-examination to ascertain their capacity and opportunity for observation.

Despite the affirmation of Amaral's conviction, the Amaral decision is significant in part because it reiterated the general principles regarding expert testimony so that they might be applied to this new type of expert: (a) the witness must be a qualified expert, (b) the testimony must concern a proper subject matter, (c) the testimony must be in accord with a generally accepted explanatory theory, and (d) the probative value of the testimony must outweigh its prejudicial effect. In addition, the court noted that the trial judge has broad discretion in whether to admit the testimony or not.

Legal scholars have analyzed the Amaral decision, pointing out in part its weaknesses. For example, Woocher (1977) noted that the decision did nothing to establish any guidelines to aid the trial judge in exercising his or her discretion. How is the trial judge to decide whether the expert witness is truly qualified or whether the testimony concerns a proper subject matter or whether it conforms to a generally accepted explanatory theory? What standards should the judge use to weigh its probative value against its potentially prejudicial effects?

Substantial disagreement exists among both psychologists and legal commentators as to the appropriateness of expert testimony on the credibility of an eyewitness. Numerous individuals have considered the four Amaral criteria and have concluded that the expert testimony is proper (Addison, 1978; Katz & Reid, 1977; Loftus & Monahan, 1980; Sobel, 1972, 1979; Woocher, 1977). In fact, some lawyers (e.g., Frazzini, 1981; Stein, 1981) and judges (Bazelon, 1980; Weinstein, 1981) have held that the expert testimony will be of clear aid to a jury. Stein (1981) notes that the *Federal Rules of Evidence* (1975), especially Rule 702, will spark use of the psychologist as expert on eyewitness testimony. The rule states: "If scientific, technical, or other specialized knowledge will assist the trier of fact to understand the evidence or to determine a fact in issue, a witness qualified as an expert by knowledge, skill, experience, training, or education, may testify thereto in the form of an opinion or otherwise."

In analyzing the expert testimony with respect to this rule, Stein asserts that in his view the expert testimony will certainly assist the fact finder. Any knowledge on the subject qualifies as an "assist," he says. He is careful to point out, however, that there is one argument against admissibility, and it can be found at Rule 403: "Although relevant, evidence may be excluded if its probative value is substantially outweighed by the danger of unfair prejudice, confusion of the issues, or misleading the jury, or by consideration of undue delay, waste of time, or needless presentation of cumulative evidence." Thus, even though evidence is relevant and will assist the jury on a relevant issue, it could arguably be excluded because it will confuse and mislead.

Weinstein (1981), a judge writing in the *Columbia Law Review,* considers a number of possible protections against the wrongful conviction of the innocent caused by mistaken identification. His views are clear: "Greater use of expert tesimony...is clearly warranted" (p. 454). He goes on to note that the *Federal Rules of Evidence* and the rules of most of the states that follow the federal rules permit this kind of evidence. He suggests, indirectly, that some courts might hold that the government is required to provide indigent defendants with experts of this kind when they are needed.

Bazelon (1980), a senior circuit judge of the U.S. Court of Appeals for the District of Columbia, has also thought a great deal about expert testimony. He states: "within our adversarial system, our only hope lies in an informed jury. Some combination of jury instructions, lawyers' arguments, and use of expert witnesses can certainly mitigate the problem" (p. 106).

Finally, Frazzini (1981) has stated: "I believe that expert psychological testimony probably is the best way for juries to learn about the unreliability of eyewitness testimony. Prosecutor and defense counsel, in questioning the expert witness, can explain to the jury both the application and the limits of experimental research in relation to the case on trial." He ends his article in this way: "For innocent men and women, wrongly accused because of mistaken identifications, expert psychological testimony still offers a beacon of hope" (p. xx).

On the other hand, some commentators have worried that the data upon which such testimony rests may be overly conflicting and inappropriate (e.g., Clifford, 1979; Egeth & McCloskey, Chapter 13 of this volume). There are other concerns, too. Some of the strongest negative language can be found in specific appellate decisions. Although the majority of the appellate comments have generally been in agreement with the Amaral decision regarding the broad discretion of the trial judge and have not taken a stand on the merits of the testimony, many courts have taken a decidedly negative posture toward the testimony. Several courts, for example, have concluded that the expert testimony on this subject is not beyond the knowledge and experience of a juror and thus is not a proper subject of expert testimony (*Dyas* v. *United States,* 1977; *State* v. *Galloway,* 1979; *Nelson* v. *State,* 1978). In *Dyas,* the court wrote, "we are persuaded that the subject matter of the proffered testimony is not beyond the ken of the average layman nor would such testimony aid the tried in a search for the truth" (p. 832). Citing from the Nelson case: "We believe it is within the common knowledge of the jury that a person being attacked and beaten undergoes stress that might cloud a subsequent identification of the assailant by the victim. As such, the subject matter was not properly within the realm of expert testimony" (p. 1021). These remarks are similar to those uttered by the Ontario Court of Appeal as it upheld the trial judge's decision to refuse the admissibility of the expert testimony: "The same can be said of stress. Knowledge by the jury that conditions of stress affect perception by the observer would add little, if anything, to what lay persons already know" (*Regina* v. *Audy*, 1977, cited by Taylor, 1980). The trial judge had refused the testimony for several reasons, one of which was lack of Canadian precedent for this type of evidence, as well as the enormous impact such evidence would have on the jury system itself (Taylor, 1980).

Why are courts so reluctant? According to speculations of Frazzini (1981) it is because of a "fear of the novel" (p. xx). Reluctance also arises from a fear that such testimony would complicate a trial or lead to the release of the guilty as well as the innocent. Frazzini further notes that court dockets are crowded, and the public wants convictions. Most people believe in eyewitness testimony, and convict on the basis of it. Despite its vagaries and unreliability, it is a proved formula for conviction, and few people want to interfere with such a success rate.

Some higher courts have been highly sympathetic to the problems inherent in eyewitness testimony but have fallen short of requiring the use of experts. Specifically, the Kansas Supreme Court recently said that juries should be warned by judges of the pitfalls of eyewitness identification (Petterson, 1981). The opinion arose out of a case involving a defendant named John Warren who was accused of aggravated robbery of the Chateau Briand Restaurant in Wichita, Kansas. The owner of the restaurant, Anthony Miller, testified that Warren was the robber who pointed a gun at him and who grabbed the bank bag from under the counter. The defendant attempted to introduce the testimony of an expert, but the trial court rejected the proffered testimony, saying that it did not think "we ought to be bringing in psychologists to say, 'well, this witness is wrong or that witness is wrong.'" The defense also requested a cautionary instruction to advise the jury as to the factors to be considered in weighing the credibility of the eyewitness testimony. The trial court refused to give such an instruction.

In discussing the question of the admissibility of expert testimony, the

Kansas Supreme Court concluded that requiring trial courts to admit this type of expert evidence is not the answer to a problem that they admitted was highly important. Rather, they felt:

We believe that the problem can be alleviated by a proper cautionary instruction to the jury which sets forth the factors to be considered in evaluating eyewitness testimony. Such an instruction, coupled with vigorous cross-examination and persuasive argument by defense counsel dealing realistically with the shortcomings and trouble spots of the identification process, should protect the rights of the defendant and at the same time enable the courts to avoid the problems involved in the admission of expert testimony on this subject.

The court went on to say that the defendant is entitled to have a cautionary instruction that includes a specific focus on the dangers of eyewitness testimony.

Impact of expert testimony

If psychologists are to be offering expert testimony in court, it behooves us to learn something about the impact of that testimony. Does the testimony have any impact on the verdict in a trial? Does the testimony have any effects on other aspects of the trial, for example, the quality of the deliberations? One anecdotal courtroom experience suggests that the testimony may influence the verdict. The trial involved was a prosecution of two ranchers, Thomas and Patrick Hanigan, who were charged with beating and torturing three Mexicans (*New York Times,* Feb. 12, 1981). They were tried in Federal Court in Phoenix, Arizona, in a trial that had one especially unique feature. Two juries sat in the courtroom at the same time, one to hear the evidence and decide on the fate of Patrick and the other to decide on the fate of Thomas. Although the evidence against the two brothers was virtually identical and consisted in large measure of eyewitness testimony by the victims, expert testimony was offered only in the case of Thomas. While his jury heard this evidence, Patrick's jury waited in the jury room. How did the two juries decide their respective cases? Patrick Hanigan was found guilty and his brother Thomas was acquitted by their separate juries. Although the differing verdicts were criticized by both sides as "bizarre" and "half-justice" (*Tucson Citizen,* Feb. 23, 1981), not to mention "the weirdest goddam thing I have ever seen" (*Arizona Daily Star,* Feb. 24, 1981), the mixed outcome has been attributed to the use of expert testimony in one case but not the other.

Although the rare two-jury case has been said to provide the "natural experiment," we obviously have only a single case here. The differing verdicts could have been due to other factors, such as differences in the likability of the two brothers or of their attorneys. Interviews with the jurors after the case might have provided further useful information, but it is not always possible to conduct them. In some cases, however, such interviews are possible, and interviews with actual jurors after a different trial (described in Loftus, 1979) suggested that the testimony may influence the jurors by affecting the deliberation process. In this particular case – a case of murder – the jurors were interviewed by the chief investigator after failing to reach a verdict. In a letter to the psychologist-expert, the investigator reported: "The most important thing was that, whether they liked you or didn't like you, they spent a great deal of time discussing your testimony" (p. 215).

This comment suggests that one possible effect of expert testimony is to increase the amount of deliberation time spent discussing the eyewitness aspects of the case. It is always risky to assume that post hoc interviews with actual jurors will provide answers to research questions, because these interviews rely on retrospective accounts. Thus, researchers have turned to another method to discover the effect of expert testimony. As with many other issues concerning the influence of some variable on the outcome of a trial, this one has been investigated in the context of a simulated jury paradigm. The simulation has the enormous advantage that the deliberations of a mock jury, unlike those of a real jury, can be recorded, dissected, and analyzed. Although one must be careful in generalizing from the simulation to the real courtroom, for the most part it is safe to take the results of simulation studies as clues to what is likely to be influential in a real courtroom setting.

Three simulation studies have been conducted recently on the impact of expert psychological testimony on eyewitness reliability (Hosch, Beck, & McIntyre, 1980; Loftus, 1980b; Wells, Lindsay, & Tousignant, 1980). These generally show that exposure of jurors to an expert reduces the effect of eyewitness testimony, perhaps by causing jurors to scrutinize the testimony more carefully. Loftus (1980b) presented written summaries of an assault case to subject-jurors, who were then asked to reach a verdict. The major piece of prosecution evidence was the testimony of an eyewitness. Half of the jurors read about the testimony of a defense expert on the reliability of eyewitness identification, whereas the other half did not. Individual verdicts were reached. The results indicated that there were fewer convictions when expert testimony was permitted. In a second study, subjects received evidence in a hypothetical criminal case and then deliberated in juries of six to reach a verdict for or against the defendant. Subject-jurors who had read about the expert testimony spent more time discussing the eyewitness account than did subjects who had not been presented with expert testimony. Loftus interpreted these results as suggesting that one consequence of presenting psychological expert testimony is increased attention given to the eyewitness accounts.

Subsequent work has generally supported this interpretation. Wells et al. (1980) had subjects view a videotaped cross-examination of an eyewitness and then reach a verdict. Prior to this, half the subjects viewed videotaped expert testimony. Again, those who viewed the expert testimony were less likely to believe the eyewitness. Finally, Hosch et al. (1980) asked community residents to serve as jurors in a videotaped burglary trial. As it happened, all juries acquitted the defendant; however, those who heard the expert testimony significantly lowered their judgments of accuracy and reliability of eyewitness identification as well as its overall importance to the trial. Further, those juries that heard the expert testimony spent a significantly longer time discussing eyewitness identification.

Conclusions

The controversy continues over the usefulness of expert testimony as a potential solution to some of the problems inherent in the presentation of eyewitness evidence in court. Will such testimony solve the problem? According to Bazelon (1980) we may never adequately solve the problem. Over time, the criminal justice system will become more sensitive to the possible weaknesses of eyewitness testimony, and this will help; but the problem will never be solved, he suggests forcefully, if we simply close our eyes to it. Clearly, expert testimony, if it is to be at least a partial solution, deserves our serious consideration. Future research should concern itself with the particular form of expert testimony, whether it be quite general or specific to the case at bar. General testimony may be somewhat useful but will need to be tied to the specific case. Specific testimony may be more relevant, but at the same time come closer to invading the province of the jury. This is only one of the many issues that now require further research if we are to tackle successfully that "greatest single cause of wrongful convictions" that has continued to plague F. Lee Bailey and countless others.

13 Expert testimony about eyewitness behavior: Is it safe and effective?

Howard E. Egeth and Michael McCloskey

Psychologists have long been concerned about the use of eyewitness testimony in the courtroom. Research on human perception and memory (for reviews see Ellison & Buckhout, 1981; Loftus, 1979; Yarmey, 1979a), as well as reports of criminal cases in which defendants were convicted on the bases of mistaken eyewitness identifications (e.g., Borchard, 1932), has led many to conclude that eyewitness testimony is inherently unreliable. Recently, it has been suggested (e.g., Ellison & Buckhout, 1981; Loftus, 1979; Loftus & Monahan, 1980; Woocher, 1977) that experimental psychologists who study normal human perception and memory should serve as expert witnesses in cases involving eyewitnesses to inform the jury about the problems with eyewitness testimony. Although the courts have often ruled this sort of expert testimony inadmissible, psychologists are testifying in an increasing number of cases (Ellison & Buckhout, 1981; Loftus, 1979; Loftus & Monahan, 1980; Woocher, 1977).

In this chapter we critically examine the arguments offered in favor of the use of expert psychological testimony about eyewitnesses. (It should be understood that we are referring only to expert testimony about perception and memory in eyewitnesses and not to other sorts of expert psychological testimony.) A basic premise of our discussion is that intervention in the operation of the justice system should not be undertaken lightly. The position we adopt is similar to the one adopted by the Food and Drug Administration in its assessment of drugs: We think expert testimony should be offered only if it clearly is "safe and effective." As we discuss in greater detail later, the use of expert psychological testimony in the absence of clear evidence of its utility would carry substantial risks both for the justice

During the preparation of this paper the authors were supported in part by NSF grant number BNS-8022670. We would like to thank John Jonides, Judith McKenna, Allyson Washburn, Elizabeth Webb, Stephen Grossman, Rod Lindsay, Elizabeth Loftus, and Gary Wells for their helpful comments.

283

system and for the psychological profession. Consequently, in the following evaluation of arguments that have been offered in favor of the use of expert psychological testimony, we ask not, Does this claim seem plausible? or Might this assumption be valid? but rather, What does the available *evidence* say about this argument? We suggest that contrary to the claims of several psychologists and lawyers (e.g., Addison, 1978; Ellison & Buckhout, 1981; Loftus, 1979; Loftus & Monahan, 1980; Lower, 1978; Starkman, 1979; Woocher, 1977), the available evidence fails to demonstrate the general usefulness of expert psychological testimony and, in fact, does not even rule out the possibility that such testimony may have detrimental effects.

It should be made clear at the outset that this chapter has been written by and (largely) for experimental psychologists. The content is psychological. We have made no effort to consider legal aspects of the problem such as, for example, laws affecting the admissibility of psychological testimony in various jurisdictions (such discussions are provided by Ellison & Buckhout, 1981; Gass, 1979; Goodrich, 1975; Loftus & Monahan, 1980; C. R. Wilson, 1975; and Woocher, 1977).

Two rationales for the use of expert psychological testimony

Two major rationales have been offered for the use of expert psychological testimony. First, the *overbelief* rationale asserts that jurors are often too willing to believe eyewitness testimony (Ellison & Buckhout, 1981; Lindsay, Wells, & Rumpel, 1981; Loftus, 1974, 1979; Loftus & Monahan, 1980; Wall, 1965; Wells, Lindsay & Tousignant, 1980). On this view an expert witness could increase juror skepticism to a more appropriate level by discussing research demonstrating the unreliability of eyewitness testimony and by pointing out aspects of the case at hand (e.g., stress experienced by the witness) that might have led to witness inaccuracy. Loftus (1979) provides a strong statement of the overbelief claim: "Since jurors rarely regard eyewitness testimony with any skepticism, the expert testimony will increase the likelihood of this happening. This is its value" (p. 197).

The second rationale for the use of expert psychological testimony asserts that regardless of whether jurors are in general too willing to believe eyewitness testimony, they cannot discriminate adequately between accurate and inaccurate eyewitnesses (Lindsay et al., 1981; Loftus, 1979; Loftus & Monahan, 1980; Wells, Lindsay, & Ferguson, 1979; Wells et al., 1980). Consequently, the argument continues, jurors often disbelieve accurate witnesses and believe inaccurate witnesses. According to this *discrimination* rationale, expert psychological testimony could improve juror discrimination by informing jurors about factors known to influence witness accuracy and by cautioning against reliance on irrelevant factors such as witness attractiveness.

Both the overbelief and the discrimination rationales make two fundamental claims: (a) jurors need help in evaluating eyewitness testimony; and (b) expert psychological testimony can provide this help. In the following section we examine these claims.

Juror evaluation of eyewitness testimony

Overbelief. Consider first the assertion that jurors are too willing to believe eyewitnesses. Several arguments have been advanced in support of this claim. One argument that is frequently implicit in discussions of juror evaluation of eyewitness testimony is that the conclusion of juror overbelief in eyewitnesses follows from research showing that eyewitness testimony is often unreliable. An important but unstated assumption here is that jurors are unaware of the unreliability of eyewitness testimony and consequently are too willing to believe such testimony.[1] There appears, however, to be no reason to assume a priori that people are unaware of the problems with eyewitness testimony. Cases of mistaken identification are often widely publicized (e.g., the recent case of Father Pagano; see Ellison & Buckhout, 1981), and wrongful conviction on the basis of mistaken or perjured eyewitness testimony is a rather common theme in fiction. In addition, there is no consensus within the legal community that jurors are unaware of the unreliability of eyewitnesses and consequently give too much credence to eyewitness testimony. For example, in ruling against admission of expert psychological testimony, the trial judge in the case of *People* v. *Guzman* (1975) stated: "It is something that everyone knows about, the problems of identification. The jurors here were well questioned regarding their experience...with having mistakenly identified people. Everyone knows these things happen" (p. 71). Thus, in the absence of evidence that jurors are unaware of the unreliability of eyewitness testimony, the conclusion that jurors are too willing to believe eyewitnesses cannot legitimately be drawn from research demonstrating that eyewitnesses are often inaccurate.

A second argument asserts that juror overbelief is demonstrated by the existence of cases in which defendants were wrongfully convicted on the basis of eyewitness testimony later shown to be mistaken. The implicit assumption here seems to be that if jurors were appropriately skeptical, wrongful convictions based upon erroneous identifications would never occur. This is not a tenable position. The degree of skepticism jurors exhibit toward eyewitnesses affects not only the likelihood that an innocent defendant will be convicted, but also the likelihood that a *guilty* defendant will be convicted. An increase in juror skepticism toward eyewitness testimony would decrease conviction of the guilty as well as conviction of the innocent, and a degree of skepticism that eliminated wrongful conviction on the basis of eyewitness testimony would also eliminate any role of eyewitnesses in the conviction of the guilty. In signal detection terms, it is unfortunate but true that except in situations involving very high signal-to-noise ratios, one cannot eliminate false alarms without also eliminating hits simply by shifting one's decision criterion.

To demonstrate juror overbelief in eyewitnesses, one must show not merely that erroneous convictions based upon eyewitness testimony sometimes occur, but that the ratio of conviction of the innocent to conviction of the guilty is unacceptably high. Documented cases of wrongful conviction resulting from mistaken eyewitness testimony obviously represent only a very small fraction of 1% of the cases in which defendants were convicted at least in part on the basis of eyewitness testimony. We cannot say what should be considered an acceptable ratio of conviction of the innocent to conviction of the guilty, as this is properly a social policy issue. Still, it would appear difficult to argue that documented cases of wrongful conviction establish that the ratio is unacceptably high. Consequently, the known cases of erroneous convictions fail to demonstrate that jurors are too willing to believe eyewitness testimony.

Our point here is not that the frequency of wrongful conviction is acceptably low but merely that known cases of erroneous conviction fail to establish that the frequency is unacceptably high. Thus our argument is not affected by the possibility that *documented* cases of wrongful conviction represent only the tip of the iceberg. In the absence of a means of estimating the number of undocumented cases of wrongful conviction, these undocumented cases cannot be used as evidence that erroneous conviction on the basis of eyewitness testimony occurs too often.

A third argument offered in favor of the overbelief claim stems from an experiment by Loftus (1974, 1979; see also Cavoukian, 1980). In this experiment, university students read a short summary of evidence presented at a robbery and murder trial and voted individually for conviction or acquittal. In the no-eyewitness condition the trial description mentioned only physical evidence against the defendant (e.g., money found in the defendant's room). Only 18% of the subjects in this condition voted for conviction. In the eyewitness condition the trial description mentioned the physical evidence and also indicated that an eyewitness had identified the defendant as the robber. In this condition, 72% of the students voted to convict. Finally, in the discredited-eyewitness condition, subjects were told about the physical evidence and the eyewitness identification. They were also informed that the defense attorney "claimed the witness had not been wearing his glasses the day of the robbery, and since he had vision poorer than 20/400 he could not possibly have seen the face of the robber from where he stood" (Loftus, 1979, p. 117). In this condition, 68% of the students voted to convict. The high percentage of subjects voting for conviction in the eyewitness condition, in conjunction with the lack of difference between the eyewitness and discredited-eyewitness conditions, it is argued, indicates that people give too much credence to eyewitness testimony.

Several recent studies cast doubt on this conclusion. First, in an experiment recently conducted in our laboratory, college students read detailed summaries (4,000–6,500 words) of a fictitious bank robbery trial and voted individually for conviction or acquittal (McKenna, Mellott, & Webb, 1981). The bank teller who was robbed chose the defendant from a lineup 2 days after the robbery and positively identified him during the trial. In addition the prosecution demonstrated that an amount of money closely matching that stolen from the bank was found in the defendant's possession.

The defense case consisted of the testimony of the defendant's mother. She stated that the money found in the defendant's possession was a loan from her so that the defendant could buy a car and that the defendant had followed his normal routine the day of the robbery, coming home from his night job in the morning, going to sleep, and getting up at 5 p.m. On cross-examination the defendant's mother admitted that she could not be sure that the defendant was at home at the time of the robbery, because his door was closed.

This study was conducted in part to examine the effect of expert psychological testimony on subjects' decisions of guilty or not-guilty. Hence, the experiment included both no-expert-testimony conditions, in which only the testimony described was presented, and expert-testimony conditions, in which the trial summaries included the testimony of an experimental psychologist concerning factors (e.g., stress) that may lead to inaccurate eyewitness identifications.

In spite of the teller's positive identification of the defendant, verdicts of guilty were obtained from only 2 of the 24 subjects (8%) in the no-expert conditions, and 3 of the 48 subjects (6%) in the conditions involving expert testimony. Examination of the subject's explanations for their decisions revealed that many subjects, including those in the no-expert conditions, thought that although the defendant may well have been guilty, it was possible that the teller had made an erroneous identification. Consequently, they were not certain enough of the defendant's guilt to vote "guilty." In subsequent experiments we have obtained similar results with adults from the Baltimore community and a trial scenario in which the defense case consisted solely of the defendant's testimony that he was at home alone at the time of the crime.

Hosch, Beck, and McIntyre (1980) obtained a similar result. In their study, subjects serving in eight six-person juries viewed a trial in which an eyewitness positively identified the defendant. Four of the juries heard expert psychological testimony, whereas the other four juries did not. After deliberating, all eight juries arrived at unanimous not-guilty verdicts. These results are somewhat difficult to reconcile with the assertion that "jurors rarely regard eyewitness testimony with any skepticism."

Other studies have examined the claim that jurors will believe even a discredited eyewitness. In an experiment in which subjects made individual guilty–not guilty decisions after reading a detailed summary of a robbery and murder trial, we found that when a prosecution eyewitness was convincingly discredited, his testimony was disregarded by the subjects (McCloskey et al., 1981). Similar results have been obtained by Hatvany and Strack (1980) and Weinberg and Baron (1982).

Thus, studies using methodologies similar to that of the Loftus (1974, 1979) experiment have shown both that a high percentage of subjects do not routinely vote "guilty" when an eyewitness has positively identified the defendant and that when a witness is discredited, his or her testimony is disregarded. Although definite conclusions about the behavior of jurors in actual trials cannot readily be drawn from these results, they fail to support the juror overbelief argument.[2]

A final argument in favor of the claim that jurors overbelieve eyewitnesses stems from a recent series of experiments by Wells and Lindsay and their colleagues (Lindsay et al., 1981; Wells et al., 1980). In these experiments subjects serving as witnesses observed a staged crime and then attempted to identify the criminal from an array of photographs. Witnesses who made accurate identifications, as well as witnesses who identified the wrong man, were then videotaped as they answered questions about the viewing conditions, the appearance of the criminal, and so forth. Additional subjects serving as jurors watched videotapes of witnesses and judged for each whether or not the witness had made an accurate identification. Under some witnessing conditions the percentage of jurors believing a witness was higher than the percentage of witnesses who made accurate identifications. For example, in one situation 50% of the witnesses made an accurate identification. Jurors viewing videotapes, however, believed witnesses from that condition 66% of the time. Lindsay et al. (1981) and Wells et al. (1980) argue on the basis of these results that jurors are too willing to believe eyewitness testimony.

Although the argument of Wells and Lindsay seems plausible, it is not entirely valid. The logic of the argument appears to be as follows: The finding that juror belief rates exceed witness accuracy rates implies that jurors overestimate the probability that an eyewitness is accurate, and this in turn implies that jurors are too willing to believe eyewitnesses.

There are some difficulties with the first step in this argument, because the finding that the percentage of jurors believing a witness was higher than the percentage of witnesses who were accurate does not necessarily imply that the jurors overestimated the probability that the witness was accurate. A simple example serves to make this point. Consider a situation in which 90% of witnesses make an accurate identification. If jurors accurately estimate the probability that a witness was accurate at .9, all jurors probably make "believe" decisions, and the juror belief rate (100%) will exceed the witness accuracy rate (90%).

Even if we ignore this problem and assume that in some situations jurors overestimate eyewitness accuracy, the conclusion that jurors are too willing to believe eyewitnesses does not follow. As we discussed earlier, to say that jurors are too willing to believe eyewitnesses means that jurors are too willing to *convict* on the basis of eyewitness testimony (or, more technically, that the weight given by jurors to eyewitness testimony results in an unacceptably high ratio of number of innocent defendants convicted to number of guilty defendants convicted).

Data suggesting that jurors overestimate the probability that eyewitnesses are accurate do not necessarily imply that jurors are too willing to convict on the basis of eyewitness testimony. The reasonable doubt criterion, among other things, intervenes between judging the likelihood that a witness is accurate and voting to convict or acquit. In our research we have frequently seen subjects arrive at not-guilty verdicts in spite of a stated belief that an eyewitness who identified the defendant was probably correct. These subjects generally say that although they believe the defendant is probably guilty, they are not certain beyond a reasonable doubt. Thus, if the criterion for decisions to convict is sufficiently stringent, juror overestimates of witness accuracy need not result in an overwillingness to convict on the basis of eyewitness testimony. More generally, our point here is that in the absence of data concerning jurors' criteria for convict–acquit decisions, we cannot determine from juror estimates of witness accuracy (or, more specifically, from the believe–disbelieve judgments collected by Wells et al. and Lindsay et al.) whether jurors are insufficiently likely, just likely enough, or too likely to convict on the basis of eyewitness testimony.

One other point should be made regarding the results of the studies made by Wells and Lindsay and their colleagues. In considering whether jurors overbelieve eyewitnesses we have focused on the question of whether juror evaluation of eyewitness testimony results in an unacceptable ratio of number of innocent defendants convicted to number of guilty defendants convicted. One may also ask whether jurors give eyewitness testimony appropriate weight relative to other sorts of evidence (e.g., the defendant's fingerprints found at the scene of the crime, money found in the defendant's possession, alibi evidence). If it could be shown that jurors give eyewitness testimony too much weight relative to some other types of evidence it might reasonably be argued that in at least some sense jurors overbelieve eyewitness testimony. (Of course, if in this situation juror evaluation of eyewitnesses produced appropriate conviction rates, it might more reasonably be concluded that the other evidence was *under*believed).

Unfortunately, the question of whether jurors give eyewitness testimony too much weight relative to other sorts of evidence is difficult to answer for at least two reasons. First, there are few studies comparing the weight given to eyewitness testimony with that accorded other types of evidence. Second, and more important, it is difficult to determine how much relative weight various sorts of evidence *should* be given. Thus, we have little to say here about juror evaluation of eyewitnesses relative to other types of evidence. We should point out, however, that the findings of Wells and Lindsay and colleagues suggesting that subject-jurors sometimes overestimate the probability that an eyewitness identification was accurate do not imply that jurors overvalue eyewitness testimony relative to other sorts of evidence. It is certainly conceivable that studies using the Wells and Lindsay paradigm, with other kinds of evidence substituted for eyewitness testimony, might show that jurors overbelieve (in the Wells and Lindsay sense) those other kinds of evidence as well. (To repeat, though, this sort of overbelief would not necessarily imply an overwillingness to convict.) Thus, the findings of Wells and Lindsay and their colleagues demonstrate neither that jurors are too willing to convict on the basis of eyewitness testimony nor that eyewitness testimony is overvalued relative to other sorts of evidence.

A discussion of juror overbelief would be incomplete without mention of two recent studies of actual trial outcomes. Both studies cast doubt upon the strong claim that "jurors rarely regard eyewitness testimony with any skepticism." Chen (1981) tabulated the outcomes of all criminal cases in the Los Angeles Superior Court from July 1977 through December 1978. With factors partialed out, the ratio of convictions in cases with at least one eyewitness identification of the defendant to convictions in cases without identification was 1.1 to 1. Similarly, Myers (1979) examined the 201 criminal cases tried by jury in Marion County, Indiana, between January 1974 and June 1976. She found that convictions were no more likely in cases involving identification of the defendant by a victim or other eyewitness(es) than in cases where there was no eyewitness identification. Of course, these sorts of results are not definitive. For example, prosecutors may bring generally weaker cases to trial when an eyewitness is available than when there is no eyewitness. Be that as it may, the Chen and Myers findings cast doubt on the strong claim that jurors rarely regard eyewitness testimony with any skepticism. A dramatic illustration of this point is provided by the case of a man who was arrested 13 times and tried 5 times in an 18-month period for a series of crimes that were later confessed to by another man. What is noteworthy about this case is that he was acquitted in all 5 trials even though one or more eyewitnesses testified against him in each (Shoemaker, 1980).

In summary, the existing evidence fails to verify the claim that jurors are too willing to believe eyewitness testimony. This does not imply that jurors exhibit an appropriate degree of skepticism toward eyewitness testimony. Our point is simply that contrary to the claims of many psychologists and lawyers (e.g., Ellison & Buckhout, 1981; Lindsay et al., 1981; Loftus, 1974, 1979; Loftus & Monahan, 1980; Wells et al., 1980; Woocher, 1977), juror overbelief in eyewitnesses has not been demonstrated. Consequently, it is by no means clear that there is a need for expert psychological testimony to make jurors more skeptical.

Discrimination. The discrimination rationale for the use of expert psychological testimony asserts that regardless of whether jurors are generally skeptical or generally credulous of eyewitness testimony, they cannot distinguish well between accurate and inaccurate eyewitnesses. According to this rationale, expert psychological testimony could improve juror discrimination.

The claim that jurors cannot readily discriminate accurate from inaccurate eyewitnesses is well founded. Cases of wrongful conviction based upon mistaken eyewitness testimony demonstrate that juror discrimination is not perfect, and the recent studies of Wells and Lindsay and their colleagues suggest that jurors' ability to distinguish accurate and inaccurate eyewitnesses may be quite poor indeed. As we mentioned earlier, these researchers conducted a series of studies in which subjects serving as jurors judged whether witnesses to staged crimes had made an accurate or inaccurate identification of the perpetrator. They found that within a given crime situation jurors were as likely to believe inaccurate witnesses as they were to believe accurate witnesses (Lindsay et al., 1981; Wells, Lindsay, & Ferguson, 1979; Wells et al., 1980).

These results are clearly disquieting. Yet the situation is perhaps not as bleak as it first appears. In the Lindsay et al. (1981) study the witnesses viewed a staged crime under one of three different viewing conditions. In the *poor* condition the criminal was visible for only 12 seconds and wore a hat that completely covered his hair. The *moderate* condition was similar to the poor condition except that the cap was worn higher on the thief's head so that physical features (e.g., hair color) were more visible. In the *good* condition the criminal's head was uncovered and he was visible for 20 seconds. Accurate identification of the criminal was made by 33%, 50%, and 74% of the witnesses in the poor, moderate, and good viewing conditions, respectively. Jurors in the study by Lindsay and colleagues (see also Wells et al., 1980) were just as likely to believe inaccurate as accurate witnesses *within a given viewing condition*. (For example, inaccurate witnesses from the good viewing condition were believed as often as accurate witnesses from the same condition.) Across viewing conditions, however, juror belief rates increased as viewing conditions improved. Specifically, juror belief rates were 62%, 66%, and 77% for witnesses in the poor, moderate, and good viewing conditions, respectively. These results suggest that jurors weighing eyewitness testimony are able to take into account at least some factors associated with witness accuracy. (It is worth bearing in mind the point we made earlier that these belief rates do not translate directly into conviction rates.)

Nevertheless, it is clear that jurors' ability to discriminate accurate from inaccurate witnesses is far from perfect. Jurors' difficulties in discrimination may, it has been suggested, stem from their failure to take into account factors that influence witness accuracy and from their reliance on irrelevant factors (Loftus, 1979; Wells et al., 1980). Some recent studies provide evidence in favor of this view. For example, O'Barr and Conley (1976) have found that judgments of witness credibility are influenced by the sex of the witness and by the way in which the witness speaks. In addition, Garcia and Griffitt (1978) have shown that witnesses described as likable were considered more credible than those described in unlikable terms. In summary, the available evidence supports the claim that jurors cannot discriminate well between accurate and inaccurate witnesses, perhaps in part because they rely upon irrelevant factors in assessing the credibility of a witness.

The effects of expert psychological testimony

Our conclusions to this point may be summarized as follows: (a) It is not clear that jurors need expert testimony to make them appropriately skeptical, but (b) there is room for improvement in the ability of jurors to discriminate accurate from inaccurate witnesses. In this section we consider the possible effects of expert psychological testimony on jurors.

Overbelief. Three recent studies suggest that expert psychological testimony may serve to make jurors more skeptical of eyewitness testimony (Hosch et al., 1980; Loftus, 1980b; Wells et al., 1980). For example, Wells et al. (1980) found that expert psychological testimony reduced the probability that a subject would believe that an eyewitness to a staged crime made an accurate identification, and Loftus reported that subjects who read brief trial summaries were less likely to vote "guilty" when the summaries included expert psychological testimony than when no such testimony was included. As with all simulations of jury decision making, problems of external validity make it difficult to extrapolate the results of these studies to the verdicts of real juries. Still, even if we accept the findings at face value, the following question remains: Given the absence of clear evidence that jurors overbelieve eyewitnesses, is it really appropriate for psychologists to offer expert testimony that serves to reduce jurors' overall level of belief in eyewitnesses? One obvious danger is the possibility that such expert testimony might make jurors more skeptical than they ought to be.

Discrimination. If we turn now to the possible effects of expert psychological testimony on jurors' ability to discriminate accurate from inaccurate eyewitnesses, we find only one relevant study (Wells et al., 1980). This study employed the basic Wells–Lindsay paradigm described earlier, in which subjects serving as jurors judged whether or not witnesses to a staged crime accurately identified the perpetrator. In the Wells et al. (1980) study half of the jurors received expert psychological testimony before judging the credibility of witnesses, whereas the remaining jurors received no expert advice. The expert testimony emphasized two general points. The first was that eyewitness identification in criminal cases is quite different from recognizing people whom one knows well, in that research using staged crimes has shown that, depending on conditions, from 15% to 85% of eyewitnesses may choose the wrong person from a lineup. The second major point was that there is considerable evidence showing that witness confidence may have little or no relationship to witness accuracy. The psychologist also mentioned that jurors should pay attention to situational factors that might affect witness accuracy.

Subject-jurors in the expert-advice and no-expert-advice conditions viewed videotapes of witnesses and made believe–disbelieve judgments. The videotapes were taken from the Lindsay et al. (1981) study in which witnesses observed a staged crime under poor, moderate, and good viewing conditions (resulting in 33%, 50%, and 74% accurate identifications, respectively).

As noted earlier, the expert psychological testimony reduced the jurors' overall willingness to believe eyewitnesses. The expert testimony had no effect at all, however, on jurors' ability to discriminate accurate from inaccurate witnesses.

In summary, the available evidence suggests that there is a mismatch between the type of help needed by jurors and the possible effects of expert psychological testimony. Specifically, jurors clearly need help in discriminating accurate from inaccurate eyewitnesses but may not need to be made more skeptical overall. Expert testimony, however, may serve to increase juror skepticism without improving juror discrimination.

Of course, firm conclusions at this point would be premature, especially with regard to effects of expert psychological testimony on juror discrimination. As we have seen, only one study relevant to this issue has been conducted (Wells et al., 1980). Furthermore, the expert testimony used in that study may not have been optimal for improving juror discrimination. Aside from the negative advice to ignore witness confidence, jurors were told only to examine "situational factors." It is certainly conceivable that expert testimony that provided a detailed discussion of specific factors that affect witness accuracy would result in better juror discrimination. Nevertheless, we must conclude that at the present time there is no evidence that expert psychological advice improves juror evaluation of eyewitness testimony.

Expert psychological testimony and lay knowledge

At this point an advocate of the use of expert psychological testimony might argue as follows: "Although the Wells et al. (1980) study failed to show an improvement in juror discrimination of accurate and inaccurate witnesses as a result of expert advice, this failure probably reflects, as you mentioned, the vagueness of the expert's remarks. There is every reason to believe that more specific expert testimony would improve juror discrimination. Empirical research has identified many variables that affect witness accuracy in ways that are not obvious to the lay juror. Expert testimony that discusses these factors in detail would, and does, increase jurors' ability to distinguish accurate from inaccurate eyewitnesses."

The validity of this argument can be assessed only through additional research. We suggest, however, that there is less reason than might be supposed for optimism about the efficacy of expert psychological testimony on juror discrimination. The claim that expert testimony would improve juror discrimination rests upon the assumption that there are many variables for which both of the following are true: (a) The relationship between the variable and eyewitness accuracy is known to psychologists as the result of empirical research, and (b) jurors do not understand how the variable is related to witness accuracy. It turns out to be surprisingly difficult to find variables of this sort. In other words, for many (if not most) variables that have been listed as suitable topics for expert testimony, either the effects of the variable on witness accuracy are not well documented, or these effects are probably obvious to the juror. A few examples will illustrate this point.

For a variable like *exposure duration* the well-documented effects are probably obvious to jurors. It is difficult to imagine that most jurors are not aware of the fact that longer exposures lead to increased witness accuracy.

Let us next consider a more subtle factor associated with the *wording of a question*. Lay knowledge of this, as well as of several other factors, has been assessed in studies in which a variety of subjects have answered multiple-choice questions (Deffenbacher & Loftus, 1982; Loftus, 1979; Yarmey & Jones, 1983). Perhaps surprisingly, over 80% of the respondents indicated an awareness of the fact that even a slight difference in wording might affect a witness's accuracy in responding. (Specifically, the question pertained to the difference between: (a) Did you see a scar on the left side of the assailant's neck? and (b) Did you see the scar on the left side of the assailant's neck?) Considering the large proportion of correct answers, it would seem unnecessary for jurors to receive expert testimony on the linguistic difference between *a* and *the*.

For *retention interval* the situation is somewhat more complex. Since the time of Ebbinghaus (1885/1964) the verbal learning literature has reasonably consistently shown that retention declines as a function of the delay between the learning experience and the subsequent test. For face recognition, there are far fewer studies, and the available data are not entirely consistent. Many studies show run-of-the-mill retention losses. For example, Shepherd and Ellis (1973) measured recognition performance a few minutes after exposure, or 6 or 35 days following exposure. Performance declined from 87% correct to 71% over that time period. Others, however, have failed to find performance declining over time. For example, Goldstein and Chance (1971) found accuracy to be unaffected by delay over the range zero to 48 hours. Similarly, Laughery et al. (1974) found no differences in recognition performance among the six retention intervals they studied (4 minutes, 30 minutes, 1 hour, 4 hours, 1 day, and 1 week). Finally, it is worth mentioning that Deffenbacher, Carr, and Leu (1981) found a reminiscence effect: Recognition performance for faces was better 2 weeks after original viewing than 2 minutes after.

There are two ways in which this situation can be assessed. First, one can conclude that at present the effects of retention interval on face recognition are not sufficiently well understood to be discussed in expert testimony. Alternatively, one could argue that the available evidence on memory overwhelmingly supports the generalization that retention declines with delay between acquisition and test. On this view the face recognition studies showing no effect of retention interval, or reminiscence, fail to reflect the true state of affairs. If this latter assessment is made, however, one is led to conclude that the true effects of retention interval on face recognition are probably not very dissimilar to jurors' beliefs about these effects, and consequently that expert testimony about retention interval may be unnecessary.

Consider now the *cross-racial identification* effect. Several studies (e.g., Malpass & Kravitz, 1969) have shown that cross-racial identifications (e.g., white witness–black defendant) are more difficult than within-racial identifications (e.g., white witness–white defendant). This result is often discussed (e.g., Loftus, 1979) as if it were not obvious to the lay juror. The claim that many jurors are unaware of the difficulty of cross-racial identification, however, is questionable at best. For example, the cliché "they all look alike to me" used in reference to members of another race suggests that there may be a general awareness of the difficulty of cross-racial identification. In fact, the Devlin report (Devlin, 1976) describes the studies of cross-racial identification as "support for what is widely accepted on the basis of common intuition" (p. 73).

Loftus (1979; see also Yarmey & Jones, 1983, and Deffenbacher & Loftus, 1982), in a study of common beliefs about factors affecting witness accuracy, found that only 55% of the subjects answered a four-alternative multiple-choice question concerning cross-racial identification correctly (b). Still, this result probably should not be taken too seriously as evidence that people do not understand the difficulty of cross-racial identification, because Loftus's question was complex and difficult to understand:

Two women were walking to school one morning, one of them an Asian and the other white. Suddenly, two men, one black and one white, jump into their path and attempt to grab their purses. Later, the women are shown photographs of known purse snatchers in the area. Which statement best describes your view of the women's ability to identify the purse snatchers?
(a) Both the Asian and the white woman will find the white man harder to identify than the black man.
(b) The white woman will find the black man more difficult to identify than the white man.
(c) The Asian woman will have an easier time than the white woman making an accurate identification of both men.
(d) The white woman will find the black man easier to identify than the white man.

It is, then, by no means clear that jurors are unaware of the difficulty of cross-racial identification.[3]

Finally, for several variables that purportedly have nonobvious effects on accuracy and consequently are cited as appropriate topics for expert testimony, there is, in fact, little empirical evidence about how (or even if) the variable affects eyewitness performance. Consider, for example, *weapon focus,* which is an alleged tendency of a person threatened with a weapon to focus on the weapon and consequently to pay little attention to the appearance of his or her assailant. Although weapon focus is frequently cited as an important factor in assessing eyewitness accuracy and has been discussed in expert testimony (see Loftus, 1979, pp. 223–224), there is virtually no evidence that the phenomenon actually occurs. The single, unpublished, experiment cited as a demonstration of weapon focus (Johnson & Scott, 1976) is "suggestive...but it is far from conclusive" (Loftus, 1979, p. 36).

As another example, it is widely maintained (e.g., Loftus, 1979; Woocher, 1977) that *stress* experienced by a witness during an event has detrimental effects on the accuracy of the witness's testimony, and this point is frequently a prominent feature of expert testimony. Unfortunately, the empirical basis of this claim is not entirely clear. Deffenbacher (1983) has recently completed a thorough review of the literature on the effects of arousal on the reliability of eyewitness testimony. He reports that of 19 relevant studies, 9 produced results suggesting that increases in arousal increase eyewitness accuracy (or at least do not decrease it), whereas 10 produced results suggesting that increases in arousal decrease eyewitness accuracy.

Deffenbacher makes two claims about these data. First, he argues that these seemingly disparate findings are, in fact, nicely consistent with the Yerkes–Dodson law, which states that the function relating stress or arousal to performance is an inverted U, such that performance is poorer at very high and very low levels of arousal than at intermediate levels. Second, Deffenbacher claims that crime situations are on the "downside" of the curve (i.e., that the level of arousal during actual crimes is beyond the optimal point so that eyewitness behavior is adversely affected).

About the first claim, it is important to note that Deffenbacher fit the empirical results to the Yerkes–Dodson law by *assuming* that a study showing an increase in accuracy with increasing arousal belongs on one side of the point of optimal arousal on the function, whereas a study showing the reverse relationship belongs on the other side of the optimal point.

Deffenbacher's second claim – that actual crime situations are located on the downside of the performance–arousal function – is also merely an assumption. Although Deffenbacher may well be right about one or even both of these claims, we as yet have no empirical basis for deciding either issue.

There may be factors that have well-documented effects that are not obvious to jurors. *Bias in identification procedures* is one possible example.

It is, however, by no means the case that there are a large number of variables with well-documented nonobvious effects.[4] Thus, the argument that expert psychological testimony could almost certainly improve juror discrimination does not appear to be well founded. Testimony that asserts as fact effects that have not been demonstrated (e.g., effects of stress or weapon focus) is clearly inappropriate (and in any event there is no reason to believe that the making of undocumented assertions would improve juror performance); testimony limited to documented phenomena, however, may tell jurors little they do not already know.

It might be argued that expert testimony about "obvious" variables, such as exposure duration, lighting, retention interval, and so forth, could be beneficial even if jurors understand the effects of these variables, because jurors might not spontaneously think about these variables when evaluating a witness's testimony. This argument ignores the fact that the defense attorney in a case involving an eyewitness identification will (in opening and closing statements, and in examination of witnesses) certainly call to the jury's attention any factors (e.g., poor lighting) that suggest that the identification may be inaccurate. Similarly, the prosecutor will point out factors (e.g., long exposure duration) suggesting that the identification is accurate. Thus, expert psychological testimony does not appear to be needed to call the jury's attention to "obvious" variables.

One final problem with expert testimony about eyewitness behavior is that it provides probabilistic information to the juror. "The law cannot assume that because eyewitnesses in general are fallible, a particular eyewitness is mistaken too" (Loh 1981, p. 688; see also Tribe, 1971, for a general discussion of trial by mathematics).

Deciding whether or not to testify

We have argued that the available evidence fails to demonstrate that expert psychological testimony will routinely improve jurors' ability to evaluate eyewitness testimony. Still, neither do the data rule out the possibility that expert testimony could have beneficial effects.

Clearly, what is needed is additional research on eyewitness behavior and on juror evaluation of eyewitness testimony. If this research establishes that jurors are too willing to convict on the basis of eyewitness testimony or that jurors give disproportionate weight to eyewitnesses relative to other sorts of evidence, then expert psychological testimony should be considered as one of several possible methods for improving juror performance. If research on the effects on jurors of various sorts of expert psychological testimony demonstrates that expert testimony can improve jurors' ability to discriminate accurate from inaccurate witnesses without producing undesirable side effects, such testimony clearly should be employed in the courtroom.

In the meantime, however, what should a psychologist do when asked to testify? When we have discussed our misgivings about expert psychological testimony with our colleagues, the reaction has often been something like the following: "Well, maybe you're right when you say it hasn't been demonstrated that expert psychological testimony helps the jury. However, it might help, and at least it can't hurt, so why not use it?"

We strongly disagree with this argument for several reasons. First, contrary to the claim that "at least it can't hurt," the possibility that psychological testimony has detrimental effects cannot be ruled out. For example, if jurors are already appropriately skeptical about eyewitness testimony, expert psychological testimony may make jurors too skeptical. It is worth mentioning here that the expert advice in the Wells et al. (1980) study apparently caused subject-jurors in at least some conditions to *underestimate* the probability that an eyewitness had made an accurate identification. In a condition yielding 50% witness accuracy, subject-jurors who heard testimony believed witnesses only about 32% of the time. Similarly, in a condition producing 74% witness accuracy, the juror belief rate was only about 53%. If we assume that jurors make "believe" decisions when they estimate the probability of witness accuracy to be greater than .5, these results suggest substantial underestimation of the probability that a witness was accurate. Of course, such underestimation does not necessarily imply underwillingness to convict. Nevertheless, the results obtained by Wells et al. (1980), which suggest the possibility that expert psychological testimony may make jurors too skeptical, deserve careful consideration.

In addition, in discussing phenomena that are incompletely understood an expert may give groundless information to the jury (see e.g., our discussion of stress and weapon focus). Thus, it is even conceivable that expert testimony could *decrease* jurors' ability to discriminate accurate from inaccurate witnesses.

A second difficulty with the argument that expert psychological testimony should be used because it might help is that a trial judge would never admit expert testimony on this basis. For expert testimony to be admitted the judge must be convinced that the testimony would benefit the jury (or at least that there is a good reason to believe that the testimony would be beneficial). Thus a psychologist who decided to testify on the basis of the "it might help and at least it can't hurt" argument would in some sense have to misrepresent his or her testimony in court.

Finally, on a more pragmatic level, the use of expert psychological testimony in the absence of clear evidence that it benefits the jury carries risks to the psychological profession as a whole. Because the effects of expert testimony are currently unclear, it is inevitable that psychologists will disagree with one another about its use. This disagreement is likely to lead ultimately to a "battle of experts" in at least some cases where attempts are made to introduce expert psychological testimony. The battle of experts could take several different forms. For example, when the defense attempted to introduce expert psychological testimony, the prosecution could use its own expert to argue that the defense psychologist should not be allowed to testify in front of the jury. The prosecution expert could state that many of the claims that would be made by the defense expert (e.g., about effects of stress or weapon focus) are not firmly established by psychological research and that the expert testimony could conceivably have detrimental effects on the jurors' evaluation of eyewitness testimony. If the judge nevertheless decided to admit the testimony of the defense expert, the prosecution psychologist could also testify in front of the jury, arguing that support was lacking for many of the defense psychologist's claims. The prosecution expert might also attempt to counter the defense expert's arguments about the unreliability of eyewitness testimony by pointing out factors in the case at hand that would facilitate eyewitness performance (e.g., long exposure duration, good lighting).

The battle of experts could also take more subtle forms. For example, a psychologist could simple serve as an adviser to the prosecutor, helping him or her to prepare an effective cross-examination of the defense expert. In any event, regardless of the form taken by a battle of experts, courtroom confrontations between defense and prosecution psychologists would almost certainly work to the detriment of the psychological profession, creating (or sustaining) the impression of psychology as a subjective, unscientific discipline, and of the psychologist as a gun for hire.

It will undoubtedly occur to the reader that battles of experts involving members of other professions (e.g., physicians, engineers) often occur. Nevertheless, these professions (with the possible exception of psychiatry) do not seem to have suffered extensive damage to their credibility. Why, then, are we so concerned about psychology? We are concerned because we suspect that courtroom battles in which opposing experts give contradictory testimony *do* decrease public respect for a profession.

Professions like engineering and medicine may escape serious loss of credibility because they, perhaps more easily than psychology, can repair the damage caused by a battle of experts. For example, suppose a reader of *Newsweek* encounters in the Justice section a report of an acrimonious battle of expert witnesses in which two physicians positively assert contradictory propositions. This may lower the reader's esteem for the field of medicine. He then turns to the Medicine section and learns about a newly developed operation that is saving the lives of previously doomed babies. This serves to raise his esteem for the field of medicine, perhaps to a point even higher than when he began reading the Justice section. The painful question we, as psychologists, must ask ourselves is, what do we have to offer the public that is as dramatic an esteem raiser as a new surgical procedure?

Quite apart from the possible effects of a battle of experts on the reputation of the field, there is also a question of what the effects of such a battle might be on the outcome of a trial. Such a battle might actually improve decision making; then again, it might not. Both experts might end up being ignored. As with many of the other questions that have been raised in this chapter, this question seems ultimately one that should be answered empirically rather than by guess.[5]

Concluding comments

In this chapter we have examined the arguments that have been offered in support of the use of expert testimony about eyewitnesses. We suggest that, contrary to the suggestions made recently by some lawyers and psychologists, it is by no means clear that expert psychological testimony would improve jurors' ability to evaluate eyewitness testimony. In fact, it is even possible that this sort of expert testimony would have detrimental effects. In short, expert testimony about eyewitness behavior has not been shown to be either safe or effective.

We suggest that a psychologist who is trying to decide whether or not to offer expert testimony should consider carefully the issues raised in this chapter. He or she should reflect on some issues that we have not discussed. Because of space limitations we can offer no more than an overview of the literature that deals with them.

Tribe (1971) and Loh (1981) discuss some of the difficulties the legal system has in dealing with the generalized or probabilistic information offered by experts when what it must do is reach particularized decisions. Meehl (1977) and Wells (1978) point up some of the problems behavioral scientists face in conducting research that will actually be legally relevant. Gass (1979) provides a valuable perspective for the experimental psychologist by discussing what is problematic about the testimony of the clinical psychologist and psychiatrist. Fersch (1980) and Morse (1978; see also Veatch, 1973) discuss a recurrent theme in the literature on expert psychological testimony: the tendency for psychologists to exceed the limits of their expertise when testifying. Fersch also provides a general discussion of ethical issues pertaining to expert testimony. Finally, for an entertaining diatribe on expert testimony given by social scientists, see Greeley (1978).

Notes

1 The argument that jurors may be unaware of the problem with eyewitness testimony is sometimes made explicitly – and strongly – as in the following quotation: "Merely to take the results of modern-day perception research seriously is to threaten the very basic nature of one's beliefs in a stable world.... When any psychologist stands up before a jury to tell its members that eyewitness testimony may be unreliable that psychologist may threaten the juror's way of perceiving the world" (Ellison & Buckhout, 1981, p. 210).

2 One question of interest at this point is, What are the reasons for the differences in results between the Loftus experiment and later studies? It is suggested (McCloskey et al., 1981) that the high percentages of "guilty" verdicts obtained by Loftus and the rare votes of "guilty" in our study and in that of Hosch et al. (1980) were a result of judges' instructions in the latter two studies, but not in the Loftus experiment, on the "beyond a reasonable doubt" criterion for voting "guilty." The reasons for the discrepancies between the Loftus study and other experiments in regard to the effects of discrediting manipulations are not clear (see Weinberg & Baron, 1982).

3 Deffenbacher and Loftus (1982) asked subjects their opinion of the cliché "they all look alike to me." Clearly, this old saw is a gross overstatement of the difficulty of cross-racial identification. Thus, it is encouraging to note that only about 20% of the respondents selected the alternative "It is true." It is less encouraging to note that this is the alternative the authors of the study deemed correct.

4 In an earlier version of this chapter, we included the relationship between witness confidence and witness accuracy as another example of a well-understood phenomenon that might not be obvious to jurors. Some recent research of ours (to be reported elsewhere), however, in conjunction with a careful reading of the literature on confidence and accuracy, leaves us doubtful that the factors affecting the degree of relationship between confidence and accuracy are, in fact, well-established and well-understood by psychologists. We say this in full appreciation of the contribution of Wells and Murray (this volume) in delineating possibly relevant factors that could determine the magnitude and even the direction of the confidence-accuracy correlation. However, until the critical studies they cite are replicated and extended we think an attitude of cautious skepticism is not unreasonable.

   To explain why we remain cautiously skeptical, we note in passing that the interpretation of one of the three crucial studies cited by Wells and Murray is by no means straightforward. Malpass and Devine (1981a) found a positive correlation between witness accuracy and confidence for perpetrator-present lineups, but a negative correlation for perpetrator-absent lineups. These investigators measure confidence in two ways that are logically similar and that are, in fact, highly correlated. For the sake of simplicity we shall describe just one method, although the same interpretive problem exists for both measures. One of the questions used to assess confidence is, How confident are you that the person who pushed over the electronics equipment is actually in the lineup? The response is to be checked on a seven-point scale which ranges from "no confidence at all" through "moderate confidence" to "absolutely certain." Consider now a trial in which the subject is absolutely certain that the perpetrator is *not* in the lineup. What would the subject's response be? We assume it would be "no confidence at all," i.e., a 1 on the 1–7 scale. The result is that this trial would be characterized as a correct, low confidence judgment. Such trials, of course, contribute to the conclusion that the correlation between accuracy and confidence is negative with the perpetrator absent. It appears to us that the response scale is just not appropriate for perpetrator-absent trials. If the scale permitted the subject to express confidence that the perpetrator was absent, rather than no confidence that the perpetrator was present, the resulting correlation between confidence and accuracy might well be positive.

5 We do not wish to leave the impression that expert psychological testimony about eyewitnesses could never be justified. In the first place, future research may clearly show that expert testimony can improve juror decision making. In the second place, even at the present time there may be certain cases in which it is appropriate to offer expert testimony. In particular, expert testimony would be appropriate in situations where psychological research clearly shows that a witness could not have seen what he said he saw. Suppose, for example, that a crucial element in a case was whether or not an eyewitness could have noted the color of a sweater worn by a defendant on a clear, moonless night (in the absence of any man-made source of illumination). Under such circumstances a psychologist could easily take measurements that might indicate that the illumination was so far below the threshold of photopic vision that the witness simply could not have correctly noted the color of the sweater.

14   A reanalysis of the expert testimony issue

Gary L. Wells

The previous chapter, by Egeth and McCloskey, outlines their reasons for believing that psychologists should not testify as experts in court on eyewitness matters. In this chapter I take each of their main arguments and provide a somewhat different perspective. Some of their points are good, but others could be misleading.

Before I address each of Egeth and McCloskey's major arguments, it is important to explore some of the implicit assumptions that pervade their thesis. First, the authors leave the impression that psychologists in general are overly eager to give expert testimony. This does not appear to be the case (Haward, 1981). The interaction begins with a request by lawyers, and because the request comes from the legal field, we might shed some light on the issue by looking at their opinions. If we examine only the legal opinions cited by Egeth and McCloskey, we might conclude that the legal field does not want or need help with its eyewitness problem. The legal view is far from one-sided. A recent U.S. Supreme Court decision (*Watkins* v. *Sowders,* 1981) indicates that the majority believe that eyewitness reliability can be assessed adequately via competent cross-examination. The dissenting opinion, however, argued that cross-examination in front of the jury is inadequate to test the reliability of eyewitness testimony because cross-examination may often be inhibited by a fear that rigorous questioning of hostile witnesses will strengthen the eyewitnesses' testimony and impress it on the jury. Thus, some Supreme Court members are content with the current ways of handling eyewitness evidence, whereas others are worried about jurors' being overly impressed. Indeed, a respectable number of lawyers (e.g., Frazzini, 1981; Stein, 1981; Woocher, 1977) and judges (e.g., Bazelon, 1980; Weinstein, 1981) have recognized the problems that arise because of faulty eyewitness testimony and have held that expert testimony would be of aid to the jury. (See Loftus, 1982, for a more extended discussion of this point.)

Another assumption that runs through Egeth and McCloskey's chapter is that faulty eyewitness testimony must result in false conviction to have any significance. By focusing only on the conviction issue (which surfaces in a superficial understanding of many cases), Egeth and McCloskey have missed a major issue. The case of Robert Dillen, described in Chapter 1 of this book, shows how false eyewitness reports create severe problems for the innocent even if the individual is never convicted. Persons who have gone through the tragedy of arrest and prosecution but are then acquitted are not typically high publicity cases. We may, therefore, underestimate the frequency of such cases. It could be argued, of course, that such events do not relate directly to the issue of expert testimony. This argument, however, overlooks the fact that properly conducted expert testimony can affect the manner in which eyewitness evidence is obtained by police investigators in subsequent cases. If the courts begin to look less favorably on certain lineup identification procedures because of expert psychological testimony, for example, then subsequent police investigators might be less likely to use these questionable procedures. As a result, false identifications may become less frequent. Thus, the issue is not simply whether or not the courts falsely convict on the basis of eyewitness evidence; the issue is also one of how to minimize the likelihood of false eyewitness evidence even in cases wherein the suspect is eventually acquitted (as happened with Robert Dillen).

A third assumption that Egeth and McCloskey make is that expert psychological testimony on eyewitness matters is biased toward discrediting eyewitnesses. On this matter it is important to keep in mind that expert testimony tends to focus on *levels* of variables (such as levels of eyewitness confidence, lighting, or lineup structure). Although it is true that a given level of one of these variables can decrease the credibility of an eyewitness, it is also true that some other level of that variable can increase the credibility of the eyewitness. An expert who speaks to the confidence–accuracy issue, for example, serves to increase the credibility of a low-confidence eyewitness relative to a high-confidence eyewitness. This may or may not serve frequently to discredit eyewitnesses, depending on the frequency distribution of confidence levels across eyewitnesses. Similarly, suppose an expert testifies that high-functional-size lineups produce more reliable identifications than do low-functional-size lineups. The effect of such testimony is to enhance the credibility of an eyewitness who identified the defendant from a high-functional-size lineup.

Critiques of the expert testimony issue have appeared elsewhere (e.g., Wells, 1978). Nevertheless, Egeth and McCloskey seem to have overplayed their criticisms. The following sections discuss each of their main points.

Critique of Egeth and McCloskey's argument

Overbelief

The overbelief issue is central for Egeth and McCloskey. Overbelief refers to the tendency for jurors to be overly willing to believe eyewitness testimony, a phenomenon that Egeth and McCloskey argue has never been demonstrated adequately. I agree that overbelief cannot be inferred automatically from research showing that eyewitnesses are often inaccurate or from the fact that there are many documented cases of wrongful conviction resulting from mistaken identification. I also agree that overbelief cannot be inferred from the experiments using written cases in which discreditation of eyewitnesses is shown to be difficult to achieve.

On the other hand, I cannot agree with the reasons used to dismiss all of the evidence on overbelief. The Lindsay, Wells, and Rumpel (1981) study is perhaps the most prominent example of support for the overbelief phenomenon. In that study, 108 unsuspecting eyewitnesses observed a staged theft and attempted an identification of the thief from a lineup. The theft was staged under three different crime conditions and yielded identification accuracy rates of 33%, 50%, and 74%. (Thus, 67%, 50%, and 26% were false identifications in these conditions, respectively.) Representative samples of these accurate–false eyewitnesses were then cross-examined from each crime condition. Subject-jurors who viewed these cross-examinations believed witnesses 62%, 66%, and 77% of the time in the 33%, 50%, and 74% conditions, respectively. Lindsay and colleagues concluded that subject-jurors were overbelieving of witnesses and that overbelief was particularly profound when the original witnessing conditions were poor. Egeth and McCloskey dismiss this study on a statistical strategy argument that seems to be quite generous to the subject-jurors. They argue that whenever the accuracy rate is above 50% (e.g., 90%), a juror could maximize hits by adopting a strategy of always believing the witness (i.e., 100% belief) even if the juror "knows" that the actual likelihood of accuracy is less than 100%. This is statistically true. The same logic, however, would predict that the juror should never believe the witness if accuracy is below 50%. Note, however, that when accuracy rates were 33%, belief rates were 62%! Their explanation does not fit these results.

At another point Egeth and McCloskey argue that the overbelief hypothesis should be tested by measuring conviction votes by subject-jurors. The question at hand, however, is concerned with overbelief biases, not overconviction biases. Apparently, even Egeth and McCloskey do not believe that the conviction-vote measure can answer the overbelief question.

As Egeth and McCloskey themselves outline, the conviction measure can never answer the overbelief question because other (circumstantial) evidence makes conviction votes impure measures of the jurors' beliefs about eyewitness testimony. Concern with overbelief is best tested by measuring actual accuracy rates of eyewitnesses and comparing those with subject-jurors' estimates of eyewitness accuracy across a wide sample of situations. To argue that conviction votes is the best way to test overbelief is to misunderstand the overbelief issue. Just as people's tendencies to overestimate distances can be tested by comparing actual distances with estimated distances, so too overbelief can be measured by comparing actual eyewitness accuracy with estimates of eyewitness accuracy. Neither an overestimation of distance nor an overbelief of eyewitnesses necessarily implies an overconviction bias. Indeed, there is no a priori reason to characterize overbelief as a factor that favors the prosecution's case – eyewitnesses sometimes testify for the defense (such as when a stranger provides an alibi).

No one study will prove to be definitive regarding the overbelief issue. Nevertheless, the discrepancy between juror belief rates and eyewitness accuracy rates in conditions that produce poor eyewitness accuracy (a discrepancy of 34% in Lindsay et al., 1981, and 25% in a replication study by Wells et al., 1980) indicates that overbelief is a problem in certain circumstances. Our task is to find those circumstances.

Discrimination

The issue of discrimination revolves around the question of whether jurors can discriminate between accurate and false eyewitness evidence, regardless of any general tendency for overbelief. On this point Egeth and McCloskey agree that the data are clear in showing that subject-jurors cannot make such discriminations (Lindsay et al., 1981; Wells, Lindsay, & Ferguson, 1979; Wells et al., 1980). The significance of these findings for expert testimony, however, is dismissed by Egeth and McCloskey on grounds that expert advice has not been shown to improve subject-jurors' discriminative abilities (Wells et al., 1980). Although this is true, one should not underplay the significance of other effects of expert testimony. Specifically, part of the expert testimony in the Wells et al. (1980) study informed subject-jurors that there was considerable evidence showing that witness confidence may have little or no relationship to witness accuracy. Those subject-jurors who received such information were able to follow that advice in that the correlation between witness confidence and jurors' tendencies to believe the witness was only .16 (vs. .59 in the no-expert condition). This was an important change in the process by which subject-jurors' ascribed credibility to witnesses. In effect, this can help pave the way for jurors to consider more diagnostic forms of information. In the long run (i.e., over many different cases) a lessened emphasis on eyewitness confidence could benefit the discriminatory powers of the trier of fact. In this regard it should be noted that the expert testimony given in the Wells et al. (1980) study not only did not harm subject-jurors' discriminations but actually improved these discriminations by an average of 6%. Although this improvement was not statistically significant, it is hardly as discouraging as Egeth and McCloskey's treatment would lead us to believe.

Lay knowledge

Egeth and McCloskey argue that there is a paucity of evidence that identifies variables that (a) are known by psychologists reliably to have a particular relationship to eyewitness accuracy and (b) are not understood already by jurors. Egeth and McCloskey acknowledge two factors that seem to qualify, namely confidence and lineup bias. They then go on to cite other factors that do not qualify (e.g., weapons focus, stress). It is not clear why a listing of factors that do not meet these criteria is an argument against expert testimony. Expert testimony could easily center on the factors that do meet the criteria. In any case, it is not clear that certain factors (e.g., question wording, cross-race effect) fail to meet the criteria.

Question wording. Egeth and McCloskey acknowledge that question wording has reliable and robust effects on eyewitness reports, but they claim that the effects are obvious to people. In support of their argument they point to studies showing that over 80% of questionnaire respondents are "aware" that slight differences in wording might affect a witness's accuracy in responding. The problem with this analysis is that a trier of fact would probably not be able to detect such wording effects in their natural context. Would a juror, for example, realize that a question such as "how tall was the person you saw?" is affecting the question respondent? I doubt that the juror would know this unless the alternative forms of the question were made salient (e.g., how short? what was the person's height?). On the other hand, if we ask people in a questionnaire whether it would make a difference in a witness's report if a question were phrased "how tall was the person?" versus "how short was the person?" we would find that the questionnaire respondent is appropriately sensitized because the alternatives are made salient. It is the latter format that characterized the questionnaire from which Egeth and McCloskey argue that people are already aware of wording effects. As outlined in Chapter 11 of this book, questionnaire items can be misleading, implying that people would be able to detect and apply the knowledge indicated by their questionnaire answers.

Cross-race identifications. Egeth and McCloskey argued that jurors need no help in judging the cross-race identification issue. Although not much can be discerned from the questionnaire results on this issue, it is not a foregone conclusion that the cross-race problem is obvious to the lay person. Many jurors might argue in deliberations that the phrase "they all look alike to me" is a racist myth. Worse, social desirability considerations may prevent the jurors from openly discussing the issue at all for fear that it would be perceived as racially biased. It seems safer to have the issue clearly aired by an expert to ensure that the cross-race factor is considered. It is probably true that the lay juror finds it very obvious when an expert says there is a cross-race identification problem; however, it would probably be equally obvious if the expert were to say that the cross-race identification problem is a common myth. As Fischhoff (1975) has shown, people are capable of holding simultaneously opposite beliefs and finding either one "obvious" after the fact.

Egeth and McCloskey try to handle these concerns by suggesting that the defense attorney will call the jury's attention to any factors that suggest that the identification may be in error. Anyone who gets calls from attorneys asking for expert testimony, however, realizes how many factors they do overlook. A common example is the attorney's lack of awareness regarding the existence of nonidentification evidence (i.e., were there eyewitnesses who could not pick the defendant out of the lineup? see Wells & Lindsay, 1980).

Even when the variables are identified by the attorney, the attorney may be unsuccessful in describing their role. Much of the time attorneys need an expert. An example was recently given to me by a defense attorney who tried to argue in court that "everyone knows that cross-racial identifications are difficult." The prosecutor countered this by arguing that such a notion is a myth and that there is generally accepted evidence that the races do not differ in the variability in facial qualities that can be used for identifications. The prosecutor was correct about his anthropometric data (see Herskovits, 1930) but wrong in his conclusions. The races are equally varied in anthropometric features, but the cross-race difficulty exists for other reasons (probably related to the way in which facial features are processed across races, see Ellis, Deregowski, & Shepherd, 1975). The defense attorney was unable to counter this misleading argument by the prosecutor.

One could assume, of course, that judges are so generally familiar with issues and arguments as to be able to keep the eyewitness arguments by prosecution and defense attorneys on track. No doubt this is true of many judges. Unfortunately it appears not to be true in all cases. Even the U.S. Supreme Court has given formal status to eyewitness confidence as a highly diagnostic factor in judging eyewitness accuracy (*Neil* v. *Biggers,* 1972). Egeth and McCloskey might, of course, consider confidence to be an exception to their argument. Nevertheless, there are other factors that are clearly misunderstood by the courts. Nonidentification evidence may be an example. In a recent court ruling (United States ex rel. *Davis* v. *Jennings,* 1976) the question arose as to whether a key eyewitness had identified the defendant from a biased lineup. Rather than analyzing a photograph of the lineup (an approach generally acknowledged by eyewitness researchers; see Doob & Kirshenbaum, 1973; Malpass, 1981a; Wells, Leippe, & Ostrom, 1979), the judge argued that *the fact that other eyewitnesses were unable to identify the defendant from this lineup was evidence that the lineup structure was unbiased.* Thus, the nonidentification evidence was functionally interpreted as incriminating evidence via increasing the credibility of the identification. We know very well from logical proofs and empirical data that nonidentifications are properly interpreted as a form of exonerating evidence (Wells & Lindsay, 1980). This is especially true if the lineup was in fact biased against the defendant! There is no way that this form of reasoning can be endorsed. (The reader might also be interested in the fact that structural lineup biases affect the distribution of identifications but do not affect whether or not an identification is made [Lindsay & Wells, 1980; Murray & Wells, 1982].)

In short, there is no guarantee that eyewitness evidence will be analyzed reasonably through normal courtroom procedures. Although there also is no guarantee that expert testimony will improve judgments of eyewitness evidence in all cases (e.g., the expert may not be a true expert or jurors may disregard the expert's emphasis on certain variables), properly delivered expert testimony can reduce ambiguity about the probable meaning of certain factors.

Probabilistic information

Egeth and McCloskey argue that expert testimony about eyewitness behavior provides only probabilistic information to the juror. Of course this is true. All science is probabilistic. But what does this mean? Imagine what it would mean if eyewitness experts could *absolutely* determine the accuracy of an eyewitness. It would mean that the case would be entirely dependent on the expert's analysis, because if the eyewitness accurately identified the defendant then the defendant would by definition be the true perpetrator. Obviously the expert's advice is probabilistic. If expert testimony were not probabilistic it would invade the province of the juror.

Interestingly, even if the eyewitness only "saw" the perpetrator in total darkness (and thus could not have identified him from memory), the question of guilt or innocence is still probabilistic. The identified person may or may not have been the perpetrator.

It is not a criticism of expert testimony on eyewitness matters to argue that it provides only probabilistic information. The eyewitness, too, is giving only probabilistic information. Surely the argument should not also apply to ruling out their testimony. A better comparison might exist with regard to engineers as expert witnesses. When an engineer analyzes debris from a crashed airplane for structural defects she or he provides only probabilistic information. Even if structural defects are "found," it could have been pilot error that actually caused the crash, yet I know of no one who would argue that such testimony should be excluded because it is only probabilistic. The courts reach decisions by reductions in ambiguity emanating from various forms of probabilistic information. Even fingerprint evidence is not direct evidence, because it proves only that a given person touched a given surface.

Deciding whether or not to testify

Egeth and McCloskey argue that expert testimony on eyewitness issues could have detrimental effects. In particular they feel that it could negatively affect the outcome of a trial by making jurors incredulous about the testimony of an eyewitness in a case where the defendant is guilty. Unfortunately, Egeth and McCloskey seem to be playing both sides of the fence in this argument. Earlier in their chapter they argued that there is no evidence indicating that eyewitness testimony has much impact on the outcomes of trials. (Egeth & McCloskey cited studies by Chen [1981] and Myers [1979] in this regard.) If that is true, then the discrediting of such testimony should also have no effects on trial outcomes. Obviously there is something inconsistent about this argument. It seems almost certain that the answer is that the study by Chen and the study by Myers fail to capture the elements that show how powerful and influential eyewitness testimony is.

There is an important factor that Egeth and McCloskey overlook about the expert testimony process, namely, that the expert is cross-examined. Under cross-examination the expert is asked questions that focus on factors that could indicate that the eyewitness was correct. An expert for the defense, for example, might be asked by the prosecution to indicate whether the odds of an accurate lineup identification are higher if two eyewitnesses made that identification than if only one did. The answer clearly is yes.

Similarly, lineups with high functional sizes (see Lindsay & Wells, 1980), short delays between time of witnessing and time of test, an absence of lead- ing questions, and numerous other factors all portend well for the likeli- hood of eyewitness accuracy relative to low functional sizes, long periods of time between witnessed event and test of witness's memory, and the use of leading questions. Thus, Egeth and McCloskey make the common error of assuming that expert testimony is biased toward discerning information that would discredit the eyewitness. That is not the way the expert testimony process operates. We must remember that the court treats expert testimony in an adversarial manner. As outlined earlier in this chapter, for each level of a variable that could make an eyewitness less credible there is a level of that variable that could make the eyewitness more credible. The task of the expert, who is examined both directly and by cross-examination, is to speak to the role played by the variables uncovered in that particular case. For example, it has been shown that jurors sometimes discount eyewitness iden- tification testimony if there is evidence that the witness has poor memory for peripheral detail; such discounting is not in line with data on this matter (Wells & Leippe, 1981). Expert testimony, therefore, could help restore eye- witness credibility in such cases. In short, Egeth and McCloskey may be stereotyping expert psychological testimony be implying that it is biased toward the defense.

Egeth and McCloskey argue that expert psychological testimony on eye- witness matters could harm the reputation of psychology by leading to a "battle of the experts." Although this also happens with the medical profes- sion and engineering, Egeth and McCloskey argue that those professions redeem themselves via significant discoveries. I suggest that the reputation of psychology has been questioned by the public for a quite different rea- son. The public expects psychologists to show applied benefits in their research. When called on to help the public, psychologists seldom respond. Thus, it is not clear to me that we are going to harm our image by helping the courts. Similarly, hiding our findings from the courts may be one of the surest ways to reinforce the public's view of us as behavioral scientists who are not interested in helping people deal with real-world problems. As for the battle-of-the-experts idea, as long as an expert testifies only with regard to reliable findings in the literature there should be little room for conflict. The "battle" will amount to little more than clarification.

There are, of course, other situations that could do some harm to the rep- utation of psychology. As noted by Haward (1981), lawyers are often unaware of the difference in training between one specialization in psy- chology and some other specialization. Although a lawyer would not ask a civil engineer to analyze a defective electrical product in a law suit, that same lawyer might ask a clinically trained psychologist to give expert testimony on eyewitness matters. In fact, however, a newly graduated experimental psychologist who has been well trained in perception, memory, and experimental social psychology is more likely to have the necessary knowledge to give good expert testimony on eyewitness matters. Even these qualifications, however, cannot guarantee that the person is an expert. There is now a technical literature on eyewitness testimony that is not a direct fall-out from traditional experimental literatures. An example was given to me by an attorney in a major American city: An experimental psychologist was asked what the effects were of high versus low physical similarity of lineup members. The psychologist, drawing on traditional memory research, explained that high similarity would make the identification less reliable because of perceptual interference. The problem here is that the "expert" psychologist failed to realize some important elements of police lineup practices. Had the expert realized that the lineup contained only one suspect who was designated a priori, he would have realized that any identification of that suspect is more rather than less reliable under conditions of high physical similarity among lineup members (see Lindsay & Wells, 1980).

Nevertheless, that there are psychologists who are willing yet not fully qualified to give expert testimony is no reason to avoid expert testimony altogether. Lawyers will have to become more sophisticated in their search for experts. In addition, psychologists should be sure that they are knowledgeable of the eyewitness literature, preferably from firsthand experience with eyewitness research, before they agree to testify.

Conclusions

Egeth and McCloskey's analysis of the expert testimony issue is a healthy thesis to which eyewitness researchers can constructively respond. Indeed, it was for this reason that we invited them to espouse their position in this book. Clearly the issue is controversial. Nevertheless, as outlined herein, we must get beyond the question of overbelief in general and realize that there are conditions in which people are overly willing to believe eyewitnesses, conditions in which people do not overbelieve eyewitness evidence, and perhaps even conditions in which people underbelieve eyewitness evidence. We must also acknowledge that people overuse certain types of information (e.g., eyewitness certainty or confidence) and that they cannot discriminate accurate from false identification testimony. Regardless of whether or not expert testimony can correct all these problems, it is difficult to justify simply sitting back and ignoring an attorney's pleas for guidance on the issues. Even the questions that are supposedly obvious (e.g., cross-race identifications) may need clarification, given that the opposite may be equally "obvious" (e.g., that the cross-race problem is a myth).

The goal of expert testimony on eyewitness matters is to decrease the likelihood that jurors will believe false eyewitness testimony and increase the likelihood that they will believe accurate eyewitness testimony. The very fact that there are studies directed at examining the effects of expert testimony on eyewitness evidence indicates a level of concern, caution, and responsibility in psychology that is unparalleled in other disciplines that give expert testimony (e.g., medicine, engineering). Although it has proved difficult to demonstrate by experimental methods that expert testimony on eyewitness matters is beneficial to triers of fact, such lack of proof should not be interpreted as evidence that expert testimony is harmful. Egeth and McCloskey's arguments about the possible negative effects is conjecture that should be weighed against the possible benefits.

15 A legal response to the inherent dangers of eyewitness identification testimony

Joseph D. Grano

Eyewitness identification testimony is more crucial in some criminal cases than in others. Its role is often minor in narcotics cases, particularly those involving possession charges, for the prosecution can usually prove the charge in such cases with evidence seized from the defendant's person, home, or place of business. Eyewitness identification testimony may loom larger in prosecutions for the sale of narcotics, for the prosecution will sometimes need the purchaser, typically an undercover agent or informant, to identify the defendant as the seller. Unlike most narcotics cases, however, prosecutions for crimes such as robbery and rape usually turn on identification evidence. Indeed, without physical evidence or an incriminating statement from the defendant, identification testimony may be the sole evidence linking the defendant to the crime. The importance of accuracy is thus apparent, especially when only one person (other than the actual offender) has witnessed the crime, as in many rape cases.

Until quite recently, the law relied exclusively on the jury, or on the judge in nonjury cases, to evaluate the reliability of eyewitness testimony. Defense counsel would try to poke holes in identification testimony by such means as demonstrating that the witness did not have a good opportunity to view the offender or by establishing inconsistency or uncertainty in the witness's testimony. If the defendant testified and claimed an alibi, the trier of fact had to compare his testimony and that of his alibi witnesses, if any, with that of the witness or witnesses identifying him. Sometimes, of course, the eyewitness testimony was greatly influenced by pretrial identification procedures conducted by the police, but the law relied on defense counsel to uncover any suggestiveness in these procedures that might have affected the eyewitness testimony, and, as stated, it relied on the trier of fact to determine whether such testimony was too unreliable to support conviction.

The legal reluctance to deal more aggressively with the dangers that attend eyewitness testimony – a reluctance that did not begin to abate until

315

the 1960s – did not stem from ignorance of the problem. For example, in what has come to be regarded as a classic study, Professor Borchard in the 1930s documented 65 cases of wrongful conviction; mistaken identification accounted for the convictions in 29 of these cases and contributed to the convictions in several others (Borchard, 1932; Frank & Frank, 1957). Borchard revealed that these mistakes occurred even in cases with more than one identification witness, and he observed that the person wrongfully identified often bore little resemblance to the real offender. Though less widely read by lawyers, psychological studies also highlighted the dangers (e.g., M. R. Brown, 1935; Feingold, 1914; Stern, 1939).

Part of the legal profession's reluctance to respond to the problem undoubtedly reflected the strong and powerful tradition of relying on the trier of fact to test the truthfulness and reliability of testimony. Conceivably, some of the reluctance to address the issue also may have stemmed from a distrust of psychologists. The legal profession always has been wary of turning to other disciplines for the resolution of legal questions, and psychological studies calling into question the law's very method of determining guilt and innocence undoubtedly hardened resistance (e.g., Rouke, 1957; Stern, 1939; for legal perspective see Wigmore, 1931). Finally, some of the reluctance to address the problem through the imposition of legal safeguards may have stemmed from a fear of unduly hampering the prosecution in its attempt to prove its case. Certainly the difficulty of proving guilt should not be underestimated, and a healthy regard for this difficulty, if not permitted to develop into intransigency, cannot be faulted.

The delay in addressing the issue at the constitutional level has an additional explanation. Most of the constitutional protections that a defendant enjoys in a criminal trial stem from the first eight amendments to the national Constitution, the amendments known as the Bill of Rights. As adopted in 1791, however, these amendments were intended to apply only against the federal government. For the most part, the Constitution did not impose restrictions on state criminal prosecutions, and because the states have primary responsibility for maintaining law and order, state prosecutions have always greatly exceeded federal prosecutions in number. After the Civil War, of course, the Fourteenth Amendment was added to the Constitution, and this amendment specifically precludes the states from depriving a person of liberty without due process of law. Nevertheless, the due process clause played a limited role in state criminal prosecutions until the 1960s, when the Supreme Court began to hold that due process requires adherence to the safeguards found in the Bill of Rights. Thus, in 1963, the Supreme Court held that the Sixth Amendment right to counsel, which already had been interpreted as providing indigents with a right to appointed counsel in federal felony cases, applied to the states as a requirement of due process of law (*Gideon* v. *Wainwright,* 1963). Until 1963, states, if they so chose, could try indigent defendants for felonies without making legal counsel available to them.

Significantly, when the Supreme Court finally addressed the problem of identification evidence, it did so through the vehicle of the Sixth Amendment right to counsel.

Use of the right to counsel to address the problem of suggestive identification procedures

In 1966, the Supreme Court agreed to review three cases involving constitutional challenges to eyewitness identification evidence. In 1967, it decided two of these cases on right to counsel grounds. In the first, *United States* v. *Wade* (1967), a man named Billy Joe Wade challenged his conviction for robbing a bank. The robber entered the bank in question in September 1964 with a strip of tape on each side of his face. At gunpoint, he forced two bank employees, the only other people in the bank, to fill a pillowcase with money. The robber then fled with an accomplice, who had been waiting in a car. The following March, the FBI obtained a grand jury indictment charging Wade and another person with the robbery. Shortly after the indictment, the FBI arrested Wade. Two weeks later, without notice to his lawyer, the FBI placed Wade in a lineup with five or six other prisoners. The FBI agent in charge had each lineup participant wear strips of tape on his face, and he directed each to repeat the words allegedly used by the robber. Both bank employees identified Wade. Interestingly, both witnesses admitted seeing Wade "standing in the hall" within sight of an FBI agent shortly before the lineup. At the subsequent trial, both witnesses identified Wade as the bank robber. After eliciting from the witnesses that they had identified Wade at the lineup, defense counsel unsuccessfully requested the trial court to exclude all the identification evidence because the lineup had been conducted in the absence of counsel.

In the second case, *Gilbert* v. *California* (1967), Jesse James Gilbert challenged his conviction for robbing a savings and loan association and murdering a police officer during the course of the robbery. Two months after the robbery, and after he had been indicted by a grand jury, the Los Angeles police placed Gilbert in a lineup with 9 to 12 other prisoners. The lineup occurred in an auditorium, and about 100 people attended, all witnesses to various robberies charged to Gilbert. The witnesses could see the prisoners, who stood on a lighted stage, but the prisoners could not see the witnesses. The police then instructed each prisoner, who bore an identifying number, to step forward; to present front, rear, and profile views; to put on various items of clothing; to answer certain questions; and to repeat words allegedly used by the robbers. After each prisoner had done this, several witnesses asked to view Gilbert and a few of the other men again. The police then put these few men, but not the other prisoners, through a similar procedure. Afterward, the witnesses talked to each other, and in each other's presence they called out the numbers of the men they could identify. At the subsequent trial, witnesses to the savings and loan robbery identified Gilbert, and at the separate sentencing hearing several witnesses of other robberies also identified Gilbert. On questioning by the prosecutor, several of these witnesses also testified to their earlier identification of Gilbert at the lineup. As in *Wade,* defense counsel unsuccessfully requested the trial judge to exclude the identification testimony because the police had conducted the lineup in the absence of Gilbert's attorney.

Before turning to the right to counsel issue in these cases, the Supreme Court rejected the claim that the lineup procedures compelled the defendants to incriminate themselves in violation of the Fifth Amendment. Relying on an earlier case (*Schmerber* v. *California,* 1966), the Court held that the Fifth Amendment protects a person only from being compelled to produce "testimonial" or "communicative" evidence. As the Court saw it, forcing a person to stand in a lineup, to wear certain clothing, and to utter words for purposes of voice identification does not violate the Fifth Amendment, for such police conduct compels the suspect only to exhibit physical characteristics and not to "disclose any knowledge he might have" (*United States* v. *Wade,* 1967, p. 222). Although there were dissents on this point, it seems unlikely that the Court will change its mind about this Fifth Amendment holding.

The Court was much more receptive to the Sixth Amendment right to counsel claim. Prior to *Wade* and *Gilbert,* the Court had interpreted the Sixth Amendment as entitling the accused to counsel not only at the trial itself but also at all "critical stages" of the criminal proceeding (see, e.g., *Escobedo* v. *Illinois,* 1964; *Massiah* v. *United States,* 1964). In *Wade* and *Gilbert,* the Court held that a postindictment lineup is a critical stage of the prosecution. Because both lineups had been conducted without notice to the defendants' lawyers, the Court ruled that both had been conducted unconstitutionally.

The Court's rationale for holding the lineups to be critical stages took account of the dangers of faulty perception and recall. The Court first observed that the annals of criminal law contain numerous instances of mistaken identification. The Court further observed that the danger of mistake is exacerbated by the suggestiveness in many pretrial identification procedures. Although the Court said that such suggestion could occur unintentionally, it also cited instances of intentional suggestiveness. These included a case in which the offender had been described as Oriental and the defendant was the only Oriental in the lineup, and another in which the offender was known to be young and the lineup consisted of the teenage defendant and several other men over 40 years old (*United States* v. *Wade,* 1967, pp. 232–233). Again, however, the Court stressed that the suggestiveness was usually more subtle and often unintentional. In *Wade,* for example, the Court pointed to the danger of permitting the witnesses to get a glimpse of the defendant in an officer's presence prior to the lineup, and in *Gilbert* it saw a special danger in permitting the witnesses to identify the offender in each other's presence. Finally, the Court worried that even without such defects, the officers' belief in the defendant's guilt might somehow be communicated to the witnesses.

Prior to *Wade* and *Gilbert,* as already noted, the law relied on the trier of fact to discount identifications produced by suggestive procedures. The Supreme Court, however, found this exclusive trust in the trier of fact to be misplaced. The Court reasoned that defense lawyers frequently have trouble getting the witnesses to describe how the lineup was conducted. As the Court put it, "neither witnesses nor lineup participants are apt to be alert for conditions prejudicial to the suspect," and even if they are alert, they are unlikely "to be schooled in the detection of suggestive influences" (*United States* v. *Wade,* 1967, p. 230). The Court also remarked that "common experience" suggests that witnesses are unlikely to recant an identification previously made. Counsel, the Court concluded, was necessary both to witness the lineup for purposes of revealing its characteristics at trial and to avert prejudice from suggestiveness even before it occurs.

Remedy for right to counsel violations

In *Wade* and *Gilbert,* the Supreme Court held that the right to counsel recognized in those cases was to be enforced by exclusionary remedies. If a lineup is conducted in violation of the right to counsel, the witnesses at that lineup are precluded from referring at trial to their lineup identifications of the defendant. Thus in *Gilbert,* it will be recalled, several of the witnesses testified about the identification they had made of Gilbert at the auditorium lineup. This testimony, the Court held, should have been excluded because the lineup was conducted in violation of Gilbert's right to counsel.

As is well known, one of the most dramatic moments in a trial occurs when a witness points to the defendant as the person who committed the crime. The Supreme Court held that even this in-court identification must be excluded if the witness attended a lineup conducted in violation of the right to counsel, unless the prosecution can prove by clear and convincing evidence that the in-court identification is sufficiently independent of the lineup observations (*United States* v. *Wade,* 1967). The Court rejected a flat per se rule that always would exclude the in-court identification. On the other hand, the Court also rejected the argument that nothing should ever be excluded other than testimony about the lineup identification itself. Such an approach, the Court reasoned, would make the right to counsel meaningless, for lineups without counsel could then be held "to crystallize the witnesses' identification for future reference" (*United States* v. *Wade,* 1967, p. 240). Moreover, defense counsel at trial would then have to struggle in the dark to reveal any possible suggestiveness at the lineup, a struggle that the right to counsel at lineups is designed to make unnecessary. The Court thus concluded that the in-court identification should also be excluded, at least in some cases.

Psychologists may find debatable the Court's assumption that an in-court identification can be unaffected by, or made independently of, a prior lineup identification. The Court's test, however, does not require complete independence; rather, it requires substantial independence. For example, an unblindfolded kidnap victim who spends a month in captivity may retain a clear mental picture of his captors, and his ability to identify them at trial may be substantially unaffected by an earlier lineup identification. On the other hand, a witness with a fleeting glimpse of a robber would normally have a much less precise mental picture of the offender, and a lineup identification could be expected to have quite an impact on subsequent identifications. That is, the risk that the witness at trial would remember the person identified at the lineup rather than the actual offender would be significant. Under the Court's test, the in-court identification would be permitted in the former example, but in all probability it would be excluded in the latter.

Without intending to be exhaustive, the Court listed some factors that would be relevant in applying its test. As the above examples demonstrate, the most obvious factor is opportunity to view the offender at the time of the crime. In addition, any discrepancy between the witness's description of the offender and the defendant's actual appearance casts doubt on the witness's ability to identify the defendant without being influenced by the improper lineup. Similarly, failure to identify the defendant on a prior occasion or identification of a different individual would make it difficult for the prosecutor to establish an independent source for the in-court identification.

It should be noted that witnesses often have poor opportunities to view offenders and poor recollections of what they do observe. Absent an improperly conducted lineup before trial, however, the law permits these witnesses to make in-court identifications, and it trusts the fact finder to evaluate the reliability of such testimony. Identification evidence is excluded under the *Wade–Gilbert* exclusionary rules only when a pretrial lineup has been conducted in violation of the right to counsel. The *Wade–Gilbert* exclusionary rules are designed to enforce the right to counsel. They are not designed to assure the general reliability of identification testimony. To the extent, however, that counsel's presence at lineups can help prevent suggestiveness that may lead to an erroneous identification, these exclusionary remedies are important.

Limits on the applicability of the right to counsel

Wade's emphasis on both the inherent dangers of eyewitness identification evidence and the additional dangers that stem from suggestive identification procedures led many legal commentators and lower courts to assume that a defendant had a right to counsel at all pretrial identification procedures, regardless of how or when conducted. This assumption turned out to be incorrect. In *Kirby* v. *Illinois* (1972) and *United States* v. *Ash* (1973) the Supreme Court held that the right to counsel applies only to certain lineups and does not apply at all to photographic identification procedures.

Kirby involved a showup (one-to-one confrontation between witness and suspect) rather than a lineup (both suspects and nonsuspects are presented to a witness), but nothing in the Court's opinion turned on this difference. After arresting two men, police learned that one of the men, Thomas Kirby, had possession of identification papers belonging to a person who had been robbed the previous day. The police then brought the robbery victim to the police station. When the victim entered the station, he observed Kirby and his companion seated at a table and immediately identified them as the robbers. Subsequently, at trial, the victim described his stationhouse identification of the men and also identified them again in the courtroom. Kirby's companion testified that he and Kirby had found the victim's papers shortly before their arrest. The jury convicted both men.

Relying on *Wade,* Kirby argued to the Supreme Court that he had a right to counsel at the stationhouse identification and that, accordingly, the victim's identification should have been excluded. A plurality of the Court disagreed. (A fifth justice, making the majority, simply refused to apply the *Wade–Gilbert* exclusionary remedies.) The plurality noted that the Sixth Amendment provides a right to counsel in "criminal prosecutions."[1] The plurality reasoned that a criminal prosecution does not begin until adversary judicial proceedings are initiated against a defendant. Although Kirby had been arrested, judicial proceedings had not yet commenced against him when he was identified in the stationhouse (*Kirby* v. *Illinois,* 1972, p. 682). In *Wade* and *Gilbert,* by contrast, indictments had charged the defendants with robbery prior to their lineups, and these indictments marked the start of adversary proceedings.

The distinction between identification procedures that occur before and after the start of formal judicial proceedings seems quite formalistic. As the *Kirby* dissenters argued, the dangers that *Wade* described are equally present regardless of whether the lineup occurs before or after judicial procedures commence. From a policy or psychological perspective, therefore, the line drawn in *Kirby* may make little sense. From a legal – especially a constitutional – perspective, the decision is somewhat more understandable. Certainly a plausible if not a conclusive argument can be made in defense of the Court's interpretation of the "criminal prosecution" terminology in the Sixth Amendment (see Grano, 1974). Moreover, the Court has applied the same line in other contexts, such as police interrogation (see Grano, 1979). Under the Court's holdings, a defendant has a Sixth Amendment right to counsel only if the police interrogation occurs after the start of adversary judicial proceedings (see, e.g., *Brewer* v. *Williams*, 1977). (*Miranda* v. *Arizona*, 1966, which provides defendants a right to counsel even during precharge custodial interrogation, is based upon the Fifth Amendment protection against compulsory self-incrimination and not the Sixth Amendment.) Whether or not *Kirby* correctly interpreted the Sixth Amendment, however, it makes the point that there are limits beyond which the Constitution is not a useful vehicle for addressing societal problems. Beyond these limits, nonconstitutional solutions must be found.

From a practical perspective, it cannot be denied that *Kirby* has substantially eroded the impact of *Wade*. Most police lineups probably occur shortly after arrest and before judicial proceedings commence against the defendant. To the extent that this is so, these lineups may now occur, at least as a matter of federal constitutional law, without counsel. Recognizing the dangers that *Wade* described, however, some state courts have provided the defendant with a state law right to counsel at these lineups (see, e.g., *Commonwealth* v. *Richman,* 1974; *People* v. *Bustamonte,* 1981), but most states have been content to accept the line drawn by *Kirby*.

The most troubling issue under *Kirby* involves identifying the point at which adversary judicial proceedings commence. Contrary to some popular understanding, an indictment is not needed to commence judicial proceedings. In *Moore* v. *Illinois* (1977), for example, the Supreme Court held that a defendant was entitled to be represented by counsel when a witness identified him at a preliminary hearing to determine whether sufficient probable cause existed to send his case to the grand jury. The Court specifically rejected the state's argument that an indictment was necessary to trigger Sixth Amendment rights. Relying on *Kirby,* the Court held that a defendant has a right to counsel at lineups or showups that occur at or after the start of formal judicial proceedings, and the Court easily concluded that in *Moore* the preliminary hearing marked the start of judicial proceedings. *Moore* also shows, of course, that the Supreme Court is not prepared to abandon *Wade* altogether.

Like *Kirby, United States* v. *Ash,* (1973), drastically limited the scope of the right to counsel. About a year after a robbery, FBI agents showed five black-and-white mug shots to four witnesses. All four made somewhat uncertain identifications of Charles J. Ash, who at that point had been neither arrested nor formally charged. On the eve of trial almost 2 years later, the prosecutor showed five color photographs to the four witnesses who previously had tentatively identified Ash. Three of these witnesses selected Ash's picture. At the subsequent trial, the witnesses identified Ash and referred to their previous photographic identifications of him. On appeal after conviction, Ash argued that the photographic display without counsel was constitutionally impermissible.

Because the black-and-white photographic display occurred before the start of judicial proceedings, Ash had to concede that under *Kirby* he had no right to counsel at that display. He argued, however, that the color display was different, because that occurred after indictment, long after judicial proceedings had commenced. *Wade* as modified by *Kirby,* Ash argued, required counsel at all identification procedures, corporeal or pictorial, that occur once judicial proceedings begin.

The Supreme Court disagreed. Turning again to the language of the Sixth Amendment, the Court observed that the Constitution provides an accused with a right to the "assistance" of counsel. The Sixth Amendment, the Court reasoned, provides counsel for the accused to assist him in coping with legal problems or in meeting his adversary. Such assistance thus requires, the Court concluded, a proceeding – a confrontation – actually involving the defendant. Unless the defendant is present or can claim a right to be present, he cannot assert a need for counsel's assistance. Because Ash was not present at the photographic display and had no right to be present, he had no Sixth Amendment right to counsel (*United States* v. *Ash,* 1973, p. 317).

Whether *Ash* correctly interpreted the Sixth Amendment may be debated. The dissenting justices, for example, took vehement exception to the Court's conclusion that an accused is entitled to counsel's "assistance" only at those proceedings at which the accused is personally present or is entitled to be present. In response to this, the majority indicated that it would be unwilling, in any event, to apply the right to counsel to photographic displays. The Court indicated that unlike the case with lineups, sufficient safeguards exist to protect against the dangers of photographic displays. The Court observed, for example, that defense counsel is always free to construct his or her own photographic displays for witnesses (*United States* v. *Ash,* 1973, pp. 317–320).

In a separate concurring opinion, Justice Stewart elaborated upon this latter analysis. He argued that "a photographic identification is quite different from a lineup, for there are substantially fewer possibilities of impermissible suggestion when photographs are used, and those unfair influences can be readily constructed at trial" (*United States* v. *Ash,* 1973, p. 324, Stewart, J., concurring). Conceding that a defendant's picture may be markedly different from others in a photographic display, and conceding also that photographs can be presented to witnesses in a suggestive manner, Justice Stewart maintained nevertheless that "these are the kinds of overt influence that a witness can easily recount" (*United States* v. *Ash*, 1973, p. 324). Immobile photographs, he insisted, are less subject to the kinds of subtle suggestion that witnesses may not even observe. Justice Stewart also expressed the view that photographs are "far less indelible" in their effects upon witnesses than are lineups. Finally, Justice Stewart observed that the photographs can be preserved for presentation at trial, thus enabling the trier of fact to observe any suggestiveness in the pictures themselves. Summarizing his view that a photographic display is thus not a critical stage requiring counsel, Justice Stewart stated that "there are few possibilities for unfair suggestiveness – and those rather blatant and easily constructed" (*United States* v. *Ash*, 1973, p. 324).

Because most of the majority's analysis in *Ash* turned upon a legalistic interpretation of the Sixth Amendment, it is not readily subject to refutation by psychologists. That is, the majority focused primarily not upon the dangers involved in photographic displays but upon the meaning of the Sixth Amendment. Justice Stewart's analysis, however, turned exclusively upon an assessment of the dangers involved, and whether Justice Stewart accurately assessed those dangers is something that psychologists are particularly well suited to evaluate. Here it suffices to note that many of Justice Stewart's assumptions may be questioned. For example, the danger of an inaccurate identification may increase when "immobile" photographs are used for identification purposes in place of a live, dynamic, three-dimensional lineup. Second, it is not obviously apparent that photographic identifications will have a less "indelible" effect upon witnesses than will lineup identifications. Third, it also is not obviously apparent that photographic displays are less subject to the techniques of subtle suggestion than are line-ups. Not only may the display itself be subtly suggestive, but as Justice Brennan noted in his dissent, "the prosecutor's inflection, facial expressions, physical motions, and myriad other almost imperceptible means of communication might tend, intentionally or unintentionally, to compromise the witness' objectivity" (*United States* v. *Ash,* 1973, p. 334, Brennan, Douglas, & Marshall, J.J., dissenting). Finally, although the photographs themselves may be preserved for trial, it is not so obvious that the witnesses will have detected subtle suggestive techniques, and the defendant, of course, will be of no help in revealing these, for unlike the case with lineups, the defendant is not present when the photographic display occurs (for a forceful criticism of Justice Stewart's analysis, see Grano, 1974, pp. 767–771).

Putting *Kirby* and *Ash* together, federal constitutional law as it presently stands guarantees an accused a right to counsel at all corporeal identification procedures – lineups and showups – that occur at or after the start of judicial proceedings. There is no federal right to counsel at such procedures when they occur, as most of them do, before the start of judicial proceedings against the accused. Finally, there is no federal right to counsel at any photographic display, whether conducted before or after the start of formal judicial proceedings. Some state courts, however, have relied on state constitutions to grant a state constitutional right to counsel in situations where *Kirby* and *Ash* would not grant a federal constitutional right to counsel. Defense attorneys cannot hope to succeed in persuading state courts to take such steps without first grounding themselves in the literature concerning the dangers that such identification procedures present.

Other right to counsel issues

Those outside the legal profession often marvel at the ability of lawyers to create complexity out of seemingly simple matters. To demonstrate that this is no less true in this area of the law, I will present here just a few issues regarding the right to counsel that have troubled the courts.

Assume, for example, that after the start of judicial proceedings, the police assemble several men, including a suspect, for a lineup. Not wanting to delay the time that would be necessary to arrange for legal representation of the suspect, the police take a Polaroid picture of the men on stage and show the picture to a witness. Can this be done in counsel's absence? It seems so. Whereas a live presentation of the men would have constituted a lineup and thus would have required counsel under *Wade,* the *Ash* case governs photographic displays. Given the rationale in *Ash,* it does not seem possible to distinguish this photographic display from any other (*Bruce* v. *State,* 1978).

Assume, instead, that the police conduct a corporeal lineup, where the accused is represented by counsel. Before the witness is asked to report whether the offender was in the lineup, the police ask defense counsel to leave. At the same time, the police remove the lineup participants, including the suspect, from the room. The police then ask whether the offender was present, and the witness responds that the person who had been standing third from the left committed the crime. Did the police violate the right to counsel? Courts are divided. Some courts have said that they will not bifurcate the observation and identification segments of the lineup, so that the right to counsel applies to the entire proceeding (see, e.g., *People* v. *Williams,* 1971). Others have said that the danger of suggestiveness is present during the presentation and observation segment of the lineup but not necessarily during the identification segment (see, e.g., *United States* v. *Bierey,* 1978; *United States* v. *Tolliver,* 1978). Some in this latter group have found support for their position in *Ash. Ash,* it will be recalled, provides a right to counsel only at proceedings where the accused is present or has a right to be present. In the facts as described, the accused was not present at the point of identification and had no right to be present. Thus, these courts reason, the accused had no right to counsel at that point. Fortunately, this issue does not arise very often, for police rarely treat defense counsel with so little regard.

Counsel's precise role at the lineup also has been subject to debate. Some view counsel merely as an observer, a person whose function is to observe whether improper suggestion occurs. Others point to *Wade's* emphasis on preventing improper suggestion and argue that counsel should play an active role in objecting to procedures or actions at the lineup that seem unfair. Again, the issue does not arise very often, for most lawyers are reluctant to accept a completely passive role, and most police at lineups are receptive to modest and reasonable suggestions for improvement when the lineup occurs (for a general discussion, see Uviller, 1978).

Use of due process principles to address the problem of suggestive identification procedures

On the same day that it decided *Wade* and *Gilbert,* the Supreme Court also decided *Stovall* v. *Denno* (1967). The Court held in *Stovall* that due process itself may require the exclusion of identification evidence produced by a suggestive pretrial identification procedure, even when the right to counsel is inapplicable. The focus of the due process inquiry, the Court indicated, is whether the identification procedure was "unnecessarily suggestive and conducive to irreparable mistaken identification" (*Stovall* v. *Denno,* 1967, pp. 301–302).

In *Stovall,* the victim, a white doctor, underwent major surgery to save her life after receiving multiple stab wounds during an unsuccessful attempt to save her husband, also a doctor, from an assailant. The police arrested Stovall, a black man, for the crime. Shortly after the arrest, five police officers and two prosecutors, all white, brought the handcuffed defendant to the victim's hospital room, where she identified him. She later identified him again at trial, and he was convicted. On appeal, the Supreme Court held that the hospital room showup did not violate due process. As the Court viewed it, the showup may have been suggestive, but it was not "unnecessarily" so:

Faced with the responsibility of identifying the attacker, with the need for immediate action and with the knowledge that (the doctor) could not visit the jail, the police followed the only feasible procedure and took Stovall to the hospital room. Under these circumstances, the usual police station lineup, which Stovall now argues he should have had, was out of the question. (*Stovall* v. *Denno,* 1967, p. 302)

The need for immediate action stemmed from uncertainty about whether the victim would survive.

Stovall is persuasive that the police had a need for immediate action, and perhaps this justified the use of the one-person showup. It should be noted, however, that such showups are extremely suggestive, for they implicitly (almost explicitly) tell the victim that the police believe that the person being viewed is the offender. Even if the police had no time to assemble a lineup in Stovall's case, however, other aspects of the showup are troubling. The police emphasized their belief in the defendant's guilt by the number of officers there to guard him and by presenting him in handcuffs. Moreover, the racial dynamic of such a presentation cannot be discounted. A procedure more conducive to mistaken identification is hard to imagine, and had there not been such an emergency need for an immediate identification, the due process result in *Stovall* undoubtedly would have been different.

After *Stovall,* some people thought that unnecessarily suggestive identification procedures would automatically require the exclusion of identification testimony at trial. In *Neil* v. *Biggers* (1972) and *Manson* v. *Brathwaite* (1977), however, the Court held that the due process test requires more than unnecessary suggestion. The Court emphasized that exclusion of testimony on due process grounds is required only when an unnecessarily suggestive procedure actually creates a substantial risk of mistaken identification.

The facts in *Biggers* illustrate how the due process test works. On January 22, 1965, a youth with a butcher knife assaulted the victim in her kitchen doorway, which was illuminated somewhat by a light in a nearby bedroom. After threatening to kill her if she did not cooperate, the youth walked the victim to a moonlit wooded area and raped her. The entire incident occurred within 15 to 30 minutes. During the next 7 months, the victim observed several lineups and photographic displays without identifying anyone. On August 17, the police summoned her to the station, and when she arrived, two detectives walked the defendant by her and directed him to say, "Shut up or I'll kill you." The victim identified the defendant. The defendant's subsequent conviction rested almost entirely upon the victim's identification of him. The state appellate courts upheld the conviction, but a federal court, in a subsequent habeas corpus proceeding, ordered the defendant's retrial because of the unnecessarily suggestive showup. The federal court of appeals upheld this action, but the Supreme Court found it erroneous.

The Supreme Court agreed with the lower federal courts that the showup was suggestive – as all one-person showups are – and unnecessarily so. The police had claimed that their small community made it impossible for them to assemble men comparable to the defendant so that a fair lineup could be held, but the Court did not find this excuse for holding a one-person showup persuasive (*Neil* v. *Biggers,* 1972). Moreover, unlike the situation in *Stovall,* the police had no emergency need for an immediate identification. Nevertheless, the Court found little danger of mistaken identification. The Court emphasized that the victim had an adequate opportunity to view the rapist both in the artificial light of her hallway and in the moonlit wooded area where the rape occurred. The Court also observed that the victim had given a "more than ordinarily thorough" description of the rapist and that she was positive in her identification of the defendant. The Court thought that the 7-month delay between the crime and the identification was a negative factor, but during that interval the victim had never identified anyone else at various identification procedures she had attended, and this, in the Court's view, bolstered the reliability of her identification (*Neil* v. *Biggers,* 1972, pp. 200–201).

Whatever one's view of *Biggers,* it demonstrates the limited utility of constitutional exclusionary rules to solve the problems that attend eyewitness identification testimony. The victim was the only witness to the rape, and excluding her testimony would have been a drastic step indeed. The judicial tendency, as noted before, is to favor submitting such cases to the trier of fact, where debate over the reliability of the identification can be waged. On the other hand, however, there is always a risk of mistake where a conviction depends primarily upon the testimony of one eyewitness, and such a risk is exacerbated when the police employ an unnecessarily suggestive identification procedure before trial. The Supreme Court in *Biggers* did not approve the procedure that the police employed, but it obviously was reluctant to require exclusion of the only evidence that could prove the defendant's guilt.

Like *Biggers, Manson* reaffirmed that the due process test focuses on unnecessarily suggestive identification procedures that create a substantial likelihood of mistaken identification. The Court once again rejected arguments that it should create a per se rule requiring exclusion of identification evidence whenever the police employ an unnecessarily suggestive procedure. Such a rule would go too far, the Court explained, for it would keep from the trier of fact identification evidence even when it is fully reliable and relevant. The Court acknowledged that such a per se rule would have more deterrent effect on the police, but it felt that its rule, focusing on the likelihood of mistaken identification, would also influence police behavior, for the police would not be inclined to take the risk that a court would suppress evidence under the more lenient due process standard. Summarizing its position, the Court said that it did not view with "unlimited enthusiasm" those "inflexible rules of exclusion that may frustrate rather than promote justice" (*Manson* v. *Braithwaite,* 1977, p. 113).

In assessing the likelihood of mistaken identification, both *Biggers* and *Manson* stressed such considerations as (a) the opportunity of the witness to view the offender at the time of the crime, (b) the witness's degree of attention, (c) the accuracy of the witness's prior description of the offender, (d) the level of certainty displayed by the witness at the identification procedure, and (e) the length of time between the crime and the identification procedure. *Manson* added that these factors should be weighed against the corrupting influence of the suggestive identification procedure. Just how this weighing is to be done *Manson* did not explain.

Because the due process focus is on the danger of mistaken identification, the suggestion has been made that external evidence of guilt – that is, evidence totally apart from the witness's ability to make an accurate identification – should be relevant to the due process test. For example, some would say that in an objective sense there is little likelihood of mistaken identification when moments after a robbery the police apprehend a person with the stolen items and a weapon in his pocket. *Manson,* however, suggested that such external indications of guilt were irrelevant, and that the due process inquiry should focus entirely on the witness's ability to make an accurate identification (*Manson* v. *Braithwaite,* 1977, p. 116; see also p. 118, Stevens, J., concurring).

A stranger-than-fiction case (*Smith* v. *Coiner,* 1973), where a rape defendant was apprehended in the victim's bed, may indicate that the suggestion in *Manson* is correct. Early one morning, a 72-year-old widow, who had cataracts and always wore glasses, awakened to the sounds of an intruder. Using a flashlight but without her glasses, the woman attempted to call her son on the telephone, but the intruder prevented her from completing the call. Before being attacked and raped, the woman looked at the assailant momentarily and determined that he was white. After the rape, the assailant apparently fell asleep. The woman then crept downstairs, slipped out a rear door, and walked to her son's house a quarter mile away. The woman did not arrive at her son's house until about 7 a.m., although she indicated that the rape had occurred about 4:30 a.m. The son called the police, and they discovered the defendant in the woman's bed at about 7:30 a.m. After routine booking procedures, the police brought the defendant in handcuffs to a doctor's office where the woman was being treated, and she identified him.

The defendant denied the crime. He claimed that he had been drinking with friends until about 2:30 a.m., when he left for home in his truck. He claimed that he picked up an older hitchhiker, who then left the truck when the defendant pulled over to sleep. The defendant claimed that the hitchhiker then returned, awakened him, and took him to a house with an empty bed. The police never investigated the hitchhiker story. Their investigation of the crime scene disclosed traces of sperm on the woman's bed but not on the defendant's shorts, which he was wearing when awakened by the police, nor on his handkerchief. Although the defendant was a young man, the woman described the rapist to her son as resembling a 50-year-old man she knew. She also described the rapist as slender and long-faced, but beyond that she could not give a description.

Putting aside the fact that the defendant was found in the woman's bed, a due process violation is apparent on these facts. A one-person showup was used when one was not necessary. The victim, who needed her glasses to see, did not get a good look at her assailant. The unnecessarily suggestive showup created, therefore, a substantial likelihood of mistaken identification. Nevertheless, some might argue that the defendant's presence in the woman's bed proves she identified the right person. But does it? The defendant gave an excuse for being in her bed. His story suggesting that the hitchhiker was the rapist may seem terribly implausible, but the inability of the police to detect any traces of sperm on his clothes must give one at least a little pause. To consider the external evidence of the defendant's being found in the victim's bed, therefore, would necessitate an inquiry into the validity and significance of the external evidence itself. Because the external evidence may not always prove what it seems to prove, this evidence, as *Manson* suggested, should properly be ignored when considering whether identification testimony must be excluded from trial under the due process test.

Cautionary jury instructions

The preceding sections demonstrate that constitutional rules, at least as they are currently defined, have only limited utility in attacking the dangers inherent in eyewitness identification evidence. Even if an accused has counsel at a lineup that is fairly conducted, the risk of an erroneous identification still exists, for the problems associated with human perception and memory remain. The constitutional rules are designed to eliminate the added danger that arises from suggestive police identification procedures, but they cannot, of course, remedy deficiencies in a witness's perception and recall. For this reason, many courts are paying increasing attention to ways of apprising the jury that eyewitness identification testimony may not be as reliable as lay individuals often assume.

The jury's function in a criminal case is to make factual findings, and in performing this function it must decide which evidence is credible or reliable and which evidence is not. In deciding what crime, if any, the defendant committed, the jury must apply the law provided by the trial judge to the facts as it finds them. Before the jury begins its deliberations, the trial judge provides it with lengthy instructions setting forth the applicable rules of law, the rules allocating the burden of proof, and the procedural and evidentiary rules that may be relevant to the determination of the defendant's guilt. Because of the dangers inherent in eyewitness identification testimony, it has been argued that the trial judge should include with his or her instructions a cautionary statement about these dangers.

In general, it may be said that courts in the United States have lagged behind those in England and some other countries in seeing the need for such cautionary instructions. Nevertheless, in 1972 a prestigious federal appellate court held that a trial judge, upon request by defense counsel and if the facts so warrant, must instruct the jury that identification testimony should be received with caution and scrutinized with care (*United States* v. *Telfaire,* 1972; see also *United States* v. *Barber,* 1971). In determining whether the facts warrant such an instruction, the judge should consider whether the witness had an adequate opportunity to view the offender, whether the witness ever failed to identify the defendant, whether the witness was certain about the identification, and whether the witness became uncertain during defense counsel's cross-examination. In other words, the trial judge should give such a cautionary instruction in cases where the identification testimony shows signs of weakness and uncertainty, and this is especially so in cases where the identification testimony is crucial or pivotal to the issue of the defendant's guilt or innocence.

A recent decision by the Kansas Supreme Court illustrates both the trend toward requiring such a cautionary jury instruction and the factual circumstances that may make such an instruction necessary (*State* v. *Warren,* 1981). The defendant, John M. Warren, and another man were charged with robbing a restaurant. At a preliminary examination, the restaurant cashier identified Warren, but on cross-examination by defense counsel, she became uncertain about her identification. Because of illness, the cashier did not testify at Warren's subsequent trial. The owner of the restaurant identified Warren as the robber who pointed a gun at him, and he made this identification both at the preliminary examination and at the subsequent trial. The defense, however, claimed that the owner's identification of Warren was mistaken. The robbery had taken less than 2 minutes, and during most of this time the owner stared at the other robber. The owner's preliminary examination identification of Warren occurred almost 5 months after the robbery, and the owner had not previously viewed a lineup or a photographic display. Before entering the courtroom at the preliminary examination, the owner was told by the police that they had arrested the robber and that his accomplice had identified him. When the owner entered the courtroom, he saw Warren sitting alone at a table. The owner had not noticed any distinguishing features on the robber's face, and he was not able to recall the color of the robber's eyes. Finally, the owner had described himself as about an inch shorter than the robber, but he was almost 6 inches shorter than Warren.

The alleged accomplice, who pleaded guilty, also testified for the prosecution, and he identified Warren as the other robber. The accomplice, however, had been living with Warren in the latter's house trailer, and he and Warren differed sharply both about the restaurant robbery and another theft. The accomplice testified that Warren had stolen a television set from the place where both men had been working, but Warren and his girl friend testified that the accomplice had brought the television to the trailer. The accomplice testified that Warren had suggested the restaurant robbery, but Warren denied knowing anything about the robbery until the accomplice mentioned it to him. The accomplice did admit that he took both the television and a bank bag that had been taken in the robbery when he moved out of Warren's trailer.

An examination of these facts reveals that the prosecution's case against Warren was not as strong as it first may have appeared. The prosecution started out with three witnesses – the cashier, the owner, and the accomplice. The cashier, however, did not attend the trial, and her earlier identification of Warren turned out to be rather uncertain. The accomplice clearly was in a position to know the other robber, but whereas he could have been telling the truth, he also could have been attempting to shift blame to Warren. The accomplice may have thought that such an effort would facilitate his own dealings with the prosecution, and, indeed, he did receive a rather favorable plea bargain: He was permitted to plead guilty to theft rather than robbery, and he received a suspended sentence with 2 years probation. On the other hand, the owner's identification of Warren tended to remove doubts about the credibility of the accomplice's story, but was his identification reliable? He was certain about his identification, but he had little opportunity to view the robbers at the time of the crime, and his first identification of Warren was not made under the most neutral of circumstances.

The Kansas Supreme Court reversed Warren's robbery conviction because the trial judge did not give the jury, as defense counsel had requested, a cautionary instruction concerning the owner's identification of Warren. The court held that a cautionary instruction must be given whenever eyewitness identification evidence is "a critical part of the prosecution's case and there is a serious question about the reliability of the identification" (*State* v. *Warren,* 1981, p. 1224). In the court's view, the owner's identification of Warren was critical because, as explained earlier, the accomplice's story may not have been believable without it. In its written opinion, the court also indicated some of the factors that trial judges should mention when giving a cautionary instruction. The court stated that the trial judge should instruct the jury to consider the opportunity of the witness to view the actual offender, the witness's degree of attention during the crime, prior descriptions given by the witness of the offender, the witness's level of certainty, and the length of time between the crime and the witness's first identification of the defendant.

Prior to *Warren,* the Kansas Supreme Court had held that trial judges had total discretion in deciding whether to grant defense counsel's request for such a cautionary instruction. In *Warren,* however, the court indicated that its prior opinions had not given "proper recognition to the potential for injustice involved in the area of eyewitness testimony" (*State* v. *Warren,* 1981, p. 1243). Thus, like other courts, the Kansas Supreme Court has become much more sensitive to and aware of the dangers that inhere in eyewitness testimony. The approach the court adopted attempts to strike a balance between the need, on the one hand, to rely on eyewitness testimony to convict a defendant and the concern, on the other hand, that such testimony may lead to the conviction of the wrong person. Although the required instruction cannot prevent mistakes from ever occurring, it should reduce the risk of such mistakes by making the jury aware of the need to give eyewitness testimony especially close scrutiny. (For a detailed model instruction on the dangers of identification testimony, see *United States* v. *Telfaire,* 1972)

Expert testimony concerning the dangers of eyewitness testimony

Many people argue that cautionary instructions from the trial judge will not do enough to alleviate the danger of mistake in eyewitness identification testimony. First, the trial judge obviously cannot testify about the danger; at most, he or she can caution the jury to look at eyewitness testimony with care. Second, the effectiveness of such an instruction may depend somewhat upon the conviction with which the trial judge gives it. Third, many cases are tried to a judge without a jury, and the possibility exists that some trial judges, like many jurors, will not sufficiently appreciate the dangers. Accordingly, many defense attorneys have attempted to use expert witnesses – usually psychologists – to testify about the inherent dangers in eyewitness testimony. Indeed, it has been argued that only through such testimony can the fact finder really be made to appreciate both the possibility that an eyewitness may be mistaken and the reasons such a mistake may occur.

Many trial judges have permitted defense counsel to call expert witnesses to testify about such matters. Quite often, however, trial judges have refused to permit such testimony, and appellate courts have generally been unwilling to find reversible error in such refusals (see, e.g., *State* v. *Helterbridle,* 1980; *United States* v. *Fosher,* 1979; *United States* v. *Watson,* 1978). The Kansas Supreme Court decision discussed in the previous section illustrates the general judicial stance on this issue. Warren's defense attorney attempted to call an expert in the scientific and psychological aspects of eyewitness identification to testify as a defense witness. In rejecting the expert's testimony, the trial judge said that it was inappropriate to permit psychologists to cast doubt on the testimony of other witnesses. The Kansas Supreme Court upheld this decision by the trial judge (*State* v. *Warren,* 1981). The court cited previous cases that had reasoned that the task of evaluating the reliability of eyewitness identification testimony is within the normal experience and qualifications of the jury. The court further stated that expert testimony is permissible only to show that a particular witness suffers from an organic or emotional disability that may affect the reliability of his testimony (*State* v. *Warren,* 1981, p. 1242). The court finally expressed the belief that its new cautionary jury instruction (see the previous section) would be sufficient to "alleviate" the dangers that inhere in eyewitness testimony.

The position of the Kansas Supreme Court, and that of other courts that have considered this issue, seems a bit curious. The Kansas court required a cautionary jury instruction precisely because of its belief that juries would not appreciate on their own the dangers that inhere in eyewitness testimony. Yet, on the issue of expert testimony, the court expressed confidence in the jury's ability to evaluate the reliability of identification evidence. Moreover, the trend of courts is to admit expert testimony not only on matters outside the average juror's ken but on any matter where such testimony might assist the jury in making a determination. Certainly it seems that expert testimony on identification testimony would "assist" the jury in evaluating the reliability of identification evidence.

Whether the judicial attitude on the question of expert testimony will change over time is not altogether clear. As expressed at the beginning of this chapter, the legal profession always has been wary of turning part of the fact-finding process over to individuals from other disciplines. In addition, courts may be concerned that juries will err on the side of overly crediting the expert's testimony, and thus become prone to acquittal. Finally, courts may be worried about the possibility of becoming a forum where experts debate conflicting viewpoints. Certainly the legal experience with psychiatric testimony in criminal cases has not been especially good, with the most cynical critics charging that an expert always can be found to testify for each side. The concern about this happening in other areas may thus partly explain the judicial reluctance to open new doors for expert witnesses. It can safely be predicted, however, that this issue will not go away, for as long as convictions must rest on the testimony of eyewitnesses, there will be pressures to adopt new safeguards to ensure that the innocent are not wrongly convicted.

Notes

1 The United States *Constitution,* Amendment 6, reads "In all criminal prosecutions, the accused shall enjoy the right. . .to have the assistance of counsel for his defense."

References

Abbell, M. Polygraphic evidence: The case against admissibility in federal criminal trials. *American Criminal Law Review,* 1978, *15,* 29–62.

Adamowicz, J. K. Visual short-term memory and aging. *Journal of Gerontology,* 1976, *31,* 39–46.

Adams, J. A. *Learning and memory: An introduction.* Homewood, Ill.: Dorsey Press, 1976.

Addison, B. M. Expert testimony on eyewitness perception. *Dickinson Law Review,* 1978, *82,* 465–485.

Alexander, J. F. Search factors influencing personal appearance identification. In A. Zavala and J. J. Paley (Eds.), *Personal appearance identification.* Springfield, Ill.: Charles C Thomas, 1972.

Alexander, L. The prehypnotic suggestion. *Comprehensive Psychiatry,* 1971, *12,* 414–422.

Allport, G., & Postman, L. *The psychology of rumor.* New York: Holt, 1947.

Alpert, M., Kurtzberg, R., & Friedhoff, A. Transient voice changes associated with emotional stimuli. *Archives of General Psychiatry,* 1963, *8,* 362–365.

American Medical Association. Medical use of hypnosis. *Journal of the American Medical Association,* 1958, *168,* 186–189.

Ansley, N. *Quick reference guide to polygraph admissibility.* Linthicum Hts., Md.: American Polygraph Association, 1980.

Arenberg, D. Cognition and aging: Verbal learning memory and problem solving. In E. Eisdorfer and M. P. Lawton (Eds.), *The psychology of adult development and aging.* Washington, D.C.: American Psychological Association, 1973.

Arons, H. *Hypnosis in criminal investigation.* Springfield, Ill.: Charles C Thomas, 1967.

Arther, R. Peak of tension: Basic information. *Journal of Polygraph Studies,* 1967, *1,* 1–4.

Arther, R. Peak of tension: Dangers. *Journal of Polygraph Studies,* 1968, *2,* 1–4.

Arther, R. The guilt complex question. *Journal of Polygraph Studies,* 1969, *4,* 1–4.

Arther, R. Peak of tension: Examination procedures. *Journal of Polygraph Studies,* 1970, *5*(1), 1–4.

Arther, R., & Caputo, R. *Interrogation for investigators.* New York: Copp, 1959.

Atal, B. S. Automatic speaker recognition based on pitch contours. *Journal of the Acoustical Society of America,* 1972, *52,* 1687–1697.

Augustynek, A. Remembering under hypnosis. *The Journal for Basic Research in Psychological Sciences, Studia Psychologia,* 1978, *20,* 256–266.

Augustynek, A. Hypnotic hypermnesia. *Prace Psychologiczno-Pedagogiczne,* 1979, *29,* 25–34.

Ault, R. L., Jr. FBI guidelines for use of hypnosis. *International Journal of Clinical and Experimental Hypnosis,* 1979, *27,* 449–451.

Babinsky, A. *Die kinderaussage vor Gericht.* Berlin, 1910.

Backster, C. Methods of strengthening our polygraph technique. *Police,* 1962, *6,* 61–68.

336

Backster, C. *Standardized polygraph notepack and technique guide.* New York: Backster Research Foundation, 1969. (a)

Backster, C. *Tri-zone polygraph.* New York: Backster Research Foundation, 1969. (b)

Baddeley, A. D. Applied cognitive and cognitive applied psychology: The case of face recognition. In L. G. Nilsson (Ed.), *Perspectives on memory research.* Hillsdale, N.J.: Erlbaum, 1979.

Baddeley, A. D., & Woodhead, M. M. *Portraiture literature and person recognition.* Unpublished manuscript, Cambridge University, 1982.

Baddeley, A. D., & Woodhead, M. M. Improving face recognition ability. In S. Lloyd-Bostock & B. R. Clifford (Eds.), *Evaluating witness evidence.* Chichester: Wiley, 1983.

Bahrick, H. P., Bahrick, P. O., & Wittlinger, R. P. Fifty years of memory for names and faces: A cross sectional approach. *Journal of Experimental Psychology: General,* 1975, *104,* 54–75.

Bailey, F. L. *The defense never rests.* New York: Stein & Day, 1971.

Baker, E. *Perceiver variables involved in the recognition of faces.* Unpublished doctoral dissertation, University of London, 1967.

Balloun, D., & Holmes, D. S. Effects of repeated examinations on the ability to detect guilt with a polygraphic examination: A laboratory experiment with a real crime. *Journal of Applied Psychology,* 1979, *64,* 316–322.

Barber, T. X. Hypnotic age regression: A critical review. *Psychosomatic Medicine,* 1962, *24,* 286–299.

Barber, T. X., & Calverley, D. S. "Hypnotic behavior" as a function of task motivation. *Journal of Psychology,* 1962, *54,* 363–389.

Barber, T. X. & Calverley, D. S. Effects of recall of hypnotic induction, motivational suggestions, and suggested regression: A methodological and experimental analysis. *Journal of Abnormal Psychology,* 1966, *71,* 169–180.

Barland, G. *The reliability of polygraph chart evaluations.* Paper presented at the meeting of the American Polygraph Association, Chicago, August 1972.

Barland, G. *Detection of deception in criminal suspects: A field validation study.* Unpublished doctoral dissertation, University of Utah, 1975.

Barland, G., & Raskin, D. The use of electrodermal activity in the detection of deception. In W. Prokasy & D. Raskin (Eds.), *Electrodermal activity in psychological research.* New York: Academic Press, 1973.

Barland, G., & Raskin, D. An evaluation of field techniques in detection of deception. *Psychophysiology,* 1975, *12,* 321–330.

Barnett, F. J. How does a jury view polygraph examination results? *Polygraph,* 1973, *2,* 275–277.

Bartholomeus, B. Voice identification by nursery school children. *Canadian Journal of Psychology,* 1973, *27,* 464–472.

Bartlett, F. C. *Remembering.* Cambridge: Cambridge University Press, 1932.

Batten, G. W., & Rhodes, B. T. UHMFS: The University of Houston mug file system. *Proceedings of the 1978 Carnahan Conference on Crime Countermeasures,* Lexington, Ky., 1978.

Bazelon, D. L. Eyewitless news. *Psychology Today,* March 1980, pp. 101–106.

Bekerian, D. A., & Bowers, J. M. Eyewitness testimony: Were we misled? *Journal of Experimental Psychology: Learning, Memory and Cognition,* 1983, *9,* 139–45.

Bem, D. J. Self-perception: An alternative interpretation of cognitive dissonance phenomena. *Psychological Review,* 1967, *74,* 183–200.

Bem, D. J. Self perception theory. In L. Berkowitz (Ed.), *Advances in experimental social psychology* (Vol. 6). New York: Academic Press, 1972.

Ben Shakhar, G., Lieblich, I., & Kugelmass, S. Guilty knowledge technique: Application of signal detection measures. *Journal of Applied Psychology,* 1970, *54,* 409–413.

Benton, A. L. The neuropsychology of face recognition. *American Psychologist,* 1980, *35,* 176–186.

Benussi, V. Die Atmungssymptome der Lüge. *Archiv für Die Gestame Psychologie,* 1914, *31,* 244–273.

Berkout, J., Walter, D., & Abey, W. Autonomic responses during a replicable interrogation. *Journal of Applied Psychology,* 1970, *54,* 316–325.

Berrien, F. Ocular stability in deception. *Journal of Applied Psychology,* 1942, *26,* 55–63.

Berrien, F., & Huntington, G. An exploratory study of pupillary responses during deception. *Journal of Experimental Psychology,* 1943, *32,* 443–449.

Bersch, P. J. A validation study of polygraph examiner judgments. *Journal of Applied Psychology,* 1969, *53,* 399–403.

Biederman, I. *A Non-obvious factor in assessing the fairness of a lineup.* Unpublished manuscript, State University of New York at Buffalo, 1980.

Binet, A. *La suggestibilité.* Paris: Schleicher Frères, 1900.

Binet, A. Le bilan de la psychologie en 1910. *Année psychol.,* 1911, *17,* 5–11.

Bitterman, M., & Marcuse, F. Cardiovascular responses of innocent persons to criminal interrogation. *American Journal of Psychology,* 1947, *60,* 407–412.

Blaney, R. L., & Winograd, E. Developmental differences in children's recognition memory for faces. *Developmental Psychology,* 1978, *14,* 441–442.

Bledsoe, W. W. *Man-machine facial recognition* (PRI-22). Palo Alto, Calif.: Panoramic Research, 1966.

Block, E. B. *Hypnosis: A new tool in crime detection.* New York: David MacKay, 1976.

Borchard, E. *Convicting the innocent: Errors of criminal justice.* New Haven: Yale University Press, 1932.

Bornstein, M. H. Name codes and color memory. *American Journal of Psychology,* 1976, *89,* 269–279.

Borst, M. Die Erziehung der Aussage und Anschauung der Schulkindes. *Die Exp. Padagogik,* 1906, *3,* 1–30.

Bortz, J. On the reciprocal relationships between rating of speakers' voices and the voice of the rater. *Archiv für Psychologie,* 1970, *122,* 231–248.

Botwinick, J. *Aging and behavior.* New York: Springer, 1973.

Bower, G. H., & Karlin, M. B. Depth of processing pictures of faces and recognition memory. *Journal of Experimental Psychology,* 1974, *103,* 751–757.

Bowers, K. S. *Hypnosis for the seriously curious.* Monterey, Calif.: Brooks/Cole, 1976.

Bradley, M. T., & Janisse, M. P. Accuracy demonstrations, threat, and the detection of deception: Cardiovascular, electrodermal, and pupillary measures. *Psychophysiology,* 1981, *18,* 307–315.

Brandon, R., & Davies, C. *Wrongful imprisonment.* London: Allen & Unwin, 1973.

Brandt, H. *The psychology of seeing.* New York: Philosophy Library, 1945.

Bray, R. M., & Kerr, N. L. Use of the simulation method in the study of jury behavior: Some methodological considerations. *Law and Human Behavior,* 1979, *3,* 107–119.

Breuer, J., & Freud, S. *Studies on hysteria (The standard edition of the complete psychological works of Sigmund Freud,* Vol. II). London: Hogarth, 1955. (Originally published, 1895.)

Brewer v. *Williams,* 430 U.S. 387, 1977.

Bricker, P., & Pruzansky, S. Effects of stimulus content and duration on talker identification. *Journal of the Acoustical Society of America,* 1966, *40,* 1441–1449.

Brigham, J. Perspectives on the impact of lineup composition, race, and witness confidence on identification accuracy. *Law and Human Behavior,* 1980, *4,* 315–321.

Brigham, J. C., & Bothwell, R. K. *The ability of prospective jurors to estimate the accuracy of eyewitness identifications.* Unpublished manuscript, Florida State University, 1982.

Brigham, J. C., Maas, A., Martinez, D., & Whittenberger, G. *The effect of arousal on facial recognition.* Unpublished manuscript, Florida State University, 1981.

Brigham, J. C., Maas, A., Snyder, L. D., & Spaulding, K. Accuracy of eyewitness identifications in a field setting. *Journal of Personality and Social Psychology,* 1982, *42,* 673–681.

Brigham, J. C., & Williamson, N. L. Cross-racial recognition and age: When you're over 60, do they still "all look alike?" *Personality and Social Psychology Bulletin,* 1979, *5,* 218–222.

Brigham, J. C. & Wolfskiel, M. P. *Opinions of attorneys and law enforcement personnel on the accuracy of eyewitness identifications.* Unpublished manuscript, Florida State University, 1982.

Brooks, L. R. Spatial and verbal components in the act of recall. *Canadian Journal of Psychology,* 1968, *22,* 349–368.

Brown, A. L. The development of memory: Knowing, knowing about knowing, and knowing how to know. In H. W. Reese (Ed.), *Advances in child development and behavior* (Vol. 10). New York: Academic Press, 1975.

Brown, E. L., Deffenbacher, K. A., & Sturgill, W. Memory for faces and the circumstances of encounter. *Journal of Applied Psychology,* 1977, *62,* 311–318.

Brown, H. B. An experience in identification testimony. *Journal of Criminal Law, Criminology, and Police Science,* 1934, *25,* 621–622.

Brown, M. R. *Legal psychology.* Indianapolis: Bobbs-Merrill, 1926.

Brown, M. R. An experience in identification testimony. *American Institute of Criminal Law,* 1935, *25,* 621–629.

Bruce v. *State,* 268 Ind. 180, 1978.

Bruce, V. Changing faces: Visual and non-visual coding processes in face recognition. *British Journal of Psychology,* 1982, *73,* 105–116.

Bryan, W. J., Jr. *Legal aspects of hypnosis.* Springfield, Ill.: Charles C Thomas, 1962.

Buckhout, R. Eyewitness testimony. *Scientific American,* 1974, *231* (12), 23–31.

Buckhout, R. Nearly 2000 witnesses can be wrong. *Bulletin of the Psychonomic Society,* 1980, *16,* 307–310.

Buckhout, R., Alper, A., Chern, S., Silverberg, G., & Slomovits, M. Determinants of eyewitness performance on a lineup. *Bulletin of the Psychonomic Society,* 1974, *4,* 191–192.

Buckhout, R., Figueroa, D., & Hoff, E. Eyewitness identification: Effects of suggestion and bias in identification from photographs. *Bulletin of the Psychonomic Society,* 1975, *6,* 71–74.

Bull, R. Eyewitnesses also have ears. In M. M. Gruneberg, P. E. Morris, & R. N. Sykes (Eds.), *Practical aspects of memory.* London: Academic Press, 1978.

Bull, R. The influences of stereotypes on person identification. In D. Farrington, P. Hawkins, & S. Lloyd-Bostock (Eds.), *Psychology, law and legal processes.* London: Macmillan, 1979.

Bull, R. Voice identification by man and machine: A review of research. In S. Lloyd-Bostock (Ed.), *Psychology in legal contexts.* London: Macmillan, 1981.

Bull, R. Gathering eyewitness testimony. In G. Breakwell, H. Foot, & R. Gilmour (Eds.), *Social psychology: A laboratory manual.* London: British Psychological Society Publications, 1982.

Bull, R., & Clifford, B. R. Identification: The Devlin report. *New Scientist,* 1976, *70,* 307–308.

Bull, R., & Green, J. The relationship between physical appearance and criminality. *Medicine, Science and Law,* 1980, *20,* 79–83.

Bull, R., Rathborn, H., & Clifford, B. R. The voice recognition of blind listeners. *Perception,* in press.

Bunge, E. Speaker recognition by computer. *Phillips Technical Review,* 1977, *37,* 207–219.

Burch, G. W. *Hypnosis; an aid to police interrogations.* Unpublished master's of science thesis, California State University, Long Beach, 1974.

Burtt, H. Further technique for inspiration-expiration ratios. *Journal of Experimental Psychology,* 1921, *4,* 106–110. (a)

Burtt, H. The inspiration-expiration ratio during truth and falsehood. *Journal of Experimental Psychology,* 1921, *4,* 1–23. (b)

Burtt, H. *Legal psychology.* Englewood Cliffs, N.J.: Prentice-Hall, 1931.

Cady, H. M. On the psychology of testimony. *American Journal of Psychology,* 1924, *35,* 110–112.

Carey, S. The development of face perception. In G. M. Davies, H. D. Ellis, and J. W. Shepherd (Eds.), *Perceiving and remembering faces.* London: Academic Press, 1981.

Carey, S., & Diamond, R. Maturational determination of the developmental course of face encoding. In D. Caplan (Ed.), *Biological studies of mental processes.* Cambridge, Mass.: MIT Press, 1980.

Carey, S., Diamond, R., & Woods, B. Development of face recognition – A maturational component? *Developmental Psychology,* 1980, *16,* 257–269.

Carlson, S. C., Pasano, M. S., & Jannuzzo, J. A. The effect of lie detector evidence on jury deliberations: An empirical study. *Journal of Police Science and Administration,* 1977, *5,* 148–154.

Carterette, E., & Barnebey, A. Recognition memory for voices. In A. Cohen & G. Nooteboom (Eds.), *Structures and processes in speech perception.* New York: Springer, 1975.

Cartwright, I. The prospective child witness. *Criminal Law Quarterly,* 1963, *6,* 196–204.

Cavoukian, A. *Eyewitness testimony: The ineffectiveness of discrediting information.* Paper presented at the meeting of the American Psychological Association, Montreal, August 30, 1980.

Cavoukian, A., & Heslegrave, R. J. The admissibility of polygraph evidence in court: Some empirical findings. *Law and Human Behavior,* 1980, *4,* 117–131.

Chapman, L. J., & Chapman, J. P. Genesis of popular but erroneous psychodiagnostic observations. *Journal of Abnormal Psychology,* 1967, *72,* 193–204.

Chapman v. *State,* 638 P.2d 1280 (Wyo.), 1982.

Chappell, N., & Matthew, N. Blood pressure changes in deception. *Archives of Psychology,* 1929, *17,* 1–39.

Charness, N. Visual short-term memory and aging in chess players. *Journal of Gerontology,* 1981.

Chen, H. T. *Disposition of felony arrests: A sequential analysis of the judicial decision making process.* Unpublished doctoral dissertation, University of Massachusetts, 1981.

Christie, D., Davies, G., Shepherd, J., & Ellis, H. Evaluating a new computer-based system for face recall. *Law and Human Behavior,* 1981, *5,* 209–218.

Christie, D. F. M., & Ellis, H. D. Photofit constructions versus verbal descriptions of faces. *Journal of Applied Psychology,* 1981, *66,* 358–363.

Clarke, F., & Becker, R. Comparison of techniques for discriminating among talkers. *Journal of Speech and Hearing Research,* 1969, *12,* 747–761.

Clarke, F., Becker, R., & Nixon, J. *Characteristics that determine speaker recognition* (Report ESD-TR-66-636). Unpublished manuscript, Air Force Systems Command, Hanscom Field, Mass., 1966.

Clay, H. M. An age difference in separating spatially contiguous data. *Journal of Gerontology,* 1956, *11,* 318–322.

Cleckley, H. *The mask of sanity.* St. Louis, Mo.: Mosby, 1964.

Clifford, B. R. A critique of eyewitness research. In M. M. Gruneberg, P. E. Morris, and R. N. Sykes (Eds.), *Practical aspects of memory.* London: Academic Press, 1978.

Clifford, B. R. The relevance of psychological investigation to legal issues in testimony and identification. *Criminal Law Review,* 1979, 153–163.

Clifford, B. R. Psychologist as expert witness in cases of disputed identification. *Legal Action Bulletin,* 1980, July, 154–157. (a)

Clifford, B. R. Voice identification by human listeners: On earwitness reliability. *Law and Human Behavior,* 1980, *4,* 373–394. (b)

Clifford, B. R. Towards a more realistic appraisal of the psychology of testimony. In S. Lloyd-Bostock (Ed.), *Psychology in legal contexts.* London: Macmillan, 1981.

Clifford, B. R. Memory for voices: The feasibility and quality of earwitness evidence. In S. Lloyd-Bostock & B. R. Clifford (Eds.), *Evaluating witness evidence.* Chichester: Wiley, 1983.

Clifford, B. R., & Bull, R. *The psychology of person identification.* London: Routledge & Kegan Paul, 1978.

Clifford, B. R., Bull, R., & Rathborn, H. *Voice identification.* Report (Res. 741/1/1) to the British Home Office, 1980.

Clifford, B. R., Bull, R., & Rathborn, H. Human voice recognition. *Home Office Research Bulletin,* 1981, *11,* 18–20.

Clifford, B. R., & Denot, H. *Visual and verbal testimony and identification under conditions of stress.* Unpublished manuscript, North East London Polytechnic, 1982.

Clifford, B. R., & Fleming, W. Face and voice identification in a field setting. *Journal of Applied Social Psychology,* in press.

Clifford, B. R., & Hollin, C. Effects of the type of incident and the number of perpetrators on eyewitness memory. *Journal of Applied Psychology,* 1981, *66,* 364–370.

Clifford, B. R., & McCardle, G. Memory for voices. *Journal of Applied Psychology,* in press.

Clifford, B. R., & Prior, D. Levels of processing and capacity allocation. *Perceptual and Motor Skills,* 1980, *50,* 829–830.

Clifford, B. R., Rathborn, H., & Bull, R. The effects of delay on voice recognition accuracy. *Law and Human Behavior,* 1981, *5,* 201–205.

Clifford, B. R., & Richards, V. J. Comparison of recall by policemen and civilians under conditions of long and short durations of exposure. *Perceptual and Motor Skills,* 1977, *45,* 503–512.

Clifford, B. R., & Scott, J. Individual and situational factors in eyewitness testimony. *Journal of Applied Psychology,* 1978, *63,* 352–359.

Cobb, N., Lawrence, D., & Nelson, N. Report on blind subjects' tactile and auditory recognition for environmental stimuli. *Perceptual and Motor Skills,* 1979, *48,* 363–366.

Cohen, D. I. An experimental investigation of hypnotic hypermnesia: The effects of hypnotic induction and regression suggestions on recall (Doctoral dissertation, University of Kentucky, 1972). *Dissertation Abstracts International,* 1972, *33,* 2339–2340 B. (University Microfilms No. 72-29, 263)

Cohen, R. L., & Harnick, M. A. The susceptibility of child witnesses to suggestion. *Law and Human Behavior,* 1980, *4,* 201–210.

Cole, P., & Pringle, P. *Can you positively identify this man?* London: André Deutsch, 1974.

Cole, R., Coltheart, M., & Allard, F. Memory of a speaker's voice: Reaction time to same- or different-voice letters. *Quarterly Journal of Experimental Psychology,* 1974, *26,* 1–7.

Cole, W. G., & Loftus, E. F. Incorporating new information into memory. *American Journal of Psychology,* 1979, *92,* 413–425.

Coleman, R. Male and female voice quality and its relationship to vowel format frequencies. *Journal of Speech and Hearing Research,* 1971, *14,* 565–577.

Coleman, R., & Lass, N. Effect of prior exposure to stimulus material on identification of speakers' sex, height and weight. *Perceptual and Motor Skills,* 1981, *52,* 619–622.

Collins v. *State,* Md. Spec. App. No. 1593, Sept. term 1981. Opinion filed July 13, 1982.

Collins v. *Superior Court of State of Arizona,* decided *en banc* on May 4, 1982, 31 Cr.L. 2156.

Commonwealth v. *Kater,* 388 Mass. 519, 1983.

Commonwealth v. *Nazarovitch,* — Pa. —, 436 A.2d 170, 1981.

Commonwealth v. *Richman,* 458 Pa. 167, 1974.

Compton, A. Effects of filtering and vocal duration upon the identification of speakers, aurally. *Journal of the Acoustical Society of America,* 1963, *35,* 1748–1752.

Cook, M. Eye movements during recognition of faces. In M. M. Gruneberg, P. E. Morris, and R. N. Sykes (Eds.), *Practical aspects of memory.* London: Academic Press, 1978.

Coombs, C. H., Dawes, R. M., & Tversky, A. *Mathematical psychology.* Englewood Cliffs, N.J.: Prentice-Hall, 1970.

Cooper, L. M., & London, P. Reactivation of memory by hypnosis and suggestion. *International Journal of Clinical and Experimental Hypnosis,* 1973, *21,* 312–323.

Courtois, M. R., & Mueller, J. H. Target and distractor typicality in facial recognition. *Journal of Applied Psychology,* 1981, *66,* 639–645.

Craik, F. I. M. Age differences in recognition memory. *Quarterly Journal of Experimental Psychology,* 1971, *23,* 316–323.

Craik, F. I. M. Age differences in human memory. In J. E. Birren and K. W. Schaie (Eds.), *Handbook of the psychology of aging.* New York: Van Nostrand Reinhold, 1977.

Craik, F. I. M., & Kirsner, K. The effect of speaker's voice on word recognition. *Quarterly Journal of Experimental Psychology,* 1974, *26,* 274–284.

Cross, J. F., Cross, J., & Daly, J. Sex, race, age, and beauty as factors in recognition of faces. *Perception and Psychophysics,* 1971, *10,* 393–396.

Dale, P. S., Loftus, E. F., & Rathbun, L. The influences of the form of the question on the eyewitness testimony of preschool children. *Journal of Psycholinguistic Research,* 1978, *7,* 269–277.

Dana, H. It is time to improve the polygraph: A progress report on polygraph research and development. In V. Leonard (Ed.), *Academy lectures on lie detection.* Springfield, Ill.: Charles C Thomas, 1958.

Das, J. P. Learning and recall under hypnosis and in the wake state: A comparison. *Archives of General Psychiatry,* 1961, *4,* 517–521.

Dauber, J. Die Gleichförmigkeit der psychischen Geschehens und die Zeugenaussagen. *Fortschr. d. Psychol.,* 1912, *1,* 83–131.

Davidson, P. O. Validity of the guilty-knowledge technique: The effects of motivation. *Journal of Applied Psychology,* 1968, *52,* 62–65.

Davies, G. Face recall systems. In G. M. Davies, H. D. Ellis, and J. W. Shepherd (Eds.), *Perceiving and remembering faces.* London: Academic Press, 1981.

Davies, G. M. Face recognition: Issues and theories. In M. M. Gruneberg, P. E. Morris, & R. N. Sykes (Eds.), *Practical aspects of memory.* London: Academic Press, 1978.

Davies, G. M., Ellis, H. D., & Shepherd, J. W. Cue saliency in faces assessed by the photofit technique. *Perception,* 1977, *6,* 263–269.

Davies, G. M., Ellis, H. D., & Shepherd, J. W. Face identification: The influence of delay upon accuracy of photofit construction. *Journal of Police Science and Administration,* 1978, *6,* 35–42. (a)

Davies, G. M., Ellis, H. D., & Shepherd, J. W. Face recognition accuracy as function of mode of representation. *Journal of Applied Psychology,* 1978, *63,* 180–187. (b)

Davies, G. M., Shepherd, J. W., & Ellis, H. D. Remembering faces: Acknowledging our limitations. *Journal of the Forensic Science Society,* 1978, *18,* 19–24.

Davies, G. M., Shepherd, J. W., & Ellis, H. D. Effects of interpolated mugshot exposure on accuracy of eyewitness identification. *Journal of Applied Psychology,* 1979, *64,* 232–237. (a)

Davies, G. M., Shepherd, J. W., & Ellis, H. D. Similarity effects in face recognition. *American Journal of Psychology,* 1979, *92,* 507–523. (b)

Daw, P. S., & Parkin, A. J. Observations on the efficiency of different processing strategies for remembering faces. *Canadian Journal of Psychology,* 1981, *35,* 351–355.

Dawson, M. E. Physiological detection of deception: Measurement of responses to questions and answers during countermeasure maneuvers. *Psychophysiology,* 1980, *17,* 8–17.

Deffenbacher, K. The influence of arousal on reliability of testimony. In B. R. Clifford and S. Lloyd-Bostock (Eds.), *Evaluating witness evidence.* Chichester: Wiley, 1983.

Deffenbacher, K. Eyewitness accuracy and confidence: Can we infer anything about their relationship? *Law and Human Behavior,* 1980, *4,* 243–260.

Deffenbacher, K., Brown, E. L., & Sturgill, W. Some predictors of eyewitness memory accuracy. In M. M. Gruneberg, P. E. Morris, & R. N. Sykes (Eds.), *Practical aspects of memory.* London: Academic Press, 1978.

Deffenbacher, K., Carr, T. H., & Leu, J. R. Memory for words, pictures and faces: Retroactive interference, forgetting and reminiscence. *Journal of Experimental Psychology: Human Learning and Memory,* 1981, *7,* 299–305.

Deffenbacher, K., & Loftus, E. F. Do jurors share a common understanding concerning eyewitness behavior? *Law and Human Behavior,* 1982, *6,* 15–30.

Dent, H. R. Stress as a factor influencing person recognition in identification parades. *Bulletin of the British Psychological Society,* 1977, *30,* 339–340.

Dent, H. R. Interviewing child witnesses. In M. M. Gruneberg, P. E. Morris, & R. N. Sykes (Eds.), *Practical aspects of memory.* New York: Academic Press, 1978.

Dent, H. R., & Stephenson, G. M. An experimental study of the effectiveness of different techniques of questioning child witnesses. *British Journal of Social and Clinical Psychology,* 1979, *18,* 41–51.

DePiano, F. A., & Salzberg, H. C. Hypnosis as an aid to recall of meaningful information presented under three types of arousal. *International Journal of Clinical and Experimental Hypnosis,* 1981, *29,* 383–400.

Devlin, Honorable Lord Patrick (chair). *Report to the secretary of state for the Home Department of the departmental committee on evidence of identification in criminal cases.* London: Her Majesty's Stationery Office, 1976.

Dhanens, T. P. The effects of several hypnotic and waking suggestions on the recall of nonsense and contextual material (Doctoral dissertation, Pennsylvania State University, 1973). *Dissertation Abstracts International,* 1973, *33,* 5546A. (University Microfilms No. 73-07, 426)

Dhanens, T. P., & Lundy, R. M. Hypnotic and waking suggestions and recall. *International Journal of Clinical and Experimental Hypnosis,* 1975, *23,* 68–79.

Diamond, B. L. Inherent problems in the use of pretrial hypnosis on a prospective witness. *California Law Review,* 1980, *68,* 313–349.

Diamond, R., & Carey, S. Developmental changes in the representation of faces. *Journal of Experimental Child Psychology,* 1977, *23,* 1–22.

Dilloff, J. The admissibility of hypnotically influenced testimony. *4 Ohio N.U.L. Rev. 1,* 1977, 18–20.

Doehring, D., & Ross, R. Voice recognition by matching to sample. *Journal of Psycholinguistic Research,* 1972, *1,* 233–242.

Doob, A. N., & Kirshenbaum, H. Bias in police lineups – partial remembering. *Journal of Police Science and Administration,* 1973, *1,* 287–293.

Dorcus, R. M. Recall under hypnosis of amnestic events. *International Journal of Clinical and Experimental Hypnosis,* 1960, *8,* 57–60.

Dristas, W. J., & Hamilton, V. L. *Evidence about evidence: Effects of presuppositions, item salience, stress, and perceiver set on accident recall.* Unpublished manuscript, University of Michigan, 1977.

Dunnaway, D. An unpublished research paper cited in E. Green, *Psychology for law enforcement*. New York: Wiley, 1976.

Duprée, E. Le temoignage: Etude psychologique et medico-legale. *Rev. d. deux Mondes,* 1910, *55,* 343–370.

Dyas v. United States, 376 A.2d 827, 1977.

Dywan, J. Hypermnesia, hypnosis and memory: Implications for forensic investigation (Doctoral dissertation, University of Waterloo, 1983).

Dywan, J., & Bowers, K. S. The use of hypnosis to enhance recall. *Science,* 1983, *222,* 184–185.

Ebbinghaus, H. E. *Memory: A contribution to experimental psychology.* New York: Dover, 1964. (Originally published 1885.)

Egan, D., Pittner, M., & Goldstein, A. G. Eyewitness identification: Photographs vs. live models. *Law and Human Behavior,* 1977, *1,* 199–206.

Egan, D. M., & Smith, K. H. *Improving eyewitness identification: An experimental analysis.* Paper presented at the meeting of the American Psychology–Law Society Convention, 1979.

Egan, J. P., & Clarke, F. R. Psychophysics and signal detection. In J. B. Sidowski (Ed.), *Experimental methods and instrumentation in psychology.* New York: McGraw-Hill, 1966.

Ellenberger, H. F. *The discovery of the unconscious: The history and evolution of dynamic psychiatry.* New York: Basic Books, 1970.

Elliott, E. S., Wills, E. J., & Goldstein, A. G. The effects of discrimination training on the recognition of white and oriental faces. *Bulletin of the Psychonomic Society,* 1973, *2,* 71–73.

Ellis, H. D. Recognizing faces. *British Journal of Psychology,* 1975, *66,* 409–426.

Ellis, H. D. Introduction. In G. M. Davies, H. D. Ellis, & J. W. Shepherd (Eds.), *Perceiving and remembering faces.* London: Academic Press, 1981. (a)

Ellis, H. D. *The performance of witnesses on identity parades.* Paper presented at the Symposium on Witness Psychology, Stockholm, 1981. (b)

Ellis, H. D. Theoretical aspects of face recognition. In G. M. Davies, H. D. Ellis, & J. W. Shepherd (Eds.), *Perceiving and remembering faces.* London: Academic Press, 1981. (c)

Ellis, H. D. The role of the right hemisphere in face perception. In A. W. Young (Ed.), *Functions of the right hemisphere.* London: Academic Press, in press.

Ellis, H. D., & Christie, D. F. M. *Some practical problems of face recall: Pictures vs. words.* Paper presented at the 22nd International Congress of Psychology, Leipzig, 1980.

Ellis, H. D., Davies, G. M., & McMurran, M. Recall of white and black faces by white and black witnesses using the photofit system. *Human Factors,* 1979, *21,* 55–59.

Ellis, H. D., Davies, G. M., & Shepherd, J. W. Experimental studies of face identification. *National Journal of Criminal Defense,* 1977, *3,* 219–234.

Ellis, H. D., Davies, G. M., & Shepherd, J. W. A critical examination of the photofit system for recalling faces. *Ergonomics,* 1978, *21,* 297–301.

Ellis, H. D., & Deregowski, J. B. Within-race and between-race recognition of transformed and untransformed faces. *American Journal of Psychology,* 1981, *94,* 27–35.

Ellis, H. D., Deregowski, J. B., & Shepherd, J. Descriptions of white and black faces by white and black subjects. *International Journal of Psychology,* 1975, *10,* 119–123.

Ellis, H. D., Shepherd, J. W., & Bruce, A. The effects of age and sex upon adolescents' recognition of faces. *Journal of Genetic Psychology,* 1973, *123,* 173–174.

Ellis, H. D., Shepherd, J. W., & Davies, G. M. The deterioration of verbal descriptions of faces over different delay intervals. *Journal of Police Science and Administration,* 1980, *8,* 101–106.

Ellison, K. W., & Buckhout, R. *Psychology and criminal justice.* New York: Harper & Row, 1981.

Ellson, D., Davis, R., Saltzman, I., & Burke, C. *A report of research on detection of deception* (Tech. Rep. N6on4–18011). Bloomington: Indiana University, Department of Psychology, September 1952.

Erber, J. T. Age differences in recognition memory. *Journal of Gerontology,* 1974, *29,* 177–181.

Erdelyi, M. H. Recovery of unavailable perceptual input. *Cognitive Psychology,* 1970, *1,* 99–113.

Erdelyi, M. H., & Kleinbard, J. Has Ebbinghaus decayed with time?: The growth of recall (hypermnesia) over days. *Journal of Experimental Psychology: Human Learning and Memory,* 1978, *4,* 275–289.

Erdelyi, M. H., & Stein, J. Recognition hypermnesia: The growth of recognition memory (d′) over time with repeated testing. *Cognition,* 1981, *9,* 23–33.

Erickson, M. H. An experimental investigation of the possible anti-social use of hypnosis. *Psychiatry,* 1939, *2,* 391–414.

Escobedo v. *Illinois,* 378 U.S. 478, 1964.

Eysenck, H. J. An experimental study of the improvement of mental and physical functions in the hypnotic state. *British Journal of Medical Psychology,* 1941, *18,* 304–316.

Eysenck, M. W. *Human memory: Theory, research and individual differences.* Oxford: Pergamon, 1977.

Fagan, J. F. The origins of facial pattern recognition. In M. Bornstein & W. Kessen (Eds.), *Psychological development in infancy: Studies in forgetting.* Hillsdale, N.J.: Erlbaum, 1979.

Fay, P., & Middleton, W. The ability to judge truthtelling or lying from the voice as transmitted over a public address system. *Journal of General Psychology,* 1941, *24,* 211–215.

Federal Rules of Evidence for United States Courts and Magistrates. St. Paul, Minn.: West, 1975.

Feingold, G. A. The influence of environment on identification of persons and things. *Journal of Criminal Law and Criminology,* 1914, *5,* 39–51.

Ferguson, R. *The scientific informer.* Springfield, Ill.: Charles C Thomas, 1971.

Ferris, S. H., Crook, T., Clark, E., McCarthy, M., & Rae, D. Facial recognition memory deficits in normal aging and senile dementia. *Journal of Gerontology,* 1980, *35,* 707–714.

Fersch, E. A., Jr. Ethical issues for psychologists in court settings. In J. Monahan (Ed.), *Who is the client? The ethics of psychological intervention in the criminal justice system.* Washington, D.C.: American Psychological Association, 1980.

Fincher, J. Presumed guilty: The ordeal of Robert Dillen. *Reader's Digest.* October 1981, pp. 104–109.

Fischhoff, B. Hindsight ≠ foresight: The effect of outcome knowledge on judgment under uncertainty. *Journal of Experimental Psychology: Human Perception and Performance,* 1975, *1,* 288–299.

Fishbein, M., & Ajzen, I. *Belief, attitude, intention, and behavior.* Reading, Mass.: Addison-Wesley, 1975.

Fisher, G. J., & Cox, R. L. Recognizing human faces. *Applied Ergonomics,* 1975, *6,* 104–109.

Flin, R. H. Age effects in children's memory for unfamiliar faces. *Developmental Psychology,* 1980, *16,* 373–374.

Forbes, D. D. S. *An investigation into pictorial memory with particular reference to facial recognition.* Unpublished doctoral dissertation, University of Aberdeen, 1975.

Frank, J., & Frank, B. *Not guilty.* London: Gollancz, 1957.

Frazzini, S. F. Review of eyewitness testimony. *The Yale Review,* 1981, *70,* 18–20.

Freud, S. *A case of hysteria. Three essays on sexuality, and other works (The standard edition of the complete psychological works of Sigmund Freud,* Vol. VII). London: Hogarth, 1953. (Originally published, 1905.)

Friedlander, B. Receptive language development: Issues and problems. *Merrill-Palmer Quarterly of Behavior and Development,* 1970, *16,* 7–15.

Frye v. *United States,* 293 F. 1013, 34 A.L.R. 145 (D.C. Cir.), 1923.

Furst, B. *You can remember.* Marple, Chesire: Psychology Publishing, 1962.

Galper, R. E., & Hochberg, J. Recognition memory for photographs of faces. *American Journal of Psychology,* 1971, *84,* 351–354.

Garcia, L. T., & Griffitt, W. Impact of testimonial evidence as a function of witness characteristics. *Bulletin of the Psychonomic Society,* 1978, *11,* 37–40.

Gass, R. S. The psychologist as expert witness: Science in the courtroom. *Maryland Law Review,* 1979, *38,* 539–621.

Gebhard, J. W. Hypnotic age-regression: A review. *American Journal of Clinical Hypnosis,* 1961, *3,* 139–168.

Geldreich, E. Studies of the galvanic skin response as a deception indicator. *Transactions of the Kansas Academy of Sciences,* 1941, *44,* 361–372.

Gheorghiu, V. Experimentelle Untersuchungen zur Hypnotischen Hypermnesie. In D. Langen (Ed.), *Hypnose und Psychosomatische Medizin.* Stuttgart: Hippokrates, 1972. Pp. 42–46.

Gibson, E. *Principles of perceptual learning and development.* New York: Appleton-Century-Crofts, 1969.

Gideon v. *Wainwright,* 372 U.S. 355, 1963.

Gidro-Frank, M. G., & Bowers-Buch, M. K. A study of the plantar response in hypnotic age regression. *Journal of Nervous and Mental Disorders,* 1948, *107,* 443–458.

Gilbert v. *California,* 388 U.S. 263, 1967.

Goldstein, A. G. The fallibility of the eyewitness: Psychological evidence. In B. D. Sales (Ed.), *Psychology in the legal process.* New York: Spectrum, 1977.

Goldstein, A. G., & Chance, J. E. Recognition of children's faces. *Child Development,* 1964, *35,* 129–136.

Goldstein, A. G., & Chance, J. E. Visual recognition memory for complex configurations. *Perception and Psychophysics,* 1971, *9,* 237–241.

Goldstein, A. G., & Chance, J. E. *Intra-individual consistency in visual recognition memory.* Paper presented at the meeting of the American Psychological Association, Toronto, 1978.

Goldstein, A. G., & Chance, J. E. Laboratory studies of face recognition. In G. M. Davies, H. D. Ellis, and J. W. Shepherd (Eds.), *Perceiving and remembering faces.* London: Academic Press, 1981.

Goldstein, A., Knight, P., Bailis, K., & Conover, J. Recognition memory for accented and unaccented voices. *Bulletin of the Psychonomic Society,* 1981, *17,* 217–220.

Goldstein, A. G., & Mackenberg, E. J. Recognition of human faces from isolated facial features: A developmental study. *Psychonomic Science,* 1966, *6,* 149–150.

Goldstein, A. G., Stephenson, B., & Chance, J. E. Face recognition memory: Distribution of false alarms. *Bulletin of the Psychonomic Society,* 1977, *9,* 416–418.

Goodman, G. S., & Michelli, J. A. Would you believe a child witness? *Psychology Today,* November 1981, pp. 82–84, 86, 90, 93, 95.

Goodrich, G. H. Should experts be allowed to testify concerning eyewitness testimony in criminal cases? *The Judges' Journal,* 1975, *14,* 70–71.

Gorenstein, G. W., & Ellsworth, P. C. Effect of choosing an incorrect photograph on a later identification by an eyewitness. *Journal of Applied Psychology,* 1980, *65,* 616–622.

Grano, J. D. Kirby, Biggers & Ash: Do any constitutional safeguards remain against the danger of convicting the innocent? *Michigan Law Review,* 1974, *72,* 717–798.

Grano, J. D. Rhode Island v. Innis: A need to reconsider the constitutional premises underlying the law of confessions. *American Criminal Law Review,* 1979, *17,* 1-13.

Greeley, A. Debunking the role of social scientists in court. *Human Rights,* 1978, *7,* 34-36, 49-51.

Green, D. M., & Swets, J. A. *Signal detection theory and psychophysics.* New York: Wiley, 1966.

Greene, E., Flynne, M. B., & Loftus, E. F. Inducing resistance to misleading information. *Journal of Verbal Learning and Verbal Behavior,* 1982, *21,* 207-219.

Griffin, G. R. Hypnosis: Towards a logical approach in using hypnosis in law enforcement agencies. *Journal of Police Science and Administration,* 1980, *8,* 385-389.

Gross, H. *Kriminalpsychologie.* Leipzig, 1897.

Gross, H. Zur Frage der Zeugenaussage. *H. Gross' Archiv,* 1910, *36,* 372-382.

Groth, A. N. The older rape victim and her assailant. *Journal of Geriatric Psychiatry,* 1979, *11,* 203-215.

Gustafson, L., & Orne, M. Effects of heightened motivation on the detection of deception. *Journal of Applied Psychology,* 1963, *47,* 408-411.

Hagedorn, J. W. The use of post-hypnotic suggestions for recall and amnesia to facilitate retention and to produce forgetting for previously learned materials in classroom situations (Doctoral dissertation, University of Tulsa, 1970). *Dissertation Abstracts International,* 1970, *30,* 4275A. (University Microfilms No. 70-7, 537)

Haggard, M. Selectivity versus summation in multiple observation tasks: Evidence with spectrum parameter noise in speech. *Acta Psychologica,* 1973, *37,* 285-299.

Haggard, M., & Summerfield, Q. *Sample size and perceptual parameters in speaker verification by human listeners.* Unpublished manuscript, Nottingham University, 1982.

Hall, D. F. *Obtaining eyewitness identifications in criminal investigations: Applications of social and experimental psychology.* Unpublished doctoral dissertation, Ohio State University, 1976.

Hall, D. F., & Ostrom, T. M. *Accuracy of eyewitness identification after biasing or unbiased instructions.* Paper presented at the meeting of the American Psychological Association, Chicago, August 1975.

Harding v. State, 5 Md. App. 230, 246 A.2d 302 (1968), 252 Md. 731, *cert. denied,* 395 U.S. 949, 89 S. Ct. 2030, 23 L.Ed.2d 468, 1969.

Harman, G., & Reid, J. The selection and phrasing of lie-detector test control-questions. *Journal of Criminal Law, Criminology, and Police Science,* 1955, *46,* 578-582.

Harmon, L. D. The recognition of faces. *Scientific American,* 1973, *229*(11), 70-82.

Harmon, L. D., & Hunt, W. F. Automatic recognition of human face profiles. *Computer Graphics and Image Processing,* 1977, *6,* 135-156.

Harrelson, L. *Keeler Polygraph Institute training guide.* Chicago: Keeler Polygraph Institute, 1964.

Hartman, D., & Danhauer, J. Perceptual features of speech for males in four perceived age decades. *Journal of the Acoustical Society of America,* 1976, *59,* 713-715.

Hastie, R. *From eyewitness testimony to beyond reasonable doubt.* Unpublished manuscript, Harvard University, 1980.

Hastie, R., Landsman, R., & Loftus, E. F. Eyewitness testimony: The dangers of guessing. *Jurimetrics Journal,* 1978, *19,* 1-8.

Hastorf, A. H., & Cantrill, H. They saw a game: A case study. *Journal of Abnormal and Social Psychology,* 1954, *49,* 129-234.

Hatvany, N., & Strack, F. The impact of a key discredited witness. *Journal of Applied Social Psychology,* 1980, *10,* 490-509.

Haward, L. *Forensic psychology.* London: Batsford, 1981.

Hayes, S. *Contributions to a psychology of blindness*. New York: American Foundation for the Blind, 1941.

Heath, H. A., & Orbach, J. Reversibility of the Necker-cube: IV. Responses of elderly people. *Perceptual and Motor Skills*, 1963, *17*, 625–626.

Hécaen, H. The neuropsychology of face recognition. In G. M. Davies, H. D. Ellis, & J. W. Shepherd (Eds.), *Perceiving and remembering faces*. London: Academic Press, 1981.

Heckel, R., Brokaw, J., Salzburg, H., & Wiggins, S. Polygraphic variations in reactivity between delusional, non-delusional, and control groups in a crime situation. *Journal of Criminal Law, Criminology, and Police Science*, 1962, *53*, 380–383.

Hecker, M. Speaker recognition – an interpretive survey of the literature. *A.S.H.A.*, Monograph 16. Washington, D.C.: American Speech and Hearing Association, 1971.

Helwig, C. V. A comparison of the effectiveness of hypnotic-motivational, task-motivational, and relaxation instructions in eliciting the recall of anxiety inducing material (Doctoral dissertation, University of Toronto, 1976). *Dissertation Abstracts International*, 1978, *38*, 6013A. (University Microfilms No. 68-7, 521)

Herskovits, M. *The anthropometry of the American Negro*. New York: Columbia University Press, 1930.

Hibbard, W. S., & Worring, R. W. *Forensic hypnosis: The practical application of hypnosis in criminal investigations*. Springfield, Ill.: Charles C Thomas, 1981.

Hilgard, E. R. *Hypnotic susceptibility*. New York: Harcourt, Brace, & World, 1965.

Hilgard, E. R., & Loftus, E. F. Effective interrogation of the eyewitness. *International Journal of Clinical and Experimental Hypnosis*, 1979, *27*, 342–357.

Hilgendorf, E. L., & Irving, B. L. Decision criteria in person recognition. *Human Relations*, 1978, *31*, 781–789. (a)

Hilgendorf, E. L., & Irving, B. L. False positive identification. *Medical Science and the Law*, 1978, *18*, 255–262. (b)

Hintzman, D., Block, R., & Inskeep, N. Memory for mode of input. *Journal of Verbal Learning and Verbal Behavior*, 1972, *11*, 741–749.

Hollander, M., & Wolfe, D. A. *Nonparametric statistical methods*. New York: Wiley, 1973.

Hollien, H., & McGlone, R. An evaluation of the voice print technique of speaker identification. *Proceedings: Canadian Conference on Crime Counter-Measures*, 1976, pp. 39–45.

Holmes, W. The degree of objectivity in chart interpretation. In V. Leonard (Ed.), *Academy lectures on lie detection*. Springfield, Ill.: Charles C Thomas, 1958.

Horvath, F. Verbal and nonverbal clues to truth and deception during polygraph examinations. *Journal of Police Science and Administration*, 1973, *1*, 138–152.

Horvath, F. Detection of deception: A review of field and laboratory procedures and research. *Polygraph*, 1976, *5*, 107–145.

Horvath, F. The effect of selected variables on interpretation of polygraph records. *Journal of Applied Psychology*, 1977, *62*, 127–136.

Horvath, F. An experimental comparison of the psychological stress evaluator and the galvanic skin response in detection of deception. *Journal of Applied Psychology*, 1978, *63*, 338–344.

Horvath, F. Effect of different motivational instructions on detection of deception with the psychological stress evaluator and the galvanic skin response. *Journal of Applied Psychology*, 1979, *64*, 323–330.

Horvath, F. Polygraphy: Some comments on the state of the art. *Polygraph*, 1980, *9*, 34–41.

Horvath, F. Detecting deception: The promise and the reality of voice stress analysis. *Journal of Forensic Sciences*, 1982, *27*, 340–351.

Horvath, F., & Reid, J. The reliability of polygraph examiner diagnosis of truth and deception. *The Journal of Criminal Law, Criminology, and Police Science*, 1971, *62*, 276–281.

Horvath, F., & Reid, J. The polygraph silent answer test. *Journal of Criminal Law, Criminology, and Police Science,* 1972, *63,* 285–293.

Hosch, H. M., Beck, E. L. & McIntyre, P. Influence of expert testimony regarding eyewitness accuracy on jury decisions. *Law and Human Behavior,* 1980, *4,* 287–296.

Hosch, H. M., & Cooper, D. S. Victimization as a determinant of eyewitness accuracy. *Journal of Applied Psychology,* in press.

Hosch, H. M., Leippe, M. R., Marchoni, P. M., & Cooper, S. D. *Victimization, self-monitoring and eyewitness identification.* Unpublished manuscript, University of Texas at El Paso, 1982.

Houts, M. *From proof to evidence.* Springfield, Ill.: Charles C Thomas, 1956.

Hoyer, W. J. The elderly: Who are they? In A. P. Goldstein, W. J. Hoyer, and P. J. Monti (Eds.), *Police and the elderly.* New York: Pergamon, 1979.

Hull, C. L. *Hypnosis and suggestibility.* New York: Appleton-Century-Crofts, 1933.

Hunter, F. L., & Ash, P. The accuracy and consistency of polygraph examiners' diagnoses. *Journal of Police Science and Administration,* 1973, *1,* 370–375.

Huse, B. Does the hypnotic trance favor the recall of faint memories? *Journal of Experimental Psychology,* 1930, *13,* 519–529.

Inbau, F. *Lie detection and criminal interrogation.* Baltimore: Williams & Wilkins, 1942.

Inbau, F., & Reid, J. *Lie detection and criminal interrogation.* Baltimore: Williams & Wilkins, 1953.

Ingeman, F. Identification of speaker's voice from voiceless fricatives. *Journal of the Acoustical Society of America,* 1968, *44,* 1142–1144.

International Society of Hypnosis. Resolution. *International Journal of Clinical and Experimental Hypnosis,* 1979, *27,* 453.

Jackson v. Denno, 378 U.S. 368, 84 S. Ct. 1774, 1964.

Jackson v. State, 239 Ala. 38, 193 So. 417, 1940.

James, W. *Principles of psychology.* New York: Holt, 1890.

Johnson, C., & Scott, B. *Eyewitness testimony and suspect identification as a function of arousal, sex of witness and scheduling of interrogation.* Paper presented at the meeting of the American Psychological Association, Washington, D.C., 1976.

Johnson, M. K., & Raye, C. L. Reality monitoring. *Psychological Review,* 1981, *88,* 67–85.

Kahneman, D., & Tversky, A. On the psychology of prediction. *Psychological Review,* 1973, *80,* 251–273.

Kassin, S. Personal written communication, 1979.

Katz, L. S., & Reid, J. F. Expert testimony on the fallibility of eyewitness identification. *Criminal Justice Journal,* 1977, *1,* 177–206.

Kausler, D., & Puckett, J. Adult age differences in memory for sex of voice. *Journal of Gerontology,* 1981, *36,* 44–50.

Keeler, L. A method for detecting deception. *American Journal of Police Science,* 1930, *1,* 38–52.

Kellogg, R. T. Is conscious attention necessary for long-term storage? *Journal of Experimental Psychology: Human Learning and Memory,* 1980, *6,* 379–390.

Kirby v. Illinois, 406 U.S. 682, 1972.

Klatzky, R. L., & Erdelyi, M. H. *The response criterion problem in tests of hypnosis and memory.* Unpublished manuscript, Center for Advanced Study in the Behavioral Sciences, Stanford, 1983.

Kleinhauz, M. *Hypnosis in criminal investigation – Ethical and practical implications.* Paper presented at the 9th International Congress of Hypnosis and Psychosomatic Medicine, Glasgow, Scotland, August 1982.

Kline, M. V., & Guze, H. The use of a drawing technique in the investigation of hypnotic age regression and progression. *British Journal of Medical Hypnotism,* 1951, Winter, 1–12.

Kline v. *Ford Motor Co., Inc.,* 523 F.2d 1067 (9th Cir.), 1975.

Kolb, L. C. Fantasy or fact as products of altering states of consciousness. In U. Neisser (Chair), *Influence of hypnosis and related states on memory: Forensic implications.* Symposium presented at the meeting of the American Association for the Advancement of Science, Washington, D.C., January 1982.

Konechni, V. J., & Ebbesen, E. B. External validity of research in legal psychology. *Law and Human Behavior,* 1979, *3,* 39–70.

Koriat, A., Lichtenstein, S., & Fischhoff, B. Reasons for confidence. *Journal of Experimental Psychology: Human Learning and Memory,* 1980, *6,* 107–118.

Kramer, E. The judgment of personality characteristics and emotions from non-verbal properties of speech. *Psychological Bulletin,* 1963, *60,* 408–420.

Kreuger, L. E. A theory of perceptual matching. *Psychological Review,* 1978, *85,* 278–304.

Kroger, W. S., & Doucé, R. G. Hypnosis in criminal investigation. *International Journal of Clinical and Experimental Hypnosis,* 1979, *27,* 358–374.

Krouse, F. L. Effects of pose, pose change, and decay on face recognition performance. *Journal of Applied Psychology,* 1981, *66,* 651–654.

Kubis, J. Electronic detection of deception. *Electronics,* 1945, *18,* 192–212.

Kubis, J. Experimental and statistical factors in the diagnosis of consciously suppressed affective experiences. *Journal of Clinical Psychology,* 1950, *6,* 12–16.

Kubis, J. *Studies in lie detection: Computer feasibility considerations* (Tech. Rep. 62–205). New York: Fordham University, Department of Psychology, June 1962.

Kubis, J. Comparison of voice analysis and polygraph as lie detection procedures. *Polygraph,* 1974, *3,* 1–47.

Kugelmass, S. *Effects of three levels of realistic stress on differential physiological reactivities* (Tech. Rep. 63–61). Air Force Office of Scientific Research, European Office. Hebrew University of Jerusalem, Israel, August 1963.

Kugelmass, S., & Lieblich, I. The effects of realistic stress and procedural interference in experimental lie detection. *Journal of Applied Psychology,* 1966, *50,* 211–216.

Kugelmass, S., Lieblich, I., Ben Ishai, A., Opatowski, A., & Kaplan, M. Experimental evaluation of galvanic skin response and blood pressure change indices during criminal investigation. *Journal of Criminal Law, Criminology, and Police Science,* 1968, *59,* 632–635.

Langdell, T. Recognition of faces: An approach to the study of autism. *Journal of Child Psychology and Psychiatry,* 1978, *19,* 255–268.

La Riviere, C. Some acoustic and perceptual correlates of speaker identification. In A. Rigault & R. Charbonneau (Eds.), *Proceedings of the Seventh International Congress of the Phonetic Sciences.* New York: Mouton, 1972.

Larson, J. Modification of the Marston deception test. *Journal of the American Institute of Criminal Law and Criminology,* 1921, *12,* 390–399.

Larson, J. *Lying and its detection.* Chicago: University of Chicago Press, 1932.

Lass, N., Hughes, K., Bowyer, M., Waters, L., & Bourne, V. Speaker sex identification from voiced, whispered and filtered isolated vowels. *Journal of the Acoustical Society of America,* 1976, *59,* 675–678.

Lass, N., Mertz, P., & Kimmel, K. The effect of temporal speech alterations on speaker race and sex identification. *Language and Speech,* 1978, *21,* 279–291.

Laughery, K. R., Alexander, J. F., & Lane, A. B. Recognition of human faces: Effects of target exposure time, target position, pose position, and type of photograph. *Journal of Applied Psychology,* 1971, *51,* 477–483.

Laughery, K. R., Fessler, P. K., Lenorovitz, D. R., & Yoblick, D. A. Time delay and similarity effects in facial recognition. *Journal of Applied Psychology,* 1974, *59,* 490–496.

Laughery, K. R., & Fowler, R. F. Sketch artist and Identi-kit procedures for recalling faces. *Journal of Applied Psychology,* 1980, *65,* 307–316.

Laughery, K., Rhodes, B., and Batten, G. Computer-guided recognition and retrieval of facial images. In G. M. Davies, H. D. Ellis, & J. W. Shepherd (Eds.), *Perceiving and remembering faces.* London: Academic Press, 1981.

Laurence, J-R. *Memory creation in hypnosis.* Unpublished doctoral dissertation, Concordia University, Montreal, 1982.

Laurence, J-R., & Perry, C. Hypnotically created memory among high hypnotizable subjects. *Science,* in press.

Lehnert, W. G., Robertson, S., & Black, J. B. Memory interactions during question answering. In H. Mandel, N. L. Stein, & T. Trabasso (Eds.), *Learning and comprehension of text.* Hillsdale, N.J.: Ablex, in press.

Leippe, M. R. Effects of integrative memorial and cognitive processes on the correspondence of eyewitness accuracy and confidence. *Law and Human Behavior,* 1980, *4,* 261–274.

Leippe, M. R., Wells, G. L., & Ostrom, T. M. Crime seriousness as a determinant of accuracy in eyewitness identification. *Journal of Applied Psychology,* 1978, *63,* 345–351.

Lenorovitz, D. R. *The discrimination of similarities and differences in facial appearance: A multidimensional scaling approach.* Unpublished master's thesis, State University of New York at Buffalo, 1972.

Lenorovitz, D. R., & Yoblick, D. A. Time delay and similarity effects in facial recognition. *Journal of Applied Psychology,* 1974, *59,* 490–496.

Levine, F. J., & Tapp, J. L. The psychology of criminal identification: The gap from Wade to Kirby. *University of Pennsylvania Law Review,* 1973, *5,* 1079–1131.

Lewis, D. J. Psychobiology of active and inactive memory. *Psychological Bulletin,* 1979, *86,* 1054–1083.

Leyra v. *Denno,* 347 U.S. 556 (1954).

Light, L., Stanbury, C., Rubins, C., & Linde, S. Memory for modality of presentation: Within-modality discrimination. *Memory and Cognition,* 1973, *1,* 395–400.

Light, L. L., Kayra-Stuart, F., & Hollander, S. Recognition memory for typical and unusual faces. *Journal of Experimental Psychology: Human Learning and Memory,* 1979, *5,* 212–228.

Lindsay, R. C. L., & Wells, G. L. What price justice? Exploring the relationship of lineup fairness to identification accuracy. *Law and Human Behavior,* 1980, *4,* 303–314.

Lindsay, R. C. L., & Wells, G. L. What do we really know about cross-race eyewitness identification? In S. Lloyd-Bostock & B. R. Clifford (Eds.), *Evaluating witness evidence.* Chichester: Wiley, 1983.

Lindsay, R. C. L., Wells, G. L., & Rumpel, C. Can people detect eyewitness identification accuracy within and across situations? *Journal of Applied Psychology,* 1981, *66,* 79–89.

Lipmann, P. Pedagogical psychology of report. *Journal of Educational Psychology,* 1911, *2,* 253–261.

Lippold, O. Physiological tremor. *Scientific American,* 1971, *224* (5), 65–73.

Lipton, J. P. On the psychology of eyewitness testimony. *Journal of Applied Psychology,* 1977, *62,* 90–95.

Loftus, E. F. Reconstructing memory: The incredible eyewitness. *Psychology Today,* August 1974, pp. 116–119.

Loftus, E. F. Leading questions and the eyewitness report. *Cognitive Psychology,* 1975, *7,* 560–572.

Loftus, E. F. Unconscious transference in eyewitness identification. *Law and Psychology Review,* 1976, *2,* 93–98.

Loftus, E. F. Shifting human color memory. *Memory and Cognition,* 1977, *5,* 696–699.

Loftus, E. F. *Eyewitness testimony.* Cambridge, Mass.: Harvard University Press, 1979.

Loftus, E. F. Alcohol, marijuana, and memory. *Psychology Today,* March 1980, pp. 42–56. (a)

Loftus, E. F. Impact of expert psychological testimony on the unreliability of eyewitness idencation. *Journal of Applied Psychology,* 1980, *65,* 9–15. (b)

Loftus, E. F. Mentalmorphosis: Alterations in memory produced by bonding of new information to old. In J. B. Long & A. D. Baddeley (Eds.), *Attention and performance IX.* Hillsdale, N.J.: Erlbaum, 1981. (a)

Loftus, E. F. Natural and unnatural cognition. *Cognition,* 1981, *10,* 193–196. (b)

Loftus, E. F. Silence is not golden. *American Psychologist,* 1983, *38,* 564–572.

Loftus, E. F., & Greene, E. Warning: Even memory for faces may be contagious. *Law and Human Behavior,* 1980, *4,* 323–334.

Loftus, E. F., & Loftus, G. R. On the permanence of stored information in the human brain. *American Psychologist,* 1980, *35,* 409–420.

Loftus, E. F., Miller, D. G., & Burns, H. J. Semantic integration of verbal information into a visual memory. *Journal of Experimental Psychology: Human Learning and Memory,* 1978, *4,* 19–31.

Loftus, E. F., & Monahan, J. Trial by data: Psychological research as legal evidence. *American Psychologist,* 1980, *35,* 270–283.

Loftus, E. F., & Zanni, G. Eyewitness testimony: The influence of the wording of a question. *Bulletin of the Psychonomic Society,* 1975, *5,* 86–88.

Loh, W. D. Psychological research: Past and present. *Michigan Law Review,* 1981, *79,* 659–707.

Lorayne, H., & Lucas, J. *The memory book.* Hillsdale, N.J.: Erlbaum, 1976.

Lower, J. S. Psychologists as expert witnesses. *Law and Psychology Review,* 1978, *4,* 127–139.

Luria, S. M., & Strauss, M. S. Comparison of eye movements over faces in photographic positives and negatives. *Perception,* 1978, *7,* 349–358.

Lykken, D. The GSR in the detection of guilt. *Journal of Applied Psychology,* 1959, *43,* 385–388.

Lykken, D. The validity of the guilty knowledge technique: The effects of faking. *Journal of Applied Psychology,* 1960, *44,* 258–262.

Lykken, D. The psychopath and the lie detector. *Psychophysiology,* 1978, *15,* 137–142.

Lykken, D. The detection of deception. *Psychological Bulletin,* 1979, *86,* 47–53.

Lykken, D. *A tremor in the blood.* New York: McGraw-Hill, 1980.

Lykken, D. The lie detector and the law. *Criminal Defense,* 1981, *8,* 19–27.

Lyon, V. Deception tests with juvenile delinquents. *Journal of General Psychology,* 1936, *48,* 494–497.

Maas, A., & Brigham, J. C. Eyewitness identification: The role of attention and encoding specificity. *Personality and Social Psychology Bulletin,* 1982, *8,* 54–59.

MacHovec, F. J. Hypnosis to facilitate recall in psychogenic amnesia and fugue states: Treatment variables. *American Journal of Clinical Hypnosis,* 1981, *24,* 7–13.

MacNitt, R. In defense of the electrodermal response and cardiac amplitude as measures of deception. *Journal of Criminal Law and Criminology,* 1942, *33,* 266–275.

Malpass, R. Effective size and defendant bias in eyewitness identification lineups. *Law and Human Behavior,* 1981, *5,* 299–309. (a)

Malpass, R. Training in face recognition. In G. M. Davies, H. D. Ellis, and J. W. Shepherd (Eds.), *Perceiving and remembering faces.* London: Academic Press, 1981. (b)

Malpass, R. S., & Devine, P. G. Realism and eyewitness identification research. *Law and Human Behavior,* 1980, *4,* 347–358.

Malpass, R. S., & Devine, P. G. Eyewitness identification: Lineup instructions and the absence of the offender. *Journal of Applied Psychology,* 1981, *66,* 482–489. (a)

Malpass, R. S., & Devine, P. G. Guided memory in eyewitness identification. *Journal of Applied Psychology,* 1981, *66,* 343–350. (b)

Malpass, R. S., & Devine, P. Measuring the fairness of eyewitness identification lineups. In S. Lloyd-Bostock & B. R. Clifford (Eds.), *Evaluating witness evidence.* Chichester: Wiley, 1983.

Malpass, R. S., Devine, P. G., & Bergen, G. T. *Eyewitness identification: Realism vs. the laboratory.* Unpublished manuscript, State University of New York, Plattsburgh, Behavioral Science Program, 1980.

Malpass, R. S., & Kravitz, J. Recognition for faces of own and other race. *Journal of Personality and Social Psychology,* 1969, *13,* 330–334.

Malpass, R. S., Lavigueur, H., & Weldon, D. E. Verbal and visual training in face recognition. *Perception and Psychophysics,* 1973, *14,* 285–292.

Mand, J. L., & Shaughnessy, J. J. *How permanent are memories for real life events?* Unpublished manuscript, Hope College, Michigan, 1981.

Mandler, G. Recognizing: The judgment of previous occurrence. *Psychological Review,* 1980, *87,* 252–271.

Mann, V., Diamond, R., & Carey, S. Development of voice recognition: Parallels with face recognition. *Journal of Experimental Child Psychology,* 1979, *27,* 153–165.

Manson v. *Brathwaite,* 432 U.S. 98, 1977.

Marbe, K. Psychologische Gutachten zum Pruzess wegen der Mullheimer Eisenbahnunglucks. *Fortschr. d. Psychol.,* 1913, *1,* 339–374.

Marin, B. V., Holmes, D. L., Guth, M., & Kovac, P. The potential of children as eyewitnesses: A comparison of children and adults on eyewitness tasks. *Law and Human Behavior,* 1979, *3,* 295–306.

Marks, E. Skin color judgments of Negro college students. *Journal of Abnormal and Social Psychology,* 1943, *38,* 370–376.

Marquis, K. H., Marshall, J., & Oskamp, S. Testimony validity as a function of question form, atmosphere, and item difficulty. *Journal of Applied Social Psychology,* 1972, *2,* 167–186.

Marshall, J. *Law and psychology in conflict.* New York: Bobbs-Merrill, 1966.

Marston, W. Systolic blood pressure symptoms of deception. *Journal of Experimental Psychology,* 1917, *2,* 117–163.

Marston, W. Psychological possibilities in the deception test. *Journal of the American Institute of Criminal Law and Criminology,* 1921, *11,* 551–570.

Marston, W. Studies in testimony. *Journal of the American Institute of Criminal Law,* 1924, *15,* 5–31.

Massiah v. *United States,* 377 U.S. 201, 1964.

Mauldin, M. A., & Laughery, K. R. Composite production effects on subsequent facial recognition. *Journal of Applied Psychology,* 1981, *66,* 351–357.

McCarty, D. G. *Psychology for the lawyer.* New York: Prentice-Hall, 1929.

McCloskey, M., Egeth, H., Webb, E., Washburn, A., & McKenna, J. *Eyewitnesses, jurors and the issue of overbelief.* Unpublished manuscript, Johns Hopkins University, 1981.

McCranie, E. J., Crasilneck, H. B., & Teter, H. R. The electro-encephalogram in hypnotic age regression. *Psychiatric Quarterly,* 1955, *29,* 85–88.

McEwan, N. H., & Yuille, J. C. *The effect of hypnosis as an interview technique on eyewitness memory.* Paper presented at the 43rd annual meeting of the Canadian Psychological Association, Montreal, June 1982.

McGehee, F. The reliability of the identification of the human voice. *Journal of General Psychology,* 1937, *17,* 249–271.

McGehee, F. An experimental investigation of voice recognition. *Journal of General Psychology,* 1944, *31,* 53–65.

McGeoch, J. A. *The psychology of human learning.* New York: Longmans, Green, 1942.

McGlone, R., Hollien, P., & Hollien, H. Acoustic analysis of voice disguise related to voice identification. *Journal of the Acoustical Society of America,* 1977, *62,* 31–35.

McKean, K. Anatomy of an air crash. *Discover,* April 1982, pp. 64–66.

McKelvie, S. J. Sex differences in facial memory. In M. M. Gruneberg, P. E. Morris, & R.N. Sykes (Eds.), *Practical aspects of memory.* London: Academic Press, 1978.

McKenna, J., Mellott, A., & Webb, E. *Juror evaluation of eyewitness testimony.* Paper presented at the meeting of the Eastern Psychological Association, New York, 1981.

Meadows, J. C. The anatomical basis of prosopognosia. *Journal of Neurology, Neurosurgery and Psychiatry,* 1974, *37,* 489–501.

Medin, D. L., & Shaffer, M. M. Context theory of classification learning. *Psychological Review,* 1978, *85,* 207–235.

Meehl, P. E. Law and the fireside induction. In J. L. Tapp & F. J. Levine (Eds.), *Law, justice and the individual in society.* New York: Holt, Rinehart & Winston, 1977, 10–28.

Mehl, P. Beitrag zur Psychologie der Kinderaussage. *Arch. F. Krim. – Antrop. u Kriminalistik,* 1912, *49,* 193.

Mehler, J., Bertoncini, J., Barrière, M., & Jassik-Gerschenfeld, D. Infant recognition of mother's voice. *Perception,* 1978, *7,* 491–497.

Melton, G. B. Children's competency to testify. *Law and Human Behavior,* 1981, *5,* 73–85.

Messerschmidt,· R. The suggestibility of boys and girls between the ages of six and sixteen years. *Journal of Genetic Psychology,* 1933, *43,* 422–437.

Miller, L. L., & Branconnier, R. J. Cannabis: Effects on memory and the cholinergic limbic system. *Psychological Bulletin,* 1983, *93,* 441–456.

Miranda v. *Arizona,* 384 U.S. 436, 1966.

Mitchell, M. B. Retroactive inhibition and hypnosis. *Journal of General Psychology,* 1932, *7,* 343–359.

Moore v. *Illinois,* 434 U.S. 220, 1977.

Morgan, A. H., Johnson, D. L., & Hilgard, E. R. The stability of hypnotic susceptibility: A longitudinal study. *International Journal of Clinical and Experimental Hypnosis,* 1974, *22,* 249–257.

Morse, S. J. Law and mental health professionals: The limits of expertise. *Professional Psychology,* 1978, *9,* 389–399.

Morton, J., Hammersley, R., & Bekerian, D. A. *Headed records: A framework for remembering and its failures.* Unpublished manuscript, MCR Applied Psychology Unit, Cambridge, England, 1981.

Mulac, A., Hanley, T., & Prigge, D. Effects of phonological speech foreignness upon three dimensions of attitude of selected American listeners. *Quarterly Journal of Speech,* 1974, *60,* 411–420.

Munsterberg, H. *On the witness stand: Essays on psychology and crime.* New York: Clark Boardman, 1908.

Murdock, B. *Human memory: Theory and data.* Hillsdale, N.Y.: Erlbaum, 1974.

Murray, D. M., & Wells, G. L. Does knowledge that a crime was staged affect eyewitness accuracy? *Journal of Applied Social Psychology,* 1982, *12,* 42–53.

Murray, T., & Cort, S. Aural identification of children's voices. *Journal of Auditory Research,* 1971, *11,* 260–262.

Myers, M. A. Rule departures and making law: Juries and their verdicts. *Law and Society,* 1979, *13,* 781–797.

Neil v. *Biggers,* 409 U.S. 188, 1972.

Neisser, U. *Cognition and reality,* San Francisco: Freeman, 1976.

Neisser, U. John Dean's memory: A case study. *Cognition,* 1981, *9,* 1–22.

Neisser, U. (Ed.) *Memory observed: Remembering in natural contexts.* San Francisco: Freeman, 1982.

Nelson v. *State,* 362 So. 2d 1017 (Fla.), 1978.

Nerbonne, G. The identification of speaker characteristics on the basis of aural cues (Doctoral dissertation, University of Pennsylvania, 1968). *Dissertation Abstracts,* 1968, *28,* (10-B), 4332–4333.

Nisbett, R. E., & Wilson, T. D. Telling more than we can know: Verbal reports on mental processes. *Psychological Review,* 1977, *84,* 231–259.

O'Barr, W. M., & Conley, J. M. When a juror watches a lawyer. *Barrister,* 1976, *3,* 8–11.

Oberman, C. The effect on the Berger rhythm of mild affective states. *Journal of Abnormal and Social Psychology,* 1939, *34,* 84–95.

O'Connell, D. N., Shor, R. E., & Orne, M. T. Hypnotic age regression: An empirical and methodological analysis. *Journal of Abnormal Psychology,* 1970, *76,* (3 Pt. 2) (Monograph).

Okun, M. A., Siegler, I. C., & George, L. K. Cautiousness and verbal learning in adulthood. *Journal of Gerontology,* 1978, *33,* 94–97.

Orlansky, J. *An assessment of lie detection capability* (Tech. Rep. 62–16, declassified version). Arlington, Va.: Institute for Defense Analyses, Research and Engineering Support Division, 1964.

Orne, M. T. The mechanisms of hypnotic age regression: An experimental study. *Journal of Abnormal and Social Psychology,* 1951, *46,* 213–225.

Orne, M. T. The nature of hypnosis: Artifact and essence. *Journal of Abnormal and Social Psychology,* 1959, *58,* 277–299.

Orne, M. T. The potential uses of hypnosis in interrogation. In A. D. Biderman & H. Zimmer (Eds.), *The manipulation of human behavior.* New York: Wiley, 1961.

Orne, M. T. On the social psychology of the psychological experiment: With particular reference to demand characteristics and their implications. *American Psychologist,* 1962, *17,* 776–783.

Orne, M. T. The disappearing hypnotist: The use of simulating subjects. *International Journal of Clinical and Experimental Hypnosis,* 1971, *19,* 277–296.

Orne, M. T. Implications of laboratory research for the detection of deception. In N. Ansley (Ed.), *Legal admissibility of the polygraph.* Springfield, Ill.: Charles C Thomas, 1975.

Orne, M. T. The construct of hypnosis: Implications of the definition for research and practice. *Annals of the New York Academy of Science,* 1977, *296,* 14–33.

Orne, M. T. The use and misuse of hypnosis in court. *International Journal of Clinical and Experimental Hypnosis,* 1979, *27,* 311–341.

Orne, M. T. On the construct of hypnosis: How its definition affects research and its clinical application. In G. D. Burrows & L. Dennerstein (Eds.), *Handbook of hypnosis and psychosomatic medicine.* Amsterdam: Elsevier/North-Holland, 1980.

Orne, M. T. The significance of unwitting cues for experimental outcomes: Toward a pragmatic approach. *Annals of the New York Academy of Science,* 1981, *364,* 152–159. (a)

Orne, M. T. The use and misuse of hypnosis in court. In M. Tonry & N. Morris (Eds.), *Crime and justice: An annual review of research* (Vol. 3). Chicago: University of Chicago Press, 1981. (b)

Orne, M. T., Dinges, D. F., & Orne, E. C. On the differential diagnosis of multiple personality in the forensic context. *International Journal of Clinical and Experimental Hypnosis,* in press.

Orne, M. T., Thackray, R., & Paskewitz, D. On the detection of deception: A model for the study of the physiological effects of psychological stimuli. In N. Greenfield & R. Sternbach (Eds.), *Handbook of psychophysiology.* New York: Holt, Rinehart, & Winston, 1972.

Patterson, K. E. Person recognition. In M. M. Gruneberg, P. E. Morris, & R. N. Sykes (Eds.), *Practical aspects of memory.* London: Academic Press, 1978.

Patterson, K. E., & Baddeley, A. D. When face recognition fails. *Journal of Experimental Psychology: Human Learning and Memory,* 1977, *3,* 406–417.

Pavlov, I. *Conditioned reflexes.* New York: Oxford University Press, 1927.

Pear, T. *Voice and personality.* New York: Wiley, 1931.

Penry, H. *Looking at faces.* London: Elek Press, 1971.

People v. *Bustamonte,* 80 Cal. 3d 239, 177 Cal. Rptr. 576, 1981.

People v. *Ebanks,* 117 Cal. 652, 49 P. 1049, 1897.

People v. *Gonzales,* 108 Mich. App. 145, 165, 1982.

People v. *Guzman,* 47 Cal. App. 3d 380, 121 Cal. Rptr. 69, 1975.

People v. *McNichol,* 100 Cal. App. 2d 544, 224 P.2d 21, 1950.

People v. *Shirley,* 641 P.2d 775 (Cal. 1982), *cert. denied,* 408 U.S. − (1982).

People v. *Williams,* 3 Cal. 3d 853, 1971.

Perry, C., & Laurence, J-R. The enhancement of memory by hypnosis in the legal investigative situation. *Canadian Psychology,* 1983, *24,* 155–167.

Peters, A. Gefuhl und Wiederkennen. *Fortschritte der Psychologie und ihrer Anwendungen,* 1917, *4,* 120–133.

Peters, R. *Studies in extra-messages: The effect of various modifications of the voice signal upon the ability of listeners to identify speakers' voices* (Project No. 001-104-500, Report No. 61). U.S. Navy School of Aviation Medical Research, 1956.

Petterson, J. Court says witnesses are fallible. *Wichita Eagle-Beacon,* November 10, 1981, p. 1c.

Phillips, R. J. Recognition recall and imagery of faces. In M. M. Gruneberg, P. E. Morris, & R. N. Sykes (Eds.), *Practical aspects of memory.* London: Academic Press, 1978.

Podlesny, J. A., & Raskin, D. C. Physiological measures and the detection of deception. *Psychological Bulletin,* 1977, *84,* 782–799.

Podlesny, J. A., & Raskin, D. C. Effectiveness of techniques and physiological measures in the detection of deception. *Psychophysiology,* 1978, *15,* 344–359.

Polk v. *State,* No. 781 (Md. Ct. Spec. App., Sept. term, 1980). Decision filed April 9, 1981.

Pollack, I., Pickett, J., & Sumby, W. On the identification of speakers by voice. *Journal of the Acoustical Society of America,* 1954, *26,* 403–406.

Postman, L., Stark, K., & Fraser, J. Temporal changes in interference. *Journal of Verbal Learning and Verbal Behavior,* 1968, *7,* 672–694.

Postman, L., & Underwood, B. J. Critical issues in interference theory. *Memory and Cognition,* 1973, *1,* 19–40.

Powers, P. A., Andriks, J. L., & Loftus, E. F. Eyewitness accounts of females and males. *Journal of Applied Psychology,* 1979, *64,* 339–347.

Ptacek, P., & Sanders, E. Age recognition from voice. *Journal of Speech and Hearing Research,* 1966, *9,* 273–277.

Putnam, W. H. Hypnosis and distortions in eyewitness memory. *International Journal of Clinical and Experimental Hypnosis,* 1979, *27,* 437–448.

Quaglino v. *People of the State of California,* No. 77-1288 (U.S. Supreme Court, October Term, 1977), *cert. denied,* 99 U.S. 599, 1978.

Rahaim, G. L., & Brodsky, S. L. *Empirical evidence vs. common sense: Juror and lawyer knowledge of eyewitness accuracy.* Unpublished manuscript, University of Alabama, 1981.

Raskin, D. Scientific assessment of the accuracy of detection of deception: A reply to Lykken. *Psychophysiology,* 1978, *15,* 143–147.

Raskin, D. C. Science, competence, and polygraph techniques. *Criminal Defense,* 1981, *8,* 11–18.

Raskin, D. C., Barland, G. H., & Podlesny, J. A. Validity and reliability of detection of deception. *Polygraph,* 1977, *6,* 1–39.

Raskin, D. C., & Hare, R. D. Psychopathy and detection of deception in a prison population. *Psychophysiology,* 1978, *15,* 126–136.

Raskin, D. C., & Podlesny, J. A. Truth and deception: A reply to Lykken. *Psychological Bulletin,* 1979, *86,* 54–59.

Rathborn, H., Bull, R., & Clifford, B. R. Voice recognition over the telephone. *Journal of Police Science and Administration,* 1981, *9,* 280–284.

Read, J. D. Rehearsal and recognition of human faces. *American Journal of Psychology,* 1979, *92,* 71–85.

Reed v. *State,* 283 Md. 374, 391 A.2d 364, 1978.

Reich, A., & Duke, J. Effects of selected vocal disguises upon speaker identification by listening. *Journal of the Acoustical Society of America,* 1979, *66,* 1023–1028.

Reich, A., Moll, K., & Curtis, J. Effects of selected vocal disguise upon spectrographic speaker identification. *Journal of the Acoustical Society of America,* 1976, *60,* 919–925.

Reid, J. Simulated blood pressure responses in lie detector tests and a method for their detection. *Journal of Criminal Law and Criminology,* 1945, *36,* 201–214.

Reid, J. A revised questioning technique in lie detection tests. *Journal of Criminal Law and Criminology,* 1947, *37,* 542–547.

Reid, J., & Arther, R. Behavior symptoms of lie detector subjects. *Journal of Criminal Law, Criminology, and Police Science,* 1953, *44,* 104–118.

Reid, J., & Inbau, F. *Truth and deception: The polygraph ("lie detector") technique.* Baltimore: Williams & Wilkins, 1977.

Reiff, R., & Scheerer, M. *Memory and hypnotic age regression: Developmental aspects of cognitive function explored through hypnosis.* New York: International Universities Press, 1959.

Reiser, M. Hypnosis as a tool in criminal investigation. *The Police Chief,* 1976, *43,* 36, 39–40.

Reiser, M. More about hypnosis (Letter to the Editor). *The Police Chief,* 1979, *46,* 10.

Reiser, M. *Handbook of investigative hypnosis.* Los Angeles, Calif.: Lehi, 1980.

Rex v. *Braiser,* 1 Leach 199, 168 Eng. Rep. 202, 1779.

Rodin, J., & Langer, E. Aging labels: The decline of control and the fall of self-esteem. *Journal of Social Issues,* 1980, *36,* 12–29.

Rosenhan, D., & London, P. Hypnosis in the unhypnotizable: A study in rote learning. *Journal of Experimental Psychology,* 1963, *65,* 30–34.

Rosenthal, B. G. Hypnotic recall of material learned under anxiety- and non-anxiety-producing conditions. *Journal of Experimental Psychology,* 1944, *34,* 369–389.

Rosenthal, R. *Experimenter effects in behavioral research.* New York: Appleton-Century-Crofts, 1966.

Rothman, H. A perceptual (aural) and spectrographic identification of talkers with similar sounding voices. In John S. Jackson (Ed.), *International Conference on Crime Countermeasures – Science and Engineering.* Lexington, Ky.: ORES Publications, 1977.

Rouke, F. *Evaluation of the indices of deception in the psychogalvanic technique.* Unpublished doctoral dissertation, Department of Psychology, Fordham University, 1941.

Rouke, F. L. Psychological research on problems of testimony. *Journal of Social Issues,* 1957, *13,* 50–59.

Rousey, C., & Holzman, P. Recognition of one's own voice. *Journal of Personality and Social Psychology,* 1967, *6,* 464–466.

Rovner, L. I., Raskin, D. C., & Kircher, J. C. Effects of information and practice on detection of deception. *Psychophysiology,* 1979, *16,* 197–198. (Abstract).

Ruback, B., Greenberg, M., & Westcott, D. *Eyewitness identification by theft victims.* Unpublished manuscript, Georgia State University, 1982.

Ruckmick, C. The truth about the lie detector. *Journal of Applied Psychology,* 1938, *22,* 50–58.

Rules of evidence for United States Courts and Magistrates. *Supreme Court Reporter,* 1973, *3.*

Sah, A. P. Perceptual suggestibility as a function of age, sex and education. *Indian Journal of Experimental Psychology,* 1973, *7,* 21–25.

Salzberg, H. C., & DePiano, F. A. Hypnotizability and task motivating suggestions: A further look at how they affect performance. *International Journal of Clinical and Experimental Hypnosis,* 1980, *28,* 261–271.

Sanders, G. S., & Warnick, D. Some conditions maximizing eyewitness accuracy: A learning/memory model. *Journal of Criminal Justice,* 1981, *9,* 136–42.

Sanders, G. S., & Warnick, D. Truth and consequences: The effect of responsibility on eyewitness behavior. *Basic and Applied Social Psychology,* 1981, *2,* 67–79. (b)

Saslove, H., & Yarmey, A. Long term auditory memory: Speaker identification. *Journal of Applied Psychology,* 1980, *65,* 111–116.

Schafer, D. W., & Rubio, R. Hypnosis to aid the recall of witnesses. *International Journal of Clinical and Experimental Hypnosis,* 1978, *26,* 81–91.

Schiffman, H. R., & Bobko, D. J. Effects of stimulus complexity on the perception of brief temporal durations. *Journal of Experimental Psychology,* 1974, *103,* 156–159.

Schmerber v. *California,* 384 U.S. 757, 1966.

Schonfield, D., & Robertson, B. Memory storage and aging. *Canadian Journal of Psychology,* 1966, *20,* 228–236.

Schwartz, M. Identification of speaker's sex from isolated voiceless fricatives. *Journal of the Acoustical Society of America,* 1968, *43,* 1178–1179.

Sears, A. B. A comparison of hypnotic and waking recall. *Journal of Clinical and Experimental Hypnosis,* 1954, *2,* 296–304.

Senese, L. Accuracy of the polygraph technique with and without card test stimulation. *Journal of Police Science and Administration,* 1976, *4,* 274–276.

Senese, L., & Buckley, J. *Research abstract: Ethnic groups and polygraph tracings.* Paper presented at the meeting of the American Polygraph Association, San Diego, August 1979.

Sergent, J., & Bindra, D. Differential hemispheric processing of faces: Methodological considerations and reinterpretation. *Psychological Bulletin,* 1981, *89,* 541–554.

Shaul, R. D. Eyewitness testimony and hypnotic hypermnesia (Doctoral dissertation, Brigham Young University, 1978). *Dissertation Abstracts International,* 1978, *39,* 2521B. (University Microfilms No. 78-21, 261.)

Sheehan, P. W. Psychology and the law: Some pitfalls of verbal testimony. *Queensland Law Society Journal,* 1982, *12,* 107–112.

Sheehan, P. W., & Perry, C. *Methodologies of hypnosis: A critical appraisal of contemporary paradigms of hypnosis.* Hillsdale, N.J.: Erlbaum, 1976.

Sheehan, P. W., & Tilden, J. Effects of suggestibility and hypnosis on accurate and distorted retrieval from memory. *Journal of Experimental Psychology: Learning, Memory, and Cognition,* 1983, *9,* 283–293.

Shepherd, J. Social factors in face recognition. In G. M. Davies, H. D. Ellis, & J. W. Shepherd (Eds.), *Perceiving and remembering faces.* London: Academic Press, 1981.

Shepherd, J. W., Davies, G. M., & Ellis, H. D. How best shall a face be described? In M. M. Gruneberg, P. E. Morris, & R. N. Sykes (Eds.), *Practical aspects of memory.* London: Academic Press, 1978.

Shepherd, J. W., Davies, G. M., & Ellis, H. D. *Identification after delay.* Unpublished manuscript, University of Aberdeen, Aberdeen, Scotland, 1980.

Shepherd, J. W., & Deregowski, J. B. Races and faces: A comparison of the responses of Africans and Europeans to faces of the same and different races. *British Journal of Social Psychology,* 1981, *20,* 125–133.

Shepherd, J. W., & Ellis, H. D. The effect of attractiveness on recognition memory for faces. *American Journal of Psychology,* 1973, *86,* 627–633.

Shepherd, J. W., Ellis, H. D., & Davies, G. M. *Perceiving and remembering faces.* Technical Report to the British Home Office, 1977.

Shepherd, J. W., Ellis, H. D., & Davies, G. M. *Identification evidence: A psychological evaluation.* Aberdeen: Aberdeen University Press, 1982.

Shepherd, J. W., Ellis, H. D., McMurran, M., & Davies, G. M. Effect of character attribution on photofit construction of a face. *European Journal of Social Psychology,* 1978, *8,* 263–268.

Shiffman, H. R., & Bobko, D. J. Effects of stimulus complexity on brief temporal events. *Journal of Experimental Psychology,* 1974, *103,* 156–159.

Shipp, F., & Hollien, H. Perception of the aging male voice. *Journal of Speech and Hearing Research,* 1969, *12,* 703–710.

Shoemaker, J. 18 months of hell for rapist's lookalike. *Chicago Tribune,* December 28, 1980, p. 18.

Siegal, S. *Non-parametric statistics for the behavioral sciences.* New York: McGraw-Hill, 1956.

Slowik, S. M., & Buckley, J. P. Relative accuracy of polygraph examiner diagnosis of respiration, blood pressure, and GSR recordings. *Journal of Police Science and Administration,* 1975, *3,* 305–309.

Smith v. *Coiner,* 473 F.2d 877 (4th Cir.), 1973.

Smith, A. D., & Winograd, E. *Age differences in remembering faces.* Paper presented at a meeting of the Southeastern Psychological Association, Atlanta, March 1977.

Smith, A. D., & Winograd, E. Adult age differences in remembering faces. *Developmental Psychology,* 1978, *14,* 443–444.

Smith, D. *Voice that gives you away: A survey of methods used in identification with suggestions for future use.* Lancashire Constabulary, 1977.

Snee, T., & Lush, D. Interaction of the narrative and interrogatory methods of obtaining testimony. *Journal of Psychology,* 1941, *11,* 229–230.

Snyder, M. Seek and ye shall find: Testing hypotheses about other people. In E. T. Higgins, C. P. Herman, & M. P. Zanna (Eds.), *Social cognition: Ontario symposium on personality and social psychology.* Hillsdale, N.J.: Erlbaum, 1981.

Sobel, N. R. *Eye-witness identification: Legal and practical problems.* New York: Clark Boardman, 1972. (Reprinted 1979 with supplement.)

Sobel, N. R., & Pridgen, D. *Eyewitness identification: Legal and practical problems.* New York: Clark Boardman, 1981.

Solso, R. L, & McCarthy, J. E. Prototype formation: A case of pseudo-memory. *British Journal of Psychology,* 1981, *72,* 499–503.

Spiegel, H. Hypnosis and evidence: Help or hindrance? *Annals of the New York Academy of Sciences,* 1980, *347,* 73–85.

Spiegel, H., Shor, G., & Fischman, S. A hypnotic ablation technique for the study of personality development. *Psychosomatic Medicine,* 1945, *7,* 272–278.

Sporer, S. L. *Toward a comprehensive history of legal psychology.* Unpublished manuscript, University of Erlangen-Nürnberg, 1981.

Stafford, C. F. The child as a witness. *Washington Law Review,* 1962, *37,* 303–324.

Stager, G. L. The effect of hypnosis on the learning and recall of visually presented material (Doctoral dissertation, Pennsylvania State University, 1974). *Dissertation Abstracts International,* 1974, *35,* 3075B. (University Microfilms No. 74-28, 985.)

Stager, G. L., & Lundy, R. M. Hypnosis and the learning and recall of visually presented material. *International Journal of Clinical and Experimental Hypnosis,* in press.

Stalnaker, J. M., & Riddle, E. E. The effect of hypnosis on long-delayed recall. *Journal of General Psychology,* 1932, *6,* 429–440.

Stankov, L., & Spillsbury, G. The measurement of auditory abilities of blind, partially sighted, and sighted children. *Applied Psychological Measurement,* 1978, *2,* 491–503.

Starkman, D. The use of eyewitness identification evidence in criminal trials. *Criminal Law Quarterly,* 1979, *21,* 361–386.

State v. *Armstrong,* 329 N.W.2d. 386, 1983.

State v. *Douglas,* Ind. No. 692-77 (Union Co., N.J.), *vacated,* May 23, 1978.

State v. *Galloway,* 275 N.W.2d 736 (Iowa), 1979.

State v. *Helterbridle,* 301 N.W.2d 545 (Minn.), 1980.

State v. *Hurd,* 432 A.2d 86 (N.J.), 1981.

State v. *Jorgensen,* 8 Or. App. 1, 492 P.2d 312, 1971.

State v. *Juneau,* 88 Wis. 180, 59 N.W.580, 1894.

State v. *Mack,* 292 N.W.2d 764 (Minn.), 1980.

State v. *McQueen,* 295 N.C. 96, 119, 244 S.E.2d 414, 427, 1978.

State v. *Mena,* 624 P.2d 1274 (Ariz.), 1981.

State v. *Palmer,* 313 N.W.2d 648, (Neb.), 1981.

State v. *Warren,* —Kan.—, 635 P.2d 1236, 1981.

State v. *White,* No. J-3665 (Cir. Ct., Branch 10, Milwaukee Co., Wis., March 27, 1979; unrep.).

Stein, J. A. Review of eyewitness testimony. *Trial Diplomacy Journal,* 1981, *4,* 61–63.

Stern, L. W. Abstracts of lectures on the psychology of testimony on the study of individuality. *American Journal of Psychology,* 1910, *21,* 270–282.

Stern, L. W. The psychology of testimony. *Journal of Abnormal and Social Psychology,* 1939, *34,* 3–20.

Stern, L. W. Zur Psych. d. Aussage. Exp. Untersuchengen uber Erinnerungstreue. *Zeits. f. d. ges. Strafrechtwissenschaft,* 1902, *22.*

Stern, L. W. (Ed.). *Beitrage zur Psychologie der Aussage,* Leipzig, 1903–1906.

Stevens, K., Williams, C., Carbonell, J., & Wood, B. Speaker authentication and verification: A comparison of spectrographic and auditory presentations of speech materials. *Journal of the Acoustical Society of America,* 1968, *44,* 1596–1607.

Stovall v. *Denno,* 388 U.S. 293, 302, 1967.

Stratton, J. G. The use of hypnosis in law enforcement criminal investigations: A pilot program. *Journal of Police Science and Administration,* 1977, *5,* 399–406.

Strong v. *State,* 435 N.E.2d 969 (Ind.), 1982.

Sturm, C. A. *Eyewitness memory: Effects of guided memory and hypnotic hypermnesia techniques and hypnotic susceptibility.* Unpublished doctoral dissertation, University of Montana, 1982.

Summary of proceedings: Workshop on crime laboratory improvement. Paper prepared by the National Institute of Law Enforcement and Criminal Justice, Law Enforcement Assistance Administration, U.S. Department of Justice, Washington, D.C., December 1977.

Summers, W. Science can get the confession. *Fordham Law Review,* 1939, *8,* 334–354.

Swets, J. A. The relative operating characteristic in psychology. *Science,* 1973, *182,* 990–999.

Taylor, J. P. Eyewitness testimony: Possible legal responses to the lessons from psychology on the fallibility of eyewitness identification. In J. P. Taylor (Ed.), *Recent developments in the law of evidence.* Vancouver: Butterworths, 1980.

Thackray, R., & Orne, M. Effects of the type of stimulus employed and the level of subject awareness on the detection of deception. *Journal of Applied Psychology,* 1968, *52,* 234–239.

Thomas, D. R., Caronite, A. D., LaMonica, G. L., & Hoving, K. L. Mediated generalization via stimulus labelling: A replication and extension. *Journal of Experimental Psychology,* 1968, *78,* 531–533.

Thompson, L. W. Testing and mnemonic strategies. In L. W. Poon, J. L. Fozard, L. S. Cermek, D. Arenberg, & L. W. Thompson (Eds.), *New directions in memory and aging: Proceedings of the George A. Talland Memorial Conference.* Hillsdale, N.J.: Erlbaum, 1980.

Tickner, A., & Poulton, E. Watching for people and actions. *Ergonomics,* 1975, *18,* 35–51.

Timm, H. W. *The effect of placebos and feedback on the detection of deception.* Unpublished doctoral dissertation, Michigan State University, 1979.

Timm, H. W. The effects of forensic hypnosis techniques on eyewitness recall and recognition. *Journal of Police Science and Administration,* 1981, *9,* 188–194.

Timm, H. W. *A theoretical and empirical examination of the effects of forensic hypnosis on eyewitness recall.* Paper presented at the 9th International Congress of Hypnosis and Psychosomatic Medicine, Glasgow, Scotland, August 1982.

Tomsho, R. Blind justice. *Pittsburgh,* March 1981, 34–40.

Tosi, O. *Voice identification: Theory and legal applications.* Baltimore: University Park Press, 1978.

Tosi, O., Oyer, H., Lashbrook, W., Pedrey, C., Nicol, J., & Nash, E. Experiment on voice identification. *Journal of the Acoustical Society of America,* 1972, *51,* 2030–2043.

Trankell, A. *Reliability of evidence: Methods for analyzing and assessing witness statements.* Stockholm: Beckman, 1972.

Tribe, L. H. Trial by mathematics: Precision and ritual in the legal process. *Harvard Law Review,* 1971, *84,* 1329–1393.

Trovillo, P. A history of lie detection. *Journal of Criminal Law and Criminology,* 1939, *29,* 848–881, and *30,* 104–119.

True, R. M. Experimental control in hypnotic age regression states. *Science,* 1949, *110,* 583–584.

True, R. M. *Limitations of hypnotic behavior.* Panel discussion presented at the New England Society of Clinical Hypnosis Workshop, Western, Mass., May 1962.

Tversky, A. Features of similarity. *Psychological Review,* 1977, *84,* 327–352.

Tversky, A., & Kahneman, D. The belief in the "law of small numbers." *Psychological Bulletin,* 1971, *76,* 105–110.

Udolf, R. *Forensic hypnosis: Psychological and legal aspects.* Lexington, Mass.: Lexington Books, 1983.

Uematsu, T. The reliability of eyewitness testimony – some results of experimental studies and their practical application. In A. Trankell (Ed.), *Reconstructing the past: The role of psychologists in criminal trials.* Deventer, the Netherlands: Kluwer, 1982.

Underwood, B. J. Recognition memory. In H. H. Kendler & J. T. Spence (Eds.), *Essays in neobehaviorism.* New York: Appleton-Century-Crofts, 1971.

Undeutsch, U. Statement reality analysis. In A. Trankell (Ed.), *Reconstructing the past: The role of psychologists in criminal trials.* Deventer, the Netherlands: Kluwer, 1982.

United States ex rel. *Davis* v. *Jennings,* 414 F. Supp. 544 (E.D. Pa.), 1976.

United States v. *Adams,* 581 F.2d 193, 198–99 (9th Cir.), 1978, *cert. denied,* 439 U.S. 1006, 1978.

United States v. *Amaral,* 488 F.2d 1148 (9th Cir.), 1973.

United States v. *Ash,* 413 U.S. 300, 1973.

United States v. *Barber,* 422 F.2d 517 (3d Cir.), 1971.

United States v. *Bierey,* 588 F.2d 620 (8th Cir.), 1978.

United States v. *Fosher,* 590 F.2d 381 (1st Cir.), 1979.

United States v. *Telfaire,* 469 F.2d 552 (D.C. Cir.), 1972.

United States v. *Tolliver,* 569 F.2d 724 (2d Cir.), 1978.

United States v. *Wade,* 388 U.S. 218, 1967.

United States v. *Watson,* 587 F.2d 365 (7th Cir.), 1978.

Uviller, P. The role of the defense lawyer at a lineup in light of the Wade, Gilbert and Stovall decisions. *Criminal Law Bulletin,* 1978, *4,* 273–282.

Van Buskirk, D., & Marcuse, F. The nature of errors in experimental lie detection. *Journal of Experimental Psychology,* 1954, *47,* 178–190.

Varendonck, J. Les temoignages d'enfants dans un procès retentissant. *Archives de Psychologie,* 1911, *11,* 129–171.

Veatch, R. M. Generalization of expertise. *Hastings Center Studies,* 1973, *1,* 29–40.

Vinokur, A., & Burnstein, E. Effects of partially shared persuasive arguments on group-induced shifts: A group problem-solving approach. *Journal of Personality and Social Psychology,* 1974, *29,* 305–315.

Wadden, T. A., & Anderton, C. H. The clinical use of hypnosis. *Psychological Bulletin,* 1982, *91,* 215–243.

Wagstaff, G. F. Hypnosis and recognition of a face. *Perceptual and Motor Skills,* 1982, *55,* 816–818. (a)

Wagstaff, G. F. Hypnosis and witness recall: Discussion paper. *Journal of the Royal Society of Medicine,* 1982, *75,* 793–798. (b)

Wagstaff, G. F., Traverse, J., & Milner, S. Hypnosis and eyewitness memory: Two experimental analogues. *IRCS Medical Science: Psychology and Psychiatry,* 1982, *10,* 894–895.

Walker-Smith, G. J. The effects of delay and exposure duration in a face recognition task. *Perception and Psychophysics,* 1978, *24,* 63–70.

Walker-Smith, G. J., Gale, A. G., & Findlay, J. M. Eye-movement strategies involved in face perception. *Perception,* 1977, *6,* 313–326.

Wall, P. D., & Lieberman, L. R. Effects of task motivation and hypnotic induction on hypermnesia. *The American Journal of Clinical Hypnosis,* 1976, *18,* 250–253.

Wall, P. M. *Eyewitness identification in criminal cases.* Springfield, Ill.: Charles C Thomas, 1965.

Wallace, W. P. On the use of distractors for testing recognition memory. *Psychological Bulletin,* 1980, *88,* 696–704.

Walsh, D. A. Age differences in learning and memory. In D. S. Woodruff & J. E. Birren (Eds.), *Aging: Scientific perspectives and social issues.* New York: Van Nostrand Reinhold, 1975.

Warnick, D., & Sanders, G. Why do eyewitnesses make so many mistakes? *Journal of Applied Social Psychology,* 1980, *10,* 362–366.

Warrington, E. K., & Ackroyd, C. The effect of orienting tasks on recognition memory. *Memory and Cognition,* 1975, *3,* 140–142.

Warrington, E. K., & Sanders, H. The fate of old memories. *Quarterly Journal of Experimental Psychology,* 1971, *23,* 432–442.

Wason, P. C., & Johnson-Laird, P. N. *Psychology of reasoning.* London: B. T. Bransford, 1972.

Watkins, M. J., Ho, E., & Tulving, E. Context effects in recognition memory for faces. *Journal of Verbal Learning and Verbal Behavior,* 1976, *15,* 505–517.

Watkins v. *Sowders,* 101 S. Ct. 654, 28 Crim. L.R. 3037, 1981.

Waxman, D. Use of hypnosis in criminology: Discussion paper. *Journal of the Royal Society of Medicine,* 1983, *76,* 480–484.

Weinberg, H. I., & Baron, R. S. The discredible eyewitness. *Personality and Social Psychology Bulletin,* 1982, *8,* 60–67.

Weinstein, J. Review of eyewitness testimony. *Columbia Law Review,* 1981, *81,* 441–457.

Weitzenhoffer, A. M. The influence of hypnosis on the learning processes. Some theoretical considerations: 2. Recall of meaningful material. *Journal of Clinical and Experimental Hypnosis,* 1955, *3,* 148–165.

Wells, G. L. Applied eyewitness testimony research: System variables and estimator variables. *Journal of Personality and Social Psychology,* 1978, *36,* 1546–1557.

Wells, G. L. Attribution and reconstructive memory. *Journal of Experimental Social Psychology,* 1982, *18,* 447–463.

Wells, G. L., Ferguson, T. J., & Lindsay, R. C. L. The tractability of eyewitness confidence and its implications for triers of fact. *Journal of Applied Psychology,* 1981, *66,* 688–696.

Wells, G. L., & Leippe, M. R. How do triers of fact infer the accuracy of eyewitness identifications? Memory for peripheral detail can be misleading. *Journal of Applied Psychology,* 1981, *66,* 682–687.

Wells, G. L., Leippe, M. R., & Ostrom, T. M. Guidelines for empirically assessing the fairness of a lineup. *Law and Human Behavior,* 1979, *3,* 285–293.

Wells, G. L., & Lindsay, R. C. L. On estimating the diagnosticity of eyewitness nonidentifications. *Psychological Bulletin,* 1980, *88,* 776–784.

Wells, G. L., & Lindsay, R. C. L. How do people judge the accuracy of eyewitness identifications? Studies of performance and a metamemory analysis. In S. Lloyd-Bostock & B. R. Clifford (Eds.), *Evaluating witness evidence.* Chichester: Wiley, 1983.

Wells, G. L., Lindsay, R. C. L., & Ferguson, T. J. Accuracy, confidence, and juror perceptions in eyewitness identification. *Journal of Applied Psychology,* 1979, *64,* 440–448.

Wells, G. L., Lindsay, R. C. L., & Tousignant, J. P. Effects of expert psychological advice on human performance in judging the validity of eyewitness testimony. *Law and Human Behavior,* 1980, *4,* 275–286.

Wells, G. L., & Murray, D. M. What can psychology say about the Neil vs. Biggers criteria for judging eyewitness identification accuracy? *Journal of Applied Psychology,* 1983, *68,* 347–362.

Wheeler v. United States, 159 U.S. 526, 1895.

Whipple, G. M. The observer as reporter: A survey of the "Psychology of Testimony." *Psychological Bulletin,* 1909, *6,* 153–170.

Whipple, G. M. Recent literature on the psychology of testimony. *Psychological Bulletin,* 1910, *7,* 365–368.

Whipple, G. M. The psychology of testimony. *Psychological Bulletin,* 1911, *8,* 307–309.

Whipple, G. M. Psychology of testimony and report. *Psychological Bulletin,* 1912, *9,* 264–269.

Whipple, G. M. Review of "Les temoignages d'enfants dans un procès retentissant," by J. Varendonck. *Journal of Criminal Law and Criminology,* 1913, *4,* 150–154.

White, R. W., Fox, G. F., & Harris, W. W. Hypnotic hypermnesia for recently learned material. *Journal of Abnormal and Social Psychology,* 1940, *35,* 88–103.

Whitely, P. L., & McGeoch, J. A. The effect of one form of report upon another. *American Journal of Psychology,* 1927, *38,* 280–284.

Wicklander, D. E., & Hunter, F. L. The influence of auxiliary sources of information in polygraph diagnoses. *Journal of Police Science and Administration,* 1975, *3,* 405–409.

Widacki, J., & Horvath, F. An experimental investigation of the relative validity and utility of the polygraph technique and three other common methods of criminal identification. *Journal of Forensic Sciences,* 1978, *23,* 596–601.

Wigmore, J. H. Professor Munsterberg and the psychology of evidence. *Illinois Law Review,* 1909, *3,* 399–445.

Wigmore, J. H. *Principles of judicial proof.* Boston: Little, Brown, 1931.

Wigmore, J. H. *The science of judicial proof.* Boston: Little, Brown, 1937.

Williams, C. *The effects of selected factors on the aural identification of speakers* (Report ESD-TDR-65-153). Unpublished manuscript, Air Force Systems Command, Hanscom Field, Mass., 1964.

Williams, G. *The proof of guilt: A study of the English criminal trial.* London: Stevens, 1955.

Wilson, C. R. Psychological opinions on the accuracy of eyewitness testimony. *The Judge's Journal,* 1975, *14,* 72–74.

Wilson, J. *The investigators.* New York: Basic Books, 1978.

Wilson, J. *Up against it: Children and the law in Canada.* Toronto: Anansi, 1980.

Winograd, E. Encoding operations which facilitate memory for faces across the life span. In M. M. Gruneberg, P. E. Morris, & R. N. Sykes (Eds.), *Practical aspects of memory.* London: Academic Press, 1978.

Winograd, E. Elaboration and distinctiveness in memory for faces. *Journal of Experimental Psychology: Human Learning and Memory,* 1981, *7,* 181–190.

Winograd, E., & Rivers-Bulkeley, N. T. Effects of changing context on remembering faces. *Journal of Experimental Psychology: Human Learning and Memory,* 1977, *3,* 397–405.

Woocher, F. D. Did your eyes deceive you? Expert psychological testimony on the unreliability of eyewitness testimony. *Stanford Law Review,* 1977, *29,* 969–1030.

Woodhead, M. M., Baddeley, A. D., & Simmonds, D. C. V. On training people to recognize faces. *Ergonomics,* 1979, *22,* 333–343.

Yarmey, A. D. *The psychology of eyewitness testimony.* New York: Free Press, 1979. (a)

Yarmey, A. D. Through the looking glass: Sex differences in memory for self-facial poses. *Journal of Research in Personality,* 1979, *13,* 450–459. (b)

Yarmey, A. D. Eyewitness identification and stereotypes of criminals. In A. Trankell (Ed.), *Reconstructing the past: The role of psychologists in criminal trials.* Deventer, The Netherlands: Kluwer, 1982.

Yarmey, A. D., & Jones, H. P. T. Is the study of eyewitness identification a matter of common sense? In S. Lloyd-Bostock & B. R. Clifford (Eds.), *Evaluating witness evidence.* Chichester: Wiley, 1983.

Yarmey, A. D., Jones, H. P. T., & Raschid, S. Eyewitness memory of elderly and young adults. In D. J. Muller, D. E. Blackman, & A. J. Chapman (Eds.), *Topics in psychology and law.* Chichester: Wiley, in press.

Yarmey, A. D., & Kent, J. Eyewitness identification by elderly and young adults. *Law and Human Behavior,* 1980, *4,* 123–137.

Yarmey, A. D., & Rashid, S. *Eyewitness identification by elderly and young adults: The misidentification of the innocent bystander.* Unpublished manuscript, University of Guelph, 1981.

Yarmey, A. D., Rashid, S., & Jones, H. P. T. *Attitudes of elderly and young adults toward jurors.* Unpublished manuscript, University of Guelph, 1981.

Yates, A. J. Hypnotic age regression. *Psychological Bulletin,* 1961, *58,* 429–440.

Yoblick, D. A. *A structural analysis of human facial features.* Unpublished doctoral dissertation, State University of New York at Buffalo, 1973.

Young, P. C. An experimental study of mental and physical functions in the normal and hypnotic state. *American Journal of Psychology,* 1925, *36,* 214–232.

Young, P. C. An experimental study of mental and physical functions in the normal and hypnotic state: Additional results. *American Journal of Psychology,* 1926, *37,* 345–356.

Young, P. C. Hypnotic age regression: Fact or artifact. *Journal of Abnormal and Social Psychology,* 1940, *35,* 273–278.

Zamansky, H. S., Scharf, B., & Brightbill, R. The effect of expectancy for hypnosis on prehypnotic performance. *Journal of Personality,* 1964, *32,* 236–248.

Zavala, R. T. Determination of facial features used in identification. In A. Zavala & J. J. Paley (Eds.), *Personal appearance identification.* Springfield, Ill.: Charles C Thomas, 1972.

Zelig, M., & Beidleman, W. B. The investigative use of hypnosis: A word of caution. *International Journal of Clinical and Experimental Hypnosis,* 1981, *29,* 401–412.

Zuckerman, M., DePaulo, B., & Rosenthal, R. Verbal and nonverbal communication of deception. In L. Berkowitz (Ed.), *Advances in experimental social psychology.* New York: Academic Press, 1981.

Name index

Subject index

accuracy vs. choice in lineups, 64–6, 71–2
acquisition, *see* encoding
age and witnessing: identification abilities
  of children, 147–8; identification abilities
  of elderly, 150–3; and leading question
  effect, 144–5; legal view of, 142–3, 149;
  questioning of children, 145–7;
  stereotypes of elderly witnesses, 149–50;
  voice recognition abilities of children,
  149; voice recognition abilities of
  elderly, 94–7
artists' drawings, 127–9
attractiveness of faces, 21–2
attributions: and confidence, 167; of
  credibility to witnesses (*see* intuition);
  about faces, effects of, 17–19

beliefs about eyewitnessing, *see* intuition
bias in lineups, *see* fairness in lineups
blind, voice recognition abilities of, 100–2
Bruce v. *State*, 325

CAPSAR, 51–63
cautions to jurors, *see* expert testimony
certainty, *see* confidence
Chapman v. *State*, 202
children as eyewitnesses, *see* age
Collins v. *State*, 202, 203, 205, 212
Collins v. *Superior Court of State of
  Arizona*, 203
color, memory for, 139–40
Commonwealth v. *Kater*, 202
Commonwealth v. *Nazarovitch*, 202
Commonwealth v. *Richman*, 322
compromise memories, 139–40
confabulation, *see* hypnosis
confidence: and age, 153; briefing effects,
  163–4; definition of, 155; and expert
  testimony, 305; and hypnosis, 192–5;
  inflation of, 163, 167–8, 192–5;
  intuitions about, 258–60, 265, 267,
  269–72, 276, 310; and lineup structure,

75–6, 162–3; measures of, 156–9; and
  realism, 164–5; reliability vs. validity of,
  156; theoretical accounts of, 165–8;
  validity of, 159–65; and voice
  identifications, 104–5, 122–3
context effects, 31–5
credibility attributed to witnesses,
  see intuition
cross-race identifications, *see* race

deception, *see* polygraph
delay effects, 23–5, 130
depth of processing, 18–19, 96–7, 103–4
descriptions of faces, 13–17, 28–9, 35,
  155, 329
diagnosticity of lineups, 72, 90
disguise: of faces, 14; of voices, 111–14
Dyas v. *United States*, 278

effective size of lineups, *see* fairness of
  lineups
encoding: drug effects on, 275; of faces,
  13–22; judgment effects on, 18–19,
  96–7, 102–4; of new information, *see*
  postevent information; of voices, 103–4
Escobedo v. *Illinois*, 318
estimator variables, 20, 66 (*see also* specific
  variables, e.g., age; attractiveness;
  confidence; sex; race)
expectations, 74–7, 175–7
experience hypothesis, 166
expert testimony (*see also* intuition):
  and cautionary instructions, 279–80;
  decision to testify, 298–301, 304,
  311–13; and detection of accuracy,
  291–2, 307–8, 313; impact of, 280–2,
  292–4, 305, 314; legal view of, 276–80,
  304; and overbelief, 285–91, 305–7,
  330–3; in practice, 274–5; and
  probabilistic information, 310–11;
  rationale for, 284–94, 314